China and Southeast Asia

Jay Taylor

The Praeger Special Studies program—
utilizing the most modern and efficient book
production techniques and a selective
worldwide distribution network—makes
available to the academic, government, and
business communities significant, timely
research in U.S. and international economic, social, and political development.

China and Southeast Asia

Peking's Relations with Revolutionary Movements

Praeger Publishers   New York   Washington   London

PRAEGER SPECIAL STUDIES IN INTERNATIONAL POLITICS AND GOVERNMENT

Library of Congress Cataloging in Publication Data

Taylor, Jay, 1931-
    China and Southeast Asia.

    (Praeger special studies in international politics
and government)
    Bibliography: p.
    1. Asia, Southeastern—Foreign relations—China.
2. China—Foreign relations—Asia, Southeastern.
3. Communism—Asia.   4. Asia, Southeastern—Politics.
I. Title.
DS518.15.T38   327.51'059   74-3511
ISBN 0-275-08910-X

PRAEGER PUBLISHERS
111 Fourth Avenue, New York, N.Y. 10003, U.S.A.
5, Cromwell Place, London SW7 2JL, England

Published in the United States of America in 1974
by Praeger Publishers, Inc.

Printed in the United States of America

for my mother and father

"If the remoter people are not submissive,
all the influences of civil culture and virtue
are to be cultivated to attract them to be so;
and when they have been so attracted they
must be made contented and tranquil."

From the Confucian Analects

FOREWORD
by Allen S. Whiting

In the first 23 years of its existence, the People's Republic of China has been the subject of much debate, some analysis, but, so far as its foreign policy is concerned, surprisingly little systematic research. A handful of books have attempted a broad exegesis of the forces and factors underlying Chinese foreign policy, drawing largely on official Chinese statements together with foreign news accounts of reported activities by Peking's diplomatic and revolutionary representatives abroad. An even smaller number have focused on specific aspects for intensive examination, through case studies of bilateral relations—whether adversary or alliance—and of multilateral diplomacy, as with the Bandung conference of 1954 and the Geneva conference of 1962.

Mr. Taylor's study is a valuable addition to the slowly growing body of literature that attempts dispassionate description and thoughtful analysis of the various components that comprise the Chinese view of the world and expectations thereof. He has chosen to focus on Peking's relations with the revolutionary movements of Southeast Asia, including the only victorious one to date—North Vietnam. He has traced these relationships as intensively as open periodicals and published sources permit, with emphasis on the 1960s. In addition he has surveyed Peking's state relations with the governments concerned and attempted to correlate all of the external and domestic factors that may have impinged on decisions and developments at particular points in time. Within this framework he has provided an account and analysis of an important area of Chinese foreign relations during the 1960s.

The question is not, Does Peking support revolutions abroad? It is rather, Under what circumstances is Peking likely to give what kind of support to which revolutionaries abroad? What are the dichotomies that exist and what tensions are produced when a large, national bureaucracy pursues simultaneously traditional state relations and revolutionary subversive relations without any serious endeavor to conceal the latter, and indeed at some times, has boasted of and even exaggerated its revolutionary support? Do the vicissitudes of domestic politics affect the weight given these two disparate thrusts of foreign policy behavior and objectives, and if so, how? How responsive are these thrusts to specific local situations as opposed to larger global calculations? Whose perspectives in Peking select and interpret information on foreign affairs in framing policy discussion and decision-making?

More narrowly, how representative is the <u>Peking Review</u> of a specifically defined policy consensus at the highest level? What audiences is it intended to serve? How much is Chinese policy the captive of its own propaganda, either by instilling belief beyond the logic of external developments or by raising expectations among foreign supplicants for "revolutionary support"? How does the competitive and conflictual relationship with Moscow compel Peking to be a more ardent champion of a particular "national liberation" group than it might otherwise choose to be?

These questions are probed by Mr. Taylor's study, which suggests that Chinese policy-making is at least as complex as that in bureaucracies of comparable size in Washington and Moscow. U.S. and Soviet elites also have their normative or ideological values, which determine foreign policy goals, proclaimed through open media and pursued through covert means. At the same time, they make choices and select priorities among a wide range of pragmatic and ideological ends-means "sets," on the basis of "reality" as perceived, interpreted, argued, and bargained over among interacting elements of their bureaucratic systems at home and abroad. The mix of precedent, tradition, organizational and idiosyncratic behavior, plus the ongoing dynamics of an international system, combine to produce the phenomena that we reify with the shorthand terms of "Washington," "Moscow," and "Peking." It is easy to exaggerate the single-mindedness of policymakers in Peking and to forget that revolutionary objectives must compete for human and material resources as well as for priorities of choice with goals of international diplomatic status, trade, and security posited by the People's Republic of China as a nation-state and argued by groups whose vested interests as well as their internalized beliefs place greater emphasis on nonrevolutionary objectives. At certain times, as during the Bandung conference and the Cultural Revolution, these tensions in general policy are more manifest. With particular countries, such as Burma, the necessity for choice is more apparent. Mr. Taylor's study indicates that Chinese policy is constantly in flux, that universally consistent behavior is seldom if ever present, and that only by taking a case-by-case approach over extended periods of time can one make valid generalizations and prognoses about the relative role of revolutionary versus nonrevolutionary objectives in Chinese foreign policy.

Mr. Taylor's study of the revolutionary component in Peking's policies also sharpens awareness of the dominant perceptions and public definition of Chinese policy held by key groups and leaders in Southeast Asia. Whatever might be their selection or distortion of evidence, the fact remains that most governments in the area have seen China's goals as threatening rather than benign. The positions of the Philippines, Malaysia, Singapore, Thailand, and since 1965

Indonesia, together with the recurring perturbations of Burma and Cambodia—even under Sihanouk—testify to the strength of this image of China as a subversive power that seeks the overthrow of existing governments by insurgent means.

To be sure, Peking has not let suppression of local communists preclude good relations with a particular regime at a particular time, as in Nepal, Burma, Cambodia, and Malaysia. Nor has it treated U.S. allies consistently as targets of revolutionary pressure—see, for example, Pakistan, the Philippines, and, in earlier years, Thailand. Some Asian leaders, such as U Nu, Ne Win, Sihanouk, Sukarno, and most recently Tun Razak, have played on the dichotomies in Peking's policy-making with varied success, steering their neutral nations between the Scylla of an American alliance and the Charybdis of a Chinese tributary.

But a wholly objective and carefully measured appraisal of how much the revolutionary factor weighs in Chinese policy would miss the perception and reaction of many, especially in Southeast Asia, who feel the long shadow of Chinese power over their future. It is easier to differentiate and discount the gap between Peking's words and deeds in the United States, separated from China by the Pacific Ocean, than in the government offices in Bangkok and Kuala Lumpur, surrounded by sizable Chinese populations in relatively close overland and overseas reach of the mainland.

These Asian perspectives were reinforced by Washington's definition of the situation, and this takes us to another important dimension of Mr. Taylor's study. Without an appreciation of the history of China's shifting relations with the communist parties of the area, it is virtually impossible to understand the basis on which three successive presidents—Kennedy, Johnson, and Nixon—expended their political capital, together with U.S. manpower and resources, in the jungle warfare of Vietnam, Laos, and Cambodia. It is too easily said that America's China policy was simply the heritage of Chiang Kai-shek's defeat, MacArthur's reversal in Korea, and the impact of Senator Joseph McCarthy. Whatever may have been the residual scars of these experiences on the political memories of men in the 1960s, the fact remains that Peking's words, and, as Mr. Taylor's study shows, to a certain degree Peking's behavior, seemed to many to reinforce the earlier assessments of a Chinese threat.

Critical inputs to this U.S. perception of China's revolutionary threat were the polemics attending the Sino-Soviet dispute and especially Lin Piao's celebrated 1965 pamphlet "Long Live People's Wars." Despite the fact that the polemic forced Premier Nikita Khrushchev to voice support for "just wars" in January 1961 and his successors to aid Hanoi with surface-to-air missiles in 1965, the major thrust of the dispute shifted the revolutionary onus, or credit as the case

may be, from Moscow to Peking. The question in Washington was not
whether the Russians did less damage than the Chinese; the Soviet
record in Cuba and Africa was certainly impressive and probably
outweighed that of the Chinese in Asia both qualitatively and quan-
titatively. Rather it was who said more about revolutionary pretensions
and objectives, Moscow or Peking. Here the Chinese in the 1960s
were the clear winners, hands down, although in terms of U.S. reaction
to the two disputants, this may well have been a Phyrric victory.

The symbolic summation of China's thrust toward world revolutionary leadership came with Lin Piao's publication, seen by high
Washington officials in 1965 as "China's Mein Kampf." Publicized
as much by U.S. propaganda as by that of the Chinese, this recapitula-
tion of Mao's long-available canons on "how to carry out revolution
yourself" handily served to document the case against Peking. But it
would be naive to think this use of this pamphlet reflected its importance in shaping official convictions. Far more relevant in this
sense were those Chinese activities, as in Thailand, spelled out in
detail by Mr. Taylor.

These three perspectives—those in Peking whose belief was
revolution-oriented, those in Southeast Asia who feared China's
subversive thrust, and those in Washington who saw America's responsibility in defeating this thrust—are rooted in the mass of material
that Mr. Taylor has painstakingly and systematically combed and
compiled for this book. Moving from perspectives to objective reality
is, of course, far more difficult because of the understandably elusive
nature of hard evidence linking local insurgency with Chinese support.
It does not suffice to show Thai or Malayan expressions of agreement
with Mao's strategy and publication by the Peking Review of Thai and
Malayan insurgent statements and claims of victory. Both parties
may find it mutually advantageous to exaggerate their respective
positions without, however, actually enjoying so firm or fruitful a
relationship.

The problem of assessing the degree of Chinese support for
foreign insurgencies somewhat resembles the argument over whether
the glass is half full or half empty. On the one hand, it is clear that,
except for North Vietnam in 1949-54 and possibly Burma in 1968-69,
Peking has never moved a decisive amount of support across its
borders on behalf of any insurgency movement. On the other hand,
some evidence for some kind of assistance from China can be found
in virtually all communist and in several noncommunist insurgencies
in Southeast Asia. More important but even more tantalizing is the
question of what will become of the revolutionary thrust now that the
Bandung policy has returned. Mr. Taylor's study cautions against
expecting a complete abandonment of this aspect of Chinese policy, if
only because bureaucratic inertia and vested interests in Peking, as

as well as demands from aspiring insurgents abroad, will keep pressure on future policy-makers.

But more fundamentally, the likelihood of some kind of continued support for foreign insurgencies is posited in the centrality of this policy in the political ethos of China. The revolutionary goals are not without utility, despite their conflict with other political and economic goals of state. Any support for revolutions abroad, whether token or substantive, extends the Chinese and others' sense of China as a power. Moreover, it clothes national interest in ideological principle, as do holy wars and democratic crusades.

Fifty years after the Bolshevik Revolution, including at least three changes in leadership, considerable political maturing, and partial economic modernization, one component of Russian foreign policy still furthers subversive and insurgent movements. Like Peking, Moscow is not a monolithic group of diehard revolutionaries prepared to take any risk in support of world revolution anywhere and at any time. Yet to overlook completely this facet of Soviet ideology and behavior is to miss an important determinant of Soviet foreign relations as perceived and experienced both in Moscow and throughout the world. Peking has shown that it can be as discriminating as Moscow in the revolutions it picks to support. The standard in both cases is national interest as defined by the dominant decision-makers.

Similarly, one can be confident that Mr. Taylor's account will remain of relevance for a considerable time after Mao leaves the scene, although changes in emphasis, focus, and implementation are certain to occur. Whether these changes will further increase the new diplomatic thrust of Chinese policy is impossible to predict with confidence. Several key variables affecting this process remain highly uncertain as of this writing, such as the composition of the post-Mao leadership and its stability, the viability of insurgencies abroad— especially on China's periphery—the individual and collective security arrangements that may prevail as counters to Chinese support, and the evolution of Sino-Soviet and Sino-U.S. relations. The constraints built into Mao's own prescription for "self-support" in "people's wars," the ethnocentrism that places Chinese internal and external state priorities above the needs of foreign insurgents, a blend of military caution and pragmatism that has so far tempered bellicose words with prudent behavior, and the possible dilution of Maoist fervor consequent from the turbulent course and aftermath of the Cultural Revolution all combine to argue against Chinese militancy and risk-taking, even with a growing stockpile of nuclear weapons.

However, former Secretary of State Dean Rusk frequently characterized the sine qua non for normalization of China's relations with the United States and the world community with the simple homily "China must leave its neighbors alone." Unfortunately the behavior of nation-states throughout this century does not augur well for the total abandonment of clandestine operations penetrating political systems lying beyond one's own borders. What can be hoped is that such activity will become secondary to other means of political influence and peaceful interaction between nations. President Nixon's trip to China in 1972 and the communiqué that he signed with Premier Chou En-lai shows that Washington now believes China meets this standard, at least as well as most countries.

Like any work which is essentially an interpretive history, this book is a synthesis of knowledge and insights gleaned from many sources. The basic research was begun in 1967-68 while I was at the Center for Chinese Studies at the University of Michigan in Ann Arbor. In subsequent years it was rewritten and brought up to date. I am indebted to the Center for Chinese Studies for its support, in particular to Professors Alexander Eckstein and Rhoades Murphy who provided guidance and encouragement.

Needless to say, the views in this book are strictly my own and do not necessarily reflect those of the Department of State or the United States Government. Likewise, while I have benefited greatly from the views of my colleagues in the foreign service, many would differ with some of the interpretations in the following pages.

Several scholars were kind enough to read portions of the draft and offer valuable criticisms and suggestions. Again, I am entirely responsible for the final product. Special thanks in this regard go to Allen S. Whiting, Richard H. Solomon, David Mozingo, Harold C. Hinton and Victor Li.

I am also grateful to Annie Lau and Janet Buechel for their help with the typing. Finally, it would not have been possible without the support and affection of my wife, Betsy.

CONTENTS

LIST OF ABBREVIATIONS

AFPFL	Anti-Fascist People's Freedom League
BCP	Burmese Communist Party
CCP	Chinese Communist Party
CONEFO	Conference of the New Emerging Forces
DRV	Democratic Republic of Vietnam
EDC	European Defense Community
GUB	Government of the Union of Burma
KM	Kabataan Makabayan, a Philippine youth organization
LPF	Lao Patriotic Front
LPM	Labor Party of Malaya
MCP	Malayan Communist Party
MNLA	Malayan National Liberation Army
MNLL	Malayan National Liberation League
MPAJA	Malayan People's Anti-Japanese Army
MPRS	Provisional People's Consultative Congress (Indonesia)
Nasakom	Sukarno's concept of nationalism, religion, and communism
NCNA	New China News Agency
OCAC	Overseas Chinese Affairs Commission
PAP	People's Action Party
PGRA	People's Guerrilla Forces of Sarawak
PKI	Indonesian Communist Party

PKP	Philippine Communist Party
PKP (ML)	PKP (Marxist-Leninist)
RGNU	Royal Government of National Union
SCMP	Survey of the Chinese Mainland Press
SCO	Sarawak Communist Organization
TCP	Thai Communist Party
TIM	Thai Independence Movement
TPF	Thai Patriotic Front
VPA	Vietnam People's Army

China and
Southeast Asia

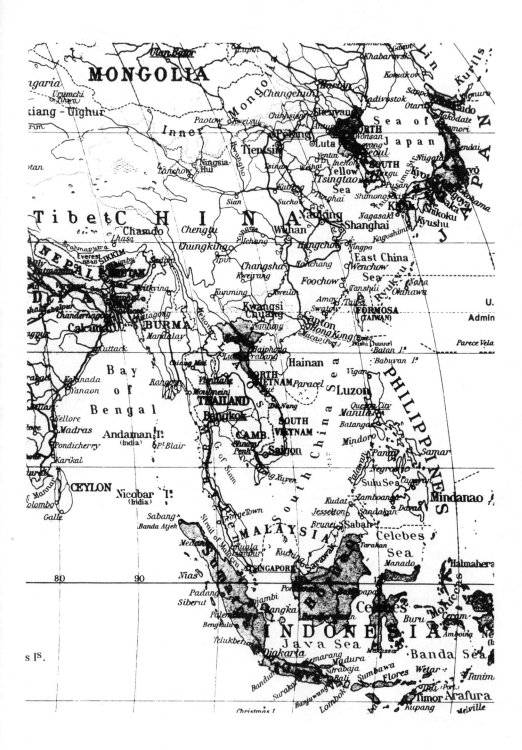

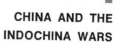

CHINA AND THE
INDOCHINA WARS

As Vietnam is bound by history and geography to China, so the communist movements of the two countries have often found their fates tied together. However, most of the political impact has been one way, that is, from China.

The Vietnamese attitude toward China has always been highly ambivalent—admiration for Chinese culture and industriousness combined with distrust of Chinese intentions and resentment of past arrogance. Today the communist government of North Vietnam retains this ambivalent view.

In this chapter, we propose to analyze China's behavior during the periods of crisis in the two Indochina wars. The political and military strategies that the Chinese and Vietnamese communists followed during the development of these periods of crisis were often consistent. Yet differences stand out that highlight the evolution of world political events, the transformation of China's global objectives and the evolving attitudes in Peking, Washington, and Moscow.

THE EARLY HISTORY

The leaders of the Vietnamese communist movement, like their colleagues in China, were naturally involved in their early years with Moscow and the Comintern. But from the very beginning, the chief Vietnamese communists, including Ho Chi Minh, Truong Chinh, Vo Nguyen Giap, and Pham Van Dong, gained their early experience and training in China.

After two years in Moscow, Ho Chi Minh in 1925 went to China to organize a communist movement in Indochina. Working in China

ostensibly as a translator at the Soviet consulate in Canton, he set
about establishing the Association of Revolutionary Youth among
Vietnamese refugees. After the Kuomintang (KMT) break with the
Chinese communists in 1927, he spent some time in Hankow but
eventually returned to Moscow, where in 1928 he became the Comintern
agent for Southeast Asia. Ho, however, left behind in China 250 Vietnamese communists who maintained a clandestine liaison with the
international communist movement and who were to become the core
of Ho's political apparatus.[1]

Taking refuge in Republican China, the Vietnamese nationalist
movement became one of the strongest in Southeast Asia. Most other
revolutionary parties of Asia lacked a similar "rear base." By 1929
some 200 Vietnamese youths are believed to have received a revolutionary education in China and to have returned home to establish a
political organization that reached into all parts of Vietnam.[2]

After directing the organizational work of the party for Thailand,
Malaya, and Indonesia, Ho went secretly to Hong Kong, where, in 1930,
he formed the Indochinese Communist Party (ICP), which was accepted
by the Comintern at the 11th plenary session of the latter's executive
committee in 1931. He was arrested by the British in Hong Kong
but was released or escaped in 1933 and again made his way to Moscow,
where he remained until 1938, when he returned to China. After a
period during which he was attached to the Chinese Communist Eighth
Route Army, he moved in 1940 to the border area to create the
guerrilla movement in Vietnam.[3]

In 1941 Ho organized the Viet Minh (Vietnam Doc Lap Dong
Minh Hoi, or League for the Independence of Vietnam) with Chinese
Nationalist support and a Vietnamese provisional government in which
the Viet Minh held a nominal minority position but in which it exercised
actual control. Brimmel has referred to this organization as a double-
deck united front; the ICP had formed a united front (the Viet Minh)
with other left-wing Vietnamese nationalists, and this organization
in turn exercised effective control in a broader united front with the
remaining nationalists to form a provisional government.[4]

With the Japanese surrender, Nationalist Chinese troops, as
agreed at Potsdam, occupied North Vietnam (plundering and gaining
considerable disrepute in the process). But the Viet Minh seized the
political initiative and proclaimed a national liberation committee.
On September 2, Ho declared the independence of the Democratic
Republic of Vietnam (DRV). To ease the way for the establishment
of a government of national union and negotiations with the French,
Ho nominally disbanded the ICP. On March 6, 1946, the French and
Ho's government signed an agreement that recognized the Republic
of Vietnam as a "free state having its own government, parliament,
army, and finances forming part of the Indochinese federation" and
the French Union.

This policy of cooperation with the French was opposed, not only by many noncommunist Vietnamese nationalists but also by militants within the Communist Party (the ICP was now called the Marxist Study Association). Ho's decision, however, was probably based in part on economic needs and on the hope of obtaining the withdrawal of the Chinese Nationalists.* It was also a policy that coincided with the objectives of the Soviet Union and the French Communist Party as well as with the requirements of the Chinese communists. Stalin at this time was primarily interested in the prospect of communist parties coming to power in France and Italy, where they had been included in popular front coalitions, and it was important that the Vietnamese communists should not cause difficulties for their French colleagues. Moreover, Ho may have been intellectually and emotionally in favor of an independent Vietnam's remaining within a French Union, provided such a union was under communist control—a possibility at that time.

The Chinese communists also had an interest in the timing of revolutionary developments in Vietnam. The forces of Mao Tse-tung in late 1945 had improved their position immensely with the capture of Japanese arms, but they were still at a decided disadvantage with the KMT, which enjoyed about a five-to-one ratio militarily. The Chinese communists were very much concerned with U.S. policy and the need to avoid direct U.S. intervention in the civil war in China. For this reason, among others, the Chinese Communist Party (CCP) displayed a cooperative attitude toward the American efforts of 1945-46 to mediate a settlement of the conflict in China.[5] As a result of General George C. Marshall's efforts in January 1946, the Chinese communists and Nationalists signed agreements on a ceasefire, a political program, and a plan for integration of the communist forces into the National Army. This political settlement, temporary as it was no doubt thought to be, was considered a significant victory by the Chinese communists. In keeping with this climate, it obviously would have been inopportune from the CCP's point of view for the Vietnamese to have launched a violent revolution in early 1946. There

---

*Many years later the party's first secretary, Le Duan, explained that the party "decided to come to temporary peace terms with the French in order to speedily get all the Chiang Kai-shek troops out of the country and sweep away all the reactionaries and their hench-men in order to gain time to consolidate our forces in preparation for the nationwide resistance against the French, which our party believed to be inevitable" (Le Duan, speech on the 40th anniversary of the Vietnam Workers Party, VNA, English, February 2, 1970). After several French concessions, the Chinese Nationalist forces were withdrawn by the summer of 1946.

is no positive evidence that this situation influenced Ho's decisions as directly as did guidance from Moscow via Paris at this time, but Ho no doubt followed events in China carefully, and in all likelihood there was liaison between the two fraternal parties.

In July, the Fontainebleau talks between Ho and the French Government broke down. The French Communist Party at this time was still reportedly urging the Viet Minh to abstain from open violence until Moscow gave its approval.[6] Moscow in fact had officially instructed Ho not to embarrass the French communists during the forthcoming elections in France.[7] Relations continued to deteriorate, however, as the French refused recognition of Vietnam's full independence under the government of national union and maneuvered to retain at least Cochin China under their control. In November 1946, the French Navy shelled Haiphong and the Viet Minh began to prepare for its counterattack, which came on December 19—a surprise attack on the French civilians in Hanoi. The Viet Minh abandoned the cities, and the people's war was on. Although this turn to violent revolution came a year ahead of the Soviet endorsement of a worldwide militant line and it did in fact embarrass the French communists, who were still part of the coalition government in Paris, it paralleled developments in China, where the ceasefire agreements of January and February had broken down. Hostilities were beginning to spread through various parts of China; and by January 1947, the U.S. mediation effort in China was officially ended.

1950: THE REVOLUTIONS LINK UP

The leader of the Vietnam People's Army (VPA), General Vo Nguyen Giap, in March 1946 told a mass rally in Hanoi that war would be disastrous without outside aid, and when war was forced by events in December, he adopted a delaying and defensive strategy.[8] For the next three years Giap followed guerrilla tactics that concentrated on building up his forces in the mountains and waiting for major assistance from China. This assistance came in December 1949, when the Chinese communist armies reached the Sino-Vietnamese border; from this point on, the nature of the war in Vietnam changed.*

------

*Twenty years later, in an article hailing the development of Sino-Vietnamese relations, the Hanoi daily Nhan Dan noted that "The success of the Chinese Revolution in 1949 broke off the encirclement of Vietnam by the imperialists, creating favorable conditions for the powerful development of the Vietnamese people's resistance war against the French" (Hanoi VNA, English, January 18, 1970).

4

There should never have been any question but that Communist China would do everything feasible to assist the Viet Minh to defeat the French. There was in this case no real or potential conflict between Peking's national and its ideological goals or between its security and its revolutionary power interests—both would be served with a communist government in Vietnam. Such a commitment was clearly consistent with the world view of all the Chinese communist leaders at that time and with their expectations as to the future. Vietnam was correctly seen as the most promising war of national liberation and as the critical wedge of the socialist camp into Southeast Asia.

The Chinese saw their assistance to the Viet Minh as taking two forms, military and political. China quickly became the "reliable rear base" for the Viet Minh.* No time was lost in pushing the war into the second or mobile stage; Chinese training and weapons quickly built the Vietnam People's Army into an efficient and modern force, and Giap began to prepare plans to liquidate the French forts along the border with China. By spring 1950, at least two military training camps had been established in China, in Yünnan and Kwangsi provinces, where young Vietnamese conscripts received three months' political indoctrination and basic training.[9] By early summer, 4,000 Vietnamese had returned to North Vietnam equipped with Chinese-furnished weapons, including U.S.-made equipment captured from the Nationalists and Soviet-manufactured items.[10] By March 1950, Viet Minh units possessed heavy mortars and pack howitzers; shortly thereafter they formed complete artillery battalions using American-made recoilless rifles and 105-mm howitzers.[11]

In the fall of 1950, French forces along the border suffered stunning defeats at the hands of about 40 battalions of well-armed Viet Minh troops. Within a few months, Giap's forces had seized all the border area and supplies, and newly trained men crossed freely from China. By the time of the ceasefire in 1954, some 40,000 Viet Minh soldiers were reported to have received training in China.[12] Chinese military personnel were also sent into Vietnam in limited numbers to provide training and technical services. Reports that Chinese "volunteers" were committed as combatants are not generally substantiated, although later in the war large numbers of Chinese truck drivers and antiaircraft personnel were apparently employed.[13] For

---

*A military aid agreement was reportedly signed between the PRC and the DRV in April 1950, during Ho Chi Minh's visit to Peking (Harold Hinton, China's Relations with Burma and Vietnam, Institute for Pacific Relations [New York, 1958], p. 18, citing a report by the French correspondent Robert Guillian, La fin des illusions [Paris, 1954]).

the movement of heavy Chinese equipment, a railway line was eventually built from Nanning to Langson and a highway from Lung Chu to Hoa Binh via Cao Bang.[14]

China and the DRV persistently denied any Chinese material assistance to the Viet Minh.[15] But the Viet Minh clearly recognized the critical importance of such aid. In a staff study presented by Giap to the political commissars of the 316th VPA Infantry Division in late 1950, it was stated that in order to carry out the general counter-offensive, which would be the third and final stage of the war, "we will have to receive aid from abroad."[16] After his final victory over the French, Giap, in his book People's War; People's Army, acknowledged, in general terms, the importance of the support of the socialist camp:

> If the Vietnamese people's war of liberation ended in a glorious victory it is because we did not fight alone but with the support of progressive peoples the world over and more especially the peoples of the socialist countries with the Soviet Union at the head. The victory of the Viet-namese peoples cannot be divided from this support; it cannot be disassociated from the . . . victories of the Soviet Red Army during the last few years.[17]

The victory of the Chinese revolution, Giap said, "exerted a considerable influence on the war of liberation of the Vietnamese people. Vietnam no longer was in the grip of enemy encirclement and was henceforth geographically linked to the Socialist bloc."[18]

Chinese intervention in Vietnam from the beginning was measured by two axioms: It was kept at a level sufficient to restore or retain the balance and the initiative with the VPA, and direct Chinese inter-vention was kept clandestine and at a minimum level. It is problem-atical what China would have done if the VPA—despite Chinese material assistance—had suffered a progressive weakening of its position. Politically and ideologically, the Chinese would have felt justified in a massive direct intervention if absolutely necessary to defeat the massive French involvement. But an invasion by Chinese volunteers would have compromised the nationalist banners of the Viet Minh, and it would have opened up China to the risk of retaliation on its own soil.

Nevertheless, Peking had run the risk of retaliation in Korea in a context that was more provocative. This precedent suggests that the Chinese were prepared to raise their involvement in Vietnam if absolutely necessary to save the VPA from complete destruction. But despite reverses for the Viet Minh from 1951 to 1953, there was never any real danger of this need arising.

Also important was the political and ideological influence of China on the Viet Minh. On January 18, 1950, the People's Republic of China (PRC) recognized the DRV (the Soviets followed on January 31), but in keeping with the policy of maintaining its official relations with the Viet Minh in as low a posture as possible, Peking did not assign an ambassador to Hanoi until the Geneva agreements had been concluded. Nevertheless, Chinese and Soviet diplomatic and political support not only raised the morale of the Viet Minh forces but also made the "dirty war" seem even more hopeless and less popular in France.

However, Chinese and Soviet political support for the Viet Minh seemed to confirm the view in the West that the issues involved in Vietnam were more than those of a colonial war; thus the Chinese commitment stimulated the U.S. Government to make greater efforts to save the French. Previously Washington had looked upon the war in Vietnam as a distasteful colonial venture that it did not oppose because of its European interests. But, with the beginning of the relatively small but important Chinese assistance to the Viet Minh, the United States responded with its own even more massive support for the French.

When Moscow and Peking recognized Ho Chi Minh's DRV in January 1950, Washington responded by recognizing the French-created regime of Bao Dai on February 7. A few days later, Secretary of State Dean Acheson, in recommending a favorable reply to the French request for assistance, wrote in a memorandum to President Harry S. Truman, "The choice confronting the U.S. is to support the legal governments of Indochina or to face the extension of Communism over the remainder of the continental area of Southeast Asia and possibly westward."[19] Vietnam had become inextricably bound up in the cold war.

THE MAOIST MODEL

The ideological and strategic influence of Maoist doctrines on the Viet Minh was also evident in the many books on the Chinese communist revolution that were translated in the early postwar years into Vietnamese, largely at Ho Chi Minh's initiative.[20] Both Giap and the party secretary general, Truong Chinh, drew heavily on Maoist concepts for their own writings and political and military strategy. After the defeat of the French, the Chinese model would be carried over into the social and economic fields.

Also important politically was the tidying up of the revolutionary model in Vietnam to fit the new situation. The principal change involved the resurrection of the Indochina Communist Party as the Lao Dong (Workers) Party in February 1951 and its open recognition as the leading element in the united front. The manifesto of the party was strictly along the lines of "new democracy," and it openly proclaimed that the ultimate, although not the present, task was the elimination of feudalism and the passage to socialism.[21]

Some have argued that the Chinese were critical of Ho for following a rightist line and for emphasizing the antiimperialist struggle to the exclusion of communist goals.[22] But Ho Chi Minh's stratagems had all along been quite consistent with Mao's. Ho's nominal disbanding of the ICP in 1945 and his seemingly pro-French attitude were, as we have seen, dictated by the need to achieve the ousting of the Nationalist Chinese (who were then supporting a nationalist Vietnamese group in opposition to the Viet Minh) as well as by the requirements of the French and the Soviet communist parties. In the same way the CCP played down its own communist ideology in the immediate postwar period both as a united front tactic and as an additional device to prevent U.S. intervention in China.

The Maoist model, however, called for the clear hegemony of the communist party over the national democratic united front.* And the emergence of the Lao Dong in the vanguard served to complete the model. It is difficult to believe that Ho and Mao were not in complete agreement on the timeliness of this move. The Viet Minh was now armed with Mao's "three magic weapons": a strong party, a united front, and an armed struggle.

THE WAR ESCALATES

Although China became heavily involved in the Viet Minh effort in 1950, it was not until the end of the Korean conflict that the Viet Minh was able to enter the decisive stage of war—the stage that depended

---

*Mao's subtle blend of ambiguity and frankness in regard to his political intentions was remarkably effective. In early 1945, for example, U.S. Ambassador Patrick Hurley was still observing that the "communists are striving for democratic principles" whereas at almost the same time Mao was repeating the Leninist dictum that "we communists never conceal our political stand, it is definite and beyond any doubt that our future or maximum program is to head China for socialism or communism" (April 24, 1945). Both quoted in Tang Tsou, America's Failure in China (Chicago: University of Chicago Press, 1963), pp. 186-187.

upon even larger consignments of Chinese weapons and materials. Beginning in the fall of 1953, the Viet Minh forces began to receive Chinese trucks, bazookas, mortars, and cannons. One study has estimated that the monthly average tonnage of Chinese military supplies going to Vietnam was between 10 and 20 tons in 1951, 250 tons at the end of 1952, and 400 to 600 tons in 1953.[23] The State Department's analysis indicated about 400 tons monthly in 1952 and about 750 tons monthly the next year.[24]

Needless to say, this Chinese aid did not compare in tonnage or firepower with the U.S. equipment that was being poured into the French war effort in Vietnam.* By 1954 the U.S. military aid program in Vietnam reached $1.1 billion, paying for 74 percent of the cost of the war.[25] Nevertheless, Chinese aid was critical to the success of the Viet Minh offensive. An ascending spiral of intervention and counterintervention by the two outside antagonists had developed.

Because of this spiral, it is perhaps impossible to say whether Chinese material aid was indispensable to the final victory of the Viet Minh, but without aid on either side the Viet Minh might have won sooner and at less cost. It is, of course, unrealistic to assume that it was at all possible for Peking not to have lent at least moral and political support to the revolution in Vietnam.

As early as 1952, Washington foresaw the possibility that the conflicting U.S. and Chinese commitments in Vietnam would escalate into a direct confrontation. At that time the U.S. Government was prepared to accept this eventuality, but given the frustrations it was experiencing in Korea, it would not contemplate again leaving China as a sanctuary. A Statement of Policy by the National Security Council in early 1952 proposed that in the event of the Chinese communist overtly intervening in the Indochina conflict or covertly participating to the point of jeopardizing retention of the Tonkin Delta area by the French, the U.S. Government should take the following actions:

1. Propose another UN resolution condemning China as an aggressor;

2. Initiate air and naval action, together with British and French forces, against China, including a naval blockade; and

3. Support Nationalist Chinese actions against China proper.

---

*Marchand estimates 10,000 tons monthly in U.S. equipment by 1953, cited by J. J. Zasloff, "The Role of the Sanctuary in Insurgency, Communist China's Support to the Vietminh, 1946-1954," Santa Monica, Cal., RAND Corporation, May 1967, p. 5. From 1950 to 1952, an estimated 100,000 tons of U.S. equipment was shipped to the French forces (New York Times, January 29, 1952).

If the United Kingdom and France refused to concur in these actions against China, the paper concluded, the U.S. Government should consider taking unilateral action.[26]

THE FINAL BATTLE

The story of the progressive Viet Minh military victories from the fall of 1953 into the spring of 1954 and culminating in Dien Bien Phu needs no retelling here. We must attempt, however, to analyze the strategic situation that China and the DRV faced in the months of crisis and the political and military strategies that they evolved. In the following analysis our intention is to show that, despite obvious differences in the priority of objectives that China, the DRV, and the Soviet Union saw in the war, the three communist governments at this time followed a generally coordinated military and political strategy in concluding the struggle. Peking and Moscow were more or less in agreement on defining the best terms possible, and Hanoi had no alternative but to accept these terms.

Obviously the DRV was concerned with the immediate objective of establishing its rule over all of Vietnam. In addition, the history of the ICP and the Viet Minh's subsequent establishment of satellite parties in Laos and Cambodia suggests a broader goal of extending Vietnamese influence of some sort over Indochina. Finally, the leaders of the DRV wanted at least as an ideal objective to promote the interests of the communist camp throughout Southeast Asia.

China's commanding national interest was the expulsion of Western power and presence from Indochina and the replacement of French control by a Peking-oriented Vietnamese regime. Moreover, China hoped to see a more accommodating, sympathetic, and neutralized Southeast Asia. With a new strategy of peaceful coexistence, China hoped to prevent the formation of a comprehensive anticommunist security community or Pacific pact in Asia. Similarly, the Soviets had set their sights on the defeat of the European Defense Community (EDC), and they, in turn, focused on Asian events likely to interfere with this objective. An integrated Western European army, including a rearmed West Germany, was seen in Moscow as a direct and menacing threat to Soviet security. While the National Assembly in Paris argued the issue of French participation in the EDC, it was made clear to the French that the quid pro quo for a satisfactory end to the war in Vietnam was French rejection of the EDC.[27]

As the last phase of the Vietnamese war began, new priorities were emerging in both China and the USSR. Stalin had died in 1953, and G. Malenkov sought a period of international relaxation. China

10

also launched its first five-year plan in 1953, concentrating on internal growth after the rigors of the Korean War. Therefore, it is likely that both countries sought compromise settlement of the Vietnamese war for domestic and foreign policy reasons.

But the most important consideration for China and the USSR was the serious risk of general war that seemed to be involved in pushing for total victory in Vietnam. Uncertainty as to the nature and extent of possible U.S. intervention became the dominating calculation in the policies of the three communist regimes. For the Chinese, this concern centered around the possible use of U.S. nuclear weapons against China. Peking could not forget that in Korea the U.S. Government had warned in 1953 that unless a ceasefire was agreed to, nuclear weapons might be employed.[28]

Following the truce in Korea, Washington focused on the role being played by China in the intensification of the war in Indochina. In a speech on September 2, Secretary of State John Foster Dulles charged that China was training, equipping, and supplying the communist forces in Vietnam, and, he said, there is the risk that "as in Korea, Red China might send its own army into Indochina." Should it do so, Dulles warned, Peking "should realize that such a second aggression could not occur without grave consequences which might not be confined to Indochina."[29]

Clearly China was faced with a delicate situation. But its determination to achieve its foreign policy goals as well as its skillful judgment of power realities was dramatically demonstrated in its handling of this first crisis of the Indochina war. At this time, Peking, Moscow, and the Viet Minh carried out a balanced and concerted political and military campaign to achieve as many of their objectives as possible. To do this, they ran considerable risk of escalating the war. But their skillful diplomacy and the nature of their aid was successful in avoiding escalation, and in the end they accepted something less than total victory.

POLITICAL AND MILITARY MOVES INTENSIFY

After the armistice in Korea in July 1953, the Chinese and the Soviets began to blame the United States for the continuation of the war in Vietnam. In the latter half of 1953 China increased its aid to the Viet Minh but at the same time hinted at a negotiated settlement. On September 2, 1953, a People's Daily editorial said that "only by applying the principle of settling international disputes through negotiations can France get out of its mess in the Vietnam war."[30]

In October Premier Joseph Laniel proposed negotiations for a "just and honorable conclusion" of the war. In apparent response, Ho Chi Minh indicated an acceptance of negotiations on condition that France "respect the independence of Vietnam." Most unusual, however, was the reference in Ho's statement that connected the end of the war in Vietnam to the issue of French participation in the EDC.

> . . . The American imperialists are forcing France to sign
> the EDC pact which implies that German militarism will
> be reborn. The struggle of the French people for independ-
> ence, democracy and peace and for an end to the war in
> Vietnam constitutes one of the major factors in the efforts
> to solve the Vietnam problem.[31]

The question of German rearmament was obviously not a major question on Ho's mind at that time, and its inclusion in his short state- ment on the possibility of peace talks suggests that the Vietnamese leader was attempting to accommodate Soviet interests.[32]

In January 1954, President Dwight D. Eisenhower approved the policy statement set forth by the National Security Council on "United States objectives and courses of action with respect to Southeast Asia." The definition of U.S. goals and policy considerations set out by the paper would guide Washington's policy for the next 15 years:

> 1. Communist domination, by whatever means, of all
> Southeast Asia would seriously endanger in the short
> term, and critically endanger in the longer term, United
> States security interests.
> a. In the conflict in Indochina, the Communist and
> non-Communist worlds clearly confront one another on the
> field of battle. The loss of the struggle in Indochina, in
> addition to its impact in Southeast Asia and in South Asia,
> would therefore have the most serious repercussions on
> U.S. and free world interests in Europe and elsewhere.
> b. Such is the interrelation of the countries of the
> area that effective counteraction would be immediately
> necessary to prevent the loss of any single country from
> leading to submission to or an alignment with communism
> by the remaining countries of Southeast Asia and Indon-
> esia. Furthermore, in the event all of Southeast Asia falls
> under communism, an alignment with the communists of
> India, and in the longer term, of the Middle East (with the
> probable exception of at least Pakistan and Turkey) could
> follow progressively. Such widespread alignment would
> seriously endanger the stability and security of Europe.

c. Communist control of all of Southeast Asia and Indonesia would threaten the U.S. position in the Pacific offshore island chain and would seriously jeopardize fundamental U.S. security interests in the Far East.

d. The loss of Southeast Asia would have serious economic consequences for many nations of the free world and conversely would add significant resources to the Soviet bloc. Southeast Asia, especially Malaya and Indonesia, is the principal world source of natural rubber and tin and a producer of petroleum and other strategically important commodities. The rice exports of Burma, Indochina and Thailand are critically important to Malaya, Ceylon, and Hong Kong and are of considerable significance to Japan and India, all important areas of free Asia. Furthermore, this area has an important potential as a market for the industrialized countries of the free world.

e. The loss of Southeast Asia, especially of Malaya and Indonesia, could result in such economic and political pressures in Japan as to make it extremely difficult to prevent Japan's eventual accommodation to communism.[33]

In February 1954, the four-power foreign ministers meeting at Berlin agreed to an international conference in April to discuss Indochina and Korea. As it would again 14 years later, the West abandoned its position that truce talks in Indochina could not take place while the communist forces were in an offensive position.[34] The week that the conference opened, another National Security Council policy paper said that the United States should consider continuing the war itself, together with the Indochinese states, if France negotiated an unsatisfactory settlement.[35]

In December, Giap had issued an order mobilizing the population,[36] and as the Geneva conference approached, the Viet Minh intensified their military activity—principally by a heavy buildup around the French garrison at Dien Bien Phu. China accordingly raised its supply effort to the Viet Minh to major proportions—nearly 4,000 tons per month.

The U.S. Government fulminated over this threatening position and the high level of Chinese material assistance—which to the Americans as well as to the French seemed to be the heart of the problem. On March 29, Dulles stressed the major, but still indirect, role played by the Chinese and revealed the frustration of the administration in attempting to deal with it.[37] For example, on April 5, Dulles told the House Foreign Affairs Committee that Chinese participation in the fighting at Dien Bien Phu looked very much like direct intervention. The secretary then charged that a Chinese general, Li Chen Hou, together with 20 technical advisers were at Giap's headquarters near Dien Bien Phu, that the enemy's radar-equipped 37-mm antiaircraft guns were serviced by Chinese, and that 1,000 Viet Minh's trucks were manned by Chinese.[38] He warned that U.S. reaction to Chinese intervention "might not be confined to Indochina." About the same time, Senate Majority Leader William Knowland warned that the "free world" might react to the threat by bombing Chinese territory, by a naval blockade of China, by unleashing Nationalist forces from Taiwan, or by joint action of the Western-aligned nations of Asia.[39]

But the fact that most frustrated the U.S. Government was that the VPA was winning without direct, overt Chinese participation. It was difficult for Dulles to justify direct U.S. involvement in combat on the basis of this sort of intervention by China. Moreover, the Americans knew that they could be accused of setting off an escalation of the war.

The January National Security Council paper recognized that "in the event the United States participated in the fighting, there is a substantial risk that the Chinese Communists would intervene." As in the early 1952 policy paper, the January document likewise concluded that in the event of Chinese intervention, " . . . the United Nations should be asked to call on member nations to 'take whatever action may be necessary . . . to meet such an aggression.' "

However, the National Security Council did not suggest the possibility of unilateral U.S. attacks against China as it had suggested in 1952.

At this point it was clear to the Chinese and the Vietnamese communists that they were playing a risky game by pursuing the campaign to wipe out the French garrison at Dien Bien Phu. Peking knew that the plight of the French would compel the United States to decide whether or not to intervene directly. The Chinese press had in fact reported Western press stories on a proposed plan for the use of U.S. tactical aircraft "to forestall a complete French collapse."[40] China had also guessed what subjects were discussed during the March visit to Washington of General Paul Ely, French chief of staff, who appealed for greater U.S. assistance to relieve Dien Bien Phu.

Washington avoided giving a formal guarantee to Paris in the event of Chinese air intervention, but it issued fresh warnings to Peking.[41] However, the most significant development of Ely's visit was the tentative proposal by the chairman of the Joint Chiefs of Staff, Admiral Arthur Radford, for several nighttime raids on the area around Dien Bien Phu by U.S. B-29 heavy bombers. This proposed operation, to be given the code name Vulture, was taken up by the French Government, and a formal request was made that it be carried out.[42]

The Chinese responded to the reports of Ely's visits and to Dulles's statements of March 29 and April 5 in defensive tones. Peking carefully avoided any threat of counterintervention or even any hint as to what its response might be if the U.S. Government did intervene with air strikes.[43] Meanwhile, the attack on Dien Bien Phu pressed on.

In early April, Operation Vulture was proposed by Dulles and Admiral Radford to a group of congressional leaders. The congressmen, however, refused to consider an authorizing resolution until three conditions had been met: approval and support from U.S. allies, complete independence for the Indochinese states, and a French commitment to stay in the war.[44] The administration could not meet these conditions because of the attitude of the British and the French, and so Operation Vulture was rejected. Washington then turned its attention to the negotiations, hoping to salvage at least part of Vietnam from a communist takeover. Nevertheless, threats of U.S. military action, including attacks on China, still played a major role in the negotiating stage.

A study in May by the U.S. Joint Chiefs on the contingency of Chinese intervention in Indochina advocated as a first stage "employing atomic weapons, whenever advantageous, as well as other weapons" against military targets in China that were being used in direct support of Chinese operations in Vietnam or that threatened U.S. and allied forces in the area. As a second stage, the study suggested the destruction of additional military targets by employing an "enlarged but highly selective atomic offensive."[45]

Seventeen years later, Peking charged that then Vice President Richard Nixon had advocated the use of nuclear weapons to save Dien Bien Phu in 1954.[46] Whether or not this is so, Dulles later included the Vietnam crisis as another example of successful "brinksmanship."

But in the spring of 1954, the PRC could reasonably calculate that the French and British would be strongly opposed to conventional escalation and most certainly to the use of nuclear weapons unless there was absolutely no other way out. The U.S. public and Congress would also clearly have been opposed to risking nuclear war in order to save the French colonials in Vietnam.

Consequently the communist strategy at the time of Dien Bien Phu was based upon the estimate that intervention by the United States on a scale sufficient to change the tide of the war in Vietnam was unlikely provided the possibility of a political settlement was kept open.

This assessment was reflected in the communist public treatment of the conflict. While pouring arms and ammunition into the Dien Bien Phu battle, China and the Soviet Union sought publicly to focus attention on the prospects of ending the war through negotiations.

Dien Bien Phu fell on May 7, the day before the conference turned to
the question of Indochina, but both Peking and Moscow treated news
of the historic victory with restraint, and one week later in Geneva,
Molotov agreed that military problems could take priority over political
ones. On May 25, the DRV premier, Pham Van Dong, implicitly
suggested a temporary military partition as the basis of a ceasefire.

THE COMPROMISE AT GENEVA

Although the communists were ready for a ceasefire, the negotiations at Geneva were acrimonious and at one point seemed on the
verge of breaking down. Nikita Khrushchev later suggested that the
communist governments, including the DRV, were from the beginning
prepared to accept a political settlement short of a total DRV victory.[47]
However, they naturally intended to come away from the conference
with as much as possible.

The first issue to be faced was the DRV insistence on recognition
of its puppet communist organizations in Laos and Cambodia, (the
Pathet Lao and the Khmer Rouge) and its refusal to contemplate
withdrawal of its own forces from these two countries. The communists
apparently were hoping for some sort of partition of Laos and Cambodia, as well as Vietnam.

Chou En-lai, in a private conversation with Sir Anthony Eden
on May 20, was inflexible on these issues, but on June 16, he asked
to see the British foreign secretary again and completely reversed
his earlier position. He also told the French that he recognized that
there were now two governments in the territory of Vietnam, the Viet
Minh Government and the Vietnamese Government (that is, Saigon).[48]
One week later Chou repeated his concessions on Laos and Cambodia
to the new French premier, Pierre Mendès-France, and agreed that
there was no urgency in holding elections in Vietnam. Chou proposed
separate talks between France and the DRV on the terms of the Vietnam
settlement.

Chou said that China would have no objections to recognizing
the kingdoms of Laos and Cambodia or to the states having forces
and arms sufficient to maintain security . . . so long as they were
not used as military bases by the U.S. Government.[49]

What had persuaded Chou and his allies to make these concessions? Apparently they feared that the conference might break down
and that U.S. conditions for united intervention might be fulfilled. Although Dulles and Eisenhower had separately confirmed on June 8
and 10 respectively that they did not contemplate asking Congress for
authority to intervene in Indochina, other steps were being taken that

16

suggested that if the conference failed to agree, such a request might be made. According to the Pentagon Papers, a draft resolution was actually prepared. On June 11, Dulles again publicly warned of U.S. intervention in Indochina if (1) it was invited by the lawful authorities; (2) such action was concurred in by the United Nations; (3) the states of Indochina were given complete independence; and (4) there was assurance that France would not withdraw.[50] On June 15, he privately informed the French that the time for intervention had run out. But to the Communist negotiators, this was still far from certain.

Paris had already met condition "3" when on June 4 it granted full independence to the Republic of Vietnam, and on June 3, at U.S. insistence, the United States, Britain, and France began preliminary military talks at the chief of staff level about Southeast Asia. During the second week of June, both the U.S. and British delegations expressed their frustration at the Geneva conference stalemate. Chou's concessions came on the same day on which it was announced that Winston Churchill and Eisenhower would meet in Washington the following week. Also on June 16, Molotov made another concession, this one on the composition of the International Control Commission (ICC).

On June 17, Mendès-France announced that he would call for conscripts to fight in Indochina and then resign if no acceptable settlement had been reached by July 20. Like President Nixon 17 years later, the French premier was under domestic pressure not only to end the fighting but to win the release of prisoners of war, of which 14,000 had been taken at Dien Bien Phu. During his conciliatory talk with Mendès-France on the 24th, Chou reiterated his concessions on Laos and Cambodia and in addition said that a "final political settlement" should be reached by direct negotiations between the two governments in Vietnam. Again he did not press for early elections.[51]

After this meeting, Chou flew off to visit India and Burma but most importantly to see Ho Chi Minh. At the same time the Eisenhower-Churchill accord of late June clearly indicated that impossible demands made upon Paris by the communist side would tend "seriously" to aggravate the international situation.[52] With the limits of settlement now defined, Chou met with Ho Chi Minh to discuss the final terms. The New China News Agency (NCNA) in announcing the meeting said only that "a full exchange of views" had taken place with respect to the question of restoring peace in Indochina. Chou returned to Geneva, and the final settlement was worked out.*

---

*The DRV proposed the 16th parallel as the dividing line and settled on the 17th, as suggested by Molotov, who also proposed that the time limit for elections be set at two years. Philippe Devillers and Jean Lacouture, End of a War (New York: Praeger Publishers, 1969), pp. 292-293.

It is widely believed that the Viet Minh were highly put out, and may have even felt "betrayed," by the terms of the settlement, feeling that their military position should have won them more concessions. This attitude was privately expressed by Viet Minh officials at Geneva to Western correspondents.[53]

The Chinese, the Soviets, and the Viet Minh viewed the ending of the war with different objectives in mind. The two powers were largely motivated by their strategic interests vis-à-vis the United States and their new united front diplomacy, while the DRV naturally sought to maximize its control of Vietnam. Nevertheless, while there was certainly disappointment among the DRV leaders at not having achieved something more in the matter of parallels and in the timing of elections, it is difficult to believe that they could actually have felt abused by the decision of their allies, upon whose support they were critically dependent.

The Viet Minh disgruntlement was no doubt in part real but also in part tactical—a continuation of the negotiation strategy in which the DRV insisted on extreme positions and Moscow and Peking intervened with compromises. The Viet Minh was at this stage highly dependent upon Chinese assistance, and calculations of the strategic situation— especially that of possible U.S. reaction—were also clearly relevant to their own judgment of how much they could win at the negotiating table. The DRV delegation itself first broached the idea of partition, and by the time of Chou En-lai's visit with Ho, it was apparent that if other compromises were not agreed to, the conference would probably break down, with the chance that joint U.S.-British-French military action would ensue. In such an event, the Viet Minh would have required even heavier Chinese support and perhaps the direct use of Chinese troops. With this consideration in mind, Ho Chi Minh probably agreed with Chou that for the movement the best bargain had been struck.* Khrushchev later reported that "we gasped with surprise and pleasure" when the French agreed to partition at the 17th parallel. This was "the absolute maximum we would have claimed ourselves."[54]

Many lower-level Viet Minh, however, were more genuinely disgruntled; thus, the DRV leadership may have felt it useful to encourage the story that the Chinese and the Soviets were to blame for having achieved less than a total victory. But if so, this explanation

---

*An official Lao Dong history, "40 Years of Activity of the Party," prepared in February 1970, explains that "By late 1954, the revolutionary forces, although having grown up, were not yet strong enough to liberate the whole country while the enemy, though having failed was not yet completely defeated. Therefore, Vietnam was temporarily divided in two zones." VNA, January 20, 1970.

was encouraged in a most unofficial and informal manner. Ho Chi Minh, in fact, explained the Geneva compromises to the Central Committee of the Lao Dong in terms of the realistic calculations discussed above. According to the communist writer Nguyen Kien, Ho told the July 15, 1954, session of the Central Committee that

> we must never forget that this strength [the DRV's] and this weakness [of the French] are all relative, not absolute. We must not succumb to subjectivism and to underestimating the enemy. Our victories have awakened the Americans. After the battle of Dien Bien Phu they changed their plans from intervention to prolonging the Indochinese war, to internationalize it, to sabotage the Geneva Conference, to seek by all means to supplant the French, . . . some people elated by our continuous victories might wish to fight at any price, to fight to the end. They see the French without seeing the Americans . . . they pose excessive conditions unacceptable to the adversary.[55]

THE INTERVENING YEARS

During the next 10 years, the DRV's relations with China and the Soviet Union continued to be characterized by Hanoi's ideological identification with both countries, its heavy economic and military dependence upon the socialist camp, and its attempt to maximize its own freedom of action. This last element provided the dynamic behind the fluctuation in Hanoi's relations between Peking and Moscow. The disputes within the North Vietnamese leadership between allegedly pro-Chinese and pro-Soviet lines were not a question of whether to promote Chinese or Soviet interests. Instead the issue was whether the DRV's own economic development goals could best be served by following the Chinese or the Soviet model and whether the major political objective of national unification could best be served by closer alignment with Peking or Moscow. In addition, there was the general question of whether to emphasize economic development in the North or the political and military tasks of unification. Finally, in the mid-1960s, the question arose as to what political and military strategies the DRV should pursue in the face of heavy U.S. intervention.

The ideological and psychological orientation of the Vietnamese was, at first, in the direction of the Chinese. The DRV's land reform and tax program that began in 1953 slavishly copied the Maoist model, although rural conditions were quite different.[56] Again following Mao's example, the DRV introduced a short-lived "hundred flowers" campaign of intellectual liberalization.

19

But the serious political and economic disruptions created by the land reform program provoked considerable skepticism about the applicability of the Chinese model. Although in 1958 Hanoi dutifully praised the Great Leap Forward, it was not tempted to copy it, and when the Great Proletarian Cultural Revolution was introduced in China, the Maoist internal model fell into even lower repute in Hanoi.

In the realm of economic aid, China was also predominant in the early postwar years. From 1955 through 1961, the DRV received more than $1 billion in communist bloc aid, of which China reportedly supplied $662 million.[57] From 1958 to 1960, however, the beginning of the Sino-Soviet rivalry stimulated Moscow's interest in the DRV, and in these years Soviet aid surpassed that of China.[58] The 1960 five-year plan in North Vietnam stressed industrialization, and it became obvious that large-scale Soviet assistance was needed, and this was apparently promised by Khrushchev.[59]

However, so long as economic development was stressed, a forward policy in the South was not advisable. But by the end of 1960 it was apparent that Hanoi—while pushing ahead with industrialization— had given the highest priority to the national goal of unification.

The leadership in Hanoi had never wavered in its deep commitment to this overriding political goal, and while there was probably disagreement as to the timing of the next step in the completion of the revolution, it seems unlikely that at any time the dominant view in Hanoi was that this goal could be achieved other than by a renewal of insurrection in the South.

This objective prejudiced Hanoi against the developing Soviet line of peaceful coexistence, détente with the United States, and relaxation of world tensions. If Hanoi was to push ahead with the war in the South, it would require the strong support of the socialist camp. However, intensification of the struggle in South Vietnam eventually proved inconsistent with Khrushchev's evolving strategy of détente.

ATTITUDES TOWARD LAOS

Peking, on the other hand, had begun to break with Moscow on the very question of relations with the United States. So long as Washington refused to extend détente to China and continued its confrontational approach to the People's Republic, Peking had nothing to gain from Khrushchev's policy of peaceful coexistence with the United States. Moscow's unilateral pursuit of accommodation with the United States was seen by the Chinese as breaking the common front of the communist powers and denying equality to Chinese interests. At the same time, Moscow denied equality to Peking within the international communist movement, for to grant it would threaten an important aspect of Soviet power and eventually Soviet control over Eastern Europe. Denied both the fruits of détente and equality of leadership within the world communist movement, China increasingly argued for a militant confrontation policy toward the United States, and on this basis it set out to challenge the Soviet leadership of the communist camp as well as Soviet influence in the Third World. Hanoi's interests were consistent with the confrontational policy, and consequently in the early 1960s the DRV was gradually drawn nearer to, although not into, the Chinese orbit.

The 14-nation Geneva conference on Laos of 1961 and 1962 proved to be the last occasion on which the Soviets and the Chinese pursued an apparently coordinated policy. The climax of that particular crisis in Laos and the new Geneva agreements on the neutralization of that harassed country came at the time of a lull in the Sino-Soviet dispute. From the early spring of 1962 to September of that year, Moscow-Peking relations appeared to be improving. Significantly North Vietnam had played some role in this development; it had proposed in January 1962 a cessation of polemics, preliminary to bilateral conversations to prepare for an international communist meeting.[60]

Moscow and Peking had quite different long-range interests in Laos at this time, but they were united on the common objective of getting the United States out of Laos without provoking direct U.S. intervention. We have observed that in the first Vietnam crisis of 1953-54, the mutual Sino-Soviet objective of promoting the DRV's interests was pursued in the context of broad and compatible strategic goals in Peking and Moscow. But by 1962 the strategic considerations of Moscow and Peking had clearly begun to diverge. Soviet action in Laos was taken in the context of its sporadic search for détente with the United States, while the Chinese position was shaped by its own national and great power interests and by the belief that because of U.S. policy toward China, these could be attained only by a strategy of resistance and struggle.

Peking and Moscow both had ideological and power motives for supporting Hanoi, but by 1962 Chinese and Soviet policies operated in the framework of a hostile rivalry. At this time the Soviet ideological commitment to Hanoi clashed with its hoped-for détente with the United States, whereas China's ideological and national interests were consistent, since accommodation with the United States was not then a possible alternative for the PRC. Nevertheless, as we shall see, Peking's commitment to Hanoi would eventually seem to part of the leadership in China to pose a threat to China's security.

21

MOSCOW MOVES AWAY FROM HANOI

Shortly after the 14-nation Geneva agreements on Laos were concluded in 1962, a series of events highlighted the issues at stake in the Sino-Soviet quarrel. These included the Sino-Indian border war and the Cuban missile crisis. In both cases Hanoi was distressed at Khrushchev's faint-heartedness. The main consideration for the North Vietnamese leaders continued to be the extent to which Moscow was prepared to back them up in the achievement of their own objectives in South Vietnam.

Khrushchev's limits were soon apparent. The DRV's goals in Laos were related first of all to Hanoi's designs in South Vietnam and secondly to its natural political interest in its small neighboring country. North Vietnam was committed to assisting the Pathet Lao in shifting the military political balance more and more to their favor after the 1962 agreement, but, more important, the continued disruption of the country and the obstruction of the work of the International Control Commission in Laos precluded any significant restraint upon the DRV's use of Laos for infiltration into South Vietnam. It is even possible that the willful attacks of the Viet Minh-encadred Pathet Lao units against the neutralist-controlled areas of Laos were in part rationalized as provoking U.S. intervention, which in turn would tend to neutralize the political effect of North Vietnamese violations of the Geneva agreements on Laos.

Khrushchev apparently began to feel by late 1963 that he was deeply committing the Soviet Union to a confrontation in which he exercised relatively little control. Consequently, the Soviet leader began to show increasingly less interest in Vietnam and Laos.

Hanoi indicated its favorable view of Peking during Liu Shao-chi's visit in May 1963 and by its opposition to the Nuclear Test Ban Treaty in the summer of that year. At the Ninth Plenum of the Central Committee of the Lao Dong in December, Le Duan spelled out the conflict of interests between Moscow and Hanoi—Soviet objectives in regard to the United States were inconsistent with North Vietnam's objectives in the South.[61] "Some people," Le Duan said, proposed a détente with imperialism above all else, and "whether you like it or not the outcome will be only to hamper the development of revolution."

In December 1963, Khrushchev divested himself of what direct leverage he had on events in Laos by turning over to Hanoi all the Ilyushin-14 aircraft that had been operating on the airlift between Hanoi and Laos since December 1960.[62] With this move Khrushchev was not only ridding himself of leverage but also shedding responsibility for what was going on in Laos.

THE STRATEGIC ASSESSMENT IN 1964

Peking and Hanoi, however, must have seen the over-all strategic situation in 1964 as analogous to the political and military circumstances they had faced 10 years earlier. The enemy's position on the battle-field in South Vietnam as well as his political foundation was rapidly crumbling; Ngo Dinh Diem's overthrow in October 1963 led to a series of coups in Saigon. The time for moving into the next phase—large-scale unit engagements or mobile warfare—was fast approaching. The "general offensive" that would lead to final victory was expected in 1965. Like the crisis 10 years earlier, 1964 was the beginning of another critical period of the war—a period again dominated by the question of whether the United States would choose massive intervention by its own forces. Thus, an astute coordination of military and political strategy was again called for. As in the war against the French, intensification of military pressure, including a sharp step-up of support from the "rear base," would be balanced with a political campaign to promote negotiations and head off intervention.

The options open to the United States in this situation were similar to the ones it had faced in 1954. The choices for the United States were outlined by the North Vietnamese themselves on February 11 as withdrawal, greatly increased aid to Saigon, or an attack on the DRV perhaps with nuclear weapons.[63] The last possibility was rated unlikely by Hanoi because the United States would have to cope with China or eventually with the socialist camp as a whole.

NCNA's summary of this Hanoi article omitted the references to China's protection of the DRV against U.S. nuclear weapons, prob-ably because Peking could not, at this time, offer any deterrent to U.S. nuclear attack.[64] Nevertheless, by 1964 an important element in Hanoi's strategy was China's commitment to defend North Vietnam. Encouraged by Khrushchev's backing down, China committed itself to providing military and economic assistance to Hanoi so that the latter could now act as the "reliable rear base" of the national liber-ation war in the South in much the same way as China had assisted the Viet Minh 10 years before. Hanoi hoped that China's guarantor role over North Vietnam would deter a U.S. attack.

It is important to note that China's strategy in Vietnam in 1964 took place against the background of impressive gains for Peking in its direct challenge to Moscow. Developments in Vietnam at this time were seen by the Chinese as a major weapon in their struggle with the Soviets for leadership of the communist movement. Success for Hanoi with Peking's backing would seem to confirm the Chinese position on almost all the major issues at stake in the Sino-Soviet dispute.

U.S. MOVES

If China in 1964 had an additional incentive to stand by its ally in Indochina, so too did the United States, which also regarded the Vietnam war as a test case. Despite assessments by the CIA and the State Department's Bureau of Intelligence and Research challenging the domino theory, Presidents John F. Kennedy and Lyndon B. Johnson continued to make decisions on the basis of the analysis given in National Security Council papers prepared as early as 1952. In March 1964, Secretary of Defense Robert Strange McNamara predicted that unless the United States created an independent noncommunist South Vietnam, "all of Southeast Asia will probably fall under Communist dominance."[65]

The administration also feared that unless the United States prevailed in South Vietnam, other wars of national liberation would break out in Asia, Africa, and Latin America. But above all these fears there loomed the persistent but vague idea of "containing China."

In 1954, the enemy had seemed to be the monolithic communist bloc, and gains for communists anywhere were considered an addition to the bloc's power—to that of both the Soviet Union and China. Although by the early 1960s it was obvious that the bloc had split apart, U.S. policy in Asia was frozen into a containment posture that appeared to assume that the Chinese or their allies, if not obstructed at every turn, would do their worst. There was little recognition in high U.S. circles that China was in part reacting to the perceived U.S. threat and the U.S. refusal to seek any accommodation with Peking while advancing détente with Moscow.

Ironically, the Sino-Soviet split was seen by some high U.S. officials not as reducing U.S. interest in the containment of China but as providing a more favorable situation for the escalation of U.S. intervention. General Maxwell D. Taylor, for example, chairman of the Joint Chiefs of Staff, in a memorandum to McNamara on January 22, 1964, said that, "It appears probable that the economic and agricultural disappointments suffered by Communist China, plus the current rift with the Soviets, could cause the Communists to think twice about large-scale military adventure in Southeast Asia."[66]

In the same month, Johnson also said that a "showdown" in the Sino-Soviet dispute was expected soon, "and action against the North will be more practicable then."[67]

These remarks suggest that the threat of Chinese expansion or aggression was indeed a chimera only vaguely conceived. The national prestige and the good word of the United States were the essential factors in the U.S. decision to stick it out in Vietnam.

Unlike the situation 10 years before, the United States in 1964 was heavily committed in Vietnam. Victory in Vietnam, the president and his aides believed, would save the U.S. reputation as a guarantor nation and would demonstrate the will and ability of the United States to have its way in foreign affairs.[68]

As the Viet Cong rebellion gained strength, the United States turned its attention to action against the North, which would force the DRV to call off the southern insurgency. Six months before the Tonkin Gulf incidents of August 1964, the United States began supporting clandestine South Vietnamese commando raids against the North in retaliation for the DRV's support of the Viet Cong. U.S.-directed air attacks against the advancing North Vietnamese and Pathet Lao in Laos also escalated, and U.S. destroyer patrols in the Gulf of Tonkin were initiated. Interest in bombing the North as the final pressure upon Hanoi to abandon its objectives in the South also accelerated during the year, and administration leaders began to talk of a draft resolution for presentation to Congress.

In June, official leaks were made to the press affirming U.S. intentions to support its allies and uphold its treaty commitments in Southeast Asia. Attention was also deliberately focused on U.S. military prepositioning moves.

To make certain that the U.S. determination was well understood in Hanoi, the Canadian representative on the International Control Commission, Mr. Seaborn, paid the first of two secret visits to Premier Pham Van Dong on June 18. Seaborn emphasized that U.S. patience was not limitless, and "in the event of escalation, the greatest devastation would, of course, result for the DRV itself."[69]

PEKING-HANOI MOVES

Neither the Chinese nor the North Vietnamese were intimidated by these U.S. moves. As with the Chinese assistance to the Viet Minh in the early 1950s, Hanoi continued to provide whatever aid was needed to keep the initiative and the momentum with the Viet Cong; Peking in turn backstopped North Vietnam. The rate of infiltration from North Vietnam of native Southerners stepped up appreciably during 1964; approximately 4,000 infiltrated in the first half of that year, as compared to about the same number for all of 1963.[70] The number of Viet Cong military attacks in the South also jumped from 3,735 in 1963 to 15,000 in 1964.[71] For the first time the Viet Cong were beginning to attack in organized units, many of which possessed heavy weapons manned by North Vietnamese regulars. On one occasion in 1964 personnel from a North Vietnamese battalion were captured in the South.[72]

As a parallel political strategy, China alternated warnings against U.S. intervention with a major effort to promote a reconvening of the Geneva conference. In June, Peking supported the DRV's call for early convocation of the 14-nation Geneva conference on Laos, and in July it gave extensive coverage to the 10th anniversary of the 1954 Geneva accords.[73] The Chinese also were obviously pleased when UN Secretary General U Thant and General Charles De Gaulle took the initiative in calling for another conference on Indochina with the same membership as the one held in 1954. At the same time, Peking officially pledged that China and the DRV were like "lips and teeth" and that it "would not look on with folded arms in the face of any aggression against the DRV."[74] To back up these warnings the Chinese, in the latter part of July, reportedly moved troops and aircraft into the southern provinces bordering North Vietnam. Construction was also begun on a number of new airfields in South China. One of these, Ningming, was located only 12 miles from the border—a vulnerable location that suggests that its purpose was for defense of North Vietnam and not of China.[75] At about the same time the lengthening and improvement of airfields were noted in North Vietnam.[76]

At this time the United States supported the demand of Souvanna Phouma that a Pathet Lao ceasefire and withdrawal from the areas that the Pathet Lao had seized during 1964 precede any new conference on Laos. The United States also believed that the increased Viet Cong attacks, the growing infiltration of communist forces into South Vietnam, Saigon's deteriorating military position and extremely shaky political situation as well as DRV and Pathet Lao violations of the Lao accords all combined to make negotiations unacceptable. Instead, the United States moved to strengthen Saigon's military position. At the end of July, Washington announced that its military mission in South Vietnam would be increased from 16,000 to 21,000.[77]

THE CLASH OF WILLS: THE LAST HALF OF 1964

The Tonkin Gulf incidents of August 2 and August 4 represent clear evidence of the Maoist-type "resolute-defensive" (or active-defense) approach to dealing with a threatening enemy who is strategically stronger. It is not our purpose here to go into the controversy on the United States side surrounding these incidents; rather, we are interested in the implications of the events for the Peking-Hanoi strategy.

North Vietnam has admitted to the first attack and justified it as retaliation for an earlier shelling of two North Vietnamese islands by South Vietnamese craft on July 31. The August 2 torpedo boat attack, then, represented a considered decision, taken at the highest level. However justified Hanoi may have felt in making the attack, it clearly did not act principally because it felt morally correct in doing so but rather because it was considered consistent with its political and military strategy. Hanoi and Peking believed that at times the enemy had to be dealt with rudely in order to awaken him to the determination of his revolutionary adversary.

This aspect of the Maoist "operational code" was dramatized in an interesting parable that appeared in the Liberation Army Daily one year later on November 26, 1965, when the issue of China's strategy in regard to Vietnam was again critical. The parable, which was subsequently republished in many other Chinese journals, was entitled "On Training in Bayonet Fighting," and the moral was that a "dare to do attitude" combined with practical caution and patience would prevail.

> In handling an enemy who is extremely savage and arrogant, the more furious he is, the more calm I remain; instead of attacking aimlessly or being afraid, extreme care should be exercised to discover his weak points and apply all possible setbacks to exploit his weak points. For instance, hit him hard several times when he comes close, thus diminishing his fighting spirit and planting fear in his heart . . . we must also remember that some things are extremely complicated, some would not be the first to attack in battle; this by no means indicates fear and poor technique. Others would start to attack at the very beginning of a battle. This does not mean that they are fearless and possess better technique.

The article stressed the need to avoid passiveness and to gain the initiative, but the choice of tactics depends upon "the enemy's situation and our own situation . . . sometimes it is better to take the defensive."

Hanoi's decision to punish the United States was perhaps also partly determined by its desire to embarrass Khrushchev and to rally the entire socialist camp to its aid. In other words, Hanoi was willing to risk provoking a retaliatory U.S. strike for it knew that an open attack against the territory of a socialist state would make Khrushchev's policy of noninvolvement increasingly costly for Soviet prestige in the communist camp. But following the one-shot U.S. retaliation on North Vietnam in August 1964, Khrushchev did not respond. In fact, against the DRV's wishes, Moscow proposed that the incident be discussed at the UN.

Peking, however, was quick to declare that "aggression of the U.S. against the DRV means aggression against China."[78] "Any time U.S. imperialism encroaches on the territorial land, waters or airspace of the DRV," People's Daily declared, "the Chinese people will abide by their pledge and give wholehearted support for the Vietnamese people's just war of resistance."[79] The Chinese dramatically demonstrated their determination by deploying twelve to fifteen MIG-15's and MIG-17's onto recently improved airfields near Hanoi.[80] Furthermore, Peking Radio within a few days announced that large-scale maneuvers were being conducted in southern China that were linked to Chinese pledges of support to North Vietnam.[81]

These steps in China were taken after Seaborn had returned to Hanoi on August 10 to pass on a new U.S. warning about the further dire consequences that would ensue if the DRV persisted in its course.

The continuation of parallel Chinese-North Vietnamese political maneuvers were manifest in Hanoi's ready acceptance of U Thant's secret proposal, first made in September, that the DRV and the United States discuss negotiations privately at Rangoon.[82] Hanoi's acceptance was consistent with its strategy of attempting to preclude U.S. escalation while itself stepping up military pressure.

The United States was again apparently unwilling to negotiate while South Vietnam's military position continued to crumble.* But even as late as January 1965, China and Hanoi were still hopeful that the United States might opt for a negotiated "graceful" withdrawal rather than a drastic escalation of its involvement. However, Seaborn's visits suggested U.S. determination to see it through, and by the fall of 1964 high U.S. officials were publicly warning that the increased pressure of the communists, including the rising scale of infiltration, could force an expansion of the war.[83] The communists were thus uncertain which course America would ultimately choose and if it did intervene, how far it was prepared to go.

The eventual U.S. decision to escalate its involvement by the "slow squeeze" method was based upon the assumption that the internal war in South Vietnam could only be won if its continuation became so costly to North Vietnam that Hanoi would discontinue its support of the struggle. As the commander of U.S. Pacific Forces, Admiral U.S. Grant Sharp, said in a secret cable of August 17: "What we have not done and must do is make plain to Hanoi and Peiping [sic] the cost of pursuing their current objectives and impeding ours."[84]

At the same time, the Hanoi (and Peking) strategy was to convince the United States of the DRV's determination to realize its objectives

---

*It is unclear, however, whether U Thant's proposal was ever brought to President Johnson's attention.

regardless of the possible cost the United States might conceivably inflict upon the North. Neither convinced the other.

HANOI SEIZES SOVIET OFFER OF SUPPORT

Thus, Chinese pledges during the latter half of 1964 to defend Hanoi were not bravado. It was clear that if the war was to be pushed ahead in the South, the risk of heavy U.S. intervention, including bombing of the North, had to be accepted. As in 1954, Mao probably estimated that if the United States did escalate, U.S. air and sea power would be directed at Vietnam and that this alone could not reduce Hanoi's position to the point that direct and massive Chinese aid would be required.

Nevertheless, as the prospect for such escalation became more real, leaders in Hanoi and some of those in Peking undoubtedly became anxious to collect what additional insurance and support they could. The sending into North Vietnam of the outdated Chinese MIG-15's and MIG-17's while a sign of determination was also a sign of China's relative weakness in the field of air defense—not to speak of nuclear weapons. If Hanoi was to seek for modern air defense support and a nuclear umbrella under which to operate, it could look in only one direction—Moscow.

But the Soviets had shown only brief concern over the Tonkin Gulf incidents, and by October, attention to Vietnamese affairs in the Soviet press was as meager as at any time since the Geneva conference of 1954.[85] At the same time Hanoi's alliance with Peking reached its closest stage, although the DRV was still careful to avoid any act that would seem irretrievably to sever relations with Moscow. Hanoi continued, for example, to avoid denunciation of the USSR or its leaders by name.

At this point there occurred for Hanoi its biggest windfall since the Chinese communists arrived on the border in 1949—the fall of Khrushchev. While the dramatic change inside the Kremlin was probably related primarily to internal Soviet affairs, Hanoi could probably claim some credit for the overthrow of China's first revisionist enemy. The new Kremlin leadership recognized the serious losses of prestige and influence that Moscow had suffered in the international communist movement in the previous two years, particularly in Asia and specifically in Vietnam. The new Soviet regime, while basically adhering to the Khrushchev foreign policy line of détente (combined with an energetic competition for influence and military superiority), devised a new strategy to combat Peking's challenge. This strategy sought to improve Moscow's political position in the camp through

29

an emphasis on reconciliation with China on a pragmatic basis and a concurrent effort to neutralize the main Chinese charges against Moscow. The Soviets therefore sought to strike a more forthcoming and dignified pose in their dispute with Peking and at the same time to demonstrate their own revolutionary respectability. The latter objective called for only a slight modification of the détente policy and some renewed attention to the interests of those communist governments that had outstanding revolutionary and national-power goals. This policy involved improvement of relations with such parties as North Korea and Cuba and most importantly North Vietnam.

At the Havana meeting of Latin American communist parties convened in November 1964, the Soviet Union, in return for Fidel Castro's acceptance of their new line on unity, pledged "new aid" to "freedom fighters" in Venezuela, Columbia, and Guatemala.[86] And in February 1965 the Soviets apparently promised new military aid to the North Koreans.[87] But the major commitment of the new Soviet leaders was to be to Hanoi.

After the fall of Khrushchev, Moscow renewed its attention to the liberation struggle in Vietnam and publicly pledged assistance to North Vietnam if the United States should attack it.[88] Moreover the National Liberation Front was allowed to open an office in Moscow.

Hanoi quickly demonstrated that its antipathy or friendship for the Soviet Union was strictly a measure of the willingness of the Russians to commit themselves to Hanoi's support. It is difficult to believe that there was any dispute in the Lao Dong Politburo on the wisdom of responding positively and immediately to the new Soviet policy. On the other hand it was unlikely that Hanoi harbored the illusion that Moscow was now committed to the achievement of the DRV's objectives in the South.

The November 1964 issue of the Lao Dong theoretical journal Hoc Tap was suddenly withdrawn in order to remove a strongly pro-Chinese and anti-Soviet article. And in early November, Premier Pham Van Dong led a party and government delegation to attend the 47th anniversary of the Bolshevik Revolution in Moscow. Presumably the Soviet leaders made a fairly firm offer of renewed support in return for North Vietnam's resumption of a position of benevolent neutrality in the Sino-Soviet dispute.

In January the DRV signed a new trade agreement with Moscow, expressed official gratitude for Soviet support, and began again to stress the need for unity in the communist camp. On February 1, 1965, Pravda announced Premier Alexei Kosygin's forthcoming trip to Hanoi. The Soviet intention of playing both sides of the street was evident when Moscow attempted to soften the impact of this announcement upon its relations with the United States by simultaneously reporting a positive response to President Johnson's appeal for close contacts and better understanding between the United States and the USSR.[89]

DECEMBER DECISIONS

What was probably expected to be the final offensive of the war was actually launched in December 1964 in central Vietnam when Viet Cong units maneuvering for the first time in regimental strength captured virtually all of the district of An Lao in the province of Binh Dinh. In January the Viet Cong scored a resounding victory at Binh Gia, wiping out a government Ranger battalion.

Until the beginning of this general offensive, regular North Vietnamese Army personnel in the South had been only communications, technical, and weapons specialists serving with Viet Cong battalions as individuals or in some cases as small support units. But according to U.S. estimates, in October 1964 the First North Vietnamese line unit—a regular infantry regiment—departed the North for the long trek to the South, crossing the border from Laos into South Vietnam in December. A second regiment followed shortly after, arriving in the South in January or February.[90] These units were presumably dispatched in order to be on hand for the final collapse of the Saigon forces, possibly as a contingency in the case of the U.S. intervention, and perhaps also to guarantee Hanoi's control of the political situation after the expected Saigon collapse. But the decision to send these units, which was presumably taken in mid-1964, made it more likely that the United States would use its own ground forces.

While the final military push was getting under way, Hanoi played its parallel diplomatic game; once again, it agreed to bilateral talks with the United States. The moment of truth was now approaching; the United States had either to cash in its chips and accept its losses or raise the stakes and commit its resources to a war limited geographically but unlimited in costs. America's objective at this point was still to protect the "security and independence of South Vietnam."

Unlike the situation in 1954, when the secretary of Defense and all the Joint Chiefs except Admiral Radford had opposed intervention, in late 1964 there was near unanimity among the civilian and military leaders of the Defense Department in favor of doing what was necessary to save the situation. The differences between 1954 and 1964 were political as well as military. A withdrawal in 1964 meant a U.S., not a French defeat, and massive intervention would be intended to save an "independent" nation, not an expiring colonial endeavor. In addition, there was no opportunity for congressional opposition like that which had blocked Secretary Dulles. The administration thought it had finessed this opposition by the mid-campaign Tonkin Gulf Resolution of August 1964, in which the Senate, by a vote of 88 to 2, authorized the president to take "all necessary requested action" in defense of South Vietnam's freedom "under the SEATO Pact." The failure to seek an open public debate and clear legislative authorization for the war against the North was probably the greatest domestic error of the Johnson Administration.*

Thus, to U.S. leaders in 1964, the objectives of the war seemed desirable, and militarily and politically it seemed feasible to escalate the U.S. commitment in order to obtain them. At this stage, Washington hoped that intervention with air power alone could save the day.

RESTRICTIONS ON THE AIR WAR

In December, the president was presented with a recommendation by his top aides that if Saigon became more effective and Hanoi did not yield on acceptable terms "or if the [Saigon government] can only be kept going by stronger action," the United States, "at a time to be determined" should enter into "a second phase program . . . of graduated military pressures directed systematically against the DRV." Such a program would consist of progressively more serious air strikes."[91]

The Joints Chiefs of Staff recommended immediate initiation of sharply intensified military pressures against the DRV. This program for a swift attack in force would be designed to destroy in the first three days Phuc Yen airfield near Hanoi as well as other airfields and major petroleum and oil facilities.[92] According to the Pentagon analysts, this plan was shunted aside because its risks and costs were too high. China was of course the risk factor that lurked in the background.

An intelligence panel consisting of the Central Intelligence Agency (CIA), the State Department's Bureau of Intelligence and Research, and the Pentagon's Defense Intelligence Agency expressed doubt that the proposed bombing would in any event succeed in breaking

---

*President Johnson later explained that not only did he believe that the Tonkin Gulf Resolution gave him all authority necessary but that he also failed to ask Congress for a formal declaration of war against North Vietnam because he feared Hanoi might have secret treaties that would automatically bring China and Russia into the fighting. New York Times, February 7, 1970, Johnson's interview with Columbia Broadcasting System commentator Walter Cronkite.

Hanoi's will. Furthermore, the panel accurately suggested that Hanoi could count on "the danger of war with Communist China" to limit war action that the United States might take against North Vietnam.

It is ironic that during the next three years the main deterrent to U.S. military action against Hanoi was fear of greater Chinese involvement, including the use of Chinese aircraft and troops. But in late 1964 and early 1965, invasion of the North was not even contemplated.

The tactic of gradual escalation of the air campaign was adopted partially in order to leave Hanoi the choice of opting out of the war without too much loss of face whenever it believed that additional damage was unacceptable (an interpretation that indicated a poor appreciation both of DRV reactions to threat situations and of the damage that could actually be inflicted by air attacks on a peasant society). But the decision for "gradualism" was probably most influenced by estimates from the Department of State that "warned constantly that air operations might prompt Peking's intervention."[93]

Two years later, the chief of staff of the North Vietnamese Army, General Van Tien Dung, in a long analysis of the air war in the North, agreed with the U.S. Joint Chiefs that escalation of the U.S. bombing "step by step made it impossible for" the U.S. Air Force "to fully develop its strength and strong points." The reason the United States had adopted this least effective approach, Dung said, was because of "the present balance of international forces."[94]

The Director of the Central Intelligence Agency, John A. McCone, believed that the restricted nature of the air campaign would encourage Chinese and Soviet support for the DRV and the Viet Cong simply because the risk would be minimum.[95]

It is uncertain how far the U.S. Government seriously pursued the question of its reaction should China intervene in the air war. The Pentagon Papers record no 1964-65 contingency plans to deal with Chinese intervention as provided in the case of the 1954 situation. But in late 1964 Washington seemed confident that this contingency could be avoided by its "slow squeeze" method, by public and private assurances that U.S. objectives were limited, and by threats of U.S. retaliation—possibly including nuclear attack—in the event of direct Chinese involvement. The breakdown of the Sino-Soviet alliance and the fact that the PRC had only exploded its first atomic device in November 1964 strengthened confidence that the tactics to avoid a direct clash with China would succeed.

A special National Intelligence Estimate of October 9, 1964 stated:

> We are almost certain that both Hanoi and Peking are
> anxious not to become involved in the kind of war in which

the great weight of superior US weaponry could be brought against them. Even if Hanoi and Peking estimated that the U.S. would not use nuclear weapons against them, they could not be sure of this. . . We believe that fear of provoking severe measures by the U.S. would lead them to temper their responses with a good deal of caution.[96]

In November, Walt W. Rostow, chairman of the State Department Policy Planning Council, warned that a basic problem was to convince Peking that "Communist China will not be a sanctuary if it assists North Vietnam in counter-escalation."[97] Rostow advocated "the introduction, into the Pacific Theatre, of massive forces to deal with any escalatory response, including forces aimed at China as well as North Vietnam, should the Chinese Communists enter the game." Earlier, Rostow had suggested that the forces to counter China could take the form of increased U.S. aircraft on Taiwan plus a carrier force off China.[98]

The joint intelligence panel in late 1964 predicted that China would not react in any major way to a bombing campaign unless U.S. or South Vietnamese troops invaded North Vietnam or northern Laos. Chinese reaction to systematic bombing of North Vietnam was expected to be limited to providing Hanoi with antiaircraft artillery, jet fighters, and naval patrol craft.[99]

Yet the Johnson Administration was always concerned that the Chinese would escalate their own participation in the air war. This was evident in Assistant Secretary of State William Bundy's secret memorandum of February 18, 1965, which said, "we do not believe" the Chinese "would engage in air operations from Communist China at least up to the point where the MIG's in the DRV were engaged and we had found it necessary to attack Fukien or possibly—if the MIG's had been moved there—Vinh."[100]

ESCALATION BEGINS

Whether or not the February 7, 1965 Viet Cong attack on the U.S. helicopter base at Pleiku was a result of local initiative or something more, we shall never know; but 12 hours after the event, U.S. carrier planes struck at Dong Hoi in southern North Vietnam. This air attack and two others that followed in February were explained by the U.S. Government as retaliatory acts, but it was clear to all the communist leaders that the U.S. Government was determined to reverse the military situation and to bring pressure on the North to abandon its objectives in the South.

34

The Soviet Union was thus forced into following through on its show of· socialist solidarity in the face of the intensifying U.S. activity (Kosygin was in Hanoi at the time). But Moscow now believed that the fighting could be contained, and it moved ahead as planned to exploit the opportunity to improve its position in the international movement vis-à-vis Peking. The Soviet Union immediately promised "together with friends and allies" to safeguard the security and strengthen the defense capability of the DRV.[101] The Soviets now concentrated on the theme that they had begun to use the previous November: socialist unity in the face of U.S. "aggression," and coordination of USSR and PRC aid to Vietnam. "United action" became the rallying cry of Moscow. The USSR proposed a conference with Peking and Hanoi and requested an air corridor through China to the DRV and apparently even suggested that Soviet aircraft use fields in the south of China.[102]

This was to prove to be an effective strategy that would increase Moscow's influence in Hanoi and its prestige in the camp at what would prove to be relatively little risk to itself or even to its détente policy. Moscow's new calculation proved correct; despite Soviet arming of the forces engaged in deadly combat with the Americans, Washington was eager to pursue détente in other fields.

At the same time, the Soviets continued to promote a political formula for the achievement of Hanoi's objectives in the South. The joint Soviet-North Vietnamese statement of February 11 again advocated an international conference on Laos and stressed both the need for unity in the camp and for settlement of international disputes through negotiations. On the same day, Kosygin stopped in Peking and urged the same strategy on Mao—unity in the camp to defeat U.S. aggression and at the same time a political policy that would allow "the U.S. to find a way out of Vietnam."[103] On February 16 the Soviets reportedly put before Hanoi and Peking their proposal to convene a new international conference on Vietnam without prior conditions—that is, without either prior U.S. withdrawal or a deescalation of DRV support to the Viet Cong.[104] Reports from Paris indicated that the USSR had in fact agreed to support de Gaulle's plans for a negotiated settlement.[105] U Thant on February 12 also called for a new Geneva conference,[106] and according to some reports Hanoi informed the UN Secretary General that it accepted his suggestion for informal negotiations.[107]

Unconditional negotiations at this point were still acceptable to the North Vietnamese, for the United States had not yet begun regular bombing of the North (that is, outside the context of retaliation for specific Viet Cong attacks) and no U.S. ground combat troops had yet arrived. If talks had taken place at this time, they would presumably have operated in the same framework as those proposed in January— that is, the United States would have been under political restraint not to escalate the war into regular bombing of the DRV and not to dispatch ground troops, while North Vietnam and the Viet Cong would have remained free to continue their offensive.

MAO REJECTS "UNITED ACTION"

As noted earlier, China had made significant gains in the international movement by its espousal of a combative anti-U.S. line, as opposed to the Soviet practice of limited détente. An essential and explicit assumption of the Maoist line was that local wars that might result from a militant revolutionary policy against "U.S. imperialism" could be contained and channeled by the decisions of the revolutionaries. On the basis of this doctrinal question of strategy, Peking had seemed, before Khrushchev's fall, to be on the way to establishing its own informal international communist movement in Asia. The fall of Khrushchev, the explosion of China's first nuclear device, and the formation of the Jakarta-Peking axis—all coming on the heels of China's political successes in the world arena—constituted a heady brew for the Maoist leadership.

In January, Mao had predicted that the United States would accept defeat in Vietnam and withdraw its forces within a year or two,[108] but when Washington confounded this assessment, Mao saw no need to revise his strategies or tactics. Certainly he was in no mood to compromise with either the revisionists in Moscow or those in Peking who advocated new policies in face of the U.S. threat. It was in fact at a "decisive meeting" on January 25, 1965 that Mao decided that President Liu Shao-chi had to go.[109]

China faced a more difficult decision in regard to the new stage of the war in Vietnam than did the Soviets. China was the rear area and at that time the principal logistical support for North Vietnam. If the United States escalated beyond Indochina, China was the logical target. Thus, Peking faced relatively great danger of a clash with the United States, a clash in which it stood practically naked in nuclear armament. Mao apparently felt that if he cooperated with the Soviets in aiding North Vietnam, it would increase the chances of escalation into China and at the same time it would be used as leverage by the Soviets to force both DRV compromises to the United States and Chinese concessions to the USSR. Even more important, "united action" with the Soviets in Vietnam would undercut the effect and destroy the foundation of China's challenge of the USSR for leadership of the communist camp. Any compromise with the Soviets by China, any acknowledgment that Moscow also was antiimperialist and sincere in assisting wars of "national liberation" would have seriously compromised the dynamics of Mao's strategy.

Mao believed that Hanoi, by fighting a protracted war with China's rear base support, could still eventually achieve a settlement on its own terms and that such a local war, in keeping with his own theories, could be contained within Vietnam. Such a victory would confirm to the communist world the validity of the militant anti-U.S. strategy espoused by Peking.

Consequently, Mao rejected "united action," and during the February 11 meeting with Kosygin, the Chinese leader reportedly took the position that Sino-Soviet unity would be reestablished only if the United States attacked one or the other.[110] The polemics, Mao said, would have to go on for 10,000 years if necessary.[111]

In regard to negotiations, too, Mao was in a dilemma. Peking in 1964, along with Hanoi, had stressed the reconvening of the Geneva conference as part of the political-military strategy employed against the United States. Mao himself, as late as January 1965 spoke favorably of unconditional negotiations on Vietnam.[112] But the chairman saw the new U.S. escalation as an attempt to strengthen its negotiating position, to win at the bargaining table what Saigon had been unable to win with limited U.S. support . . . independence from the North. Peking rejected a political settlement on February 19, at a time when North Vietnam apparently still believed it to be at least tactically advantageous to support negotiations.

Successful reengagement of the Soviet Union into the issue was also an important factor in Chinese policy on negotiations. Mao evidently now saw a negotiated settlement, even one that covered a U.S. withdrawal, as implying an ideological triumph for the Soviet Union.

A FLAW IN THE MAOIST STRATEGY

Some of the party chairman's colleagues saw a serious danger in Mao's interpretation of the situation, and in particular his assumptions about U.S. actions. What if the United States should attempt to cut off Peking's support for Vietnam by bombing Chinese supply lines or air bases? What would China's next move be? If it were to attack U.S. planes or to send troops to Vietnam, the United States might launch nuclear attacks on China's nuclear and military installations, heavy industry, and communications. The United States probably would not, however, commit troops to the Chinese mainland, leaving "people's war" as an irrelevant strategy.

The reply to this eventuality, spelled out on several occasions by Chinese spokesmen, was to warn that in any future war the United States could not expect to set the limits. If the United States launched air and sea attacks against China, the Chinese might retaliate with masses of troops in Southeast Asia and possibly in Korea. At this point Mao's strategy seemed to be inconsistent, for in addition to being a poor deterrent to nuclear attacks, this reaction would necessarily consist of Chinese fighting not a "people's war" in their own country, but a positional ground war in foreign lands against massive U.S. firepower and, possibly, tactical nuclear weapons. This would amount to a Korean-type engagement with the significant difference that China would probably find itself outside the Soviet strategic system. In such an eventuality, the Chinese military leadership would have to assume that there would be relatively little restraint on U.S. employment of tactical and perhaps strategic nuclear weapons.

THE OPPOSITION VIEW

Although we do not know the details, there is evidence to suggest that throughout 1965 and into early 1966 there was continued debate and increasing disagreement among the Chinese leadership with Mao's Vietnam strategy and his policy toward the Soviets. The opposition group included President Liu Shao-chi; mayor of Peking Peng Chen; Army Chief of Staff Lo Jui-ching; and Party Secretary General Teng Hsiao-ping. The views of these leaders probably varied widely and may have changed over time; they may also have disagreed with Mao for different reasons and to varying degrees. The purpose here is not to attempt to analyze in detail their possible individual positions, but generally to analyze what appeared to be a polarization of the leadership on critical foreign policy questions.[113]

It seems clear that a serious dispute was going on that was vaguely reflected in the Peking press from February 1965 to March 1966. In this dispute, the opposition group's members apparently urged a partial détente with the USSR in the interests of China's national security. They apparently took the position that, with intensification of the war on China's borders, it was critically important to renew the credibility of the Soviet nuclear umbrella. In addition, they apparently argued, if the PRC accepted the Soviet offer of "united action," China could more effectively struggle to redirect misguided Soviet policies and more effectively aid the DRV.

They argued that the post-Khrushchev leadership in Moscow was not implacably revisionist and could be won over to the revolutionary path. They rejected the theory that cooperation with the Soviets in Vietnam would increase the chances of U.S. attacks on China. On the contrary, they argued that if China persisted in rejecting any compromise or rapprochement with the Soviets, not only would it find its position increasingly weakened in the Afro-Asian and communist worlds but also further U.S. "aggression" would be encouraged. Finally they rejected Mao's theory that the conflict in Vietnam had to be seen primarily in the context of China's broad strategic struggles with both the United States and the USSR. Whereas Mao stressed the long-term aspect of the struggle with the U.S. "imperialists," he gave primacy to the principle of no compromise with the heretical Soviet "revisionists"; his opposition within the party emphasized that a war with the United States was a possibility and that this was the overriding consideration.

The existence of this split in the leadership is suggested by subsequent attacks in the Peking press on Liu Shao-chi, which accused Liu of exaggerating the threat from U.S. imperialism in 1965 and of having advocated compromise with the Soviet revisionists at that time. The People's Daily, for example, has charged that in 1965 Liu took the position that China could work with the new Soviet leadership, and that at the same time he had warned that "the U.S. is very powerful; it is the strongest country in the world."[114] Despite obvious distortions in the charges against Liu, other evidence tends to bear out the essential point about Liu's alarmist views on the security situation in 1965 and early 1966.

The most convincing piece of evidence that Liu favored rapprochement with Moscow is the analysis provided by Edgar Snow following his long stay in China in the fall and winter of 1970. Basing his remarks on talks with Mao, Chou En-lai, and other Chinese leaders, Snow said that there were two issues in the Cultural Revolution. The first was Mao's conviction that the party was following the revisionist (Soviet) path to capitalism. The second and closely linked issue was that posed by "Liu's search for a compromise in the Sino-Soviet impasse." When the United States seemed to be threatening China with war, Snow reported, Liu wanted to send a Chinese delegation to the 1966 Soviet 23d Party Congress and to reactivate the Sino-Soviet alliance.[115]

Shortly after Liu's purge, some Soviet writers emphasized the split in Peking over the question of "united action" with the USSR:

> Differences arose in the Chinese Party leadership between those who desired more active resistance to US imperialism on the basis of unity with the socialist camp, and the Maoists, who counted on attaining their goals by balancing between the socialist camp and the USA, halting active support for the struggle of the Vietnamese people and demonstrating their anti-Sovietism.[116]

Moscow, however, did not give prominence to this interpretation of Liu's fall until after the purge of his rival, Lin Piao, in 1971. Moscow

Radio Peace and Progress, for example, on November 18, 1971, in a Mandarin broadcast told its Chinese listeners, "As you know, the already purged President Liu Shao-chi was in favor of adopting a friendlier policy toward Moscow." Subsequent Moscow comment continued to expound the line that the Cultural Revolution had been launched to "get rid of those opposed to Mao Tse-tung's foreign policy"[117] and that Liu Shao-chi and Teng Hsiao-ping had in fact favored "united action" with the Soviets in Vietnam.[118]

Red Guard posters two years after Liu Shao-chi's fall charged that the month after the U.S. bombing of North Vietnam began in 1965, Liu removed the central government files from Peking to the mountains and established "special international telephone links with which to ask help of an unnamed foreign power"—the Soviet Union.[119] Posters claimed that these moves were related to a coup attempt Liu was plotting for February 1966.[120] While it is not impossible that Liu was hatching a plot against Mao, it seems more likely that Liu's measures in 1965 were not part of any plan to seize power but rather resulted from apprehension that a U.S. attack on China was an imminent possibility.

AN ABORTED MOVE TO "UNITED ACTION"

Immediately after the dramatic change in the Vietnam war and the Soviet offer of "united action," signs appeared that suggested the possibility of policy changes in Peking that might lead to at least temporary unity between China and the USSR. Those within the CCP who advocated a limited rapprochement with the Soviet Union were in control of the party and government machinery, and they seemed possibly to be pushing ahead with a conciliatory policy toward Moscow, as shown by the treatment of the 15th anniversary of the Sino-Soviet treaty on February 13. Delegations of ministerial rank were exchanged to mark the occasion, and representatives of both countries waxed enthusiastic over the importance of the treaty in the face of the "imperialist danger" and over the need for "unity against the enemy."[121] Although the People's Daily in its February 14 editorial called for communist unity on the basis of the CCP's general line, it proclaimed that "History has proved that all those who try to undermine the alliance and unity of China and the Soviet Union will inevitably end up with a bloody nose and meet with utter failure."[122]

According to this editorial, the enemy feared the Sino-Soviet treaty, and that was "precisely why we treasure it." The implication in this article was that while China was not prepared to change its basic position on the questions at issue with Moscow, it was prepared to strengthen the alliance in the face of the common danger.

A message from the Chinese leadership to the Soviet leaders also proclaimed that "the consolidation and strengthening of the great Sino-Soviet alliance is beneficial to the common cause of opposing our common enemy."[123] In his reply, Brezhnev appeared to smooth the way for rapprochement by pledging that the Soviet Union would "support in every way possible the great revolutionary struggles" in Asia, Africa, and Latin America.[124]

During the first two weeks following the U.S. bombing of North Vietnam, Peking media emphasized China's alliance with the Soviet Union, rejected negotiations that were approved by both Hanoi and Moscow, and at the same time adopted a militant posture toward U.S. action in Vietnam . . . more militant than that of Soviet Russia. "Aggression against the Democratic Republic of Vietnam means aggression against the Chinese People's Republic," a slogan that was first heard during the Tonkin Gulf incident in 1964, was the favorite summing up of the Chinese position in the first half of February 1965. This position appeared to contrast with Mao's statement the previous month to Edgar Snow that only a U.S. attack on China would bring war over Vietnam.[125]

On February 19 there was another strong editorial in the People's Daily on the Vietnam issue, but from that date until March 1, there was a strange silence in the Peking press on this critical question.

On February 25, however, Peking suddenly blasted Moscow. NCNA charged that the "sinister spirit of Khrushchev had not departed," and the next day People's Daily attacked "Khrushchevism without Khrushchev." By March the Sino-Soviet struggle had resumed in earnest—the Chinese having found, or more likely manufactured, a suitable cause célèbre, the Soviet "suppression" on March 4 of an anti-U.S. demonstration by Chinese and other foreign students in front of the U.S. embassy in Moscow. Twelve months later, the 16th anniversary of the Sino-Soviet treaty would be marked only by a prefunctory cocktail party, and in 1967 it would not be noted at all, as the Soviet Embassy at the time was just coming out from an 18-day seige by Red Guards.

MAO IMPLEMENTS HIS STRATEGY

Although opposition within the CCP to Mao's strategy in dealing with the Vietnam crisis continued for the next 12 months, the chairman had apparently succeeded in imposing his basic policy in regard to the Vietnam war. He proceeded substantially to raise China's material assistance to the DRV and urged the North Vietnamese to respond to U.S. escalation with a "protracted people's war" and to avoid a Korean-

41

type positional war. He rejected the various Soviet proposals for an international conference and a multilateral statement of support for North Vietnam. He decided against air defense from China of North Vietnam's air space; he scornfully turned down Moscow's request for an air corridor and an air base in China. He did sign an agreement with the USSR for rail transport of Soviet equipment to Hanoi, but at the same time he denigrated the quantity and quality of Soviet aid and, in various ways, may have impeded its delivery.126 Mao's policy was to provide as much Chinese aid as possible to the DRV and to act as its "rear area" of support but at the same time to urge reduction in the pace and scale of the war and to avoid involvement that might provoke U.S. attacks on China. From Peking's public declarations came the message that China would not initiate an attack on U.S. forces.

Although Mao intended China to remain true to its revolutionary principles by assisting the Vietnamese war of "national liberation" and by rejecting unity with the revisionists, he had decreed a policy of prudence and patience. As long as the danger of a clash with the United States could be avoided, Mao and his supporters probably saw other important advantages in the continuation of the conflict in Vietnam. It served to undermine U.S.-USSR peaceful coexistence; it created internal and external contradictions for the United States; it aroused revolutionary and anti-U.S. fervor in China and abroad; and it served as a model and an inspiration for other wars of "national liberation." But Mao also apparently saw the Vietnam war, together with the concurrent Indonesian campaign against Malaysia, as the political and psychological instrument for the creation of an anti-U.S. united front in Asia and for the renewal of armed struggle by pro-Peking insurgents throughout Southeast Asia.

THE NATURE OF THE OPPOSITION

Although the dissidents in Peking naturally did not directly spell out their views, factional lines apparently began to harden during the year on four issues, all directly or indirectly related to the Vietnam war: relations with Moscow, with the "moderates" advocating a limited rapprochement; the nature of the internal class struggle, with the "moderates" opposing an intensive political campaign at home at a time of national crisis; China's strategy in the Afro-Asia world, with the "moderates" urging a more broad-based appeal in order to elicit wider support in the struggle against U.S. "imperialism"; and the structure of the military establishment in China, with the "moderates" promoting "regularization" and "modernization" of the army so as to adopt a conventional rather than a guerrilla-type defensive strategy.

We do not know the manner in which these differences were aired or the dynamics of the personal relationships involved, but at least until September 1965 the debates within the Chinese leadership proceeded in the context of party discipline and of an acceptance of Mao's ultimate authority. The opposition may not have disagreed with Mao's basic objectives, but it believed that his methods were increasingly dangerous. As the forces that were inclined to more traditional approaches occupied the top civilian and party positions, they had ample opportunity to attempt to lay down policies and courses of action consistent with their own perceptions of China's interests. One presumes that only when major decisions were called for or at high-level party conferences would Mao himself intervene to reverse a policy trend or to dictate a course of action. Something like this may have happened in February 1965, when Mao reversed the official actions and statements outlined above that seemed to suggest a partial acceptance of "united action" with Moscow.

Some observers have urged that by the end of 1965 two distinct opposition groups had evolved in Peking that embraced "dramatically opposed views on the desirability of reconciliation with Moscow."[127] This view maintains that there were "hawks" in the Chinese military who desired a "tougher policy" on Vietnam and sought a rapprochement with Russia for this reason; and that there were "doves" in the party who wanted to concentrate on economic development and thus desired to make up with the Soviets for this purpose. A third group, the "dawks," or those in the Maoist faction, are identified in terms somewhat similar to our own analysis of the Maoist position. In addition, these observers suggest that there was another view, expressed by Peng Chen, who was also extremely anti-Soviet and who allegedly called for rapprochement with the United States.[128] While these arguments are presented persuasively, their conclusions are misleading.[129]

First of all, it is difficult to believe that there was any disagreement upon the basic policy that China should do what was feasible and prudent to help North Vietnam achieve its objectives in the South and to resist U.S. "aggression." In all likelihood, there was probably no serious opinion group in the Chinese leadership that argued for a compromise that would surrender Hanoi's ultimate goals. It also seems unlikely that there were any serious differences on the type of strategy that Hanoi should follow—that is, a protracted guerrilla strategy rather than intense mobile warfare. Those who have discovered "hawks" in the 1965 Peking leadership on the question of Vietnam have yet to spell out what hawkish military actions this group proposed to take in Vietnam that the situation required and that were desired by the North Vietnamese. The threat to send Chinese troops if needed seemed clearly to refer to the contingency of a U.S.

invasion of the North; certainly no Chinese leader would have recommended that Chinese combat troops be used in South Vietnam. What then would Chief of Staff Lo Jui-ching and his fellow hawks have done to help Hanoi that Mao did not do?

Direct air defense over the DRV from bases in China is, of course, one possibility, but this could not have been done effectively without large-scale Soviet involvement and planes. China at this time had the capability of manufacturing MIG-19's but not MIG-21's, of which it possessed only a handful. This strategy however may have been supported by some advocates of "united action," who may have urged acceptance of the reported Soviet offer to provide cover from bases in South China.

It seems fairly clear that all groups in Peking agreed that China should act as Hanoi's "rear base." The dispute was simply whether or not such a step was so risky that a limited rapprochement with the Soviet Union was necessary. In addition the Maoists opposed Soviet aid to North Vietnam and attempted to persuade Hanoi that the political consequences of such aid surpassed its military benefits. But some of the Chinese military and party leaders probably put more value on Soviet military aid for North Vietnam, and on this question they may also have disagreed with Mao and his supporters.

There was certainly a functional distinction among the evolving opposition in Peking. One opposition group consisted of military leaders and another represented officials concerned with party and government matters. There were those in the military who disagreed with Mao and Defense Minister Lin Piao on the structure of the People's Liberation Army (PLA) and the general strategy that should be followed in the event of a U.S. attack. More concerned than Mao with the possibility of a U.S. attack, this military group, led by Lo Jui-ching, advocated immediate and extensive defense preparations. They sought to improve China's air defense capability and the firepower of the People's Liberation Army. They proposed that in the event of a U.S. nuclear attack on China followed by a ground invasion, the PLA should be prepared to fight a conventional war with modern weapons. Thus, they stressed the creation of a professional and modern army with modern weapons.

To Mao and Lin Piao, this meant that Lo was opposing "absolute party leadership" and political work for the army and that he was attempting to promote "regularization" and the creation of a "bourgeois army."[130] They feared "that the adoption of Lo's proposals would force the disengagement of the PLA from domestic political activity and might, by increasing the ratio of military to political training, reduce the PLA's political reliability."[131] The Maoists emphasized a revolutionary and highly politicized people's army ready to fight a people's guerrilla war, as in the struggle against Japan.[132]

This struggle between the two lines in the military (professional versus revolutionary) was said to have been the third great contest of its kind in the long history of Mao's leadership of the party. The first struggle came after the Korean War, when those with a "slave mentality" promoted "regularization and modernization" of the PLA and attempted to make the PLA "a carbon copy of foreign practice." This effort was defeated at the 1958 enlarged session of the CCP's Military Affairs Committee. The second struggle involved the "anti-party clique" of former Defense Minister Peng Te-Huai, which also allegedly attempted to abolish political work and the party's absolute leadership over the army. Peng was ousted in the August 1959 Lu Shan plenum. The third big struggle came to a head during the summer of 1965; as before, the "revisionist line" was routed.[133] (As we will see, the fourth struggle was to come in 1971.)

Disputes within the party over economic and social policy during the years had also involved the same basic struggle between Maoism and revisionism, between boldness and caution, and between pragmatism and adherence to the long-range goal.[134] The fundamental disagreements among the leadership were apparently on these internal issues of military, economic, and cultural policies, but the most emotional aspects were probably on foreign affairs.

Dispute over these issues whirled around the hidden intrigue of a struggle for power. Mao was striving to restore his personal authority over the party and the government—an authority that had been weakened as a result of the failures of the Great Leap Forward. Lin Piao had been chosen by Mao to consolidate the chairman's authority over the PLA and eventually to spearhead the campaign to eliminate Liu Shao-chi and Teng Hsiao-ping, and to purge the party, the government, and the army of their supporters. As Snow reported, Mao had decided that Liu had to go one month before the war escalated. Like Stalin in 1936, Mao's purpose was to destroy the autonomous character of the bureaucracy, eradicate the personal alignments and cliques that had been built up, and "achieve the complete ascendancy of the thought of Mao" and of Mao the leader.[135]

For the ambitious Lin Piao, it was essentially a struggle for the succession. Lin was to use the Cultural Revolution to purge his rivals from leading positions and to replace them wherever possible with members of his own Fourth Army clique. Lin hoped to consolidate his dominant role in the PLA and also extend his influence into the party and government structures.

While all sides in this developing power contest no doubt seized opportunities to attack one another on various internal matters, the most dramatic issues—the Vietnam war and relations with the USSR— would have been the most lethal weapons that could have been employed. Those who saw themselves threatened by Mao and Lin in 1965 very probably began to unite on the question of the Vietnam war and on the need for a limited rapprochement with the Soviets.

WAR AND DISSENT INTENSIFY

Dissent from Mao's strategy in Vietnam continued to be expressed through the spring and summer. Chief of Staff Lo Jui-ching's article of May 10, 1965, for example, may be interpreted, in part, as a veiled attack on the Maoist concepts. Lo compared the United States with Nazi Germany, and he praised Stalin for identifying the principal contradiction or threat that faced his nation and in rallying forces in a united front against imperialism and fascism. Lo urged "bearing this experience in mind," and he urged that U.S. war plans could be defeated provided "we are good at uniting the socialist camp." Recalling Neville Chamberlain and Edouard Daladier's rejection of a Soviet alliance, he noted that Hitler "struck at them first and caught them unprepared." This message was probably intended as a gentle lesson not only to present-day "appeasers" in the Kremlin but to dogmatists in Peking who rejected a similar alliance against "aggression."[136]

On June 1, 1965, an "Observer" article in the People's Daily talked of the likelihood of a U.S. escalation of the war into a Korea-type localized struggle and the creation of a pretext for spreading the war into China. Yet there was no hint that Hanoi or Peking should adopt a more defensive policy. The North Vietnamese, "Observer" stated, "have no further restrictions whatsoever in assisting their compatriots in the South." Moreover, the Chinese people were said to "have secured the right to do all in their power to aid the Vietnamese people in hitting back at the aggressors."

Statements by various Chinese leaders and in the Peking press continued to warn of the possibility of China sending volunteers to fight in Vietnam if required . . . and the inference was that such a contingency caused by a U.S. effort to destroy the DRV was very possible. Premier Chou En-lai, who was in Albania in March, told a rally in Tirana that China was "prepared to send our personnel to fight alongside the South Vietnamese,"[137] but this phrase was omitted from the NCNA version of his speech. The same sort of pledge, however, was frequently renewed during the next several months, presumably to Mao's alarm. In March, Chen Yi said that China stood ready to dispatch its "men to fight shoulder-to-shoulder with the South Vietnamese people whenever the latter require."[138] Similar statements were made by Chief of Staff Lo Jui-ching, on May 10;[139] by Foreign Minister Chen Yi on May 29;[140] by the People's Daily on

April 11; by Vice Premier Li Hsien-nien on June 2;[141] in a Foreign
Ministry statement on June 18; and in a Chinese Government statement
on August 7.[142]

In June, however, Mao was quoted as saying that "it is not necessary for China to dispatch volunteers to North Vietnam so long as the
armed forces of North Vietnam are strong."[143]

A rather defensive joint editorial on June 14 in People's Daily
and Red Flag also implied that there was still a dispute on whether
the struggle against revisionist influence in China was to be carried
through while the imperialists were at China's doorstep. The editorial
implied that some Chinese leaders were mistakenly calling for flexibility in relations with the Soviets, and it stressed the importance of
not giving in on principle: "It would be wrong to exercise unprincipled
flexibility to create ambiguity and confusion on questions of principle
on the pretext of flexibility."

Meanwhile, the U.S. bombing of the North not only failed to
intimidate the North Vietnamese leaders but also encouraged greater
material and political support from the Soviet Union to the DRV and
served to soften the impact on world opinion of Hanoi's clandestine
invasion of the South. On April 1, President Johnson reportedly decided
to use two marine battalions, which had been in South Vietnam since
March 8, in active rather than passive defensive action.

In May and June, came the disastrous defeats for Saigon by Viet
Cong (not North Vietnamese) units at Ba Gia in Quang Ngai Province
and in Dong Xoai north of the South Vietnamese capital. The momentum
of the communist offensive was thundering ahead, and Saigon again
teetered on the verge of collapse.

Air power had failed, and the inevitable logic of escalation, as
foreseen earlier by Under Secretary of State George Ball, was in
command. The Joint Chiefs of Staff once more recommended a greatly
intensified air campaign to isolate North Vietnam from China. This
plan was rejected again "because of the concomitant high risk of
inviting Chinese intervention."[144]

President Johnson was once more faced with the alternatives
of cutting losses and withdrawing or of substantially expanding the
U.S. presence and role in the war. In late July he chose the latter
course[145] and more U.S. combat troops were rushed into South Vietnam
to stave off defeat. But the first major clash between the Americans
and the North Vietnamese did not come until the fall.

Hanoi realized that the U.S. had heavily committed itself to final
victory by its involvement in the ground fighting. The North was no
less determined, however, to push on with its offensive.

The situation was now different from that of January or early
February, when Hanoi indicated a willingness to accept unconditional
talks. The absence of conditions for negotiations now implied that the

47

United States could resume the bombing, and it was reasonable to conclude that it would do so if Hanoi failed to scale down its own efforts. Negotiations under these conditions would imply that the DRV was on the defensive. The initiative had to be retained for the revolutionary forces; Hanoi ignored President Johnson's appeal for negotiations and his five-day total pause in the bombing in May and instead increased its attacks.

In June, the People's Daily "Observer" asked if the Johnson Administration was not preparing "to spread the war in Indochina to the rest of Southeast Asia, and even to China?"[146] And in July an editorial in the same paper warned Washington that the People's Liberation Army stood ready in "battle array," but it repeated, "we will not attack unless we are attacked; if we are attacked we will certainly counterattack."[147]

Civil defense and some military preparations were noted in China during the summer of 1965, with special attention paid to the role of the militia. The Chinese however avoided a frenetic war atmosphere. As the U.S. build-up in Vietnam continued, China's previous pledge to send volunteers if requested by the DRV was played down, and after August no Chinese statement suggested any such commitment to the DRV. War with the United States was only certain if Washington insisted on forcing it on China.

Nevertheless, China's support of the DRV war effort was to be on a scale substantially greater than that which it had provided to the Viet Minh against the French. As in the early 1950s, the nature and the amount of Chinese material support was consistent with the needs of the situation; Peking did what it thought necessary to offset U.S. intervention and to retain the initiative with the Vietnamese communists—never any more. If there was a need for more Chinese anti-aircraft or engineer units in the North, they would be sent; if there was the need to place North Vietnamese MIG's in China, they would be received. In the fall of 1965, Chinese logistic, engineer, and anti-aircraft troops began to arrive in North Vietnam. Ultimately they totaled between 30,000 and 50,000 men.

But at the same time, Mao aimed at avoiding a confrontation with the United States if at all possible. He did not intend to repeat the Korean War and see the Soviet Union sit back while China and the United States wasted themselves in conflict. Such a development would have served Soviet interests in more ways than one. Most certainly, it would have increased pressure for rapprochement with Moscow.

Mao's approach was reflected in the Chinese reaction to the few direct clashes that took place between the United States and China in the air war. From the beginning, China treated these incidents with caution, consistent with its resolute defensive strategy. In the first few months of the air campaign in 1965, Peking reported having shot down four unmanned U.S. aircraft, one jet, and one U-2 reconnaissance plane that had allegedly violated Chinese air space. Lin Piao termed these incidents "provocations" that had been soundly rebuffed. He carefully refrained from suggesting, however, that more aggressive action by the Chinese air force was justified.[148] Other incidents in August, September, and October of that year were similarly treated as attempts by the United States to "impose" war on China.

LIN PIAO'S ADVICE

Peking presumably expressed its ideas on how the war should be conducted directly to Hanoi. But Mao also gave a public analysis of the new stage of the war in the September 3, 1965 V-J Day anniversary article by Defense Minister Lin Piao. Lin, who at this point could see the way opening to the succession, was vigorously siding with Mao.

In addition to its graphic presentation of the then current Maoist world view as an overlay of the Chinese revolution, Lin's article carried a clear message to Asian revolutionaries on the strategy they should follow. The lesson was drawn for the benefit of the Indonesian Burmese, Malay, and Thai communist leaders. But it was mostly intended for the instruction of the North Vietnamese.

Lin's article may be interpreted as an attempt to put the Vietnam conflict into the broader context of the world revolutionary struggle and to urge the North Vietnamese into a self-reliant and protracted "people's war" that would wear down the United States rather than provoke it into further escalation. For the further instruction of the Vietnamese, Mao's 1938 article on "Problems of Strategy in the Guerrilla War Against Japan" was reprinted at this time in Red Flag, whose editor noted that Mao's theory of people's war had "particular practical importance today for those oppressed nations struggling against U.S. imperialism."[149]

Lin in his article stressed that a people's war of annihilation against a stronger enemy should not only be protracted but also largely self-reliant. Lin promised necessary "aid and support" from China, but he made no reference to the possibility that China would send its men to fight "shoulder-to-shoulder" with the Vietnamese. After Lin's speech no such pledge was in fact made again.[150]

But Lo Jui-ching's V-J Day speech (September 2)[151]still reflected differences with Lin and thus with Mao over the nature and imminence of the U.S. threat. Both Lo and Lin asserted that the United States might extend its ground war into China, but Lo was more worried that Washington might "in order to save itself from defeat . . . go mad."

Lo was concerned about an irrational U.S. air attack on China, and he called for urgent preparations to meet it. Lin on the other hand implied that China was well organized to meet the threat.[152]

GIAP's ASSESSMENT

The North Vietnamese obviously did not accept the general strategy proposed by Lin Piao.[153] General Giap, with his understanding of the psychology of the Western powers, as well as of relative strengths, judged that the United States could not be defeated strategically but had to be defeated tactically and politically. Giap saw the crucial omission in Lin Piao's description of how the Chinese communists by a protracted and defensive policy had achieved victory in the war against Japan—the Red Army of course had not actually defeated the Japanese.

Lin conveniently neglected to mention the critical U.S. and Soviet roles in Japan's collapse. Since there was for Hanoi no similar savior in sight willing and able to administer a strategic defeat to its enemy, a defensive and waiting strategy was inadvisable. The massive military and economic resources that the United States could concentrate on the pacification of South Vietnam also suggested that the U.S. goal was feasible when compared with the enormous problems Japan faced in pacifying China in the 1930s. The advance in military technology, especially air power, also indicated a much more difficult path for a purely guerrilla war. The United States, in Giap's view, had to be forced in the matter of a few years to abandon its objectives.

In 1969, General Giap summed up the strategic problem that always faced the DRV as follows:

> The realistic situation of the national liberation war . . . has posed to our people, a people whose population is not very big and whose territory is not very large, the strategic requirement to defeat enemies having large armies and economic and military potentialities many times greater than ours. Confronted with this strategic requirement, our forefathers to achieve victory, created the art of using a weak force to fight a strong enemy, using a small force to fight a bigger one and waging short battles to win protracted wars. . .[154]

Using a small force to fight a bigger one, Giap said, "means using a small force to win big victories." It does not mean, he said, carrying out only small offensives; but also "medium and big offensives."[155]

50

In war, parallel with wearing out and annihilating small
portions of the enemy in widespread guerrilla actions, the
most concentrated armed forces . . . particularly the main
force units . . . must resolutely wipe out increasingly more
important parts of the enemy.[156]

The new situation in the summer of 1965 was of course obvious
to Hanoi. The United States had moved from a "special war" in which
it employed advisers and air power to a "limited" or a "local" war
in which it employed its own ground forces on a large scale. The
all-out U.S. intervention, which the DRV and China had striven to avoid
for over 10 years, had now occurred. A quick victory was no longer
possible, but a total reversion to a Yenan-type strategy was also seen,
probably correctly, as an unpromising alternative.

In December 1965 the Lao Dong convened its 12th plenum and
discussed the question of over-all strategy. The party's decision
was a compromise intended to gain "a decisive victory in a relatively
short time" but within the framework of protracted struggle.[157] In
this approach both guerrilla and mobile warfare would be employed
as the situation required. The party's assessment was that continued
military pressure combined with the political, economic, and psychological contradictions inherent in the U.S. policy would achieve
ultimate success in a few years' time.

Hanoi remained optimistic and uncompromising. Thus it failed
to respond to the 37-day bombing pause (December 24, 1965 to January
30, 1966) and to the "14 points" put forward by the U.S. Government
as a basis for negotiation. On the contrary it exploited the bombing
halt to push a steady stream of supplies and men toward the demili-
tarized zone (DMZ) and along the Ho Chi Minh trail.[158] Hanoi would
not be prepared for negotiations until its military forces were exerting
their maximum pressure and the United States was weary of the war.
At the beginning of 1966, neither condition existed.

Thus the North Vietnamese strategy at this point was, as
Chalmers Johnson described it, "not to defeat the U.S. and allied
forces militarily but to convince the Americans through the use of
violence, both pervasively and at selected points, that their position
[was] hopeless."[159] This approach, contrary to all the Maoist dictums
on guerrilla war, required that the North Vietnamese accept many
more casualties than the United States; in addition, it also involved
a greater risk of escalation, and it required the kind of heavy material
and economic assistance that could only be provided by Moscow, not
Peking.

It was therefore natural that Peking opposed Giap's compressed
version of the protracted strategy. The degree of friction between
Peking and Hanoi on this question of strategy may have been exaggerated

in the West, but in the last half of 1965 it was serious. At that time the fear of some Chinese of expansion of the war intensified. At this point, the views of the North Vietnamese and the evolving opposition to Mao inside China coincided; both believed that Peking-Moscow cooperation was necessary to prevent further escalation.

NO TO "UNITED ACTION"

On November 11 a major article probably written by Mao again categorically rejected the idea of "united action" with the Soviets.[160]

The article charged that because the Vietnamese people were successful, the new Soviet leaders had come "to realize that it was no longer advisable to copy Khrushchev's policy of disengagement" and had switched to a policy of involvement, "that is, getting their hand in." "United action," the article said, was a "fraud" and an attempt by Moscow to recover its position as the "Father party."

The article stressed the importance of the Sino-Soviet rivalry in the Vietnam question proclaiming that the present world situation was in a "process of great upheaval, great division and great reorganization" on the basis of "opposition to or alliance" with the United States. The "sharpest difference of theory and line" between Moscow and Peking, the article stated, concerned "precisely the question of handling relations with enemies and friends, in other words, the question of whether or not to oppose or unite with U.S. imperialism." On this basis the Marxist-Leninist parties of the world were to draw a "clear line of demarcation both politically and organizationally" between themselves and the revisionists. On this basis, Peking still hoped to challenge Moscow for leadership of the antiimperialist Third World as well as the communist camp.

OTHER FAILURES STRENGTHEN THE DISSIDENTS

In addition to the increased war threat, more grist for the opposition mill in Peking was provided by the series of reverses to the PRC's external relations that occurred throughout 1965 and that, in large measure, resulted from Mao's pursuit of his quarrel with the USSR and his attempts to polarize the Afro-Asian as well as the communist world. Peking's tactics in attempting to bar Soviet participation in the aborted second Bandung conference and its demand that the condemnation of the United States be the number-one order of business alienated many Afro-Asian leaders. Mao's relentless crusade against both Moscow and Washington compelled him into an increasingly radical course. Failures in Africa, although coincidental to Chinese activities were numerous . . . Algeria's Ahmed Ben Bella was overthrown, and the Chinese communists were tossed out of Burundi and later lost their position in Dahomey, the Central African Republic, and Ghana. Chinese support for opposition forces undermined their position in Kenya and Egypt (the arrest of an anti-Nasser plotter was reportedly connected to the hasty departure of the Chinese Ambassador and the NCNA correspondent). Although the Chinese apparently were only marginally involved in the Congo rebellion of 1964, they had high hopes for it, and its dissipation by the fall of 1965 could be counted as another failure.

A particularly heavy blow was the suppression of the Indonesian Communist Party (PKI) and the collapse of the Peking-Jakarta axis following the aborted coup against the Indonesian Army of September 30, 1965. The resultant smashing of the PKI and Sukarno's loss of power destroyed Mao's most valuable ally and dealt a severe blow to the vision of a Peking-centered antiimperialist Asian front arrayed against Washington. The PRC's seemingly provocative but unsuccessful role in the Indian-Pakistani conflict in August and September of 1965 was another attempt to counter USSR and U.S. influence, which resulted in considerable loss of prestige by Peking. In the communist camp, the new Soviet tactic of "united action" and Mao's rejection of it were increasing Moscow's influence in several communist parties, notably in North Vietnam, North Korea, and Japan. In the movement, Peking could now only depend upon little Albania, the insignificant Communist Party of New Zealand, and the insurgent parties of Malaya, Thailand, and Burma.

THE INTERNAL STRUGGLE BEGINS

Although the outside world hardly noticed a ripple, by September 1965, struggles within the party over the planning of the Cultural Revolution, relations with Moscow, the Vietnam war, and strategy within the Afro-Asian camp had apparently reached a serious stage. Sometime from late September to early October, a high-level party meeting took place in Peking including all regional bureau party chiefs. It was probably at this meeting that Mao demanded a drastic rectification campaign at home, and he may have attacked those in the cultural organs and in the party who had only given lip service to his demands for a Cultural Revolution. The opposition at this time was outspoken. Red Guard posters in 1967, for example, charged that Teng Hsiao-ping coldly rebuffed Mao on the need for educational reform. While this charge may be a distortion of the facts, it seems clear that there was serious obstruction, if not opposition, to Mao's call for an intensification of the class struggle at home, while a war threat loomed on the horizon.

The chairman became alert to what he saw as a revisionist cancer throughout the party. While he had already decided to get rid of Liu Shao-chi and his associates, Mao now determined to carry out a far-reaching rectification campaign that would clear the way for the radical social reforms he had been planning. We now know that at this time Mao appointed, possibly as an entrapment strategy, an important member of the Liu camp, Peking Mayor Peng Chen, to head the First Cultural Revolution group. Peng's recommendation, which was dismissed by Mao as revisionist and bourgeois drivel, was submitted in February 1966, at the same time as a crisis over "united action" in Vietnam was coming to a head.

JAPANESE COMMUNISTS SUPPORT THE OPPOSITION

One of the best sources as to the nature of the foreign policy disputes involved in the intraparty struggle in Peking at this time is the polemics between the Chinese and the Japanese communist parties. For several years, the Japanese Communist Party (JCP) had sided with Peking in its fight against Soviet "modern revisionism." Moscow in turn had supported a splinter pro-Soviet faction that in December 1964 broke away from the main body of the JCP. Nevertheless the JCP continued to be concerned about the question of unity in the socialist camp, and it never fully accepted Mao Tse-tung's formulation that the "broad united front against imperialism" could not include the USSR. In late 1965, the JCP was apparently disturbed by the aborted coup in Indonesia and the destruction of the Indonesian Communist Party. In addition, the JCP also wished to move to a position with more appeal to Japanese public opinion.

In February 1966, the Japanese communists made an effort to change Peking's attitude. After spelling out its position in a February 4 article in its journal Akahata, the JCP sent a delegation led by Secretary General Kenji Miyamoto to China, North Vietnam, and North Korea to push for some accommodation between Peking and Moscow. In early February 1966, Peng Chen traveled to Shanghai to greet the JCP delegation. Peng had been closely associated with the JCP leaders and had been scheduled in 1965 to head the Chinese delegation to the JCP Congress but was refused a visa by the Japanese Government. It seems likely that Peng encouraged the JCP's visit to China in early 1966 to support the position of those who were opposed to Mao's Vietnam policies.

54

There is evidence to suggest that this visit of the Japanese communists to China may actually have been an important catalyst in the intense struggle within the CCP on the question of "united action." Despite its previous hard anti-Soviet line, People's Daily, which at that time apparently still reflected the orientation of Peng Chen and Liu Shao-chi elements, reprinted in full the Akahata February 4, 1966 article "For Strengthening International Unified Action and United Front Against American Imperialism." On the other hand the ideological journal Red Flag under the editorship of Chen Po-ta, the future militant director of the Cultural Revolution group, printed a long article on "Soviet-U.S. Collaboration," which categorically rejected the argument for "united action." The biweekly issue of Red Flag that carried this article was scheduled for release about February 11, 1966, the day of the arrival of the JCP delegation, but the issue was held up without explanation until February 27. During March there also occurred a hiatus in press attacks on Peng Chen's associate, vice mayor and playwright Wu Han, which had been appearing since November.

These events suggest that in February and March 1966 the developing internal power struggle was in a critical and uncertain stage and that the group or groups opposed to Mao may have been maneuvering against him, exploiting the issue of China-USSR relations and the war in Vietnam.

After visiting North Vietnam, the Japanese delegation, on March 3, held formal talks with Chinese leaders, including Liu Shao-chi, Teng Hsiao-ping, and Peng Chen. According to articles that appeared almost a year later in Akahata, the JCP and the CCP were sharply divided on the question of whether or not the new leadership of the Communist Party of the Soviet Union should be included in the international united front against U.S. imperialism in Vietnam or whether a struggle should be launched for a united front against both the United States and the USSR by placing the Soviet Communist Party and U.S. imperialism on the same level. However, a Japanese report of these meetings stated that Peng, Chou, Liu, and Teng demonstrated a sympathetic understanding of the JCP position.[161]

These talks closed on March 8, with the two sides unable to reach agreement on a communiqué.[162] On March 11, Miyamoto and his colleagues went to North Korea, whose government had for many months taken a similar line on the question of the need for "united action" in the socialist camp. On March 22, after the return of the JCP delegation from Pyongyang to Peking, the "Chinese side," according to later reports by the Japanese communists,[163] made a new proposal on the drafting of a joint communiqué. At this time, both Liu Shao-chi and Teng Hsiao-ping were out of the Chinese capital, and the "Chinese side" referred to by the Japanese included Chou En-lai and Peng Chen.

As a conciliatory gesture, the JCP headquarters announced on March 25 that the Japanese party would not, contrary to former expectations, attend the forthcoming meeting of communist parties in Moscow. On March 26, Peng Chen's Peking Municipal Committee held a mass rally in honor of the JCP delegation. Peng and Miyamoto both addressed the rally, and the core of both speeches was a paraphrase of the 1960 Moscow declaration that denounced "modern dogmatism" as well as "modern revisionism." (The former was generally understood to mean Maoist dogmatism.) On March 27 the JCP group again held a formal discussion with a CCP delegation led by Chou En-lai and including Peng Chen, Kang Sheng, Liu Ning-i, and Liao Cheng-chih. The group approved a joint communiqué that denounced "modern revisionism" for shirking and obstructing the struggle against U.S. imperialism but also stressed that it was more and more necessary to step up international aid to the Vietnamese people and that it was an important international task to unite the people of the world into the broadest international front against U.S. imperialism. This wording seemed to be a compromise in favor of those who advocated "united action." According to the Japanese, Chou En-lai proposed a toast to the agreement on the joint communiqué, which he said would "give a blow to our enemy and courage to our friends."[164] Later the JCP accused Chou of attempting to evade responsibility for the drafting of the communiqué.[165]

The communiqué, however, was never issued. The Japanese later claimed that prior to their departure, an interview was arranged for them with Mao Tse-tung. To the surprise of the JCP delegation, at the very beginning of their meeting, Mao said that he could not consent to the publication of a joint communiqué that did not condemn the Soviet leadership by name. The chairman allegedly demanded a large-scale revision of the contents of the communiqué. The Japanese rejected this demand. Mao thereupon reportedly said that there was no need to issue a communiqué and to forget about the meeting.[166]

On March 29, Miyamoto and his delegation were seen off at Peking airport by Peng Chen. Significantly, this was the last public appearance of the mayor until he was "dragged out" by the Red Guards in December 1966. Subsequently, relations between the Japanese and the Chinese communist parties sank to a remarkably low level of vituperation.

In their subsequent polemics with the Chinese, the Japanese communists implied that the basis of Mao's position was his theory that the Vietnam war had to be seen in the context of the world revolutionary struggle against revisionism as well as against imperialism. The Japanese indicated that Mao accused them, and presumably his internal opponents as well, of being afraid of holding to principles, of advocating compromise with revisionism, and of refusing to build for the inevitable, but distant, world revolution. The JCP in turn accused Mao of being afraid to oppose the United States in Vietnam.[167]

WAR AND REVOLUTION

The leadership of the CCP was welded together by the strength of its common commitment to Chinese nationalism and to a neo-Marxist ideology, by the nature of its Leninist organization and by the mystique of its ultimate leader. The self-interest of this group and its idealistic aspirations required a perpetuation of this solidarity. Such an elite organization could be split by a power struggle or by a serious threat that seemed to pose the choice between the security of the regime itself and the purity of ideological principles. The escalation of the Vietnam war in 1965, like the failure of the Great Leap Forward in 1958, posed such a dilemma.

The intensification of the conflict in Indochina and the implied threat to China served to exacerbate the internal split in China as well as that between China and the USSR and finally between China and the DRV. It was at this time that the Soviet Union began to build up its military forces along the China border. It would be four years, however, before this border conflict became the major threat.

With his internal opposition on the run, Mao moved to define more clearly the limits of Chinese intentions in dealing with U.S. actions in the Vietnam war. During the February 1966 Sino-U.S. ambassadorial talks in Warsaw, China and the United States again had an opportunity to inform each other of their respective positions on the war. According to unconfirmed reports, China indicated that it would not intervene directly, provided the United States did not attempt to invade the DRV or bring about the collapse of the Hanoi regime. The United States was said to have "taken note" of China's position and to have indicated in turn that if China did intervene directly in the war, the United States would regard the conflict and the weapons to be used as unlimited.[168] Whether or not such direct statements as these were actually made at the Warsaw meetings, they reflect the actual attitudes of the two sides.[169]

In April 1966, Chou En-lai made a four-point statement on China's policy toward the United States. In a nonpolemical interview with the Pakistani newspaper Dawn, Chou said that China would not take the initiative to provoke a war with the United States, and he pointed to Peking's continued willingness to negotiate the problem of Taiwan as "very good proof" of this. Chou indicated, however, that if the United States imposed air attacks on China, the latter would retaliate with ground forces, presumably in Southeast Asia. "If you come from the sky," he said, "why can't we fight back on the ground."[170]

The U.S. side also made its position clear: It too wished to avoid a Sino-U.S. conflict. As early as February 1965, it informed the Chinese that the United States "had no designs on the territory of North Vietnam nor any desire to destroy the DRV."[171] However, the State Department on April 26, 1965 reiterated that planes attacking allied aircraft over North Vietnam would be pursued into the territory of their home "sanctuary," if necessary. No such incidents apparently arose, and Chinese aircraft did not pursue intruding U.S. planes back over the border.[172] U.S. planes also attacked the Chinese engineer units in Vietnam and in turn were shot down by Chinese gunners protecting these units. But neither government publicized these incidents.

Mao saw the war in terms primarily of China's rivalry with the USSR for leadership of the anti-U.S. forces in the world and secondarily in terms of China's immediate security interests.

Mao's opponents in Peking wished to reverse this order of priorities. But for Mao, China's great power interests—the challenge to Moscow—transcended the question of the unification of Vietnam or securing a nuclear shield against the U.S. threat. He sought to exploit the political and psychological climate of a prolonged war in Vietnam to further his own international strategies, while at the same time avoiding an expansion of the fighting into China. He wished Hanoi to fight an extended war of attrition, without Soviet help and without compromise with the United States.

Consequently the major causes of strain between Hanoi and Peking were the role of Moscow in the war (the question of "united action") and the question of when to launch a "general offensive." In addition, the unleashing of the Cultural Revolution in China beginning in late 1966 not only raised ideological tensions between China and Vietnam but at one time reportedly interfered with the passage of Soviet aid for Hanoi.

Despite Peking's differences with Hanoi, China continued to assist North Vietnam on the same principle it had always employed. Mao felt justified in providing a level of support sufficient to keep an intensive guerrilla war going in the South and to counter U.S. air attacks on the North, but no more than that. In the first four years of the war, China's support remained at about the same level—two railway engineer and two antiaircraft artillery divisions consisting of from 30,000 to 50,000 thousand men were stationed in the North.[173] During this period DRV aircraft occasionally staged into South China, and several thousand North Vietnamese troops were trained in China, mostly in technical fields. China supplied Hanoi with important quantities of light weapons, ammunition, trucks, large quantities of coastal and patrol vessels, and some of the 100 MIG-15 and MIG-17 fighters in the DRV air force.[174] But total Chinese military and economic aid was about (U.S.) $200 million a year while a U.S.

Government estimate put Soviet aid at $1 billion annually in the early years of the war and about half that in later years.[175] Moscow supplied most of the heavy and sophisticated military equipment for the DRV, including MIG-21 fighters and surface-to-air missiles. In addition, the Soviet Union was also said to have had about 2,000 non-combat military personnel in North Vietnam.[176]

After purging Lo Jui-ching and Peng Chen, Mao and Lin Piao, with control of army headquarters and public media, turned to the Red Guards in 1966-67 as a novel instrument with which to rid themselves of Liu Shao-chi and his clique. From 1967 to 1969, China's attention and energies were consumed in the Cultural Revolution, which in part was an ideological reformation and in part an intense power struggle.

The political dynamics of the Cultural Revolution reinforced the rationalism of China's foreign policy and the principle of opposing both the United States and the Soviet Union—making opposition of "U.S. imperialism" the foundation of Peking's challenge to Moscow.

The North Vietnamese, however, pushed on with their own strategy.

HANOI'S STRATEGIC ASSESSMENT

In any violent conflict where there is a fairly clear and mutual understanding of intentions, as in the Vietnam war, compromise settlement becomes possible when the two adversaries arrive at approximately the same assessment of the physical possibilities. What also seems possible, however, is a measuring of resolution and of political strengths and weaknesses—qualities that are difficult to assess.

Before discussing the next period of the second Vietnam war, a brief review of the development of the opposing strategies is in order. In the simplest terms, the basic situation in Vietnam was that Hanoi wished to unify the country under its rule and the United States intended to deny it this goal. In 1964 both sides attempted to demonstrate that they were willing to pay a high cost to achieve their respective but mutually exclusive objectives; neither of course convinced the other, and the inevitable test of wills and strength began.

North Vietnam had been hopeful that the general offensive would be launched and carried through to victory in 1965. The initial phase of the U.S. bombing strategy did not alter this optimistic assessment in Hanoi, and, as suggested, it was perhaps useful as a political smoke screen to cover the clandestine invasion of South Vietnam by regular DRV forces. The subsequent U.S. assumption of the main burden of combat, its decision to accept the cost of a "limited war," only changed Hanoi's calculations in terms of the time span required and the cost involved. The DRV leadership was still determined to push for a "decisive victory" but in a relatively compressed "protracted war." Hanoi was not prepared to discuss a political settlement, much less to accept a ceasefire until the United States had been psychologically beaten and militarily put on the defensive.

The official U.S. assessment of the military situation during this period likewise remained grimly optimistic. The United States naturally sought a stand-down in the fighting. This position was made clear in the 14 points of late December 1965 as well as in the communiqué of the Manila conference in the fall of 1966. The United States agreed in principle to withdraw its forces if North Vietnamese regular units were withdrawn, although the former move was not to come until six months after the latter. As a first order of business, the United States was also prepared to discuss a ceasefire. Such a settlement of course would have frozen the situation, with Saigon in control of most of the population and with an opportunity to consolidate its position. The communists controlled but did not occupy significant territory.

Hanoi was determined not to agree to a ceasefire under these conditions. When substantive negotiations finally began in 1969, these policy positions still characterized the two sides: The U.S.-Saigon side sought to have the conference first discuss military measures leading to deescalation while Hanoi and the NLF insisted on first taking up political matters. Hanoi would not and could not agree to a military stand-down until it was convinced that it had maximized its gains.

In late 1967, communist forces in South Vietnam gave the appearance of pulling back into sanctuaries in Laos and Cambodia. These movements were in preparation for the general offensive Giap and the Hanoi high command had decided to launch in early 1968. The DRV leaders knew that after almost three years of fighting the United States had paid a heavy price in lives, money, and prestige for its commitment to Vietnam and that it was torn by heated and occasionally violent domestic opposition to the war. Giap and his colleagues calculated that the time had come to make a major effort to shatter the American will.[177]

The DRV strategy of a compressed version of the protracted war emphasized taking the initiative and developing a small, limited offensive position into a widespread and comprehensive one in defiance of the enemy's superior troop strength, firepower, and mobility.[178] The great "leap-and-bound" of 1968 was to be a critical test to Hanoi's strategy.[179]

Thus for a combination of reasons, but essentially because it was inherent in Giap's strategy, the decision was made. The "general offensive and uprising," postponed or cut short in 1965, was launched on January 30, 1968 with the first of a series of sustained assaults against centers of allied strength. During the next 14 months, the DRV put its resources into four campaigns aimed at escalating casualties and destruction. Hanoi's gamble was that the sacrifice of 200,000 or 300,000 or even a million of its own men would eventually buy a political and psychological victory if, in the process, they could kill one-tenth that number of Americans.

Although China opposed Giap's compressed version of "protracted strategy," it agreed with Hanoi's political principle that negotiations should not begin until a decisive military position had been won or the United States had despaired of the war. The disagreement between Peking and Hanoi was over how this situation could best be achieved, a divergence based on different assessments of the situation and dissimilar priorities.

When Hanoi, in early 1968, moved into the third stage of the people's war and launched a limited general offensive, Peking had serious objections. The Chinese had always opposed the compressed strategy of protracted war as well as the regular-force tactics that the North Vietnamese had mixed in with their guerrilla campaigns. Mao saw Hanoi's decision to throw its troops in larger units against the allied strongholds as both premature and dangerous. Mao had argued that the extent of the Vietnam war, like other local wars, could be controlled by the decisions of the revolutionary forces, but Hanoi's strategy threatened this control.

Peking praised the "victories" of the Tet attack, but shortly afterwards, its distaste for the strategy was heightened by apprehension that the offensive was intended as a prelude to peace talks. After the DRV accepted the offer of preliminary negotiations, apparently without prior consultation with the Chinese Government, Peking-Hanoi relations became more chilled than ever before and China made clear its extreme displeasure with the negotiations.

For six months Peking failed to inform its people that the Paris talks had even begun, and during this time Hanoi censored Peking's references to the "peace talks fraud" and the "bombing halt hoax." At the same time China's reporting of the fighting in South Vietnam tapered off, and NCNA began to pay much more attention to the relatively small-scale struggles of Maoist insurgents in Thailand and other areas of Southeast Asia.[180] Hanoi's support for the Soviet invasion of Czechoslovakia further irritated the Chinese, and the DRV delegation at Peking's October 1 celebrations that year were ranked behind the Australian Communist Party.

The fourth round of Hanoi's general offensive was launched in February 1969, but Peking media did not mention the event. In a long article on the "Asian Revolution" in April, Peking Radio failed to list Vietnam as one of the "storm centers" of revolution on the continent.[181]

On the formation in June 1969 of the "People's Revolutionary Government" in South Vietnam, Peking showed mistrust and offered only belated and unenthusiastic recognition.

This behavior suggests some of the calculations that lay behind Mao's opposition from 1965 to 1969 to negotiations. Mao and the radicals who won control of foreign affairs in 1967 feared that a settlement would threaten to end the "great upheaval" in world forces on which they placed such hopes.[182] A compromise settlement in Vietnam while the United States continued to exclude China from its policy of détente would further have isolated Peking and would have represented a victory for Moscow.

The Vietnam war also served as both an inspiration and a justification for the China-oriented insurgent groups in Southeast Asia in which Chinese interest had increased partially as a response to the U.S. containment effort and partially as a result of the militant ideological line taken by Peking to contrast with the alleged collusion policy of the Soviet Union. The upsurge in radicalism in 1967 inside China had also sparked new interest in the revolutionary parties of Southeast Asia and in attacking the peaceful coexistence policies of Liu Shao-chi (and Chou En-lai). A negotiated settlement in Vietnam would have destroyed much of the psychological impetus of these Maoist liberation wars and of the anti-U.S. basis of their respective united fronts.

RETURN OF THE PRAGMATISTS

The Cultural Revolution power struggle resulted in the emergence of a coalition of radicals, moderates, and military cliques bound together by shared interests but still affected with the strains and tensions of a fight for power.

Important groups and factions opposed to the radicals and Lin Piao made up an important element in the coalition. Mao and his personal coterie held the balance. Many powerful regional military commanders, like Hsu Hsih-yu in Nanking and Chen Hsi-lien in Shenyang who were not part of Lin Piao's clique, constituted major powers. Chou En-lai, through his political acumen, his personal prestige, his numerous friendships, and his accepted loyalty to Mao, also retained considerable power at the center. After 1967 Chou began slowly to recover his authority in foreign affairs.

Cross-currents were again at work within the hierarchy. The most radical aspects of the Cultural Revolution began to be reversed. Chou En-lai's administrators and planners together with the security-minded regional military leaders formed or gradually evolved into a new coalition in opposition to the Cultural Revolution group of radical ideologists. Those who had responsibility for the achievement of concrete objectives—national defense, economic development, and foreign relations—began to recover power from those whose interests lay in intellectual, ideological, and cultural affairs. Lin Piao at this time probably took an ambivalent position, lending some support to his erstwhile radical allies but also perhaps adjusting to the new situation. In any event, he must have been defensive about rejection of some of the radical policies in foreign as well as domestic affairs with which he had been identified.

The Soviet invasion of Czechoslovakia in August 1968 and Peking's unprecedently cool relations with Hanoi provided the first impetus for a hard-headed and realistic foreign policy that would maximize China's diplomatic options and end its isolation among the great powers. The 12th plenum of the 8th Central Committee of the CCP in October 1968 marked a watershed in the evolution of foreign policy during the Cultural Revolution. Although the radicals continued to influence foreign policy, a more supple and subtle style to deal with both the United States and the USSR began to emerge.

In foreign affairs the communiqué of the 12th plenum returned to the central theme of forming a "broad united front" to maintain "close unity with all Marxist-Leninists and the masses of the revolutionary people of the world. . . ." Nevertheless the communiqué's formulation of the broader-based united front was not categorical in that it referred to "all peoples" and not to all countries or governments as well. The phraseology employed by the 12th plenum was similar to that used in the August 1966 communiqué of the 11th plenum, which had formally opened the Cultural Revolution. The main difference was that in 1968 those with whom common cause could be made against Soviet revisionism were not limited to "revolutionary Marxist-Leninists" (that is, pro-Peking communists), as had been stipulated in 1966.

During and following the 12th plenum, two major revisions were made in policy that pointed toward a major effort to maximize China's diplomatic support and that were essentially related to the fear in Peking, after the invasion of Czechoslovakia, of a growing threat from the USSR. In October 1968, the PRC, for the first time, took cognizance of the Paris peace talks, and in early November it reprinted statements by both sides at the talks. Shortly afterwards, a Foreign Ministry statement (November 26) on the Warsaw talks renewed the pre-Cultural Revolution position that the United States and the PRC should conclude an agreement on peaceful coexistence. This position contrasted with a People's Daily article a year earlier that had attacked Liu Shao-chi for alleging that Sino-U.S. relations could improve once the Taiwan question was settled, a line that had been depicted as ignoring China's international proletarian responsibilities. Simultaneous with the issuance of the November 1968 statement on the Warsaw talks, Peking attempted to rationalize its reversal by republishing a March 1949 statement by Mao in which he referred to the permissibility of negotiations with the "enemy."

The revolutionary line of hostility to "U.S. imperialism"as the core of China's foreign policy, however, was far from dead. The broad united front policy was omitted from the December 31, 1968 joint New Year's editorial, which again simply referred to the great struggle by "genuine Marxist-Leninists" and revolutionary people. In January there were vitriolic attacks on the new American president, and the Warsaw talks scheduled for February were abruptly cancelled (on the pretext of a defection of a Chinese official in the Netherlands). Lin Piao and the radicals at this time may have seen Chou's attempts to redirect China's international line as aimed in part at discrediting them. Presumably at this point Mao had not yet been fully won over to Chou's new line but had adopted a wait-and-see attitude. Moscow, however, was to convince him.

1969: FOCUS ON THE SOVIETS

During 1969, Chinese attention focused on the Soviet Union and the menace from the north. Although the Soviets had been building up their forces along the border since 1965 and were engaging in what the Chinese considered provocative patroling in disputed areas, it seems fairly clear that the Chinese side launched the action of March 2 on Chenpao (or Demansky) Island. This bold strike was in keeping with the Maoist "operational code" in dealing with or deterring a superior and threatening enemy: When the enemy adopts a threatening posture, he must be awakened to the determination of his adversary.

The Soviet bear, however, reacted with rage to this "pinking," and on March 15 he struck back on Chenpao Island and other points with overwhelming force. More alarming, he began to send up signs of preparing a preemptive war against China.[183] Faced with the most serious threat to the PRC since the Korean War, the mainstream group in Peking came to the fore and focused on military preparedness and internal unity. In addition, it began to win Mao's approval of a foreign policy that would maximize international support for China and concentrate on diverting and weakening the Soviet Union.

The advancement of the united-front line was expressed in Lin Piao's report to the Ninth Party Congress of the CCP in April in which he again emphasized the goal of forming "the broadest possible united front" opposed to both the United States and the USSR. Lin included in this front all countries as well as all peoples who had a common interest in resisting the dominance of "imperialism" and "social-imperialism." Nevertheless, Lin made clear that the main target was still the United States. The revolutionary line was also continued in Lin's separate pledges of support to the "revolutionary people of all countries," mentioning, among others, Burma, "Malaya," Indonesia, and India. The continuing influence of the Cultural Revolution group was also indicated by the election at the Party Congress of Chen Po-ta and K'ang Sheng to the five-man Politburo Standing Committee. The Ninth Congress was the peak of Lin's career.

The trend to a pragmatic and expedient line in dealing with the Soviet threat resulted in China's efforts to defuse the border situation and eventually in its acceptance in September 1969 of negotiations with the Soviets. Hanoi apparently played an important role in drawing its two big allies away from the brink of war. Although the DRV benefited from the rivalry of the communist giants, it was disturbed by the fact that actual hostilities between China and the Soviet Union would have profound consequences for its own war effort. Following the death of Ho Chi Minh, the DRV leaders took advantage of the presence in Hanoi of the Soviet and Chinese premiers to press them to begin negotiations.

A PRC Government statement of October 7, 1969 declared that normal state relations should be maintained between China and the Soviet Union on the basis of peaceful coexistence despite "irreconcilable differences of principles." Subsequently, Chinese anti-Soviet polemics were reduced, but at the same time Peking began to develop its diplomatic, as distinct from its former ideological, offensive within the communist camp. A main objective of this diplomatic campaign was to improve relations with North Korea and North Vietnam. Advances were to be made in both areas in 1970, but the Chinese could not hope to reconstruct the informal alliance that they had begun to develop with these communist states in 1964 against Soviet revisionism.

THE AMERICAN EQUATION

Concurrent with its perception of increasing danger from the Soviet Union, Peking also began to calculate that the U.S. "threat" was diminishing and that U.S. policy toward China was in fact beginning to change.

As we concluded earlier, Peking's opposition to Hanoi's political-military strategy during 1968 was based on its fear that the general offensive was a highly provocative policy and its suspicion that the strategy was a prelude to a negotiated compromise settlement. Even when it became clear that the Johnson Administration had adopted a defensive posture and in effect had abandoned its 1964 goal of militarily defeating the communists in the South, the Chinese were still concerned that the new Republican administration would threaten new weapons or a new strategy. China's experience in the Korean War with the Eisenhower-Nixon Administration's threat to use nuclear weapons unless compromises were forthcoming probably influenced Peking's fears. The Chinese possibly also remembered that Nixon as vice president in 1954 at one point was strongly in favor of Radford's plan for massive U.S. air intervention.[184] This fear of the new Nixon Administration very likely lay behind China's studied silence on the February 1969 DRV offensive.

But by the spring of 1969 Hanoi's compressed version of the protracted war culminating in four campaigns of the 14-month general offensive had not excited U.S. military intensification from either the Johnson or Nixon Administrations but had won a series of political concessions and the beginning of the withdrawal of U.S. forces.

In May 1969, President Nixon's national security adviser, Dr. Henry Kissinger, met secretly with the DRV negotiator Le Duc Tho in Paris and began talks that would eventually lead to a U.S. offer of total troop withdrawal from South Vietnam in return only for the release of U.S. prisoners and a ceasefire, and not for a North Vietnamese withdrawal. The month before, the president had proclaimed the "Nixon doctrine," which promised a "low-profile" U.S. policy in Asia. In June, Nixon announced his program of withdrawing U.S. forces from South Vietnam unilaterally.

The Chinese assessment of American intentions began to change. The U.S. failure to retaliate for the North Korean destruction of an American reconnaissance plane over international waters on April 14, 1969, also probably indicated to Peking that the new administration would not be easily provoked. Even more important was the failure of the United States to try directly to exploit the Sino-Soviet conflict of 1969.

But next to the war scare with the Soviets, the most potent ingredient in the 1969 mixture of political developments for China was the first secret approach by Nixon "to communicate our new attitude . . . and to seek contact with the People's Republic of China."[185] According to Nixon, his first secret contact with Peking was made within two weeks of his inauguration, and "the two sides began clarifying their general intentions."

THE VIEW FROM WASHINGTON

For 20 years the formal basis of U.S. policy in Indochina had been the assumption that behind the ambitions of Hanoi lay the power of Communist China. For the first half of this period, it was further believed that behind Peking was the power of Moscow. It was thought that an extension of the DRV's control to South Vietnam would be an extension of China's power and influence and ultimately that of the USSR. Victory for the communists in Vietnam, it was feared, would also undermine the credibility of the Western collective security system in Asia and somehow excite Chinese efforts to intimidate and perhaps overthrow other noncommunist governments of the region.

The Nixon Administration, however, was faced with the economic and political impossibility of continuing the large-scale U.S. involvement not only in Vietnam but throughout the world. Finances and the American public demanded retrenchment, and so it became necessary to divorce the Vietnam war from the China problem.

An enormous U.S. commitment to the security of Southeast Asian countries against both direct aggression and internal communist revolt only made sense if its aim was to contain Chinese aggression. The Nixon doctrine, which sought to disengage the United States from direct participation in the internal wars of Asia, implied that the loss of any one country to a local communist rebellion was not necessarily calamitous for U.S. interests. If the Nixon doctrine was to promote stability in Asia, the goal had to be accommodation with China rather than containment of her influence. Washington's justification of its diminishing role in Vietnam now focused not on the reasons given for the original military commitment but on the need for its "honorable" termination.

Likewise, it was apparent that before such an "honorable" end could be achieved, it was essential to isolate Hanoi diplomatically from its two major allies and to reduce its ability to play them off against each other. This meant that Peking had to be given a stake in its relations with the United States, which would override Chinese interest in a clear victory for Hanoi. This could only be achieved by the United States extending détente to Peking and offering to accommodate some of China's broader goals and specifically to seek a compromise on the issue of Taiwan.

The desire for Sino-U.S. accommodation, however, involved a reassessment of goals on the Chinese side as on the American. The Chinese attempt from 1963 to 1968 to construct an Asian communist system centered on Peking seemed to lend credence to the American fear that China represented the main danger to stability and peace. During most of the 1960s, Peking sought to build its own international movement and an informal alliance system on the militant exploitation of the outstanding revolutionary goals of ruling and nonruling parties. Mao sought to build a community of common interests among the communists of Asia by directing them along the proper path to power and by encouraging militant struggle with "U.S. imperialism."

The dreams of polarizing the communist movement in Asia fell to pieces over the adroit post- 1964 Soviet response to the Vietnam war, and as described in Chapter 2 below, over the collapse of the Peking Jakarta axis. The truth was that no Asian communist party had a common interest with Peking in continued hostility toward Moscow so long as the Soviets were prepared to provide equal or greater support than was Peking. Only the Southeast Asian insurgent parties that were ignored by Moscow, such as the communist parties of Burma and Malaysia, continued to pay homage to China. By 1970 there was no compelling political or ideological reason for China to maintain a militant stand against the United States and deny itself leverage with both of its adversaries as well as the opportunity to achieve objectives vis-à-vis the United States in regard to Taiwan, Japan, the United Nations, and the U.S. containment policy.

The third crisis of the Vietnam war ended, in Peking's eyes, on some unmarked day in mid-1969. The threat that U.S. involvement in Vietnam might lead to conflict with China seemed to Peking finally expunged when Nixon failed to retaliate against the DRV-Viet Cong offensive of February 1969 and instead proposed total withdrawal of all U.S. forces and at the same time made his first move toward accommodation with China. The danger of a U.S. attack on China had seemed serious to the Chinese leaders at the time of the DRV general offensive in 1968, but by mid-1969, it probably appeared all but certain to the professional Chou En-lai group that the Republican administration in Washington also had no intention of escalating the objectives of the war but like the previous administration had concluded that the primary goal "should be to level off our involvement and to work toward gradual disengagement."[186]

While the United States hoped that "Vietnamization" would continue to deny Hanoi its goals in the South and although there remained the threat of a resumption of regular U.S. bombing of the North, it must have seemed to Chou En-lai in 1969 that there was relatively little chance of a U.S. invasion of the North or of U.S. attacks against China. At just this time the Chinese were preparing for and expecting a Soviet attack on China. A new sort of "upheaval" was taking place in world politics.

PEKING-HANOI TIES IMPROVE

By mid-1969 Hanoi had enjoyed for one year the circumstances it had always sought for the discussion of political terms: maintaining its military pressure at a high level while denying the enemy opportunity for consolidation. But the general offensive had achieved its political objectives at a horrendous price. The campaigns of January-February, May, and August 1969 had taken an estimated 150,000 to 180,000 North Vietnamese and Viet Cong lives . . . more than the total number of young men who reached draft age during that year.[187] Most damaging was the loss of much of the Viet Cong superstructure in the villages and the death of many of the party's local cadres. The intensity of the attacks began to wane; the last assault of the campaign, which came in February 1969, was on a notably smaller scale than the other three. In addition, the February 1969 offensive, which was the first test of the Nixon Administration, involved few frontal attacks on fortified allied positions.

During the remainder of the year, it became clear that the first general offensive, a 14-month campaign, had been concluded and that the communist forces in 1970 were stressing a more moderate mixture of guerrilla and mobile warfare in order to economize their forces. Policy directives from Hanoi began to emphasize a longer-range military and political effort.[188] Throughout 1969 no more massive assaults took place, and the total number of communist forces in the South shrank to about 240,000, compared to 290,000 the previous year.

In December, General Giap in a series of seven articles outlined the DRV's response to its severe manpower shortage and its answers to the problems of dealing with continued U.S. military superiority and with the U.S. political strategy of Vietnamization. In the new situation, Giap said, it was necessary to create new tactics and skillfully coordinate armed struggle with political struggle in order "to create favorable conditions for carrying out more important leaps and bounds."[189] Giap emphasized the need to apply the protracted war strategy and to "gain time" in order to score even greater victories. The stress on the offensive remained, but for the next two years tactics were to be more flexible and on a smaller scale; the timetable for victory was once again extended.

Consequently, Giap was compelled to stretch out further his compressed version of the protracted-war strategy. This meant that temporarily the war would proceed more in keeping with the Maoist model and that the threat of a major escalation would not come until the spring of 1972.

In the last half of 1969, there was a notable warming in Hanoi-Peking relations. Differences and strains that had existed seemed to be melting away. Hanoi media began to praise the thoughts of Mao and the "great successes" of China's Cultural Revolution. The two Chinese nuclear explosions in September were described by Hanoi as a new blow at U.S. imperialism and as having brought "into bold relief the superiority of the new regime . . . headed by Chairman Mao Tse-tung."[190] Peking, too, began to give more coverage to the Vietnamese struggle, and in their celebration of current revolutionary wars, Chinese commentators in the summer of 1969 restored the Vietnam conflict to its former place of honor.[191]

Peking's position was spelled out in an official message on the 24th anniversary of the DRV. The message, signed by Mao, Lin Piao, and Chou En-lai, expressed confidence that the DRV would win total victory "by persevering in protracted war, persevering in maintaining independence and the initiative in their own hands and persevering in self-reliance." The Chinese people, the message concluded, "firmly stand on the side of the Vietnamese people and resolutely support them in carrying the war through to the end until final victory."[192]

The same theme was expressed in the condolence message of the Central Committee of the Chinese party on the death of Ho Chi Minh. This message also reiterated that the vast expanse of China's territory was the "reliable rear area" of the Vietnamese people.[193] The DRV readily recognized that its "victories" were "closely associated with the very great support and assistance from China and the other socialist countries."[194] After Ho's death, the DRV leaders, including Premier Pham Van Dong, Lao Dong First Secretary Le Duan, and Chairman of the National Assembly Truong Chinh expressed their nation's "heartfelt thanks" for China's "whole-hearted support and assistance."[195]

The Viet Cong delegation to China's National Day Celebrations on October 1, 1969 received the most attention of all the foreign guests, and the statements by Chou En-lai and Pham Van Dong during the latter's two separate visits to Peking in October reflected no differences of opinion on the state of the war and its future direction.

THE 1970 VIEW IN PEKING

Peking's joint New Year's editorial for 1970 reflected the continuing evolution in China's foreign policy. For the first time since 1966, peaceful coexistence was mentioned in the New Year's message and, as a new departure, was even said to be the basis of China's relations with "all countries"—that is, with socialist and "revisionist" countries as well as with those with different social systems. This broad definition of peaceful coexistence appeared to rationalize efforts to improve state relations with the East European states, as well as negotiations with the USSR and the United States. Nevertheless, the editorial continued to speak of world revolution and armed struggle in terms that suggested the imminence of class warfare and to hail the "great division and great reorganization" within the international communist movement.

The radicals, with the support of Lin Piao's military clique, fought a rear-guard action on foreign affairs throughout the first half of 1970—as we will see, they tried to seize the initiative with the Cambodian affair. But Chou En-lai was in firm control of the Foreign Ministry, and he continued steadily to restore the multifaceted diplomacy of the international united front.

With the threat from the Russian north as the overriding foreign policy consideration, Chou was eager to encourage Sino-U.S. détente as a counter to the Soviet Union. The Chinese obviously could not hope for U.S. military assistance in the event of a Soviet attack, but once Sino-U.S. relations had been improved, they could expect that the United States would view with the greatest alarm any Soviet move to restore by force of arms a monolithic Moscow-controlled Eurasian bloc. The Russians could not be sure that a nuclear onslaught on China would eradicate either the Chinese challenge or the Sino-American effort at détente. More likely, a shattered China would survive, and the result would be to repolarize the world, this time with China and the United States allied.

Nixon by open measures as well as contact through third parties had continued throughout 1969 to express his desire for a rapprochement with Peking. In July 1969 Washington relaxed the trade embargo on Chinese goods, and in the fall it canceled regular U.S. naval patrols in the Taiwan Straits. In December, U.S. subsidiaries abroad were permitted to engage in commerce with China.

China's perception of an emerging independent threat from Japan also provided further sanction for Chou and his group's practical approach to maximizing China's diplomatic options. With the Sato-Nixon communiqué of November 1969, the Chinese began to fear that as part of the Nixon Doctrine, Japan would assume a portion of U.S. security responsibilities in Asia, most likely over South Korea and Taiwan. To counter this threat, an active diplomacy with both Japan and the United States was necessary as well as a settlement of the Taiwan issue.

The PRC agreed to a resumption of the Warsaw talks with the United States in January. Promising ambassadorial talks were held on January 20 and February 20, 1970. Although these were broken off after the Cambodian episode in the spring, according to Edgar Snow, Nixon had already succeeded in communicating his desire to end the deadlock in Sino-U.S. relations, clear up the question of Taiwan, see Peking enter the United Nations, and establish normal U.S.-PRC relations.[196]

NOTES

1. Robert Shaplen, The Lost Revolution (New York: Harper and Row, 1966), p. 70.

2. J. J. Zasloff, "The Role of the Sanctuary in Insurgency, Communist China's Support to the Vietminh, 1946-1954," RAND Corporation memorandum RM-4618TR, Santa Monica, Cal., May 1967, p. 5.

3. King C. Chen, Vietnam and China (Princeton, N.J.: Princeton University Press, 1969).

4. J. H. Brimmel, Communism in Southeast Asia (London: Oxford University Press, 1959), p. 177.

5. Tang Tsou, America's Failure in China (Chicago: University of Chicago Press, 1963), p. 401.

6. Virginia Thompson and Richard Adloff, The Left Wing in Southeast Asia (New York: Institute for Pacific Relations, 1950), p. 40.

7. Harold Isaacs reports having seen these orders, which were passed to the Vietminh by French CP agents in Saigon. No Peace in Asia (New York, 1948), pp. 173-174.

8. Melvyn Gurtov, The First Vietnam Crisis (New York: Columbia University Press, 1967), p. 5.

9. Bernard Fall, Street Without Joy: Indochina at War, 1946-1954 (Harrisburg, Pa.: Stackpole, 1961), p. 27. A training camp was at Nanning, an artillery range at Ching-Hsi, and a tank school at Wu Ming.

10. Shaplen, op. cit., p. 69.

11. Fall, op. cit., p. 29.

12. Zasloff, op. cit., p. 19.

13. Ibid., p. 20, reports his interviews 10 years later with "highly placed French intelligence officers" in December 1946, which confirm the judgment in most literature on the subject that the small number of Chinese personnel in Vietman had "largely technical and advisory roles." One French officer told Zasloff (p. 23) that Chinese material never exceeded 20 percent of the Vietminh's total supplies. It is not clear however whether this total includes foodstuff, which could have made up the bulk of the tonnage. During the war, of course, official French reports tended to exaggerate the Chinese role, primarily for the effect on Washington.

14. Harold Hinton, China's Relations With Burma and Vietnam (New York: Institute for Pacific Relations, 1958), pp. 18-19.

15. Ibid., p. 18, cites a DRV broadcast of April 20, 1953, which in passing stated that "China will grant facilities to its brother fighters who are able to ask for aid such as the aid given to the fighting forces in Vietnam."

16. Fall, op.cit., p. 30.

17. Vo Nguyen Giap, People's War, People's Army (New York: Praeger Publishers, 1962), p. 36.

18. Ibid., p. 22.

19. The Pentagon Papers, as published by the New York Times (New York: Bantam Books, 1971), p. 9.

20. Hsiao Yang, Chieh-fang Chung Ti Yueh-nan (Vietnam in Liberation) (Shanghai, 1951), cited in Gurtov, op. cit., p. 15.

21. Robert V. Daniels, ed., A Documentary History of Communism vol. 2 (New York: Random House, 1962), pp. 779-782.

22. See for example, Hoang Van Chi, From Colonialism to Communism: A Case History of North Vietnam (New York: Praeger Publishers, 1964), p. 71.

23. George K. Tanham, Communist Revolutionary Warfare: The Vietminh in Indochina (New York: Praeger Publishers, 1961), pp. 68-69. Tanham had access to French Army records in Paris, and he describes these figures as reliable. He also cites reports that 75 percent of this aid consisted of ammunition and petroleum products and 25 percent weapons and medical and signal equipment. Zasloff, op. cit., p. 22, also cites a French general's estimate that Chinese aid was 2,000 tons monthly in 1953, having risen from a previous average of 1,000 tons.

24. Draft dated March 24, 1954, of Overseas Press Club speech by John Foster Dulles, March 29, p. 5, in Dulles's papers (Princeton University, Princeton, N.J.), file 1.B cited by Gurtov, op. cit., p. 170.

25. Pentagon Papers, op. cit., p. 10.

26. Ibid., pp. 31-32.

27. Daniel Lerner and Raymond Aron, eds., France Defeats EDC (New York: Praeger Publishers, 1957).

28. New York Times, January 13, 1954.

29. Ibid., September 3, 1953.

30. People's Daily, September 2, 1953; Survey of the Chinese Mainland Press (SCMP), no. 643, September 1953.

31. Text in Alan B. Cole, ed., Conflict in Indochina and International Repercussions (Ithaca, N.Y: Cornell University Press, 1956), pp. 148, 149.

32. Charles B. McLane, Soviet Strategies in Southeast Asia (Princeton, N.J.: Princeton University Press, 1960), p. 464. McLane reports that Soviet commentaries on Ho's statements also related the two issues.

33. Washington Post account of the "Pentagon Papers," June 18, 1971.

34. Gurtov, op. cit., p. 72.

35. Pentagon Papers, op. cit., p. 11.

36. For the text of Giap's mobilization order, see Jules Roy, The Battle of Dien Bien Phu (New York: Harper and Row, 1965).

37. New York Times, March 30, 1954.

38. Department of State Bulletin 30, 713 (April 19, 1954).

39. Quoted by Philippe Devillers and Jean Lacouture, End of a War (New York: Praeger Publishers, 1969), p. 81.

40. NCNA, April 4, 1954; SCMP, no. 781, April 4, 1954.

41. Devillers and Lacouture, op. cit., pp. 71-89.

42. Ibid.

43. See for example NCNA comment on Dulles speech, April 1, 1953.

44. Chalmers M. Roberts, "The Day We Didn't Go to War," in Roberts, Marcus G. Raskin, and Bernard B. Fall, eds., The Vietnam Reader (New York: Vintage, 1965), pp. 57-60.

45. Pentagon Papers, op. cit., pp. 45-46.

46. NCNA, February 8, 1971.

47. Khrushchev Remembers (Boston: Little Brown and Co., 1970), pp. 481-482. Some observers question the authenticity of these memoirs, but most specialists believe they are authentic although not necessarily accurate.

48. A June 1954 cable from U.S. Ambassador to France Douglas Dillon to Dulles, quoting a French diplomat, Jean Chauvel. Reported in the Washington Post's account of the "Pentagon Papers," June 18, 1971.

49. Cable from Undersecretary Walter Bedell Smith to Dulles, in ibid.

50. Department of State Bulletin 30, 783 (June 28, 1954): 971-973.

51. Washington Post Reports of the "Pentagon Papers," June 18, 1971.

52. New York Times, June 29, 1954.

53. Tillman Durdin, in New York Times, July 25, 1954. This notion has become part of accepted wisdom. See for example Seymour Topping, in New York Times, February 4, 1966.

54. Khrushchev Remembers, op. cit., p. 483.

55. Nguyen Kien, Le Sud-Vietnam Depuis Dien Bien Phu (Paris, 1963), pp. 27-29.

56. P. J. Honey, Communism in North Vietnam (Cambridge: MIT Press, 1963), p. 46.

57. Bernard Fall, The Two Vietnams (New York: Praeger Publishers, 1967 ed.), p. 175.

58. Honey, op. cit., p. 49.

59. Ibid., p. 78.

60. This was revealed in a Lao Dong statement on February 10, 1963, issued by the Vietnam news agency in English to Europe and Asia. For discussion of this period, see William E. Griffith, The Sino-Soviet Rift (Cambridge: MIT Press, 1964), pp. 33-42.

61. Donald S. Zagoria, The Vietnam Triangle (New York: Pegasus, 1967), p. 110.

62. Arthur Dommen, Conflict in Laos: The Politics of Neutralization (New York: Praeger, 1964), p. 224.

63. Hoc Tap, February 1964, in Harold C. Hinton, Communist China in World Politics (Boston: Houghton Mifflin, 1966), p. 361.

64. Ibid.

65. Pentagon Papers, op. cit., p. 278.

66. Ibid., p. 276.

67. Ibid.,

68. Ibid., p. 255.

69. Ibid., p. 256.

70. New York Times, February 1, 1965.

71. Fall, Two Vietnams, op. cit., p. 358.

72. This statement is referred to in the Department of State's "White Paper" of February 1965, publication 7838.

73. Mass rallies were held throughout China to mark the occasion. See for example People's Daily editorial of July 20, 1964, SCMP, no. 3264, July 1964.

74. See Chen Yi's reply to the DRV foreign minister in NCNA, July 8, 1964, and PRC statement of July 19, 1964 (NCNA, July 19, 1964).

75. Allen Whiting, "How We Almost Went to War with China," Look, April 29, 1969.

76. Washington Post and Times Herald, July 26, 1964, cited by Hinton, Communist China, op. cit., p. 363. McNamara also referred to the work on these fields in his press conference of August 7, 1964 (New York Times, August 12, 1964).

77. New York Times, July 28, 1964.

78. People's Daily, August 7, 1964.

79. Ibid., August 6, 1964.

80. New York Times, August 12, 1964, citing a report of the Department of State.

81. Ibid., August 14, 1964.

82. Eric Sevareid, "The Final Troubled Hours of Adlai Stevenson," Look, November 20, 1965, p. 84.

83. William P. Bundy, in New York Times, October 2, 1964.

84. Pentagon Papers, op. cit., p. 299.

85. Charles B. McLane, "USSR Policy in Asia," Current History (October 1965), pp. 214-220.

86. William E. Griffith, Sino-Soviet Relations 1964-65 (Cambridge, Mass.: The MIT Press, 1967), p. 82.

87. Ibid., p. 78.

88. See TASS release of November 27, 1964; Kosygin's first report to the Supreme Soviet on December 9, 1964; and Foreign

Minister Gromyko's statement on December 20, 1964, all cited in
McLane, "USSR Policy in Asia," op. cit.

89. New York Times, February 1, 1965.

90. U.S. Department of State, "Working Paper on the North
Vietnamese Role in the War in South Vietnam," Saigon, May 1968.

91. Pentagon Papers, op. cit., pp. 373-378.

92. Ibid., p. 378.

93. US News and World Report, August 18, 1969, p. 26.

94. General Van Tien Dung, "Some Great Experiences of the
People's War," Quan Doi Nhan Dan (Hanoi), June 1967.

95. Pentagon Papers, op. cit., p. 441.

96. Ibid., p. 420.

97. Ibid., pp. 420-421.

98. Ibid., p. 419.

99. Ibid.

100. Ibid., p. 430. Presumably Bundy meant Yünnan Province,
where DRV MIG's were stationed, and not Fukien, which is opposite
Taiwan.

101. New York Times, February 9, 1965.

102. These secret Soviet overtures of April 3 and April 17,
1965 were publicized by European communist parties and reported
by Edward Crankshaw in the Observer, November 14, 1965. A Peking
spokesman, Liao Cheng-chih, in July 1966, told Japanese newsmen
that China had rejected the Soviet proposal for an airbase in Yünnan
because it doubted Soviet "sincerity" (Tokyo Domestic Television
Service, in Japanese, 1000 GMT, July 15, 1966, NHK Correspondent
Kobayashi).

103. People's Daily—Red Flag, November 11, 1965.

104. Ibid.

105. Times (London), Paris dispatch, February 25, 1965.

106. New York Times, February 13, 1965.

107. Ibid., February 26, 1965.

108. Edgar Snow, "Interview with Mao," New Republic, February
27, 1965.

109. Edgar Snow, "Aftermath of the Cultural Revolution," New
Republic, April 3, 1971. Snow was told this by a "very responsible
person" in Peking.

110. Griffith, op. cit., p. 75.

111. Edgar Snow, "A Conversation with Mao Tse-tung," Life,
April 30, 1971. When Kosygin asked if this could not be shortened,
Mao agreed to knock off 1,000 years.

112. Snow, "Interview," op. cit.

113. For one perceptive but still I would suggest tentative
analysis of the personalities and positions of the various factions,
see Zagoria, op. cit. Uri Ra'anan has provided an even more detailed

content analysis in Tang Tsou's China in Crisis, vol. 2 (Chicago: University of Chicago Press, 1968), pp. 23-72.

114. People's Daily, April 5, 1967.

115. Snow, "Aftermath," op. cit.

116. B. Zanegin, A. Mironov, and Y. Mikhailov, Developments in China (Moscow, 1968), cited by Harry Harding and Melvin Gurtov, "The Purge of Lo Jui Ch'ing," Santa Monica, Cal., RAND Corporation, 1971, p. 49. The authors, however, strongly believe that relations with the Soviets were not an important issue in Lo's purge, and they point out that Soviet media in its rare references directly to the purge victims have, in fact, attacked Lo as well as Liu Shao-chi for being anti-Soviet.

117. Moscow Radio, in Mandarin, December 3, 1971.

118. Ibid., January 16, 1972.

119. Tanjug dispatch from Peking, April 17, 1967.

120. Prague CTK, in English, January 24, 1967.

121. NCNA, February 13, 1965.

122. People's Daily, February 14, 1965.

123. NCNA, February 13, 1965. The fact that Mao's name headed this message obviously weakens our argument. However, the reader is referred to the short discussion of the dynamics of Mao's role at this time on page 44, which may offer some explanation. In addition, as noted, Mao had told Kosygin that Sino-Soviet unity would be reestablished only if the United States attacked one or the other. Mao at this point saw the treaty as useful but not warranting compromise on these issues.

124. Ibid.

125. New York Times, February 12, 1965.

126. Peking Review, "Malinovsky Is a Liar," May 3, 1966. China vigorously denied it had ever delayed such shipments.

127. Zagoria, op. cit., p. 91.

128. Ra'anan, op. cit.

129. Michael Yahuda, "Kremlinology and the Chinese Strategic Debate, 1965-1966," China Quarterly, January-March 1972.

130. Liberation Army Daily, August 1, 1966.

131. Harry Harding and Melvin Gurtov, "The Purge of Lo Jui-ch'ing: The Politics of Chinese Strategic Planning," Santa Monica, Cal., RAND Corporation, 1971, p. vi.

132. Morton Halperin and John Lewis, "New Tension in Army-Party Relations in China, 1965-1966," China Quarterly, May 25, 1966.

133. See the Liberation Army Daily, August 1, 1966, for a discussion of these struggles and an article by Marshal Ho Lung on August 1, 1965, which warned of attacks on the party-committee system in the army.

134. See People's Daily, July 1, 1966, for a review of the series of challenges to Mao's policies.

135. Leonard Schapiro and John W. Lewis, "The Roles of the Monolithic Party Under the Totalitarian Leader," China Quarterly, October-December 1969.

136. Lo Jui-ch'ing, "Commemorate the Victory over German Fascism," Peking Review, no. 20, May 14, 1965, pp. 7-15. An editorial from the People's Daily that also appeared in this issue of PR seemed to lay much greater stress on the battle with revisionism and specifically rejected "united action." For a good analysis of Lo's article, see Donald S. Zagoria, Vietnam Triangle (New York: Pegasus, 1967).

137. Radio Tirana, March 29, 1965.

138. NCNA, March 28, 1965.

139. Red Flag, no. 5, 1965.

140. NCNA, March 29, 1969.

141. Ibid., June 2, 1965.

142. Ibid., August 7, 1965.

143. Kyodo, June 14 report of Arudji Kartawinta, speaker of the Indonesian National Assembly, interview with Mao on June 10.

144. Pentagon Papers, op. cit., pp. 383, 397.

145. Johnson described these alternatives in an article that appeared in the February 1969 issue of Reader's Digest. See also Chapter 7 of the Pentagon Papers, op. cit.

146. People's Daily, June 1, 1965.

157. Ibid., July 13, 1965.

148. NCNA (English), April 18, 1965.

149. For a discussion of Lin's article, see David Monzingo and T. Robinson, "Lin Piao on People's War; China Takes a Second Look at Vietnam," RM8414-PR, Santa Monica, Cal., RAND Corporation, November 1965.

150. One of the last such pledges was on August 7, 1965, when a PRC government statement warned that "we the 650,000,000 Chinese people have repeated pledges to the Vietnamese people our all-out support and assistance up to and including the sending according to their need of our men to fight shoulder to shoulder with them to drive out the U.S. aggressors. We warn the U.S. aggressors once more. We Chinese people mean what we say!" (Peking Review, August 13, 1965).

151. People's Daily, September 3, 1965.

152. For an excellent analysis, see Harding and Gurtov, op. cit.

153. Lin's article was not republished in North Vietnam.

154. Vo Nguyen Giap, "The Party's Military Line Is the Ever Victorious Banner of People's War in Our Country," carried in Nhan Dan, broadcast on Hanoi Domestic Service, December 19, 1969.

155. Ibid.

156. Ibid.

157. This decision was revealed in a captured top-secret resolution of COSVN (Central Office for South Vietnam), the political and military coordinating body between Hanoi and the Viet Cong. See John C. Connell and Melvin Gurtov, "North Vietnam: Left of Moscow, Right of Peking," Santa Monica, Cal., RAND Corporation, February 1968, p. 43. For a public explanation of the North Vietnamese strategy, see Le Duan's speech on Radio Hanoi, July 26, 1966, and Nguyen Chi Thanh's article in the July 1966 issue of Hoc Tap.

158. According to Theodore H. White, President Johnson was reported to have once said, "Every time I stop the bombing of North Vietnam they run those trucks of theirs right up my ---." Theodore H. White, The Making of the President 1968 (New York: Atheneum, 1969), p. 103.

159. Chalmers Johnson, "Third Generation of Guerrilla Warfare," Asian Survey 8, 6 (June 1968): pp. 447.

160. "Refutation of the New Leaders of the CPSU on 'United Action'," People's Daily-Red Flag, November 11, 1965.

161. Asahi, December 18, 1966, quoting a "Japanese police report" on these meetings.

162. Akahata, January 24, 1967 quoted in Asahi Evening News, January 24.

163. Ibid.

164. Ibid.

165. Ibid.

166. Akahata, September 9, 1971.

167. See particularly the long Akahata article of August 8, 1966 entitled "On Consolidation of International Unified Action and United Front Against American Imperialists."

168. This "understanding" reached at Warsaw has been frequently referred to in the press but never confirmed; at best it was very likely vague and indirect. For one version of this meeting, see John Gittings, "A Diplomatic Thaw," Far Eastern Economic Review, December 19, 1969. The Paris Match editor in January 1966 reported that China's conditions were that the United States should not invade China or North Vietnam and would not bomb the dikes. United States Senate, Committee on Foreign Relations, Background Information Relating to Southeast Asia and Vietnam (Washington, D.C: U.S. Government Printing Office, 1968) p. 35

On May 23, unidentified State Department officials reportedly stated that if the PRC intervened in Vietnam with massive forces, the United States would have to take action with everything it had. Ibid., p. 41.

169. Yahuda, "Kremlinology and Chinese Strategic Debate,"
op. cit., points out that both sides knew that the talks were bugged by
the Polish authorities.

170. People's Daily, May 10, 1966. The interview was given on
April 10.

171. Pentagon Papers, op. cit., p. 395.

172. NCNA, May 13, 1966.

173. Institute for Strategic Studies, The Military Balance 1968-69
(London, 1969).

174. Ibid. China reportedly supplied the DRV 4 fast patrol boats,
18 motor gunboats, and 3 P-6 motor torpedo boats. The Soviets provided 3 coastal escorts and 8 P-4 motor torpedo boats.

175. Department of State, Background Notes: People's Republic
of China (Washington, D.C., August 1971).

Estimated Military and Economic Aid to North Vietnam
(millions of dollars)

	1967	1968	1969	1970
PRC	225	200	195	180
USSR	705	530	370	430

176. Far Eastern Economic Review 1969 Year Book (Hong Kong),
p. 224.

177. Giap in Nhan Dan, December 16, 1969.

178. General Van Tien Dung, "Under the Party's Banner,
Vietnam's Military Art Has Constantly Developed and Triumphed,"
Nhan Dan, December 18, 1969.

179. There was reportedly heated disagreement, however, in
Hanoi on the timing of the general offensive. Newsweek, March 10,
1969, reported that U.S. intelligence had pieced together from war
prisoners and other sources the story of the serious split in Hanoi's
"middle-level leadership" over the decision made in late 1967 to
launch the general offensive.

180. On October 19, NCNA made its first direct reference to
the Paris talks, and on November 3 it carried the complete text of
President Johnson's speech announcing the total halt of bombing as
well as the text of the DRV statement.

181. Peking Radio (English), April 4, 1969. Lin Piao in his
political report to the CCP's Ninth National Congress included Vietnam
in the list and repeated China's "firm support for the Vietnamese
people in carrying their war of resistance through to the end." NCNA,
April 27, 1969.

182. NCNA, December 20, 1968. One Chinese official spoke
directly to the point when he described the peace talks as America's

"vain attempt to gain at the conference table what it has failed to get in the battlefield, force the Vietnamese people to abandon their war . . . and to divide the Vietnamese people."

183. Harold Hinton, "Conflict of the USSR: A Clash of Nationalisms," Problems of Communism, January-April 1971. An excellent survey of the border clash and related developments.

184. Nixon told the American Society of Newspaper Editors on April 16, 1954, that if prevention of a communist conquest of Indochina required the dispatch of U.S. forces, the U.S. Government would have to "face up to the situation" (New York Times, April 18, 1954). Nixon also reportedly informed the French Ambassador that he favored the Radford plan (Devillers and Lacouture, op. cit., p. 92). A few days later, Nixon changed emphasis and said that the objective was to seek an "honorable and peaceful settlement" in Geneva (New York Times, April 21, 1954). As noted previously, in 1971, Peking charged that Nixon in 1954 had advocated the use of tactical nuclear weapons to save Dien Bien Phu.

185. "Foreign Policy Report to Congress," Documentation, February 9, 1972, USIS Hong Kong, February 10, 1972.

186. Clark Clifford, "A Vietnam Reappraisal," Foreign Affairs, July 1969.

187. U.S. officials estimated in 1969 that a total of about 1 million North Vietnamese had been inducted into the armed forces since 1965 and that roughly half of them had been killed, wounded, or discharged as sick or disabled (New York Times, May 28, 1969). In 1969, Giap also reportedly confirmed in an interview with an Italian journalist in Hanoi that the communists had suffered half a million dead (International Herald-Tribune, February 13, 1970.).

188. New York Times, December 14, 1969. A high-level Viet Cong document, Resolution no. 9, of COSVN, dated July 1969, took this line.

189. Nhan Dan, December 18, 1969.

190. Ibid., October 6, 1969.

191. See for example NCNA, September 15, 1969.

192. Ibid., September 1, 1969.

193. Ibid., September 4, 1969.

194. Nhan Dan, September 28, 1969.

195. NCNA, September 22, 1969.

196. Snow, "Conversation with Mao," op. cit.

2

THE COLLAPSE OF THE
PEKING-JAKARTA AXIS

The celebration of the Chinese communist regime's 16th anniversary took place in Peking on a bright October 1 in 1965. Prominent among the foreign guests in attendance was Cambodia's Prince Sihanouk, but dominating the visitors' gallery were no less than 17 different delegations of Indonesians including government, military, and communist party representatives. This large contingent of Indonesians was dramatic evidence of the importance of their country to Peking's foreign policy in that critical year. On September 30, the Chinese and their Indonesian visitors had signed seven separate agreements on economic, technical, corporation, and trade matters. These documents only added to the pile of agreements, protocols, and joint communiqués between the two governments that had been produced with increasing frequency over the previous 12 months.

But before the ink was dry on these latest documents and before the guests could settle themselves into their upholstered chairs on the reviewing stand in the Square of Heavenly Peace, dramatic events began that would eventually destroy the foundation of China's evolving partnership with Indonesia.

On the morning of the anniversary celebration, the Chinese informed the visiting Indonesians of the 7:30 a.m. news from Radio Jakarta that a "September 30 movement" headed by a Lieutenant Colonel Untung had acted to forestall an allegedly U.S.-sponsored coup by a "Council of Generals." However, by 9:00 p.m. the Indonesian Army under General Suharto recovered the radio station in Jakarta, announced that the general situation was again under control, and denounced the September 30 movement as counterrevolutionary.

The next morning Harian Rakjat (the official paper of the Indonesian Communist Party, PKI) went on the streets supporting Untung's movement and thus sealed the fate of the PKI. The Chinese Government maintained official silence on these events, but on October 3, its leaders sent a message of "regards and heartfelt wishes" to Sukarno on learning of his "good health."[1] The PRC Embassy in Jakarta also made its sentiments known by being the only diplomatic mission in Jakarta to refuse to fly its flag at half mast in honor of the slain generals. A few days later the Indonesian parlimentary delegation to Peking returned home, but before it departed it signed a communiqué with the PRC reaffirming Indonesia's support for China on all major international issues.[2]

From that point on it was all down hill for the Peking-Jakarta axis. Within two weeks, the PRC protested against a wave of "anti-China and anti-Chinese activities condoned by the government of Indonesia," and in turn, the Chinese were being accused by official Indonesian papers of complicity in the aborted "Gestapu" (the Indonesian abbreviation for the September 30 movement). During the next year and a half, as Sukarno gradually lost effective power within Indonesia, relations between China and the Government of Indonesia were marked by increasing hostility. By the time Sukarno was officially stripped of power in March 1967, Peking was publicly pledging itself to support the PKI in its proclaimed intention of overthrowing the Suharto government. In October of the same year, diplomatic relations between the two countries were finally "suspended." The Peking-Jakarta Axis, like other alliances, had proved sensitive to internal political changes in both countries and subject to overnight collapse.

Its creation had been several years in the making. Perhaps most fundamental to development of the axis was the fact that Jakarta and Peking in the mid-1960s perceived a common interest in driving the United States and the United Kingdom from Southeast Asia by a policy of struggle and confrontation. China's policy was in part the result of the failure of the Bandung line to achieve any substantial new breakthrough, except in Indonesia and Cambodia, in the U.S. policy of quarantining the PRC. U.S. military presence was steadily expanding in Indochina and Thailand while Washington continued to seek détente with Moscow but not Peking. Attempting to turn this situation to its advantage, Peking had launched its challenge to Soviet leadership of the communist and antiimperialist camps on the basis of alleged U.S.-Soviet collusion. Peking proclaimed in 1963 that peaceful coexistence could not be applied to the imperialists or their lackeys. Opposition to U.S. imperialism became the banner under which the Chinese hoped to form an informal alliance of communist and "progressive" states in Asia.

The Chinese objective of asserting political influence in Asia through struggle with the United States was perceived by the leadership in Jakarta not as contradicting but as complementing Indonesia's desire to assert its authority in the Malay world and to influence world politics. Indonesia's community of interest with China at this time rested on Sukarno's belief that the power of the imperialists in Southeast Asia served as both the physical obstacle to and the rallying cause for the achievement of his country's international objectives.

In addition, Sukarno's ideological and psychological proclivities were compatible with those of revolutionary China and with those of the post-1951 leadership of the Indonesian Communist Party, a party that he believed had become "Sukarno-ized." Consequently, Sukarno's assessment of China as the inevitable dominating force in Asia was paralleled by his attitude toward the PKI's role in Indonesia.

THE KEY POSITION OF THE PKI

By the end of 1964 China appeared to be doing well in its challenge to Moscow for the support of the Asian communist parties. Those ruling parties that had an interest in maintaining a hard line against the United States, particularly North Korea and North Vietnam, had sided with the Chinese. The Japanese party and a significant faction of the Indian party had also aligned themselves with China in the international communist movement. Moreover, in Southeast Asia, the insurgent parties of Burma, Thailand, Malaya, Laos, and Vietnam all had a similar stake in the adoption of a hard line by the socialist camp. The leaders of these insurgent parties, hiding out in the jungles of Southeast Asia, saw that a détente with the United States implied rapprochement with their respective "reactionary" governments and consequently the end of their hopes for power. In addition, by the early 1960s China was the only possible source for these parties of external political and, in some cases, financial support.

The key to China's capture of the Asian communist camp, however, was the Indonesian Communist Party. The checkered history of the PKI has been detailed and analyzed by several distinquished Western scholars and there is no need for us to presume to add anything to their accounts.[3] However, a summary of the PKI's history is necessary to our story.

SUKARNO AND THE PKI

The early PKI leaders, like the founders of the Chinese party, were victims of their own dogmatic faith in Moscow. The PKI's original antireligious orientation, for example, while in strict accord with

Marxist theory, served to restrict the party's influence among the general populace as well as among the Moslem-oriented elite group, and the ill-timed Indonesian communist uprising of 1926 (begun against the advice of the Comintern) failed to arouse significant popular support.

The PKI did not reappear on the scene as a serious political contender until after World War II. Its ineffectiveness as a nationalist force after 1926 was demonstrated by its adherence from 1935 to 1939 to the Comintern's united front line, which actually called for a policy of cooperation with the Dutch.[4] After the 1939 Nazi-Soviet pact, the PKI called for a new struggle against the Dutch only to reverse its line again in 1941, when it attempted to rally the people to fight the Japanese.

During the period of revolutionary struggle, 1945 to 1947, the PKI was split and lacked a strong organizational or ideological basis. The strategy during these years was to create a front group of various nationalist organizations whose leaders were secret members of the PKI. After a period of uncertainty, an Indonesian communist group in 1948 attended the Calcutta meeting of Asian communist parties and returned with a hard line against the national bourgeois. The PKI's policy of seizing power by armed struggle and taking over the revolution from the "reactionary" nationalist leaders was, of course, part of the general Asian communist pattern at that time. The struggles against the Dutch and the bourgeois nationalists were to be carried out concurrently—a classic strategy of "united-front-from-below."

On September 14, 1948, an attempt to remove procommunist elements from a division of the republican army stationed in Madiun sparked a communist uprising that was immediately endorsed by the PKI's leadership. Sukarno broadcast an appeal for the populace to choose between himself and the PKI, and by December 7, 1948, the rebellion was ended and the PKI leader Musso was killed. Before the end of 1952, a new line of action for the international communist movement had been declared by Stalin. The new strategy for communist countries and communist parties of peaceful coexistence with the national bourgeois governments was most appropriate to the program that the PKI's new leader, D. N. Aidit, wished to follow in Indonesia. One observer commented prior to the 1965 destruction of the PKI, that the Indonesian communists were lucky to have been so mightily and decisively defeated in the 1948 rebellion, for they did not, like the insurgents in Burma, Malaya, and the Philippines, hang on to a policy of violent opposition long after it was clear that there was no hope of its success.[5] In other words, the party, with no assets for armed struggle, was able to move easily to a classic right strategy and operate as a legal political party. It had, however, also lost its source of independent armed strength.

Aidit, who became the party's secretary general at the age of
31 in January 1951, proclaimed a policy of noninterference in the
affairs of other parties, a national-democratic united front, and full
support for Sukarno. The PKI endorsed Sukarno's "Pantjasila," a
series of five principles: belief in God, nationalism, humanism,
democracy, and social justice. In addition, the party eventually sub-
scribed to Sukarno's concept of Nasakom—nationalism, religion, and
communism—as the three pillars of the nation. With this framework
the PKI under Aidit's leadership entered into a period of remarkable
growth. One Western scholar has described the party's new image
as

> fervently patriotic, sympathetic to religion, peaceful in
> pursuit of its goals, painstakingly solicitous of the small
> problems consciously felt by its potential supporters,
> moderate in demands and self-effacing in the friendliness
> shown toward most other Indonesian political forces.[6]

In the 1955 general election, the party won more than 6 million
votes, more than 15 percent of the total votes cast. In overpopulated
central Java, which contains a large percentage of Indonesia's total
population of 115 million, the PKI built its center of support, and in
the local elections of 1957 received the largest number of votes of
any party, although not yet a majority. By 1965, Aidit claimed 2 million members in the party, compared to the total of 8,000 in 1952.
In addition, the various front organizations claimed a total of 16 million members. These fronts included a communist peasant organization (BTI) of some 8.5 million; a communist trade union organization
(SOBSI) of 3.5 million; the youth organization (the Pemuda Rakjat) of
2 million; and a women's organization (Gerwani) of 2 million.[7]
Whereas Sukarno had often been the enemy of the old PKI, he
looked with favor on this new party, which did not challenge his "concepts and teachings"—teachings he hoped would live a thousand years.[8]
Unlike the old PKI, the new party made it increasingly clear that the
Communist Party of Indonesia was no obedient follower of any foreign
power. In this regard the Sino-Soviet dispute and the PKI's rejection
of the Soviet line seemed to demonstrate the party's independence.
Moreover, the party's extraordinary flexibility on religion and other
internal matters was seen as evidence that the PKI had been Indonesianized and "Sukarno-ized." Sukarno was not won over to the PKI, but
rather he gradually became convinced that the PKI was developing
into the disciplined revolutionary nationalist party of the masses
that he himself had dreamed of leading.

"GUIDED DEMOCRACY" GIVES NEW STRENGTH
TO SUKARNO AND THE PKI

There were two major trends in Indonesia's domestic politics in the period of "guided democracy" (which began officially in 1959). The first was the increasing personal power position of Sukarno, and the second was the marked improvement of the PKI's political position under his sponsorship. After 1962, Sukarno became more explicit in identifying himself with the communists.

One might argue that Sukarno's promotion of the PKI was simply redressing the balance between the army and the communists. But it seems evident that after 1962, the scale was being tipped heavily in the direction of the communists. As Herbert Feith suggested in August 1964, Sukarno's moves to strengthen the PKI were not simply a balancing act but a result of the fact that by 1963 he had become secure enough in his position to be able to fashion policies on the basis of his own ideas and attitudes about the future.[9] In other words, Sukarno's new power position provided him the freedom in which he could express his own ideological and psychological predilections; and it is evident from Sukarno's own testimony that these predilections had all along been revolutionary and Marxist.

Sukarno, for example, proclaimed that he was "inspired, fascinated . . . completely absorbed . . . crazed and obsessed by the romanticism of revolution."[10] As an aroused Marxist and a revolutionary romantic, it was natural that Sukarno would identify with the PKI once he was convinced that it had been domesticated and "Sukarno-ized." Thus it was natural that he would attempt to weaken the conservatively inclined army and strengthen the PKI to whatever degree seemed consistent with avoiding a violent breakup of national unity. It seems that by 1964 Sukarno had decided that Nasakom, the five principles of Pantjasila, and the "socialist stage" of the Indonesian revolution were embodied in and could be realized only through himself and the PKI. In this scheme of things, the army had to be remolded to serve, not as a source of political power, but as an obedient instrument of nationalist policy.

It is safe to assume that Sukarno did not envisage the casting aside of Nasakom and the donning of a purely communist garb. However, he did believe that it was time "to turn the wheel" and to begin the socialist revolution in Indonesia. This called for a continuation of a united-front Nasakom government, but one that was under the effective control of Sukarno and his PKI allies.

It is of course hazardous to speculate about Sukarno's vision of Indonesia's future. But the picture that emerges from his statements of 1964 and 1965 is that of a radical but unique state in which there would be a broad dynamic consensus on the need to carry out Sukarno's will. In this vision the PKI would provide the base of mass support and administrative and political discipline, and the army would serve as the willing tool of the revolution at home and abroad. Sukarno must also have contemplated the possibility that he would not live to see the fulfillment of his revolutionary dreams. His frequently proclaimed desire "to complete the revolution" in Indonesia and his perception of his own immortality in history as the "great leader" of this revolution must have played an important role in his decisions in the 1960s. He certainly did not want the army to succeed him, backed as it was by his political and ideological enemies; but if the PKI succeeded him, he was in danger of being relegated to the status of an Indonesian Sun Yat-sen, while Aidit, or some other PKI leader, would become its Mao Tse-tung. The only solution to this dilemma was an acceleration of the revolution so that Indonesia would enter "the socialist stage" under the leadership of Sukarno.

But the radicalization of internal policies in Indonesia could only be achieved by the parallel pursuit of a confrontation foreign policy. This is not to say that Sukarno's militant foreign policy in the 1960s was constructed simply to serve his internal objectives, but domestic and foreign policy were, as elsewhere, inextricably linked together.

CHINA AND THE PKI

Sukarno's apparent objective of moving into the next stage of the revolution together with the PKI gave him the same interests as the communists in a confrontation policy and in rejection of peaceful coexistence—the same interests in uncompromising pursuit of a militant struggle against imperialism, colonialism, and neo-colonialism (or Nekolim). This, of course, was also compatible with the national and ideological interests of the Chinese communists in the 1970s.

Because the PKI publicly proclaimed an internal evolutionary strategy, unlike the other parties of Southeast Asia, it had nothing to gain by supporting a militant line on domestic matters. Such a public position in fact would have worked to undermine the PKI's insistence that it adhered to Sukarno's Nasakom concept of national unity and would have welded together the anticommunist forces in the country. But the question of armed struggle was only one part of the broader issue of united-front strategy, which in the Maoist view did not necessarily mean violence, but only the preparation for violence.

For the PKI, the critical question was whether it was to continue a basically "right" strategy within the national democratic united front or whether conditions required that it should move to a Maoist-type model. In the early 1960s the PKI's general strategy was to continue to build its strength on national rather than on communist sentiment, to attempt to excite or exploit a climate of imperialist danger in which the party could become the leading champion of the nationalist cause, to increase its agitational work among the peasantry and maintain its own program as distinct from the government, and to attempt to establish an autonomous source of armed power.

The objective of creating a base of independent armed strength was the principle departure from the party's previous policy, and it was to become the focus for the gathering storm in Indonesian politics. It was this objective that created the PKI's community of interest with China as well as the ideological empathy between the two parties. If the PKI was to succeed in establishing its own power base, it could only do so in a climate of national crisis and confrontation and not in a situation of relaxation of international tension. Both the Chinese and the Indonesian communists probably saw the same great potential for the PKI in the "crush-Malaysia" campaign as the Chinese party in the 1930s and 1940s had found in the "resist-Japan" movement in China. Thus, the PKI eventually came to oppose a limited détente between the socialist and "imperialist" camps and instead sought to exacerbate contradictions between Indonesia and the "imperialists."

The promotion of confrontation with the "imperialists" had, since 1951, served the PKI's general strategy of stressing its nationalist leadership, and at the same time it had occupied the attention of the army. But in the case of the Malaysian confrontation, the most important factor would be the justification of the arming of the PKI, an increasingly pressing objective in the eyes of the party.

Despite and perhaps because of its growing popular support, the PKI was increasingly apprehensive that the anticommunist forces, mobilized and supported by the army leadership might eventually attempt a physical suppression of the party. The stronger the PKI became, the more likely the conservative forces were to be provoked into suppression. One solution to this problem was infiltration of the military itself. By 1964 a part of the air force leadership appeared to have been won over; but in the more important ranks of the army only a few officers and a fair number of NCO's could be considered sympathetic. Therefore in early 1964 Aidit reportedly formed a new body within the party, the Bureau for Special Affairs, to intensify penetration of the army. Aidit's intention was to create a clandestine corps of sympathetic "progressive officers" to assist the party in its political struggle with the military.[11]

There were three other direct measures that might have neutralized the power of the army—the establishment of a commissar or political cadre system within the military, the creation of a popular armed force under the control of the PKI, and the removal of the anti-communist generals. While the Bureau for Special Affairs expanded its list of progressive officers, Aidit began to focus on the second course of action as the prerequisite for ultimately attaining the third.

Because of his own experience with the Kuomintang in the 1920s, Mao Tse-tung was aware of the danger to the PKI, and in 1965 he personally urged the PKI "to enhance its fighting capacity."[12] Mao also attempted directly to aid the Indonesian party in this objective.

Aidit, however, needed little encouragement from the Chinese. In 1963, he probably calculated that the crisis with Malaysia would provide the opportunity to achieve a quasimilitary force for the party. The escalation of the war in Vietnam in 1965 further stimulated and justified this course.

As the crisis over Malaysia developed, the PKI position moved closer to that of the Chinese. The PKI had previously accepted the concepts of peaceful transition and peaceful coexistence, and during the early years of the Peking-Moscow dispute the party had striven to maintain a balance position between the two capitals and had repeatedly affirmed that "the conflict was an honorable one, that is, concerning the fastest way to bury capitalism, and could be resolved through friendly discussion."[13]

Aidit's first hint of a more militant internal and external strategy closer to the Maoist interpretation came in February 1963 shortly after the Brunei revolt and the beginning of the confrontation crisis.[14] As the dispute with Malaysia developed during the first half of 1963, Peking and the PKI gave all-out support to Sukarno. But in the July-August summit meeting between the Indonesian, Malaysian, and Philippine leaders, the crisis seemed virtually settled. Aidit was in China during most of September, and his speeches in the first part of the month, when the Malaysian crisis appeared to have been resolved, reflected a relatively moderate analysis of the "protracted and complex" Indonesian revolution, and a neutral position on the Sino-Soviet dispute. Aidit failed, for example, to denounce the nuclear test ban treaty.[15]

But on September 16, when Malaysia was formally proclaimed, Sukarno was enraged at the procedure, which he claimed violated the Manila agreements, and he immediately relaunched his "crush-Malaysia" campaign. Again both the PRC and the USSR publicly supported the Government of Indonesia. But on September 28, Aidit indicated a new partisan line on the Peking-Moscow conflict in favor of the Chinese. He denounced revisionism and stated that the international movement was undergoing a period of "selection, crystallization, and consolidation." For the first time Aidit indicated on which side the PKI stood.[16]

The Soviets were able and probably prepared to provide much more material aid to Indonesia in its new confrontation than were the Chinese. Why then did Aidit choose this moment to move into the Chinese camp and thus dampen Moscow's reluctant enthusiasm for the "crush-Malaysia" policy? The answer lies in the different objectives of Peking and the PKI (and eventually Sukarno), on the one hand, and the USSR, on the other, in the confrontation with Kuala Lumpur. The Soviet Union was motivated principally to protect its investment and influence in Indonesia, and to this end it was prepared to assist Jakarta in gaining independence for the former British Borneo territories or possibly even in bringing the area under Indonesian control. Peking and the PKI, however, were much less interested in the avowed objective of simply breaking up Malaysia than they were in exploiting the issue to intensify the struggle against the imperialists and to excite the national crisis in Indonesia, a crisis that would be conducive to the development of the PKI's political strategy.

In the last half of September, the PKI chairman must have held long discussions with leaders in Peking on the consequences and possibilities of the impending conflict over Malaysia. In his last speech in the Chinese capital that month, Aidit could only hint at the party's new militant policies, for presumably such an important shift had to be discussed and approved by the Politburo.

This approval was apparently obtained, and in December 1963 Aidit openly attacked the Soviet Union and made explicit the party's rejection of peaceful transition and peaceful coexistence.[17]

The Chinese responded to the PKI's position with effusive praise of Aidit and his strategy. In May 1963, the Chinese party's ideological journal Red Flag, hailed the PKI for having adopted the correct political line in its internal political strategy as well as in the international communist movement.[18] The strategy of the PKI was elevated to the status of a model for other parties whose national situation was parallel, presumably referring to countries like Pakistan and Malaysia where organized religion was a major cultural force.[19]

By the spring of 1965, when the PKI was leading the whole nation in a frenzied anti-U.S. campaign, Aidit proclaimed that the position of the Chinese Communist Party in the international movement constituted "a red beacon light, a signal that will become our line and guiding light."[20]

The Chinese apparently looked upon the PKI's acceptance of Sukarno's Nasakom as similar to their own expedient acceptance of Sun Yat-sen's "Three People's Principles" in the 1924-27 as well as the post-1936 united front. In other words, the Chinese clearly appreciated the reality of the PKI's position and the unique political situation in which it operated. Mao was not so foolish as to insist that the PKI take to the hills and begin shooting, nor was such violence necessarily required by his revolutionary model. On the contrary, Mao himself, as late as May 1965, praised the PKI for "creatively applying and developing Marxism-Leninism in the light of revolutionary practice in its own country." He expressed confidence that the party would "continue to consolidate and expand the national democratic united front."[21]

THE PKI's INTERNATIONAL ROLE

Closely related to the national strategy of the PKI and in particular the "crush-Malaysia" campaign was the party's evolving perception of its international role as the leader of the Marxist-Leninist movement in the entire Malay region, including Malaya, Singapore, North Borneo, and the Philippines. Such a role required the assertion of PKI patronage over the largely ethnic Chinese communists of Malaya and Sarawak as well as over the Philippine communists. By 1965 the PKI may have gained Peking's acceptance of its leadership position in the Malay world in return for its agreement to accept China as the center of the communist movement.

After returning from Peking in September 1963 and aligning his party with China, Aidit proclaimed a radical view of revolutionary prospects in Southeast Asia:

But the fact is that at present the most acute anti-imperialist struggle is in Asia, especially in Southeast Asia, where the sound of gun fire has not stopped since the end of World War II. The peoples of South Vietnam, Laos and other places in Southeast Asia have been waging an armed struggle. This is also the case with the Philippines and Malaya where the people's armed struggles are still continuing even though on a small scale.

In Southeast Asia there are already a socialist country and large scale revolutionary movements of the masses. There are also Communist parties which exert a very broad influence on the revolutionary movement, like the Communist parties of Indonesia, Burma and other countries. It may be said that all the Communist parties of Southeast Asia are holding high the banner of Marxism/Leninism. There is no market for revisionism in Southeast Asia.[22]

Indonesia's revolutionary role in Southeast Asia as well as the PKI's adherence to the Peking line were confirmed by the plenum of the PKI, which met from December 23 to 26, 1963. The plenum declared that the party had "tremendous responsibility" in the independence struggles of Southeast Asia, and it called for strengthened cooperation among the peoples and the Marxist-Leninist parties of the area.[23]

The rejection of peaceful coexistence as the general line of the international movement was consistent with the PKI's new attention to its external role, but even more important it was essential to the achievement of the party's internal objectives. It was also at the December 1963 plenum that Aidit clearly indicated that on internal policy the PKI was also discarding the Soviet theory of peaceful transition in favor of a more militant doctrine.

An informal understanding in regard to PKI-Indonesian leadership of the Malay world was probably worked out by the Indonesian and Chinese communist parties sometime in 1963, and it may have been proposed or perhaps only indirectly suggested to Sukarno and Foreign Minister Subandrio at the end of 1964—by which time these Indonesian leaders had come to see their community of interests with China and the PKI.

SUKARNO AND PEKING

After the proclamation of Sukarno's "guided democracy" in July 1959, Indonesia's foreign policy was increasingly characterized by Sukarno's personal dominance and by the extension of his revolutionary concepts to the international plane.[24] "International Nasakom," as described by the president in May 1965, meant largely the same as Mao Tse-tung meant by his broad international united front—a political alliance of diverse states joined together on the basis of all-out opposition to imperialism and neocolonialism. Although Sukarno, since 1956, seemed to have become a real and increasing admirer of Mao Tse-tung and the Chinese revolution (an admiration that coincided with his growing respect for the new PKI), there should be no doubt that he came to his "confrontation policy" largely guided by his own ideological and psychological inclinations—specifically a thirst to assert himself and his nation in the world—and by his perception of Indonesian national interests in the establishment of an Indonesian sphere of influence.

Although Sukarno was a neo-Marxist, his fervent nationalism precluded his support for the communist party until it had become a completely national party at least giving the appearance of complete loyalty to him. Likewise he would not knowingly subordinate Indonesia to a satellite role in any international movement. Nevertheless it seems highly unlikely that Sukarno would have pressed his radically militant policy abroad without the support and encouragement of one of the great powers, and by late 1963 it was clear that he would have to turn to China.

Having implemented "guided democracy" at home, and as a consequence exercising for the first time full authority over foreign affairs, Sukarno was free to carry out a confrontation foreign policy. The roots of Sukarno's switch from nonalignment to confrontation, as well as the launching of his claim for a leadership role in Asia can be traced to his speech on the occasion of the gathering of chiefs of state at the UN in September 1960. In this speech, Sukarno called upon the new nations to join in the crusade against all the bulwarks of power controlled by the capitalist nations of the West.

Sukarno's speech at the Belgrade conference of nonaligned nations in September 1961 clarified the progression of his position. Sukarno's stress at this conference was on the necessity to combat Western imperialism and not on cold war mediation.

At the second conference of the nonaligned held in Cairo in October 1964, Sukarno ridiculed the idea that nonalignment still had a role to play and instead focused on imperialism as the threat to peace.[25] The ultimate expression of this sentiment was Indonesia's withdrawal from the United Nations in January 1965, and its planning for a new Conference of the Emerging Forces (CONEFO) scheduled to take place in August 1966. For both of these moves, Sukarno received Chinese support.

THE CRUSH-MALAYSIA CAMPAIGN

In order to achieve the goals of taking West Irian from the Netherlands, Indonesia in 1961 and 1962 had acquired large-scale Soviet military aid as well as U.S. diplomatic support. Both of these were achieved by means of a bold and striking diplomacy in which Indonesia shrewdly exploited cold war considerations as well as the fear existing in both Moscow and Washington of growing Chinese influence in Indonesia.[26]

After the victorious settlement of the West Irian issue in August 1962, Sukarno seems to have vacillated between pursuing a policy of domestic economic development and a bold foreign policy. His decision in September 1963 to crush Malaysia marked the beginning of a new militant stage in Indonesia's confrontation policy and in Indonesia's close relationship with China.

Just prior to this dramatic development, a climactic meeting had been held in Manila between Sukarno, Tunku Abdul Rahman of Malaya, and President Diosdado Macapagal of the Philippines, from July 31 to August 5. This conference ratified a formula under which it appeared Indonesia and the Philippines (which had laid claim to parts of North Borneo) could accept the formation of Malaysia. The three nations agreed to group themselves under a loose organization to be called Maphilindo, and Sukarno won recognition from the Tunku and Macapagal that Western bases in their countries were "temporary."

The significance of the Manila agreements seemed to be portentous. Sukarno's acceptance of these agreements also appeared "to indicate his preference for a peaceful extension of his influence into Southeast Asia within a Maphilindo framework rather than aggressive pursuit of influence by means of confrontation."[27] To some observers the entire performance, from the Brunei revolt to the Manila conference, seemed like another stunning victory for Indonesia's crisis diplomacy. By an adroit mixture of brinksmanship and reasonableness, Sukarno seemed to have prepared the way for the gradual achievement of his major goal—the withdrawal of Western power from Southeast Asia and the assertion of Indonesia's leading role in the Malay world.

Sukarno at this time was also choosing between an American-backed program of economic stabilization and the communist-supported policy of opposing Malaysia. The PKI during the spring of 1963 had led the opposition, both to the U.S. economic program and to Malaysia.[28] The PKI at first also opposed publicly the Maphilindo idea. Aidit proclaimed that the policies of the three countries were in conflict. But before the completion of the Manila conference, Aidit radically altered his stand, and the PKI warmly endorsed the concept.[29]

Peking's silence on the Maphilindo project is surprising, especially considering the interpretation of the pact in Western, Filipino, and Malay newspapers as being principally directed at containing China and Chinese influence.

This development also came at the time of the major crisis and perhaps the decisive turning point in the Sino-Soviet dispute—the nuclear test ban treaty, which had been agreed to in July. Unprecedentedly bitter public exchanges between Moscow and Peking ensued, and finally in September China decisively launched itself onto a separate road with its reply to the open letter of the CPSU Central Committee of July 14, 1963.

The peaceful settlement of the Malaysia issue and the prospect of a more restrained Indonesian foreign policy thus came at a particularly bad moment for the Peking leadership. There was no public Chinese comment on the Manila meeting or on its agreements. Likewise in Chinese messages and speeches marking Indonesia's independence day on August 17, 1963, there was no mention of the "crush-

Malaysia" campaign. Peking however, like the PKI, seemed either prepared to let Sukarno call the shots or else was confident that the moderation of Sukarno's confrontation policy was only a temporary ploy.*

There is no evidence that would indicate precisely why Sukarno chose to react as he did to the announcement of Malaysia on September 16, 1963.[30] Most likely it was an impulsive reaction to the superficial UN survey held in Sarawak and Sabah (August 27-September 5) and to the (to Sukarno) provocative manner in which Jakarta's protests were overridden and Malaysia was hurriedly proclaimed. Until other evidence is available, we will have to accept the view that Sukarno's response was largely impulsive although taken in the context of PKI and Chinese encouragement.

Nevertheless the circumstances cited above suggest the possibility that the Maphilindo agreement may have been another example of clever agitational diplomacy by Sukarno and Subandrio. It is not unreasonable to conjecture that Sukarno may have agreed to the Manila talks and to Maphilindo (which anyway was Macapagal's inspiration) as an attempt to win the sympathy and support of the Philippines or at least to keep them neutral while intending all along to wreck the agreements with Malaya and informing the Chinese of his intentions.[31] During 1963 Indonesia paid considerable attention to forging close ties with the Philippines, and these efforts continued after the renewal of the campaign against Malaysia. In January 1964, for example, Sukarno paid his fourth visit to Manila within a year. Indonesia also held out the prospect that its former trade with Singapore could be diverted to the Philippines.[32]

---

*A denunciation of Liu Shao-chi in 1967 revealed what was probably Peking's, or at least Mao Tse-tung's, real assessment of Maphilindo:

"In the course of his [Liu's] visit [to Indonesia in April 1963], the Khrushchev of China played the shameful broker for U.S. imperialism. At that time U.S. imperialism was scheming to organize a so-called Federation of Malaya, Philippines, and Indonesia. This was an intrigue to suppress revolution in this region, to strengthen U.S. imperialism's encirclement of China in Asia and to undermine the national independence of Indonesia. This scheme was resolutely opposed by the Indonesian people and the peoples of other countries in the region." (Peking Domestic Radio, July 13, 1967, article by a member of the Revolutionary Rebel Liaison Center of the Ministry of Foreign Affairs on the reactionary film, A Visit to Indonesia.) Actually Liu had heaped praise upon Indonesia for its "just stand of opposing the neocolonialist scheme of Malaysia and supporting the just struggle of the people of North Kalimantan."

Whether impulsive or well-calculated, Sukarno's decision in September 1963 represented a windfall opportunity for the national as well as the international strategy of the Indonesian Communist Party, and this fact was immediately reflected in Indonesian politics. In September, a distinct new swing to the left began, which was to continue with increasing velocity for the next two years. The removal of strong anticommunist regional functionaries was resumed after September, and in a government reorganization General Adul Haris Nasution, Defense minister, was not included in a newly formed three-man presidium of deputy prime ministers. Paradoxically, it was the formation of Malaysia—on the basis of mostly false assumptions (see Chapter 5)—that created the proper context and the necessary pretext for the choice of both Sukarno and the PKI for a militant revolutionary policy and a close relationship with China. Whereas the PKI's decision came in the last quarter of 1963, Sukarno apparently did not fully commit himself until one year later.

In the 12 months following the formation of Malaysia, the campaign against the federation was paralleled by various unsuccessful efforts at mediation and negotiation.

But in August 1964, Sukarno significantly escalated the conflict in both political and military terms by extending guerrilla attacks from the Borneo territories to the Malay peninsula.

During this 12-month period (September 1963 to August 1964), one of China's most important moves to strengthen its relationship with Jakarta was its decision in March 1964 to cease operations of the Bank of China in Indonesia. This institution had served as the principal channel through which financial assistance was rendered indirectly to the Indonesian Communist Party (overseas Chinese loan recipients were expected to donate to the party), and its voluntary liquidation was an important gesture of China's identity of interest with the Sukarno government[33] and also of the PKI's independence of Chinese influence.

Indonesia dramatized its own strong pro-Peking line at the second conference of the nonaligned nations in Cairo in October 1964.[34] Having previously recognized the North Korean Government, Jakarta in August exchanged diplomatic relations with Hanoi and in November recognized the National Liberation Front of South Vietnam.

After the escalation of confrontation in August 1964, there ensued a flurry of high-level visits between China and Indonesia, which continued for the next year. But Peking was probably disturbed when in October 1964 Sukarno visited Moscow and conferred with Khrushchev, who promised support and assistance to Indonesia's struggle. In return, Sukarno supported the test ban treaty and implied support for Soviet participation in the Afro-Asian Conference.[35] After the Cairo nonaligned conference, Sukarno flew to Shanghai, and there he held an important meeting with Chou En-lai.[36]

The Chinese had apparently decided to raise substantially their commitments to Indonesia in the economic, political, military, and perhaps even nuclear fields. Precisely what reciprocal commitments the Indonesians made is not known; but concurrent events suggest that Sukarno's decision to withdraw from the UN, his banning of anticommunist organizations, and the beginning of the campaign to arm the PKI were related to the dramatic escalation of the Chinese commitment. It is important to remember that Sukarno's stop in China was made while he was in a state of euphoria over what he believed was his domination of the Cairo conference and immediately after China's first atomic explosion and the fall of Khrushchev. The Chinese may have picked this time to unveil for Sukarno the design of a Peking-Jakarta axis—the vehicle for a new order in Asia.

A few weeks after Sukarno returned to Jakarta, Foreign Minister Chen Yi paid another flying visit to Indonesia (November 27-December 3) and agreed in principle to a (U.S.) $50 million economic aid agreement, which was formally concluded in January. One press report claimed that spheres of influence were decided upon at the meeting.[37] A joint press statement of December 3 revealed that the two sides had discussed "ways of raising the level of struggle."[38] One report, quoting diplomatic sources in Washington, stated that Chen advised Sukarno to shift from guerrilla raids to a new strategy of massing conventional forces on the frontier in Borneo to strain Malaysian and British resources and to encourage insurrection in Sarawak and Sabah.[39] Subsequently, Indonesian forces in the Sarawak border area reportedly increased from about 2,000 men to 15,000-20,000.[40]

On January 23, Foreign Minister Subandrio and an Indonesian Government and military delegation arrived in Peking for what was hailed as a visit of "great significance."[41] Subandrio explained that the two sides talked about the problem of "carrying out a policy of mutual assistance to clear imperialism, headed by the U.S. and Britain, out of Southeast Asia."[42]

In the joint statement issued on January 28, 1965, the two parties stressed that "no peaceful coexistence is possible between the new emerging forces and the old established forces or between the imperialist forces and the antiimperialist forces."[43] The Government of Indonesia reaffirmed its "persistence in the struggle against Malaysia," and while the PRC did not specifically offer to join in the fight, it declared that should the United States or Great Britain attack Indonesia, "the Chinese people will absolutely not sit idly by."[44]

What had previously been a community of interest between China and Indonesia based upon diplomatic expediencies and sympathetic ideological orientations now became a working, informal alliance founded upon compatible strategic interests. The previous collaboration between Peking and Jakarta, based largely on tacit understandings had probably developed, by January 1965, into a close coordination of tactics and strategies. Government-to-government coordination now paralleled that which had existed for some time at the party level.

PART OF A "PEOPLE'S OFFENSIVE"
IN SOUTHEAST ASIA

The Chinese, by this time, had committed themselves in direct and concrete ways to the struggle against Malaysia. January 1965, however, was a critical juncture in the communist struggle in South Vietnam, and very likely the Chinese and the Indonesians agreed to coordinate the struggle against Malaysia with developments in the revolutionary wars in the other parts of Southeast Asia, specifically Vietnam, Laos, and Thailand. "The anti-imperialist revolutionary movements of all peoples form an integral whole," the joint communiqué of January 28 said, and "they should support and coordinate with each other."[45]

In this strategy Indonesia and the China-oriented Sarawak communists would keep the pressure on in Eastern Malaysia. At the same time the Indonesians would step up infiltration of the Malayan peninsula and, in cooperation with the Malayan Communist Party (MCP), attempt to give the revolution a new Malay-oriented direction. The Indonesian and PKI leaders apparently believed that as Malays themselves they could succeed where the Chinese-led MCP had failed.

The PKI established influence with the remnant band of MCP guerillas in the heavily Moslem southern provinces of Thailand. This influence was suggested when the MCP set up such political organizations as the People's Party of Thailand and the Southern Thai National Party.[46] These parties followed the PKI Nasakom approach by pledging support to the Moslem religion and to the Malay irredentist sentiment among the inhabitants. A new Malay-oriented front for the MCP, the Malayan National Liberation League, was created in the spring of 1964, and in January 1965 an aborted attempt was made to promote the formation of a national front by pro-Indonesia Malayans and to incite a rebellion among the Malays in coordination with infiltrators from Indonesia and the MCP.*

---

*Leaders of the pro-Indonesian and extremist Pan Malay Islamic Party (PMIP) and of the leftist Socialist Front were arrested in Malaya in January 1965. Some of those arrested allegedly confessed to receiving several hundred thousand dollars in support from the Indonesian Government. A new national front was reportedly established by this

The "crush-Malaysia" campaign was considered by both Peking and Jakarta as an integral part of the wider confrontation in Southeast Asia and as a major instrument for the restructuring of the Asian political order. Peking at this time saw its relations with Indonesia in terms of its ideological and political challenge to the Soviets and its power struggle with its number-one enemy and national threat, the United States. The alliance with Jakarta was the key to break the U.S. encirclement and containment of China in Southeast Asia. Sukarno hoped that out of his own confrontation policy would come a Jakarta-dominated Malay world allied to China.[47]

A RIVAL TO THE UNITED NATIONS

Sukarno's decision in January 1965 to pull out of the United Nations appealed to Mao as a "bold revolutionary move." The United Nations after all was hardly a revolutionary organization; on the contrary it was dedicated to promoting the general détente that Peking at that time opposed (as we have suggested, largely because the United States refused to extend its own détente policy to China). China's attitude toward the United Nations had in fact all along been an ambivalent one. On the one hand, it was strongly motivated to claim its position in the United Nations and most particularly in the Security Council as one of the major world powers. On the other hand, exclusion of the People's Republic of China was proof to the Chinese that the United Nations was under the dominance of the U.S. "imperialists," who, together with the Soviet revisionists, exploited the organization to serve their own interest.

Consequently, the proposal for a rival organization was appealing. It was no doubt compatible with Mao's own increasingly combative and activist view of the world struggle, and it also reflected increased frustration and anger at China's failure to gain admittance to the established organization. The proposal also had utility as a pressure tactic.

As suggested earlier, Indonesia's plan to walk out of the United Nations may have been promoted by China as early as November 1964. When Indonesia did withdraw from the United Nations in early January,* the People's Daily and the Chinese Foreign Ministry hailed

_____

group in January with the objective of launching armed struggle to overthrow the Alliance government-in-exile. See Government White Paper in Straits Times, March 1, 1965 and Chapter 6.

*Indonesia withdrew over the seating of Malaysia in the Security Council.

it as "revolutionary action" and as a major contribution to the anti-imperialist cause.[48] About the same time, Mao told Edgar Snow that it was now practical to consider forming a union of nations excluding the United States. Mao mentioned the Afro-Asian Conference as a possibility for the nucleus of such an organization.[49] During Subandrio's visit to China in the latter part of January, Chou En-lai hinted at a new world organization when he warned that "another United Nations, a revolutionary one, may well be set up so that rival dramas may be staged in competition,"[50] and on January 30, People's Daily officially endorsed this idea of a revolutionary rival to the UN.

During the Subandrio visit, China apparently agreed to help Sukarno in the financing of his Conference of the New Emerging Forces (CONEFO), which was slated to be held in August 1966 and which Sukarno hoped would turn out to be the rival organization Chou had proposed. The ground-breaking ceremony for the enormous building complex for CONEFO, patterned on the UN headquarters in New York (including a 2,500 seat Assembly Hall), took place in April, at which time Sukarno announced that Chinese engineers and materials were being used on the project.[51] In April, Chou and Chen Yi were both in Jakarta to attend the 10th anniversary celebrations of the first Bandung meeting. Dr. Ali Sastroamidjojo (minister and vice chairman of the People's Congress) quoted Chou as having said that "China will no longer insist on being seated as a member of the United Nations now that Indonesia has withdrawn . . . instead we are considering the creation of a new world body which is progressive and revolutionary in nature."[52] This statement was hailed by the Indonesian Herald as proof of the imminent collapse of the "decadent" world organization.[53] The Mid-East News Agency also quoted Chou as proposing a new revolutionary UN "to help and strengthen the voice of the Afro-Asian people."[54] The Peking press, however, apparently carried no mention of Chou's remarks and in fact did not broach the notion of a rival UN for the rest of that year.

In his August 17 National Day speech, Sukarno did not specifically state that CONEFO could replace or compete with the United Nations, but the vision he outlined was quite clear. Sukarno explained again his concept of "international Nasakom" as a combination of the nationalist states with the religious and the communist countries joined together on a world scale "to batter the neo-Colonialists and imperialists and to build the world anew. . . ." The significance of CONEFO, Sukarno claimed, was that it would bind together all of the international revolutionary forces.[55] In early September, Subandrio said that Indonesia was not planning to set up a rival United Nations, but that if many UN members became dissatisfied and wanted to do so, then "it would be another question."[56] And in the middle of September, Chinese aid to the CONEFO building project was stepped up.[57]

We have no way of knowing how seriously China took Sukarno's CONEFO as a possible revolutionary rival to the United Nations and thus as an institutional framework for Mao's anti-U.S. international united front. The evidence of public statements, however, suggests that after its initial enthusiastic response to Indonesia's "revolutionary action" of January 1965, China took a prudent position on the question of a rival United Nations and never displayed much enthusiasm for the CONEFO project.

China's diplomatic campaigning in the months prior to the aborted second Afro-Asian conference may have confirmed what the PRC already suspected, that at the time there was little hope of enticing any major nonaligned or neutral Afro-Asian nation or perhaps any nation at all into leaving the United Nations. It was obviously not the time for China, or Indonesia for that matter, to commit itself to such a task, desirable as its achievement might be. Instead, China's policy was to maintain its maneuverability and to go along with CONEFO and see what developed; in the meantime, it would exploit all possible opportunities to polarize the Afro-Asian world. One such opportunity was presented at the second Afro-Asian conference, which was scheduled to be held in June in Algiers.

BANDUNG TWO FADES AWAY

During the first half of 1965, Indonesia and China concentrated their diplomacy in the Third World on the second Afro-Asian conference, sometimes known as Bandung Two. The decision to hold the conference at all was itself largely the result of the persistence of Indonesia and China, both of whom hoped to isolate their respective enemies and to promote their "two-camp" world view. The escalation of the Vietnam war in February 1965 had increased the hopes and the determination of both China and Indonesia that together they could dominate the conference and turn it into an antiimperialist and anti-U.S. forum.

China was infuriated, however, with the Soviet decision to participate presumably in order to prevent Chinese dominance of the meeting. Peking thus began a vigorous campaign to exclude the Soviets, while at the same time Indonesia maneuvered to exclude Malaysia.* Both China and Indonesia, however, seemed to be in a minority position in regard to their demands to keep out their respective enemies. The question thus arises as to why they were the only powers except

---

*Indonesia never publicly opposed Soviet participation.

Algeria that were so insistent on continuing with the conference after the overthrow of Ahmed Ben Bella's government and why, by the following September, China changed its mind.

The majority of the countries attending the conference seemed positively relieved that the June 19 coup of Haouri Boumédienne in Algeria had provided an excuse for not having the meeting. China, however, which had considered the Ben Bella government one of the most promising revolutionary governments in Africa, recognized the new Algerian regime in less than 24 hours and—within 48 hours of the coup—began lobbying for a decision to proceed with the meeting as scheduled. Indonesia also extended recognition to the new government, and Aidit went so far as to claim that the Boumédienne coup had "rescued the Algerian revolution from Ben Bella's deviations."[58] According to the London Times, only China, Indonesia, North Korea, North Vietnam, and Algeria were actually supporting the holding of the conference at that time.[59] The conference was finally postponed until November; but by the end of September, China had reversed its position.

On September 8, Chou declared that Soviet nonparticipation was a matter of principle concerning which China would "carry the struggle to the end."[60] In his press conference of September 29, 1965, Foreign Minister Chen Yi stated that "the foremost task of the Afro-Asian Conference is to denounce U.S. imperialism; otherwise there will be no sense in convening the conference." Chen also emphasized the importance of keeping out the Soviets and said that the conference should not be held until "the conditions are ripe"—that is, until a majority agreed that the conference should be principally an anti-U.S. forum and that the Soviets should be excluded.

Chen's statement came after his September travels to Pakistan, Syria, Algeria, Mali, Guinea, and Afghanistan, where he had tested official sentiment on these two questions. In none of the capitals visited, however, was a communiqué issued, a fact demonstrating China's militant and often high-handed insistence on its own view.

China well understood that its prestige was not what it had been at the beginning of the year. One important factor was Peking's adamant refusal of "united action" with the Soviets in Vietnam. Concurrently the Soviets had improved their own revolutionary image. China's (and to a lesser extent, Indonesia's) strong backing for Pakistan in September during the Indo-Pakistani war also seemed, to many neutral governments, an inflammatory act. China's ultimatum to India on September 19 failed to achieve the desired results and drew a bad press in most Afro-Asian nations.[61]

Indonesia was in full accord with Peking on the Indo-Pakistani war and, like China, contributed not only strong diplomatic support but also military assistance to Pakistan. If the Pakistani effort, backed up by China's threat, had even partially succeeded, Peking might well have pushed for the holding of the second Afro-Asian conference in November, at which time it might have expected to dance on the grave of the Indian union. However, not only did Pakistan fail in its objectives, but Soviet prestige was greatly increased as a consequence of the crisis—this time in the role of peace-maker. Faced with these setbacks vis-à-vis the Soviets, Peking must have decided against a new polarization move in the Third World for a while. Indonesia, however, apparently felt that a failure to hold Bandung Two would prejudice the successful convening of a CONEFO meeting in August 1966. In September Indonesia indicated continued support for the conference,[62] and after the September 30 coup failure, Sukarno publicly supported the Algerian policy in favor of the meeting.[63]

THE NUCLEAR GIFT PUZZLE

One of the most extraordinary aspects of Sino-Indonesian diplomacy from 1964 to Gestapu involved the possibility of Chinese assistance for an Indonesian nuclear test program. During the first three quarters of 1965, Indonesian officials continually claimed that Indonesia was on the verge of producing its own atomic bomb. If the facts behind these claims were known, they would probably throw some light on the internal events that culminated in the September 30 movement and provide some insight into China's real position at that time on the question of nuclear proliferation.

Indonesia signed the nuclear test ban treaty in the summer of 1963. This was the period in which Indonesia's foreign policy still seemed unsure. It was the interregnum between Indonesia's successful completion of its campaign for West Irian and the beginning of the extremely violent stage of the "crush-Malaysia" campaign. But by the time of the first Chinese nuclear explosion on October 16, 1964, Sukarno's confrontation policy was entering its final and most militant stage and the Peking-Jakarta friendship was rapidly developing. On October 18, NCNA quoted a number of second-rank political figures in Indonesia as praising the Chinese explosion. Both Subandrio and Sukarno were then out of the country, but when Subandrio returned a few days later he seemed somewhat uncertain of the line he should take. After all, earlier in the month, Sukarno had reaffirmed Indonesia's support of the test ban treaty in his joint communiqué with Khrushchev. So Subandrio told newsmen that the Chinese explosion might expedite disarmament, but "in general, Indonesia is inclined to prevent such blasts, especially when the explosions are conducted near Indonesian territory."[64] After Sukarno returned on November

5 in a euphoric state over his chat with Chou En-lai, no more critical remarks were made concerning the Chinese test. In fact, the Indonesians almost immediately began to boast of their own nuclear weapons development.

In November, Brigadier General Hartono, director of the Indonesian Army Arsenal, bemused the world when he announced that Indonesia planned to explode a nuclear bomb in 1965.[65] Shortly after this claim, at the end of November, Chen Yi made his visit to Jakarta, and, according to at least one report, he pledged that China would train Indonesian technicians at its nuclear plants.[66] If true, this arrangement presumably was in keeping with some commitment made to Sukarno in China earlier the same month.

Early in 1965, Hartono announced that 200 Indonesian scientists were working to make the country's first A-bomb, and he coyly promised a "surprise" at Indonesian Armed Forces Day on October 5, 1965.[67] This statement, coming from a responsible official source, seemed fantastic in view of the scientific and industrial capability of Indonesia,* which could not even make its own cars or trucks, much less a nuclear device. Diplomatic speculation was that China, in order to cement its axis with Indonesia, might conduct a nuclear test somewhere in the Indonesian islands and allow Indonesia to take the credit for it. Generally, however, this hypothesis was dismissed as incredible.

Closer military and scientific cooperation between China and Indonesia, as noted earlier, did begin about this time, but it is unknown whether the public exchanges and agreements that followed had anything to do with nuclear weapons or tests. The January 1965 Subandrio-Chen Yi communiqué included the pledge that both sides would strengthen "friendly contacts in the military field."[68] (Hartono's statement about the 200 scientists followed this communiqué.) In February a Chinese scientific and technical delegation visited Indonesia and signed a scientific agreement calling for the exchange of scientists, scientific data, and specimens.[69]

---

*Indonesia possessed a 250-kilowatt research reactor purchased from the General Atomics Division of General Dynamics Corporation under the U.S. Atoms for Peace Program. In addition a 2,000-kilowatt reactor was being provided by the USSR. These were small subcritical assemblies suited only for training and research purposes (Business Week, February 6, 1965). In October 1964 the U.S. State Department denied Senator Barry Goldwater's charge that the United States had provided materials with which Indonesia could make atomic weapons. U.S. officials said the reactor was too small (New York Times, October 23, 1964).

During the summer months of 1965, there were many more public claims made by high Indonesian officials, including Sukarno, about the imminence of an Indonesian atomic bomb. On July 24, Sukarno, addressing a religious conference in Jakarta, said that Indonesia "will shortly succeed in producing its own atom bomb," but he promised it would be used only for defense.[70] Within a few days Sukarno followed this statement with a message to the Tokyo International Conference Against Atom and Hydrogen Bombs, in which he took the Chinese line that a distinction must be made between nuclear weapons in the hands of the New Emerging Forces (NEFOS) and those in the hands of the Old Established Forces (OLDEFOS).[71] Within a few days, Hartono was quoted as saying that the first nuclear test would be held in November.[72]

During August there was a further escalation of Indonesian boasting of its nuclear weapons development. The vice chairman of the National People's Congress, Li Hsueh-feng, flew to Jakarta to attend Indonesia's 20th anniversary celebrations and on August 7 gave a speech to the Indonesian Parliament in which he stressed the need to arm the people. If the time and place of Li's remarks seemed significant, so too did those of Minister Coordinator and Speaker of the House of Representatives Arudji Kartawinata on the occasion of a dinner in honor of the visiting Chinese official. Kartawinata proudly announced in Li's presence that Indonesia "before long will explode its first atomic bomb," but perhaps more to the point he proclaimed that China's atomic bomb not only benefited the Chinese people but was also "owned by the other people of Asia and Africa."[73]

Shortly afterwards, it was announced that Chen Yi would head another Chinese delegation to attend the celebration, and the Chinese foreign minister arrived in Jakarta in the middle of August. In his August 17 National Day speech, Sukarno warned that Indonesia would "defend freedom to the death, if necessary with atom bombs."[74] During the next few days, Chen Yi conferred with Sukarno, Aidit, and Subandrio in a series of meetings that lasted more than nine hours. One U.S. reporter quoted "well-informed sources" to the effect that the Indonesian leaders at this time had pressed Chen for facilities and resources to explode a nuclear device.[75] Chen returned to Peking on August 23. The next day Sukarno seemed more confident than ever when he told a group of Japanese visitors that "Indonesia's preparations to explode its first A-bomb were progressing smoothly."[76] Subandrio followed up this comment with a statement that in effect renounced Indonesia's adherence to the nuclear test ban treaty. On August 25, 1965, he acknowledged that Indonesia had signed the test ban treaty two years before, but, he said, "the world situation has developed rapidly, bringing changes in our thoughts regarding the world." Indonesia, he said, could not keep on tolerating other countries using nuclear weapons to blackmail and threaten the nuclear have-nots. That, he explained, was why Indonesia "was striving to produce an atomic bomb."[77]

Apparently nothing further was said on this matter until September 29 (one day before the coup attempt in Jakarta), when Chen Yi, in answer to a question in the course of his press conference, appeared to dismiss the possibility of China's providing nuclear weapons assistance to other countries. China was ready, he said, to render assistance on the peaceful use of atomic energy, but "as for the request for China's help in the manufacture of atom bombs, this question is not realistic. China hopes that Afro-Asian countries will be able to make atom bombs themselves, the more the better."[78]

This strange chain of events leaves us with the possibility that Sukarno was not simply bluffing to intimidate the Malaysians and the "imperialists." The evidence for our conclusions is mostly circumstantial, mixed with some unconfirmed third-hand reports of discussions between the Chinese and the Indonesian leaders (for example, as reported in the New York Times from "diplomatic sources"). However, we can conclude that Sukarno, incredible as it may seem, was probably pressuring the Chinese to conduct a nuclear test in Indonesia's name, presumably in Indonesian territory. Sukarno's objective was certainly to enhance his and Indonesia's prestige among the NEFOS and perhaps to deter the OLDEFOS from any rash decision to use nuclear weapons on Indonesia. There was occasional talk in Kuala Lumpur at this time of "retaliation" for the Indonesian attacks on the Malay peninsula.[79] The OLDEFOS of course would know that Indonesia could not make atom bombs itself, but if one were exploded in Indonesia, they could never be sure that another weapon did not exist that might be employed against them.

While these foreign policy objectives were important, perhaps the most pressing reason for Sukarno's efforts to achieve a nuclear "capability" by proxy were internal. Sukarno may have held out the prospect of a Chinese-provided nuclear explosion and the consequent enhancement of army and air force prestige as a device to dislodge the generals from their strong opposition both to the PKI Fifth Force and to the alliance with China. In July the generals were adamant on the question of the Fifth Force, but training of the PKI youth groups was already under way. In August, as we will see, the decision was made to accept Chinese weapons to arm popular units of the PKI. Sukarno may have hoped that the explosion of an "Indonesian" nuclear weapon would be the crowning glory of the army's prestige, as well as adding to his own reputation as a leader who could achieve miracles. It would thus make more palatable the alliance with China. Such a tour de force could help Sukarno during the most dangerous transitional period in the Indonesian revolution.

We still do not know if China would actually have agreed to such an unprecedented step. Chen Yi's answer in his September 29 press conference does not rule out the possibility; in any circumstance his answer presumably would have been the same. No doubt it was a difficult decision for the Chinese. Sukarno was publicly challenging China with its own statement that the more nuclear armed nations among the NEFOS, the greater the chance for world peace. One can imagine the arguments Sukarno, and probably Aidit, were pressing upon their uneasy Chinese allies. Peking as early as November 1964 seems to have tried to put Sukarno off by offering to train Indonesian nuclear scientists, but by the summer of 1965, Jakarta (as the statements of Sukarno and Subandrio suggest) was apparently putting the pressure on for the whole show.

The Chinese leadership was probably divided on this question itself. There is no indication of the position of Lin Piao's military clique, but the radical elements, who, together with Lin, were to dominate the party's foreign and internal policies within a year, may have supported the Indonesian request. Others, including Chou En-lai and Liu Shao-chi, probably argued that such a move not only might boomerang and make both Indonesia and China look ridiculous, but also that it entailed serious risk. Such an act would reflect on China's responsibility as a nuclear power, and thus it could provide a pretext for an "imperialist" preemptive attack on China's nuclear facilities. Political problems, it was probably argued, would in any event be tremendous—Pakistan, the UAR, and other friendly countries might demand similar demonstrations in their own countries. It is reasonable to suspect, therefore, that the moderates overrode the radicals and that by September 30 Peking had already replied to Jakarta's request with a polite but definite "no."*

INTO THE LAST ACT

From the escalation of confrontation in August 1964 until the final dénouement on September 30, 1965, Indonesian domestic politics

---

*Another possible explanation is that the PRC and Sukarno were collaborating in creating the illusion that such a development was a real prospect in order to strengthen Sukarno's hand during the critical period of arming the PKI. Uri Ra'anan suggests that the PRC actually intended to bill its next test as a joint Sino-Indonesian endeavor ("The Coup That Failed," Problems of Communism April/May 1966, pp. 37-43). Chen Yi, however, appeared categorically to deny this possibility in his September 29, 1965 statement.

was dominated by Sukarno's increasing identification with the PKI, the dramatic deterioration of the political position of the noncommunist elements, and the launching of an extraordinarily intense anti-American campaign. In his August 17, 1964 Independence Day address, Sukarno described the stages of the Indonesian revolution: How before 1959 it had been a revolution adrift, but since that time it had again become "a revolution of romanticism, dynamism and dialectics." Sukarno also implied, in a theme that was to become recurrent, that the next stage of the Indonesian revolution was due. In December, Sukarno banned the newly established anti-PKI group that had called itself the "Body for the Support of Sukarnoism."[80] In January he outlawed the influential Murba Party and closed down all anticommunist publications, proclaiming that the country could no longer afford freedom of the press.* A cabinet reshuffle at the end of March demoted the anti-communist ministers Chairul Saleh and Adam Malik, while further strengthening Subandrio.[81]

Sukarno's speech in August 1964 signaled the start of an anti-American campaign that swept into a frenzy in 1965. After Chen's visit in November, Sukarno strongly denounced U.S. policy in the Congo and, for the first time, proclaimed the slogan "crush America." In December, the campaign flared up with the burning of the USIS Center. The government closed all USIS libraries in February, and a mob attacked the U.S. Consulate in Medan, the fifth such attack on American property in six months.[82] In March, Sukarno's agitational diplomacy began to take extreme forms; demonstrators actually invaded the home of U.S. Ambassador Howard P. Jones, and communist labor unions cut off utilities and mail to the U.S. Embassy apartment building. (After U.S. protests to Subandrio, services were eventually restored.) The PKI was attempting to force the United States to break or suspend relations in order to intensify the air of hostility and to provide more credibility to the picture of Indonesia threatened by the imperialists. Evidence indicates that Sukarno was himself directing the campaign against the United States.

In an effort to salvage something of the situation, Ambassador Ellsworth Bunker flew into Jakarta on April 1 as a special envoy of President Johnson. (Bunker had mediated the West Irian dispute.) After some two weeks of talks it was announced that the two governments would "try to minimize irritants" in their relations. This was to be done by reducing even further the U.S. presence in Indonesia. The U.S. Government had decided to lay low as much as possible and see what the storm would bring.

---

*The shift in the political balance is dramatized by the contrast with the period 1960-62, when the army was banning many communist organizations and periodicals.

As Bunker was flying away from Jakarta, Chou-En-lai and Chen Yi were just arriving to attend the 10th anniversary celebrations of the 1955 Bandung meeting. In a talk over Jakarta Radio, Chou stressed Indonesia's and China's mutual belief in the dictum that "there can be no talk of peaceful coexistence with imperialism."[83] Sukarno affirmed his own faith in this doctrine by his direction of the anniversary celebrations, which was turned into an anti-U.S. forum. In speeches in April and July, Sukarno spoke of Indonesia's entry into the socialist stage and implied that the entry might be a violent one.*

Likewise, in May, Aidit told the fourth plenary session of the Central Executive Committee of the party that Indonesia was in an "ever-increasing and maturing revolutionary situation" and that "our task at the present time is to step up the revolutionary offensive, continue to develop the revolutionary situation, and bring it to a state of maturity."[84]

In May, Sukarno, addressing the 45th Anniversary Celebrations of the PKI, first launched his idea of extending the Nasakom concept to relations among states. The president by this time was becoming virtually ecstatic about the PKI. "PKI go ahead," he said "onward, onward, onward, never retreat."[85] In his own message to the PKI, Mao Tse-tung praised the party for having "Indonesianized Marxism-Leninism with outstanding success."[86] Peng Chen, who was attending the party's celebrations, also applauded the PKI for having achieved national unity on the basis of Nasakom.[87]

Although the postponement of the Afro-Asian conference in Algeria was a lost opportunity to intensify confrontation with the imperialists and to polarize the Afro-Asian world, the anti-Western campaign was maintained at a fast clip within Indonesia. Sukarno and Subandrio began to claim that the imperialists feared Indonesia more than the communist states and to warn of a possible attack on their country. In the summer, a press campaign against the United States and Britain was stirred up with the publication of an alleged photocopy of a letter from British Ambassador Sir Andrew Gilchrist to the British Foreign Office suggesting a British-U.S. plot to invade Indonesia, with the aid of "our local army friends."[88] About the same time, rumors spread about the existence of a council of generals who planned a coup d'état.

In August Sukarno completed his withdrawal from the Nekolim world by taking Indonesia out of the International Monetary Fund, the World Bank, and Interpol.

---

*On April 11, 1965, Sukarno spoke at the Provisional People's Consultative Congress (MPRS) and on July 26 at the PKI anniversary celebration.

Singapore's withdrawal from Malaysia on August 9 was interpreted by Sukarno as a confirmation of his confrontation policy, and on August 17 Sukarno for the first time spoke of the "Jakarta, Phomn Penh, Hanoi, Pyongyang axis." This axis, he said, was "most natural" and had been "formed by the course of history itself."[89]

THE SHORT LIFE OF THE FIFTH FORCE

Sukarno's increasingly radical pronouncements created growing apprehension among the noncommunist forces in Indonesia over the domestic consequences of his confrontation diplomacy. During these last few months, the struggle against internal reactionary forces had intensified. In May, Aidit called for an increased revolutionary offensive against the bureaucratic capitalist enemies.[90] And it was clear that the bureaucratic culprits he was referring to were in the top ranks of the army. Sukarno adopted the PKI terminology and lashed out at the "swindlers and corrupters." In the countryside there was also increasing PKI agitation against the "perfidious landowners" and the "rural capitalist bureaucrats." In his August 17 speech Sukarno again predicted that the time would come when Indonesia would build socialism and there would be no more capitalism and the land of the landlords would be redistributed.[91]

The issue that probably played the critical role in the apprehension of the noncommunist forces was the question of arming the peasants and workers—that is, the PKI mass organizations. As the "crush-Malaysia" campaign intensified, the PKI began to agitate for an armed militia as well as for the institution of a political commissar system in the army. The army fully recognized that the establishment of a large militia outside its chain of command was meant to neutralize its own power and provide the PKI with its long sought independent power base.[92] General Abdul Haris Nasution and the other generals took the position that the Indonesian Army was already a people's army, and therefore no militia was needed.

Sukarno, as much as the PKI,* felt the need for an armed force with which to balance the army. The president's direct authority over armed units had always been small but had actually declined since 1958. At that time there were several regional commanders who had sided with Sukarno on some of the important issues between himself

---

*On January 17, 1965, Aidit said that millions of organized workers and peasants were ready to take up arms to oppose the imperialists.

and the army. But after the rebellion was suppressed, the unity of the army was strengthened and these commanders were removed.[93]

Sukarno's public position on the arming of the masses underwent a gradual change from mild rejection in January 1965 to the assertion in August that the creation of a new people's militia, or Fifth Force, was his own idea. Probably, by the beginning of 1965, he had already committed himself to this project, and he was only searching for the most politic way to achieve it.

Beginning in the summer of 1965, China also was publicly identified with the proposal. Sukarno in a speech to the National Defense Institute on May 31 revealed that Chou En-lai had told him (apparently in April) that the Indonesian armed forces should become a "people's army" built around a volunteer armed service. Sukarno at this time implied that he approved of the idea.[94] As previously mentioned, Mao Tse-tung in his public message to the PKI in May 1965 expressed confidence that the party would "enhance its fighting quality." And on May 25 at a Peking reception, Peng Chen proclaimed that "in active response to the PKI's fighting call for arming the workers and peasants and for holding a rifle in one hand and a spade in the other, the broad masses are heightening their vigilance."[95]

During the summer months, as Sukarno and his top officials began to boast that Indonesia would soon enter the nuclear club, they also began to talk more about the Fifth Force, and in early August, the Chinese returned to the issue when Li Hsueh-feng in a speech in Jakarta emphasized the need for "the people of all countries to arm themselves . . . as in China the whole population becomes citizen soldiers."[96] According to press accounts of the talks between Li and Third Deputy Prime Minister Chaerul Saleh, the subject of the Fifth Force was discussed; both agreed that it was feared by the imperialists.[97] In his August 17, 1965 address, Sukarno indicated that the Fifth Force was his own idea, and, citing the danger posed by the imperialists, he quoted the 1945 constitution, which provides that "every citizen shall have the right and the duty to participate in the defense of the state." Sukarno said that "after an even more thorough consideration of this question, I will make a decision in my capacity as supreme commander of the armed forces."[98]

On September 10, Sukarno received the Chinese Ambassador, and on September 15 the procommunist air force commander, Via Marshal Omar Dhani, flew secretly to Peking in Sukarno's private plane to arrange among other things for the supply of small arms.[99] Meanwhile, members of the PKI youth (Pemuda Rakjat) and the women's organization (Gerwani) were organized in September into a special reserve force at the Halim Air Force Base while some militia training of laborers, farmers, and persons associated with various PKI mass organizations had already begun in July at Halim Air Base.*

ANTICIPATING THE GENERALS

The speeding up of the plan to arm the PKI took place against the background of an increasingly tense political situation and a sudden scare over Sukarno's health. In early August, Aidit returned from Peking and called three Politburo meetings between August 17 and August 28 to discuss the dramatic events that were developing. Aidit told the Politburo that the health of the president had taken a turn for the worse; the party chairman had in fact brought back with him by "special plane" from Peking the Chinese doctors who had previously treated Sukarno. Although Sukarno recovered from this attack (presumably related to his kidney problem), a possibly fatal recurrence was feared.

Aidit also discussed with the Politburo the alleged plan by a "council of generals" to launch a coup after the death or incapacitation of the president. Finally the PKI leader informed his colleagues of the existence of a group of "progressive officers" in the army who were prepared to foil the plan of the "council of generals." The general subject of these meetings were later testified to by three PKI Politburo members, Sudisman, Njono, and Sakirman.[100] Sudisman's testimony, as reported in the communist journal Tricontinental, revealed that

----

*Dhani testified at his trial in December 1966, that he was sent by Sukarno to Peking to discuss with Pakistani and Chinese officials the question of Indonesian military aid to Pakistan. Dhani stated that in addition he discussed with Chou En-lai the alleged promise Chou had made to Subandrio nine months earlier to provide 100,000 small arms to Indonesia. Dhani apparently made arrangements for the delivery of 25,000 of these arms slated for the air force, an arrangement that, he implied, was unknown to the armed forces staff. He testified that he reported the results of his talks with Chou only to Subandrio. (Jakarta Domestic Service in Indonesian, December 6, 1966). This could hardly be considered subversion, as China was dealing with the established government.

After "gestapu," some Indonesian sources reported that Chinese weapons had been found among materials for the CONEFO site. But this report was never substantiated. See John Hughes, The End of Sukarno: A Coup That Misfired (London: Angus and Robertson, 1968).

In the meeting of the Political Bureau of the Central Committee of the PKI, Comrade D. N. Aidit explained that
there were several progressive officers in the Army who
wanted to forestall the Council of Generals and keep it
from staging a coup d'état.

Therefore, Comrade Aidit gave the order to send
a number of activists to the provinces severals days
before the beginning of the 30th of September movement.
They were instructed to listen to the broadcasts of the
RPI [Radio Indonesia] from Jakarta and to support a
Council of revolution.[101]

The army must have had some inkling about what was going on
at Halim since July and what had transpired in Peking in September.
In any event, the PKI and Sukarno fully appreciated the provocativeness
of their move in regard to the Fifth Force. Even if the generals did
not know about these developments, Aidit and Sukarno must have been
extremely nervous about the possibility; rumors of coups and plotting
and counterplotting were running thick during the summer months in
the capital, and Sukarno's ill health at this time made everyone nervous.[102] Sukarno and Aidit knew that in the next few weeks or months,
until the arming of the PKI was a fait accompli, they would be in their
most dangerous position. Within this context, Aidit, probably with
Sukarno's approval, instructed the commander of the presidential
palace guard, Colonel Untung, to prepare a contingency plan together
with the group of "progressive officers" and the PKI to be used as a
preemptive blow to eliminate the army generals should a coup seem
imminent. The organizing agency for the plan was the PKI Special
Affairs Bureau. Because of the situation, such a contingency plan
would seem to have been a logical precaution. Aidit and the PKI
Politburo in its August meetings agreed that the PKI would cooperate
with the "progressive officers" in planning a preemptive strike at
the generals to be carried out if necessary.[103] The Politburo approved
preparations, which included a 2,000-man reserve force.[104] Again
according to Tricontinental, Sudisman admitted that "some PKI leaders
including myself were involved" in the September 30 movement, as
were the progressive officers led by Colonel Untung.[105]

I made decrees and drew up the plan for the council of
revolution and was present in Halim, Lubang Buaja and
Pondok Gede (Auri base) at the time the 30th of September Movement began. All responsibility should fall
on my shoulders, not on the Party's since all actions
were executed by individuals who happened to be members of the PKI.[106]

114

Throughout the months of August and September, Untung met
with his small band of conspirators. The plotters, according to Untung,
included the commander of the first infantry brigade of the Jakarta
garrison, a representative of General Dhani, and two representatives
of the PKI Special Affairs Bureau.

The generals very likely were considering contingency plans
to be implemented in the event of Sukarno's death, but it is unknown
whether in fact they were preparing to move against him and the PKI
while he was still in command. Sudisman, in fact, testified that Aidit
offered no evidence of any coup plan. Moreover, the army's reluctance
to attack the president was indicated by its failure to oust him after
September 30; and certainly none of the generals were expecting anything unusual on the night of September 30 when they were caught in
their beds. But it is not clear whether Sukarno or Aidit really believed
the generals were ready to strike or which one of the two was responsible for ordering the execution of the preemptive strike that they had
been planning for more than a month. Perhaps it was Untung or the
personnel of the Special Affairs Bureau who, anxious not to let their
moment of glory pass, encouraged the decision to move. On the other
hand, some of the testimony given by PKI officials during the trials
before the Supreme Military Tribunal indicated that Aidit, guided by
information received from the PKI Special Affairs Bureau and from
Subandrio's central intelligence body, believed that the generals were
planning to strike on October 3 or October 5. This testimony also
suggests that as early as August 28 Aidit had decided that the leftist
forces should "anticipate" the generals. Peres Pardede, a candidate
member of the Politburo, quoted Aidit as saying that he "personally
would prefer to anticipate" the generals.[107]

Sudisman, however, implied that the responsibility was Sukarno's.
He defended the movement as "working for the security of the President," and he claimed that movement was loyal to Sukarno, as proved
by the fact that "Colonel Untung obeyed every decision of the President, no matter what it was." The Politburo member devoted an important part of his declaration to attempting to prove the existence
of the conspiracy of the council of generals and that the movement
was just and legitimate because it began with "the aim of aborting
that conspiracy."

As Sudisman pointed out, events after September 30 showed
that the PKI was in a passive state and offered no resistance. "Once
you have taken up arms," he said, "you must not play with them, but
must go on [to] the end." Sudisman was attempting to prove his point
that the PKI was not "completely involved" and that the party "cannot
be held responsible." The error of the PKI, Sudisman hinted, was
in allowing itself to become involved in a movement that was "isolated
from the masses," that lacked revolutionary skills, and that failed

to calculate correctly the correlation of forces and the relative strengths of the PKI and its enemies.[108]

Our own review of the history of events leading up to the September affair suggests that Sukarno remained the major actor in Indonesian events at least up until the night of September 30 and that the PKI had fully committed itself to Sukarno and vice versa. No matter how cynical the PKI may have been about its relationship to Sukarno, in this situation it had absolutely nothing to gain and everything to lose by involving itself in the September 30 coup without Sukarno's full support and, very likely, his leadership.[109]

THE PKI AND GESTAPU

Untung's testimony at his trial and interrogation clearly implicated the PKI as being involved in the coup. But this evidence could be of questionable value. To be objective, we should also set aside the confessions of some of the PKI officials, such as Aidit, which military authorities reportedly passed on to a Japanese reporter.[110] But there is other convincing evidence to indicate that the PKI was deeply involved in the planning and execution of the murder of the generals. It is certain that members of Pemuda Rakjat and Gerwani PKI organizations received weapons training at Halim airbase sometime before September 30 and together with members of Untung's palace guards made up the assassination teams and took part in the torture and murder of the generals. In addition Aidit was at Halim airbase on October 1 (one report claims he had arrived there at 11 the previous night)[111] and fled to central Java when the coup failed. Furthermore the PKI newspaper Harian Rakjat in its edition issued October 2 editorially approved and supported the action taken by the September 30 Movement,[112] and while it stated that this was an internal army affair, it did not renounce the inclusion on Untung's revolutionary council of a PKI member (Tjugito), the Pemuda Rakjat secretary general (Sukanto), the Gerwani chairwoman (Mrs. Suharti Suwarto), or that of another prominent PKI member (Hardojo).[113] On October 1, the east Java branch of Pemuda Rakjat issued a statement of full support for the September 30 movement, presumably before it would have had a chance to have read the Harian Rakjat editorial.[114] A rump central committee of the PKI operating out of Peking and headed by Politburo member Yusuf Adjitorop in a number of statements after 1965 clearly stated that the party's failure was in involving itself in the "adventure" of the September 30 movement. This Peking-based PKI group, for example, admitted that "the party leadership had been engaged in adventures which violated organizational rules and they

116

had also involved themselves in the September 30 movement which was not based on the high consciousness and condition of the masses."[115] A pro-Soviet PKI group likewise talked of the party's complicity as a fact. Finally, there is the testimony of Sudisman, which has been accepted in communist journals, and the credible evidence of Njono and other unrepentant PKI leaders.

The least that can be said on the basis of this evidence is that the PKI knowingly participated in the planning and creation of a coup force and in its activity during the night of September 30; moreover the party on October 2 deliberately identified itself with the attempted coup. The leadership of the PKI understood the seriousness of these events and that it could no more be only "slightly involved" in such an affair than a Gerwani member could be "slightly pregnant." The PKI's limited but fateful direct involvement in the actual violence, its failure to exploit its resources, and the confusion of the coup forces on October 1 suggest that the party was following Sukarno's lead.

It is certainly implausible to propose, as some observers have, that the coup attempt was an "internal army affair" and that the PKI was innocent of involvement. Sukarno and the PKI obviously could have thought of a better way to get rid of the generals. Sukarno simply could have forced them to retire or arrested them one by one, backed in each case by mass demonstrations of popular support arranged by the PKI.[116] This neater, more Sukarno, and more Indonesian way was most likely the path that the president and the PKI planned to follow, after they had taken out an insurance policy in the form of arming the PKI with Chinese-supplied weapons. In the meantime, the revolutionaries covered themselves with an all-conceived contingency plan. But the momentum of the revolutionary offensive and Sukarno's illness made the leftists increasingly fearful, and they struck out—perhaps needlessly.

CHINA'S ROLE

Can the debacle in Indonesia be laid in any way at China's door? Perhaps in a very limited sense, but not in the same way that Stalin's strategy was responsible for the CCP's own castastrophe in 1927. China had no direct responsibility for the events of September 30, 1965. There has been speculation that Peking had foreknowledge of the coup, as suggested by the manner of its announcement of the event to its foreign guests on the morning of October 1. The British historian H. R. Trevor-Roper, for example, received the impression that the Chinese were taking credit for the coup as the culmination of some deliberate policy of their own.[117] Given the Chinese role

in the arming of the Fifth Force, it seems likely that either Aidit or
Sukarno or Subandrio informed the Chinese Embassy of the plans being
worked out between the PKI and the "progressive officers." Although
probably not informed of the details or timing of the blow and perhaps
not knowing whether the coup forces were to "anticipate" the generals
or to be held in reserve, the leaders in Peking were nevertheless not
taken by surprise when informed of the events in Jakarta, and, misled
by early reports, they were naturally pleased that the coup seemed
to be going smoothly.

But it is clear that the PKI was its own master and that it decided
on its own to push for the Fifth Force. Mao encouraged Aidit and
Sukarno in this venture, and perhaps he pushed them along faster than
they otherwise would have gone, for the preparation for armed violence
was at the core of Mao's model for the seizure of power. We also
know that he and his colleagues, beginning at least in the spring of
1965, began adding their own pressures to the PKI campaign for the
Fifth Force. It seems possible that it was Sukarno who was most
affected by the Chinese enthusiasm for the Fifth Force, that the overly
anxious Chinese encouraged the Indonesian president into his decision
to go ahead with the arming of the PKI without the approval or knowledge of the army.*

Why was Mao in such a hurry? Apparently his interpretation
of the PKI's potentially dangerous position was basically the same
as that of Aidit, although Mao's fears were perhaps exaggerated by
his own party's experience in 1927. But perhaps most important was
the deterioration of China's international position that began with the
escalation of the Vietnam war in February 1965.

The importance of Indonesia's close cooperation thus became
even more critical than before. Peking was more anxious than ever
to protect its huge stake in the PKI and in Sukarno's confrontation
policy. Faced with setbacks abroad and dissent within his own leadership group at home, Mao in particular was eager for the victorious
consummation of the Peking-Jakarta axis as a blow to both the United
States and the Soviet Union.

The escalation of the Vietnam war in February 1965 and the
consequent heightening of the confrontation with imperialism also

---

*Chou En-lai's remarks to Sukarno in the spring and the public
statements made in the summer by Chinese officials urging the Indonesians to create a "people's army" could not have been intended to
persuade the generals but presumably were aimed at encouraging
Sukarno. One possibility is that Sukarno's request for a Chinese
nuclear test may have been linked in some reciprocal fashion to
China's request that he arm the PKI.

gave Mao and Sukarno an added interest in and cause for rushing through the revolution in Indonesia. The final battle to drive the United States and Britain out of Southeast Asia seemed joined. But Indonesia could not be a fully reliable partner in the struggle so long as the revolutionary forces in Indonesia were not in control of the national democratic front. On the contrary, it seemed they were constantly in danger of violent suppression by a "reactionary" army leadership.

The U.S. escalation in Vietnam in 1965 had a major, if negative, effect on the momentous events in Indonesia. Not that the Indonesian generals would have responded in a different way had the United States chosen the other alternative in Vietnam—negotiation of a withdrawal pretty much on Hanoi's terms—but events would probably not have built up to such a crisis pitch in Indonesia. Sukarno and the PKI would have felt less able to push the revolutionary campaign at home; consequently, the dizzying spin to the left would have been slowed, the secret attempt to arm the "masses" perhaps would not have been ventured, and the PKI would have gone back to its longer-range program, which some reports say envisioned a takeover by 1970. Having made tremendous gains in weakening the anticommunists, the PKI and Sukarno could well have afforded to have taken a step backwards. Had they done so, the final leap forward was much more likely to have succeeded.

If the United States in 1965 had seemed unwilling or unable to deny Hanoi's own confrontation policy the achievement of its objectives in South Vietnam, Sukarno's world view would have seemed confirmed to many Indonesians. His prestige, as well as China's among most Indonesians, including the generals, would have been increased by an important degree. This would have strengthened Sukarno's hand and that of the PKI, but it is impossible to say what turn events would then have taken.

IF THE COUP HAD SUCCEEDED

Had the September 30 movement succeeded, the effect on the world scene would have been serious. The movement would not have been a PKI takeover, nor was it portrayed as such. Sukarno simply wanted to eliminate those generals who were in the way of his great Indonesian revolution. He wanted to neutralize the army as a political force and to make it his obedient instrument, just as he believed he had "Sukarno-ized" the PKI. Sukarno had envisaged himself as leading Indonesia into socialist revolution and into the battle for a new world order with the PKI and the army as his dedicated tools. He dreamed of international Nasakom and Indonesian ascendancy in the Malay areas of Southeast Asia.

119

In 1964, Herbert Feith suggested that Sukarno might move Indonesia into a position somewhat like that of Cuba.[118] Sukarno was certainly similar to Castro in that he was an avowedly Marxist revolutionary whose ambitions and goals transcended those of his own nation. The ideological and psychological sympathies of both Castro and Sukarno lay with the socialist camp, but, more important, both of these leaders had come to see that their broader goals, their intense desire to spread their own revolution and influence throughout their respective areas, could only be achieved by militant struggle with the United States and thus through alliance with the Soviet Union and China, respectively.

Had the September 30 movement succeeded, events in Indonesia might have paralleled those in Cuba, particularly in foreign policy. There are, of course, important differences in the situations of the two countries and in their internal political circumstances. Had Sukarno succeeded in bringing the army completely under his control, he would have been still more constrained than Castro by the need to appease various political, regional, and ethnic groups. (One possible result of the coup could have been dissident rebellions in the outer islands and the eventual balkanization of Indonesia.) Sukarno may have wanted in any event to have maintained his Nasakom system. Because of its sheer size and its geopolitical position, Indonesia would not have become nearly so dependent on China for economic aid and military protection as Cuba has been on the Soviet Union.

Sukarno probably would have been able to attain the position that Castro still desires—affiliation with the communist camp against the United States but complete freedom of action to spread his own brand of revolution in his own area. In this optimum situation, Indonesia, for strategic ideological reasons, would have wished to maintain some leverage with Moscow. Jakarta was in debt to Moscow for nearly $2 billion of military aid, and in 1965 it was not meeting its repayment schedule. The Indonesian armed forces, particularly the air force, were heavily dependent upon Soviet replacement and spare parts equipment, which China probably could not have provided. The Soviets had also been more generous than the Chinese in economic aid.* Consequently, we may assume that Indonesia in the socialist camp would

---

*In addition to its immense military aid, Soviet economic aid to Indonesia by 1965 totaled $270 million with about $100 million drawn and some 700 Soviet advisers and technicians in the country. China, on the other hand, had committed so far $108 million, of which about $40 million had been drawn, and there were only about 40 Chinese technicians in the country at that time. (New York Times, August 25, 1965).

have inclined toward Peking but would not have wished for complete alienation from Moscow.

Sukarno certainly did not anticipate becoming a satellite of China; on the contrary he sought an equal position of revolutionary leadership with China in the entire Afro-Asian world. And Peking after 1960 was always careful to pander to Sukarno's world power ambitions, for example, by underwriting his games of the New Emerging Forces and his grandiose CONEFO, as well as frequently employing his jargon.

Up until the September 30 movement, the highest Chinese officials, including Mao, had praised Sukarno as a creative revolutionary and had lauded the PKI for developing Marxism-Leninism within the Nasakom concept. Almost certainly, Peking would have accepted Sukarno's claim that he was building socialism. It is true that China's rejection of the Soviet theory of the progression of a "national democratic state" into the socialist revolution made the PRC reluctant to acknowledge that Cuba was building socialism after Castro had first claimed that it was doing so. Nevertheless, it probably would not have had any serious doctrinal difficulty in accepting Sukarno's new regime as a legitimately Marxist-Leninist one, had Sukarno declared it as such. While the Russians might have claimed that the victory for socialism in Indonesia had followed the evolutionary pattern, the PKI would not have confirmed this analysis but would have argued that the victory came through the application of a Maoist strategy and that the arming of the party, the ability to meet counterrevolutionary violence with revolutionary violence, had been the factor that had secured the victory of the proletariat in Indonesia.

Friction, however, would have inevitably appeared between Peking and Jakarta. Strains would have developed over questions of strategy and tactics as well as over conflicts generated by the vanities and ambitions of the two leaders. While Sukarno genuinely seemed to admire Mao, the serious-minded Chinese leader probably had little use for Sukarno's personal peccadillos and ideological pretensions. After Sukarno's loss of power, the Peking press again referred to him as a "bourgeois-nationalist" and demeaned both his "teachings" and his claim to have been the "great leader of the revolution."[119] On Sukarno's death in June 1970, Chou En-lai in a condolence message praised him for having worked for Indonesian independence but did not refer to any revolutionary characteristics.[120]

Political disputes over spheres of influence and the question of overseas Chinese were the most serious potential sources of friction. Indonesia and China both had compelling national interests in Malaya, Singapore, and the Borneo territories, and sensitive issues could have exploded at any time. Nevertheless, while conflicts of interest would have been inevitable, they would not necessarily have led to a breakdown in effective cooperation between the two capitals.

We have suggested that Peking and Jakarta, or at least the CCP and the PKI, had agreed that Indonesia would become the dominant power in the Malay world. As David Mozingo has speculated, Peking was apparently willing to concede the Malaysian area to Indonesia as an acceptable price for a long-range alignment in excluding Western "imperialism" from eastern Asia.[121] In this political picture, Indonesia would have controlled its own sphere—a "Greater Indonesia"— under a larger international grouping that would have had Peking as its center. There is admittedly no documentary evidence to support the conclusion that spheres were agreed to, but it seems reasonable to believe that some sort of understanding on the subject was necessary.

EFFECT ON THE CHINESE LEADERSHIP*

Moscow propaganda organs charged that the PKI was on the parliamentary road to victory but that it got off the tracks and fell into a "Peking adventurist line," with terrible consequences. The September 30 movement, Moscow Radio said, was "inspired by Peking and provoked by Western intelligence."[122] In 1967, the Soviets unveiled their own PKI group to do verbal battle with the pro-Peking Indonesians. The French Communist Party newspaper L'Humanité on December 11 published a document from the "Marxist/Leninist group of the Indonesian Communist Party" blaming pro-Chinese elements for the party's catastrophe.[123] The document recalled that leaders of the PKI visited China the summer before the aborted coup. They came home, the article charged, "to undertake an adventure that had nothing to do with Marxist theory of armed insurrection. The mass of the people was not ready for armed action."[124] A Soviet commentator

---

*At the time of the troubles in Indonesia in the fall of 1965, one member of the PKI Politburo, Yusuf Adjitorop, was in China. He remained there and continued to issue statements in the name of the PKI Central Committee. Peking Radio and NCNA, beginning in January 1967, quoted at length from a new organ of the exiled PKI, Indonesian Tribune, which was published in Albania. In addition, NCNA quoted from a publication called Voice of Indonesian Youth and from statements reportedly made by Indonesian groups in organizations like the Afro-Asian People's Solidarity Organization. The Chinese interpretation or "line" on the September 30 movement was embodied in these "PKI" and Indonesian-exile statements as well as in Peking-originated comment.

concluded that the main cause of the PKI's collapse was its pro-Chinese orientation and its alignment with Sukarno.[125]

In response, Peking in 1967 stated its position with remarkable clarity. Despite the PKI's electoral victories, the Chinese argued, the party could never have made a peaceful transition to power in Indonesia until it had taken over the army and/or established its own independent armed force, the "Fifth Force."

> If the proletariat fails to take over the army and the police and other instruments of national dictatorship, then such victories (as that of the PKI in 1957) are nothing more than idle chatter. Making revolution, a proletarian party must vigilantly train the popular masses, organize and amass revolutionary forces, meet counterrevolutionary violence with revolutionary violence, and take power by violent revolution. In other words, it must embark on the path of armed struggle.[126]

As we have seen, this seems to have been just what the PKI was doing. The party had launched itself onto the road of armed struggle by training the popular masses and taking the first steps toward organizing a revolutionary force so that it might meet counter-revolutionary violence with revolutionary violence. Unfortunately for the PKI and Sukarno, the creation of a people's armed force had only begun when the "counterrevolutionary elements," the generals, excited by this very move, decided on a violent suppression—or so the revolutionary leaders, including both Sukarno and Aidit, believed or were told by Untung or Subandrio.

But although the line the PKI was following coincided with the Maoist model, in 1967 the Chinese party and the rump PKI central committee in Peking denounced the Aidit leadership for having adopted "the revisionist Soviet line of peaceful transition" and then having compounded this sin by involving itself in a "putschist adventure," which "violated organizational rules."[127] In addition they condemned the Aidit leadership for accepting the Nasakom slogan, turning itself into an appendage of the national bourgeois (Sukarno) and losing independence within the united front, putting Sukarno's teachings on a par with those of Marx, adopting the line of achieving socialism peacefully, and failing to prepare for the possibility of a nonpeaceful path.[128]

As shown, these charges of revisionism and "apostolism" are glaringly inconsistent with the previous Peking line on the PKI. But it is not unusual for a big-brother party to make a scapegoat out of the leader of an associated party for failures in carrying out a mutually agreed-upon policy. It is a pattern most reminiscent of Stalin's reaction to the communist disaster in China in 1927. Stalin would have put all the blame on the CCP leadership in any event, but he was greatly stimulated to look for a scapegoat by the relentless attacks of Trotsky, who used Stalin's failure in China to attack the dictator's political position.[129] Was there any similar split on basic policy on Indonesia within the CCP?

Before September 30, 1965, there was no evidence of any serious disagreement in the Chinese leadership over the general policy in Indonesia—consolidating the alliance with Sukarno and approving and attempting to promote the PKI's internal strategy. But we now know that a bitter struggle was already developing at that time within the Chinese Communist Party.

The collapse of China's hopes in Indonesia coincided with the meeting in Peking in which festering opposition to Mao was more or less openly manifest. We have already speculated about divisions within the Chinese leadership at this time on the questions of Vietnam and internal policies and possibly on the issue of carrying out a nuclear test explosion for Indonesia. Similar differences may have also occurred on other questions related to Indonesia, such as the rushing through of the Fifth Force,* support for a rival UN, and the holding of Bandung Two. But it was not until the radicals and supporters of Lin Piao had seized control of the Foreign Ministry in Peking that retroactive charges about this period appeared. Although it is apparent that Mao approved in general of Aidit's policies in 1964-65, the radical coalition with whom Mao was then allied tried in 1967-68 to exploit the PKI's failure in order to incriminate alleged revisionists at home and abroad. Aside from attacking the Aidit leadership for having tied itself too closely to Sukarno, the radicals also attacked Liu Shao-chi for having "prettified the bourgeois politician Sukarno" and having promoted the Maphilindo concept.[130] Liu and Aidit were both retroactively accused of having followed a Soviet revisionist line in Indonesia. As in the case of Burma, these attacks on the earlier policies were probably aimed also at Chou En-lai and Foreign Minister Chen Yi.

In sum, we may conclude that up until September 30, 1965 there were probably minor but no serious disagreements within the Chinese leadership on the general line in Indonesia. In this case, the factors that shaped Peking's policy were China's struggle with the United States and its rivalry with the USSR. After the collapse of the coup attempt, the Cultural Revolution faction within the CCP attempted to exploit the Jakarta failure as another weapon against the foreign affairs establishment.

---

*It is interesting to note that in May 1965, both Mao and Peng Chen, one of the first major victims of the 1966 purge, publicly urged the PKI to arm the masses.

The effect of the PKI disaster on Mao was probably profound. The chairman at the time was concentrating his thoughts and energies on the problem of internal revisionism allegedly led by Liu Shao-chi, and he probably interpreted the catastrophe in Indonesia in terms of this preoccupation. The Indonesian events may have appeared to him as a confirmation of the danger of compromising revolutionary principles. Despite the fact that Mao himself had approved the PKI's united front with Sukarno, the collapse of the strategy may have hardened his determination to pursue a path of revolutionary purity in China and the rest of the world.

THE END OF THE AFFAIR

In the months following the aborted September 30 movement, Sukarno in vain demanded an end to attacks on Chinese nationals and to the violence being wreaked upon PKI members.[131] Moreover, as the political base of his revolutionary design was being decimated, he continued to reveal the depth of his alliance with the PKI and China. In November, for example, he told a meeting of 400 military officers that as long as he was leader, Indonesia would have some form of communism in its government,[132] for if he eliminated communism, "there would be no Indonesia."[133] His country, he proclaimed, would remain a "leftist nation" forming an "axis with Communist China."[134]

While Sukarno was still struggling to protect the PKI and to regain the upper hand from the army, China continued to be deferential to him. The PKI's hope throughout most of 1966 was that somehow Sukarno's political wizardry could balance off the army's power. But as Sukarno's struggle appeared more and more futile and as the power of the radicals in Peking grew, China and the exiled PKI grew markedly less interested in maintaining the illusion of revolutionary comradeship with the old engineer. An NCNA article in March 1967 protested against his allegedly illegal ousting, but little further mention was made of the "great leader of the Indonesian revolution" except in the context of denunciations of the Aidit leadership.

Thus, by 1967, China as well as the PKI (both inside and outside Indonesia) had given up hope of reestablishing influence through a united-front-from-above with Sukarno. Theoretically, the Chinese might have done as the Soviets did—tolerate suppression of the PKI and attempt to maintain some influence and leverage for the long run by maintaining working relations with the new military government. But the loss had been too great for Peking easily to adopt a united-front-from-above strategy in Indonesia. In the context of the heated disputes then raging within the Chinese party as well as within the international communist movement over the correct path for revolution, it was virtually impossible for Peking to support even minimum cooperation with the Suharto government. The killing of thousands of overseas Chinese during the rampages of late 1965 further stimulated Peking's animosity toward the new order.[135]

The suppression of the PKI became another hot issue in the Moscow-Peking conflict, with each side accusing Aidit of having followed the other's policy to disaster. The Soviets attacked the PKI for straying from the parliamentary path, while the Chinese had no alternative but to denounce their former friends for following the Soviet road of peaceful transition. Thus, Peking's ideological contest with Moscow, its political radicalization at home, and its emotional involvement forced it openly to support a united-front-from-below strategy in Indonesia: the establishment of PKI base areas in the countryside, the creation of a peasant army, and the unleashing of violent struggle.

After Sukarno's overthrow in March 1967, Peking, then in the throes of the Cultural Revolution, began openly to proclaim armed violence as the new strategy for the revolution in Indonesia. In April a Chinese Foreign Ministry statement proclaimed Chinese support for the new revolutionary era that was dawning in Indonesia:

> We are firmly convinced that a new revolutionary high
> tide is bound to arrive in Indonesia and that the Indo-
> nesian people will eventually overthrow the reactionary
> rule. . . . The Chinese people . . . firmly support the
> Indonesian people in their revolutionary struggle . . .
> for freedom and liberation. We are determined to pro-
> vide this support . . . deeply convinced that through
> joint struggles the day will soon come when the sun will
> shine forth in full splendor.[136]

This statement came in the midst of intensifying polemics between China and Indonesia concerning incidents of violence to Chinese residents, the repatriation of several thousand Chinese (mostly from Medan, Sumatra),* and demonstrations against their respective embassies. Overseas Chinese in Indonesia were promised the "powerful backing" of their motherland and the Jakarta government was warned that "the Chinese people are determined to hit back."[137] Suharto

---

*The PRC transported 4,251 to China. At the end of 1967 over 6,000 remained in special barracks awaiting repatriation. These were apparently still there in 1970. (Jakarta Domestic Service, May 9, 1970.)

was pictured in a then typical rush of metaphors as the "despicable pawn and lackey of the U.S. and the USSR . . . a national traitor . . . and a lap dog in human skin."[138] Relations were finally "suspended" by Indonesia in October.

The PKI Central Committee echoed the Maoist line, and during 1967 as the Cultural Revolution swept through China, the Indonesian party took up the cry for the building of armed bases in the country-side and the initiation of actual violence. In May the party promised to follow "the road of people's war as charted by Mao Tse-tung."[139] In July as extremists virtually took over the foreign affairs and propaganda sectors of the Chinese Government, Peking called for a general uprising throughout Indonesia, to which it again offered the "firm support" of the Chinese party and people.[140] Partially inspired by the rhetoric from Peking Radio, the 700-800 Sarawakian Chinese communists in West Kalimantan joined by some PKI elements formed the People's Guerrilla Forces of Sarawak (PGRS) and initiated a terrorist offensive in West Kalimantan (See Chapter 5).

At the end of the year the radicals in Peking seemed optimistic:

> The year 1967 has witnessed an important new start in the Indonesian revolution . . . armed struggle waged by the Indonesian communists and revolutionary people in the rural areas of several major islands in the country. The Indonesian guerrilla fighters have solemnly proclaimed to the world through their revolutionary gunfire that they are determined to take the road of the Chinese revolution paved by the great leader of the world's people, Chairman Mao Tse-tung, that is, to rely on the peasants, wage armed struggle, set up rural revolutionary base areas, overthrow the Suharto-Nasution fascist military regime and carry the revolution to victory.[141]

In a February 1968 article in People's Daily, Yusuf Adjitorop, from his Peking exile, boldly announced that the Indonesian revolutionaries were "wiping the blood off their bodies" and rallying their forces for a new armed struggle. Adjitorop stressed the importance for the Indonesian revolutionaries of the support of the new militant China:

> Today, the center of world revolution has moved to China. Under the leadership of Chairman Mao Tse-tung, China, as the bastion of world revolution, is developing steadily and is being increasingly consolidated. This is a factor most favorable to the world communist movement especially to the communists now engaged in armed struggle.[142]

In its anniversary statement of May the PKI Central Committee reiterated that the main form of struggle was now the "armed agrarian revolution."[143] Although the PKI remnants in Indonesia were still preoccupied with survival and rebuilding the framework of an organization, the party stirred itself once again and in response to these appeals rushed onto the path of armed terrorism. As promised by the pro-Maoists, "terrifying flames of revolution" flared up in East Java in the summer of 1968: "In East Java, the people's revolutionaries are accelerating their armed struggle, and are actively carrying out guerrilla activities, killing the wicked landlords and cruel chieftains in the broad rural areas."[144]

A PKI underground armed force of several hundred had in fact been slowly built up in the South Blitar region of East Java, and in early 1968 it launched a terrorist campaign against the local leaders, which resulted in the killing of about 70 people. Presumably its intention was to create, as urged by Peking Radio and the pro-Maoist PKI, a rural guerrilla base for the party. The result however was the exposure of a budding underground organization and further suppression of the PKI by the Indonesian Army. Within a few weeks the South Blitar communist organization in East Java had been virtually wiped out, and the rear base was no more. From 800 to 2,000 PKI members were captured or killed, including the new party leader Oloan Hutapea, who had replaced Sudisman, and nine of the new ten-man Politburo.[145] Moreover this action led directly to the arrest of 600 members of the East Java Military Command suspected of having links with the communist organization and to the detention or dismissal of thousands of alleged PKI agents and sympathizers in the government. Moscow was quick to charge Peking again with direct responsibility for the disaster. In September, Pravda accused Peking of provoking the PKI's outburst of armed terrorism and thus leading it to another smashing defeat.

At the same time the Sarawak communists in West Kalimantan including PKI components were also being harassed by the Indonesian Army and plagued by factionalism, disease, and a lack of food.

THE PKI SPLITS

A schism on the question of the Peking line began to develop within the underground PKI elements in Indonesia. According to one analysis, the PKI remnants in East and Central Java were pro-Peking while PKI elements in the capital and its vicinity were under the influence of "another" communist party (that is, the Soviet party).[146] The pro-Peking committee implied that the pro-Soviet group was making headway:

Soviet revisionists also resort to activities designed to
divide the Indonesian revolutionary forces and try in
vain to divide the Indonesian Communist Party. By
diabolical activity, they are trying to gather a handful
of Indonesian Communist Party renegades in Moscow,
picking them out from history's rubbish heap, and using
them for their increased activities directed at the schism
of the Indonesian Communist Party and the Indonesian
revolutionary people.[147]

The pro-Soviet position was spelled out in a statement of the
"Marxist-Leninist Group of the PKI" in June 1969:

It is the opinion of Indonesian Marxist-Leninists that
before thorough and revolutionary preparations are
made, before a revolutionary crisis has actually
emerged which, in turn, produces a revolutionary situation, before an organized and highly influential Marxist-
Leninist party has been formed which can serve as a
nucleus of the vanguard of an armed struggle and which
is assured of mass support from forces united with the
working class . . . and this mass support is absolutely
necessary for the success of a revolutionary action . . .
armed action is premature.

Nevertheless, at the mid-1969 World Communist Conference
in Moscow, pressure for a more militant line, possibly from the pro-
Soviet Indonesians in Moscow, and the perceived need to undercut the
appeal of Peking's armed-struggle line resulted in a partial modification of the Soviet-endorsed political program. A new program by
the pro-Moscow group proposed the rebirth of the PKI on revolutionary
lines. While still taking Peking to task for adventurism in its advocacy
of immediate violence, Moscow in the last half of 1969 was proposing
that the PKI prepare itself for eventual armed struggle.[148]
    This partial shift came at the most critical stage of the Sino-
Soviet border war and at a time when Moscow was hinting at the possibility of a massive attack on the PRC. The Soviet party was therefore
particularly anxious to win support from the communist world for its
policy toward China and to belie Peking's charges of revolutionary
desertion.
    However, in 1970, the British withdrawal and the U.S. retrench-
ment from Southeast Asia enhanced Soviet interest in taking up the
resultant political slack. The build-up of Soviet naval activity in the
Indian Ocean inevitably increased Moscow's interest in improved ties
with the Indonesian Government. The first big step was taken in

August 1970, when Moscow agreed to reschedule repayment of Indonesia's debts on virtually the same terms as those accorded by the West. It was also agreed that a Soviet technical team would survey the rusting $36 million Soviet steel plant at Tjilagon in West Java.

In keeping with this emphasis on state relations, Soviet comment dropped the themes of the previous year on preparation for armed struggle and instead emphasized the need for the PKI to focus on united front activity with other progressive forces. At the end of 1971 the Soviets were still stressing PKI efforts to reorganize and reunite all democratic, patriotic, and antiimperialist forces. Moscow avoided the subject of armed struggle and again denounced the Maoists for expounding "the rotten theme of Indonesia being in the midst of violent revolution and that history obliges the PKI to embark on the road of armed struggle."[149]

SHIFTING INTERESTS

Adjitorop and the pro-Peking PKI had pinned their hopes on Chinese support during the 1968 uprisings in Indonesia, although it is not clear in what form they expected this aid to materialize. In his congratulatory message on the 12th plenary session of the Eighth Central Committee of the CCP (held October 13-31), Adjitorop focused on the passage in the session's communiqué that "reiterated that the Chinese Communist Party and Chinese people will render in accordance with proletarian internationalism, resolute backing and genuine support to the revolutionary people the world over . . ."[150]

Adjitorop again pointedly emphasized the importance of China's resolute support, and he reminded the CCP of its explicit pledge to the PKI in May 1967:

The Indonesian Communists and revolutionary people, in their struggle for emancipation, have from the outset deeply realized the significance of the resolute backing and genuine support rendered by the Chinese Communist Party and the Chinese people. At a time of setbacks in the Indonesian people's revolutionary struggle, which is carried out under the leadership of the Indonesian Communist Party, Red Flag, organ of the Central Committee of the Communist Party of China explicitly stated in the editorial in its 11th issue, 1967: "The Chinese Communist Party and the Chinese people constantly have the fight of the Indonesian Communist Party and the Indonesian people in mind. Our hearts are closely linked with the hearts of our class brothers in Indonesia.

"We stand unflinchingly on the side of the Indonesian
Communist Party, on the side of the Indonesian revolutionary people and firmly support the Indonesian Communist
Party in leading the Indonesian people's struggle to overthrow the Suharto-Nasution fascist regime and establish
a completely independent and democratic new Indonesia."
The resolute backing and genuine support from the Communist Party of China and the 700 million Chinese people
have greatly inspired the Indonesian Communists and
revolutionary people in overcoming various difficulties
they encounter in the protracted and tortuous armed
struggle to overthrow the Suharto-Nasution fascist military regime and to build a people's democratic regime
of Indonesia.[151]

In 1969, however, PKI statements began to play down the role
of China in the Indonesian armed struggle, and both Peking and PKI
comment painted a stark picture of the "long, difficult, tortuous and
twisting" path of armed revolution.

In his report to the Ninth Party Congress on April 1, 1969, Lin
Piao noted that armed struggle was steadily growing in Thailand,
Burma, Indonesia, and other countries, but he did not discuss the
Indonesian case nor refer directly to China's support for these strug-
gles.

Nevertheless, the PKI described Lin's statement as having
reiterated the "clear-cut attitude" of the Chinese party in supporting
the revolutionary struggle of the Indonesian people. The PKI still
proclaimed that the PRC, "the most dependable bulwark of world
revolution," stood firmly on the side of the Indonesian people and
consistently supported the Indonesian revolution.[152] However, it
was stated that the greatest assistance that the Chinese people rendered
was the thought of Mao Tse-tung.[153]

During the summer, as Sino-Soviet tensions reached their peak,
the Chinese stepped up their castigation of Soviet relations with Jakarta.
Peking denounced the "Suharto fascist military clique" as a "faithful
running dog" of both U.S. imperialism and Soviet revisionism, and
Moscow was charged incorrectly with having supplied large quantities
of weapons and ammunition and many military advisers to the Suharto
regime.[154] The Soviet and Indonesian Governments were accused
of a "blood dripping friendship":

. . . the "problems faced by" the Indonesian reactionaries
are becoming increasingly serious. After the counter-
revolutionary coup d'état, the revolutionary people of
Indonesia were neither cowed, conquered nor exterminated.

They picked themselves up, wiped off the blood, buried
their fallen comrades, and, holding high the great standard of armed struggle, went into battle again. The counter-
revolutionary rule of the fascist Suharto regime has
brought darkness to Indonesia and destitution to its people.
That regime is ridden with deep political-economic
crisis . . .
   The great leader Chairman Mao has pointed out:
"Those who are backed by imperialism are the very
ones spurned by the masses." The Suharto fascist military clique, ardently flirting, is a pack of executioners
whose hands are dripping with the blood of the Indonesian people. . . . They are already besieged by the
broad masses of the Indonesian people. The Soviet
revisionist renegade clique will come to no good end by
intensifying its counterrevolutionary collusion with the
Suharto clique.[155]

In 1970, the year of the U.S. incursion into Cambodia, Peking's
comment on Indonesia shifted to the U.S. role there. In addition, there
was increasing concern in China about the expansion of Japanese
economic influence in Indonesia as well as throughout Southeast Asia.
The Chinese feared that, as elsewhere, Japanese economic power in
Indonesia would be reflected eventually in the political and security
fields.
   The PKI was visibly excited by the Cambodian events of 1970,
apparently hoping that somehow this affair would catch up the Jakarta
government in the Indochina conflict and provide Peking with enhanced
interest in assisting the revolutionary movement. The pro-Peking
PKI issued a statement hailing the April summit conference of the
Indochinese people and firmly supporting the joint declaration of the
conference. The Indonesian communists also denounced the Suharto
regime for allegedly sending "military advisers" and shipping arms
to the Lon Nol government in Cambodia. The Jakarta authorities
were even said to have been preparing to send troops to help the Phnom
Penh regime. The PKI hopefully predicted that the raging struggle
in Indochina would "have far-reaching influence on the struggle of
the peoples of the various Southeast Asian countries, particularly
the struggle of the Indonesian people."[156]
   On the heels of the Cambodian incursion, Adjitorop enthusiastically termed Mao's May 20 statement calling for the world's people
"to unite and defeat the U.S. aggressors and all their running dogs"
as a "new clarion battle call . . . encouraging the proletariat and the
revolutionary people of the world . . . to intensify their struggle. . . ."[157]
The revolutionary people of Indonesia, Adjitorop proclaimed, had

been greatly inspired by the new revolutionary developments in Indo-china.

Nevertheless, armed struggle within Indonesia was being placed in more realistic perspective. On its 50th party anniversary, the PKI Central Committee explained that the "general principle" guiding the party at the present time was to stress party-building and under-ground work in the countryside rather than actual violence.[158] State-ments by Adjitorop increasingly downplayed the theme of "protracted war."

Peking meanwhile was beginning to separate its national from its ideological goals in regard to Indonesia. By 1970 the Chinese seemed more interested in discouraging Jakarta from aligning itself with the United States and from establishing close ties with the USSR and Japan than in fulminating about the social revolution in Indonesia. Chinese verbal attacks on the Indonesian Government no longer stressed evils within Indonesia but focused on Jakarta's foreign policies.

In May 1970, Peking accused Foreign Minister Adam Malik of running errands for the United States by putting forward the idea of a "conference of Asian countries on the situation in Cambodia." If the Indonesians dared pull chestnuts out of the fire for the United States on the Cambodian question, People's Daily warned, "they will end up ignominiously in the same grave. . . ."[159] But Peking, unlike the PKI, did not directly link the Indochina conflict with the revolution-ary struggle in Indonesia. In May 1970 the Chinese party greeted the PKI anniversary but made only a vague pledge that the Chinese would "resolutely support" the revolutionary struggle of the PKI.

After this, Peking media coverage of Indonesian affairs dropped off sharply. Following the August-September plenum of the CCP's Central Committee, which criticized leading radicals in the CCP and apparently endorsed Chou En-Lai's united-front peaceful coexistence diplomacy, there was no report on Indonesian affairs until January 1971. (On China's October 1, 1970, National Day, no message of greet-ing was published from the PKI, although Adjitorop appeared on the rostrum.) Significantly, the subject of Peking's renewed attention in January was a report that the Indonesian Government was training "Lon Nol puppet troops."[160] Likewise in May, Peking expressed alarm over press reports that Japan was planning to train Indonesian Army officers.[161]

Although PKI hopes of greater Chinese commitments were again temporarily excited by Saigon's incursion (with U.S. backing) into Laos in the winter-spring of 1971, the Indonesian Party continued to receive progressively less attention in the Peking press. For the first time in many years, the PKI anniversary in May 1971 went un-noted in Chinese media.

The Peking-based PKI Central Committee's message to the Chinese party on the latter's 50th anniversary (July 1, 1971) proclaimed that the Chinese Communist Party had "always firmly and resolutely supported the struggle of the Indonesian people and the Indonesian Communists." The message again described China as the "reliable and invincible bulwark of world revolution."[162] But the major editorial in Peking marking the party anniversary did not make such a claim for China and failed to mention Indonesia. Following the July elections in Indonesia, which were swept by the government vehicle, Golkar, broadcasts from China attacking the government virtually disappeared. In addition, China's implicit acknowledgment in 1971 of "Malaysia's" legitimacy closed the book on the "crush-Malaysia" period in Sino-Indonesian relations.

Peking's shift away from its openly hostile policy toward the Jakarta government was a result of its acceptance of realities in Indonesia, the purge of the radicals and Lin Piao within the Chinese leadership, and the great changes that had taken place in Sino-U.S. and Sino-Soviet relationships. Moscow was now perceived as the principal threat to China while the United States was seen as abandoning its containment posture. Détente in Asia rather than confrontation was viewed by the Chinese as again offering the best possibility of furthering China's security and expanding its influence.

JAKARTA REVIEWS THE SITUATION

While China turned its attention away from the battered PKI, some elements in the Indonesian Government began to favor an improvement of relations with Peking. This view found expression primarily in the Indonesian Foreign Ministry, which apparently sought to provide additional leverage and balance in Jakarta's relations with the great powers and to improve Indonesia's reputation as a nonaligned state. U.S. retrenchment in Asia and the sharp rise in China's prestige and international position provided a stimulus for this view.

In 1969, Foreign Minister Malik said that Indonesia would welcome restoration of relations provided the PRC stopped its subversive activities in Indonesia and its anti-Indonesian propaganda.[163] Throughout 1970 Malik repeated this position. And in April 1971, following the first signs (on the ping pong table) of Sino-U.S. rapprochement, Malik said that Indonesia also was taking certain unspecified initiatives to normalize relations with China. Earlier, the foreign minister had called for direct trade with China, stating that Indonesia indirectly imported more than $40 million worth of Chinese goods and that China could purchase up to 100,000 tons of Indonesian rubber annually.[164]

In Hong Kong, Malik said that while Indonesian trade with Taiwan had increased, the Government of Indonesia had never officially recognized Taiwan, and thus this issue would pose no problem in Peking-Jakarta relations.[165] Later, Malik said that his country rejected the concept of two Chinas and recognized only the PRC.[166] During May and June, Malik toured several East European countries including Rumania and Yugoslavia, where he may have discussed the prospects of improved PRC-Indonesian relations and probed for Peking's own intentions. In October, Malik, sitting as president of the UN General Assembly, ruled against an effort by the U.S. delegation to vote separately on the two sections of the Albanian resolution to seat China, thereby stymying a last-ditch U.S. effort to prevent the expulsion of Taiwan. When the Chinese vice foreign minister, Chiao Kuan-hua, arrived in New York in November, his first call at the UN was on Adam Malik.

Despite these signs of interest in normalization of relations with China, there was still strong opposition to any such move among the military and Moslem leaders of Indonesia. In addition to the ideological differences, there were persistent fears of China's political intentions and of the effect of diplomatic ties on the local Chinese.

The Indonesian generals largely accepted the dubious theory that China had played a leading role in the 1965 coup attempt. In any event, China's close relations with President Sukarno and the PKI and its support of the Fifth Force left the anticommunist military leaders with no love for the People's Republic. The strong anti-Chinese feelings among the Moslem leaders and the latter's desire to seize control of commerce from the overseas Chinese was another important reason for moving slowly.

In addition, the Indonesians still looked upon themselves as the major power in Southeast Asia, and the generals, unlike Sukarno, viewed China as their principal rival. They were not, therefore, anxious to hasten China's diplomatic reemergence into the Southeast Asia area. Finally, given Indonesia's size and its fairly safe distance from China, the Jakarta leaders felt less compulsion than the Malaysians or even the Filipinos to arrive at some modus vivendi with China.

After China's victory in the UN (Indonesia abstained on the Albanian resolution to seat the PRC and expel the Chinese Nationalists) and as Sino-U.S. détente loomed on the horizon, the Indonesian leaders, afraid that events were getting out of hand, tried to dampen the China mood in Asia. Jakarta refused to authorize Indonesian participation in a Peking-sponsored Afro-Asian table tennis tournament held in November 1971, and at the Association of Southeast Asian Nations (ASEAN) meeting that year in Kuala Lumpur, Indonesia was one of the conservative forces that attempted to water down the neutralization declaration approved at the session.

Consequently, by the end of 1972, it was uncertain whether Indonesia would participate in, much less lead the way toward, a new Bandung. But the Indonesians still aspired to a nonaligned image, and they did not wish to be left too far behind the Malaysians and others who were busily promoting the concept of neutralization and pursuing the path of accommodation with China.*

Meanwhile, for an important element of the old axis, the PKI, it was time for a long march.

NOTES

1. NCNA, October 4, 1965; U.S. Consulate General, Hong Kong, Survey of the Chinese Mainland Press (SCMP), October 1965, no. 3554.

2. New York Times, October 8, 1965.

3. Ruth T. McVey, The Rise of the Indonesian Communist Party (Ithaca, N.Y.: Cornell University Press, 1965); Donald Hindley, The Communist Party of Indonesia 1951-63 (Berkeley and Los Angeles: University of California Press, 1964); Justus M. van der Kroef, The Communist Party of Indonesia (Vancouver: University of British Columbia Press, 1965); J. H. Brimmel, Communism in Southeast Asia (London: Oxford University Press, 1959).

4. Ibid., p. 145.

5. Ruth McVey, "The Southeast Asian Insurrectionary Movements," in Cyril E. Black, ed., Communism and Revolution (Princeton, N.J.: Princeton University Press, 1964), p. 179.

6. Hindley, op. cit.

7. John Hughes, Indonesian Upheaval (New York: David McKay, 1967), p. 83.

8. Sukarno's August 17, 1965 speech, Antara, August 17, 1965.

----

*President Suharto in his August 1972 speech on the 27th anniversary of Indonesian independence recalled the intimate Sino-Indonesian friendship of 1965 but charged that Peking had supported the PKI in launching the coup. This experience, he said, would be a bitter lesson, but this did not mean Indonesia did not want to establish friendly relations with countries having the same ideological concepts as the PKI. A thaw in Sino-Indonesian relations, he said, depended on their "attitude towards us." A nonhostile attitude and noninterference in Indonesia's internal affairs were conditions for friendly relations, Suharto said. (Hong Kong Standard, August 17, 1972.)

9. Herbert Feith, "Sukarno, the Army and the Communist Party," Asian Survey, August 1964, p. 978.

10. Sukarno's National Day speech, Antara, August 17, 1964.

11. The director of the Special Affairs Bureau, Ahmad Kamarazaman, alias Sjam, described the bureau in the course of his trial. Radio Jakarta, February 19-24, 1968.

12. SCMP, May 1965, no. 3465.

13. Donald Hindley, "The Indonesian Communist Party and the Conflict in the International Communist Movement," China Quarterly, July-September 1964, p. 114.

14. Dare, Dare and Dare Again! (Peking: Foreign Languages Press, 1963).

15. D. N. Aidit, The Indonesian Revolution and the Immediate Tasks of the Communist Party in Indonesia (Peking: Foreign Languages Press, 1964).

16. Hindley, "Indonesian Communist Party," op. cit., p. 109.

17. D. N. Aidit, Set Afire the Bandung Spirit! Ever Forward No Retreat! (Peking: Foreign Languages Press, 1964).

18. Red Flag, May 20, 1965.

19. The PKI was recognized as having "ever increasing attraction for the Communist world and revolutionary people of the capitalist world, particularly of the Asian, African and Latin American countries. Its great success and rich experience . . . are of great international significance for the International Communist movement." Speech by Kang Sheng, NCNA, September 2, 1963, quoted by David P. Mozingo, "Sino-Indonesian Relations, An Overview 1955-65," Santa Monica, Cal., RAND Corporation, RM 4641-PR, July 1965.

20. SCMP, May 1963, no. 3470.

21. Ibid., May 1965, no. 3465.

22. Van der Kroef, op. cit., p. 287; Aidit, Set Afire, op. cit.

23. Ibid., pp. 288, 292-298.

24. In this section I have drawn heavily on the excellent study of "Guided Democracy, Foreign Policy, 1960-65," by Frederick P. Bunnell in Indonesia, vol. 2, Modern Indonesia Project (Ithaca, N.Y.: Cornell University Press, October 1966), pp. 37-76.

25. Ibid., p. 67.

26. Ibid., pp. 50-54.

27. Bunnell, op. cit., p. 60.

28. Feith, op. cit., p. 970.

29. Arnold C. Brackman, "The Malay World and China," in A. M. Halpern, ed., Policies Toward China (New York: McGraw-Hill, 1966), p. 266.

30. See Bunnell, op. cit., for a balanced discussion of the issues involved.

31. Mozingo, op. cit., p. 60, suggests that Sukarno had informed the Chinese that his purpose was to draw both the Philippines and Malaysia away from the West. In either case, the Chinese may have warned Sukarno that the conciliatory approach would not work.

32. Parker, op. cit., p. 693.

33. Mozingo, op. cit., pp. 66-67. It should also be noted that the PRC turned over the Bank of China branch in Burma when the Burmese Government nationalized all banks.

34. Harold C. Hinton, Communist China in World Politics (Boston: Houghton Mifflin, 1966), p. 440.

35. Joint communiqué, Antara, October 6, 1964. On October 5, General Nasution stressed the cooperation of the Soviet Union and indicated that its material assistance would be stepped up.

36. Hinton, op. cit., p. 440.

37. Arnold Beichman, New York Herald-Tribune, February 7, 1965, reported a secret briefing on this subject by Subandrio to Indonesian diplomats assembled in New York on December 9. According to this version Indonesia was to have all the island territories while Malaya would be in China's sphere.

38. Mozingo, op. cit., p. 70; NCNA, December 3, 1964.

39. New York Times, January 8, 1965.

40. Ibid.

41. People's Daily, January 23, 1965; SCMP no. 3387.

42. SCMP, no. 3389, January 1965.

43. Ibid., no. 3390.

44. Ibid.

45. NCNA, January 28, 1965.

46. Arnold C. Brackman, Southeast Asia's Second Front: The Power Struggle in the Malay Archipelago (New York: Praeger Publishers, 1966), p. 255.

47. This dream was expounded by Sukarno at a meeting of the Investigating Committee for Preparation of Indonesia's Independence set up by the Japanese occupation near the end of the war. At that time Sukarno declared:

"I myself am convinced that the people of Malaya feel themselves as Indonesians, belonging to Indonesia and as one of us. Even if we do not take this reason into account, despite the danger of my being accused as an imperialist, Indonesia will not become strong and secure unless the whole Straits of Malacca is in our hands" (Investigating Committee for Preparation of Indonesia's Independence meeting of July 11, 1945, issued in English by the Federal Department of Information, Kuala Lumpur, 1964).

On July 10, 1964 Sukarno said that Indonesia was ready to join a Federation of "free" Malaya, Singapore, Sabah, Brunei, and Sarawak.

Indonesia's desire for expanded influence was not limited to Sukarno. Lieutenant General Yani, one of the victims of the September 30, 1965 coup, on August 4 told a senior seminar of naval officers that "our defense conception must cover all of Southeast Asia." He said that Indonesian kingdoms had exercised hegemony over Southeast Asia for centuries through control of the seas. And "the Indonesian people will not ignore the demands of history and it has been my conclusion since 1963 that at some time the Indonesian navy will take over the role of the U.S. Seventh Fleet and the British Far East Fleet in Southeast Asia." General Nasution also told the same seminar that the strategic goal of the armed forces must be to knock out the British bases at Singapore and break out of the containment represented by the British-protected Federation of Malaysia. (New York Times, August 25, 1965.)

48. People's Daily, January 10, 1965.

49. New York Times, February 12, 1965.

50. SCMP (NCNA, January 24), no. 3387, January 1965.

51. Antara, April 22, 1965.

52. Ibid., April 27, 1965.

53. Ibid., April 30, 1965.

54. Quoted by China News Analysis, no. 574, July 30, 1965.

55. Antara, August 17, 1965.

56. Ibid., September 1, 1965.

57. SCMP (NCNA), no. 3541, September 14, 1965.

58. Antara, June 24, 1965.

59. Times (London), June 23, quoted in China Quarterly, no. 23, July-September 1965, p. 218.

60. NCNA, September 12, 1965.

61. See Klaus H. Pringsheim, "China's Role in the Indo-Pak Conflict," China Quarterly, no. 24, October-December 1965, p. 170.

62. Indonesian Herald, "The Second Afro-Asian Conference," September 17, 1965, referred to in William E. Griffith, Sino-Soviet Relations 1964-65, (Cambridge, Mass.: The MIT Press, 1967), p. 128.

63. Griffith, op. cit., p. 128.

64. Antara, October 22, 1964.

65. New York Times, November 16, 1964. The head of the Indonesian Army Information Service said only that "the possibility could not be excluded" (Antara, November 20, 1964). A few days after the Chinese test, Indonesia announced that it had achieved its first chain reaction (with the help of U.S. scientists and a U.S. research reactor). New York Times, October 21, 1964; Antara, October 21, 1964.

66. New York Times, January 8, 1965 (article referred to previously, which quotes diplomatic sources in Washington).

67. Business Week, February 6, 1965; New York Times, February 2, 1965.

68. SCMP (NCNA), no. 3390, January 28, 1965.

69. Ibid.

70. Antara, July 24, 1965. On July 25, Sukarno told an Indonesian National Party (PNI) rally that independence had to be won with "the use of rifles, guns or even nuclear weapons." Indonesian Herald, July 25, 1965.

71. Antara, July 26, 1965.

72. New York Times, July 29, 1965.

73. Indonesian Herald, August 10, 1965.

74. Antara, August 17, 1965.

75. Seymour Topping in New York Times, August 25, 1965.

76. Ibid., August 24, 1965.

77. Ibid., August 25, 1965. The United States apparently was not concerned that Indonesia itself was making a weapon, for in September it extended the Atoms for Peace Pact with Jakarta for five more years. New York Times, September 9, 1965.

78. This quote is the NCNA version of Chen's remarks released a few days after the press conference. According to the Akahata account of the conference, Chen merely said that China had not been asked for nuclear aid.

79. See for example report in Indonesian Herald, July 12, 1965 on "British plan" to bomb Indonesia.

80. New York Times, December 18, 1964.

81. Ibid., April 1, 1965.

82. Ibid., February 19, 1965.

83. SCMP, no. 3447, April 1965.

84. D. N. Aidit, "Perhebat Ofensif Revolusioner Disegala Bidang," cited by Victor Fic, "September 30th Movement in Indonesia: 1965 Gamble That Failed," paper given at International Conference on Asian History, August 1968, University of Malaya.

85. Denis Warner, "The Peking-Jakarta Axis," The Reporter 35, no. 5 (September 23, 1965), p. 25

86. SCMP (NCNA), no. 3465, May 22, 1965.

87. Ibid., (NCNA), no. 3468, May 26, 1965.

88. New York Times, July 23, 1965.

89. Antara, August 17, 1965.

90. Ibid., May 14, 1965.

91. Ibid., August 17, 1965.

92. Arthur J. Dommen, recalls that Hatta's program for disbanding regular partisan units controlled by the communists was one of the causes of the 1948 Madiun rebellion. "Attempted Coup In Indonesia" China Quarterly (January-March, 1966).

93. Herbert Feith, "Dynamics of Guided Democracy," in Indonesia, Ruth McVey, ed. (New Haven, Conn.: HRAF Press, 1963), p.
337.

94. Warner, op. cit., p. 25.

95. SCMP (NCNA), no. 3468, May 25, 1965.

96. SCMP (NCNA), no. 3516, August 8, 1965.

97. Indonesian Herald, August 11, 1965.

98. Antara, August 17, 1965,

99. Nugroho Notosusanto and Ismail Seleh "The Coup Attempt
of the September 30 Movement in Indonesia" (Kuala Lumpur: Khee
Meng Press, distributed by Indonesian Embassy).

100. Sudisman's interrogation (December 7, 1966), Njono's
preliminary investigations (January 3, 9-12, 1966), and Sakirman's
interrogation (October 4, 1966), all cited in ibid. In contrast to some
other testimony and confessions, Sudisman's is most convincing in
that he maintained a defiant attitude throughout the trial, denouncing
the Suharto government as a "lackey of imperialism" and warning
that the PKI would rise again. Njono's trial testimony is also convincing, as he repudiated much of an earlier alleged confession. As
noted, Sudisman's statements were accepted by the communist journal
Tricontinental (Havana).

101. Tricontinental (Havana) July-August 1968.

102. Sukarno appeared to dramatize his ill health during August
and September. For example, in the middle of a speech in late September, Sukarno suddenly excused himself as not feeling well and
temporarily left the platform to recover, an action that set all Jakarta
abuzz. One might speculate that he was possibly feigning his ill health
as another device to hold back the generals from any precipitate move.
Sukarno could reasonably have deduced that if the generals were indeed planning an anti-PKI coup, they would prefer to wait until after
his death, if convinced that such was in fact imminent, and thus assume
the mantle of his legitimacy.

Victor M. Fic indicates that the medical records introduced
in the later military trials did not support a gloomy prognosis. Fic
offers the conjecture that the Chinese doctors had really "doctored"
their assessment in order to encourage or justify Aidit's proposals
to the Politburo for a preemptive strike. Fic, op. cit., p. 148.

103. An article by the delegation of the PKI Central Committee
resident in Peking in July 1968 denounced the Aidit leadership for
thus having relied on "enemy troops" (that is, units led by "progressive officers" but not actually military units of the communist party):

"The revisionists [that is, Aidit] dreamed of the coming of a
nationwide revolutionary crisis and of achieving victory in the whole
country simultaneously and easily through the method of combining
'peasant's struggle in the countryside,' 'workers' struggle in the

cities,' with 'work within the armed forces of the enemy.' . . . the 'theory of the method of combining the three forms of struggle' also spread the illusion of relying on enemy troops. This actually denied the necessity of building up a people's army under the absolute leadership of the Indonesian Communist Party." (NCNA English, July 19, 1968.)

104. According to the Jakarta account of the trial, Sudisman said the meeting of August 28 "discussed a plan for a military operation by progressive officers to frustrate any action by the so-called 'council of generals.' " After the meeting Sudisman said he gave instructions for the creation of the special reserve force. (Jakarta Domestic Service in Indonesia July 6, 1967.) Sudisman also described Aidit's instructions on the necessary preparations (see Sudisman's Interrogation December 7, 1966, in Notosusanto and Saleh, op. cit., pp. 2-3).

105. Tricontinental, op. cit., pp. 10, 13.

106. Ibid., p. 19.

107. Notosusanto and Saleh, op. cit., p. 81, testimony of Pardede, third session, February 15, 1966.

108. Tricontinental, op. cit., pp. 9, 18.

109. For the most detailed exposition of the planning and execution of the coup, see Fic, op. cit., who argues that the coup was almost entirely a PKI-conceived operation carried out without Sukarno's foreknowledge. Also see Guy J. Pauker, "The Rise and Fall of the Communist Party of Indonesia," RAND Corporation, memorandum RM-5753-PR, February 1969, Santa Monica, Cal.

110. See Dommen, op. cit., for the text of this confession as it appeared in Asahi Evening News.

111. John Hughes, The End of Sukarno: A Coup That Misfired (London: Angus and Robertson, 1968).

112. For text, see Indonesia, vol. 1, Modern Indonesia Project (Ithaca, N.Y.: Cornell University Press, April 1966), p. 184.

113. It was not until October 5 that the PKI central committee issued a statement denying involvement and claiming that the names included on the revolutionary council were done so without authorization (ibid., p. 188). The PKI had always been anxious about a second "Madiun provocation," and it is interesting to compare the party's reaction to a similar event of August 1951 with its reaction to the September 30 movement. On August 6, 1951, an armed attack was reported on a police station by forces wearing a hammer and sickle symbol. The PKI at once denied any connection and declared it could not be dragged into the affair. (Hindley, Communist Party of Indonesia, op. cit., p. 53.) The point is that the PKI's great fear of provoking a "white terror" would have precluded its ex-post-facto support for such a coup or its acquiesence in the use of the names of PKI officials if in fact it was not involved.

114. Indonesia, vol. 1, op. cit., p. 185.
115. "Self-criticism of the Central Committee of the PKI,"
September 1966, quoted by Radio Tirana in English, May 1967 from
an article in the Indonesian Tribune published in Albania by the exiled
PKI Central Committee. It has also been declared that "The 'left'
opportunism which found expression in the putsch of the 30th of Sept.
movement, was the continuation of right opportunism carried out
before. After the defeat of the 30th of Sept. movement the Party made
another deviation by completely capitulating to the bourgeoisie."
Indonesian Tribune 1, 8-9 (June-July 1967): 27.
    This "self-criticism" was apparently written by Sudisman before
his capture and was circulated clandestinely in Java.
116. The though is that of Ruth McVey.
117. H. R. Trevor-Roper, "Understanding Mao, or Look Back
to Stalin," New York Times, September 7, 1965.
118. Feith, op. cit.
119. Red Flag, 11th issue, July 7, 1967. One cannot resist the
analogy of the Hitler-Mussolini relationship.
120. NCNA, English, June 27, 1970.
121. Mozingo, op. cit., p. 63.
122. Radio Moscow, March 16, 1967.
123. The first mention of the "Marxist/Leninist group of the
PKI" appeared in the pro-Soviet Indian weekly Mainstream, March
11 and 18, 1967.
124. Agence France Presse, Paris, December 11, 1967.
125. A. B. Reznikov, in Narody Azii Afriki, no. 1, 1968.
126. Radio Peking in Russian, October 24, 1967.
127. Radio Tirana, May 8, 1967 quoting Indonesian Tribune
Review.
128. "People of Indonesia Unite! Fight to Overthrow the Fascist
Regime," Red Flag, no. 11, July 1967. Yusuf Adjitorop in an article
in People's Daily, February 21, 1968, charged that "The united front
policy followed by the PKI leadership in the more than a decade before
1965 especially the policy of forming a united front with Sukarno was
in essence a policy of class collaboration." NCNA, February 21,
1968.
129. Trotsky's attacks against the Stalin line in China were
remarkably similar to Peking's indictment of Aidit. See Leon Trotsky's
Problems of the Chinese Revolution (Ann Arbor: University of Michigan Press, 1967).
130. Peking Domestic Radio, July 13, 1967, article by member
of "Revolutionary Rebel Liaison Center," op. cit. In December 1968,
People's Daily again resurrected the case of Liu's visit to Indonesia
when it charged that he "committed high treason." (NCNA, English,
December 13, 1968.) The same subject was treated in Peking Domestic
broadcasts of December 6 and 13, 1968.

131. New York Times, October 17, 22, 23, 24, 28, 1965.

132. Ibid., November 21, 1965.

133. Ibid., December 12, 1965.

134. Ibid,, November 21, 1965.

135. For relations after the coup, see Justus M. van der Kroef, "The Sino-Indonesian Rupture," China Quarterly, no. 33 (January-March 1968), pp. 17-46; and Sheldon W. Simon, The Broken Triangle (Baltimore: John Hopkins Press, 1969).

136. NCNA (English), April 26, 1967.

137. Ibid., August 8, 1967.

138. Ibid., April 13, 1967.

139. Statement of the Central Committee of the PKI, NCNA (English), May 23, 1967.

140. Red Flag, no. 11, July 1967.

141. NCNA (English), December 23, 1967.

142. People's Daily, NCNA (English), February 21, 1968.

143. May 24 Statement by PKI Central Committee, NCNA, May 25, 1968.

144. Radio Peking in Indonesian, GMT 0500, June 28, 1968.

145. New York Times, July 12, October 29, 1968.

146. Jakarta Domestic Service, September 16, 1968.

147. Tirana ATA (English), October 18, 1968.

148. See article by Arnold Brackman, in Straits Times, December 12, 1969.

149. Moscow Radio in Indonesia, July 9, 1971.

150. NCNA (English), December 1, 1968.

151. Ibid.

152. Ibid., June 4, 1969.

153. Ibid.

154. People's Daily, August 8, 1969.

155. Ibid., September 1, 1969.

156. PKI Central Committee Statement, NCNA (English), May 8, 1970.

157. Ibid., May 28, 1970.

158. Ibid., May 23, 1970.

159. People's Daily, May 2, 1970.

160. NCNA (English), January 17, 1971. The Cambodian foreign minister, Koun Wick, visited Indonesia January 12-17, 1971.

161. NCNA, May 9, 1971.

162. PKI Central Committee letter, June 30, 1971; NCNA July 2, 1971.

163. Malik's interview with Kyodo News Agency, Jakarta Domestic Service, November 27, 1969.

164. Hong Kong Standard, April 17, 1971.

165. Ibid., April 24, 1971.

166. South China Morning Post, September 13, 1971.

3

THE WAR IN CAMBODIA—BACKGROUND

During the summer of 1967, Prince Norodom Sihanouk was increasingly agitated by the Cultural Revolution-type activities of the Chinese Community and Chinese officials in Cambodia. At the same time, a communist insurgency, led by the Khmer Rouge, was growing in Battambang province. To make matters worse, Peking media, now in the hands of the radical faction, began to call for revolutionaries everywhere—presumably including Cambodia—to follow the path of Mao Tse-tung.

The prince restricted the wearing of Mao badges and the distribution of Mao's published "Thought." He dissolved the Sino-Cambodian Friendship Association, along with all other similar associations, and closed down all nongovernment newspapers, including five Chinese-language pro-Peking journals. On September 11, 1967, he publicly denounced China's interference in Cambodian affairs and sacked two pro-Peking members of his cabinet—Minister of the Economy Chau Seng[1] and Minister of Health So Nem.

In addition, three prominent leftist members of the National Assembly, Hou Yuon, Khieu Samphan, and Hou Nim, under threat of arrest, fled the capital. Three years later these men were to take leading positions in Sihanouk's exile government, headquartered in Peking.

Shortly after chastising the Chinese, the prince was infuriated when he interpreted a message to the defunct Chinese-Cambodian Friendship Association from the Peking Chapter of the same organization as a challenge to his authority to disband the Phnom Penh branch. Finally, Sihanouk threatened to withdraw the Cambodian Embassy staff from Peking out of fear that it would be abused as had other foreign missions in the Chinese capital.

With the radicals at least physically out of the Foreign Ministry in Peking, Chou En-lai moved to mollify the prince. He called in the Cambodian Ambassador on September 14 and, according to Sihanouk's public account, pledged that China had no intention of intervening in Cambodian internal affairs. Chou said the incident that had disturbed Sihanouk was an isolated case and that China had not published the prince's speech "lest publication . . . bring about consequences favorable to our common enemy." Finally Chou asked the prince to reconsider withdrawal of the embassy.[2] Sihanouk replied,

> What matters to such old friends as Chou En-lai and Chen
> Yi is their own skins first and I think that there is neither
> time nor the possibility for them to save Sihanouk's skin.
> I have respect and sympathy for Chou En-lai and Chen
> Yi and I will continue to do so, no matter what may happen
> to my seniors. However, I understand them, I know that
> my friends are overcome by the Cultural Revolution and
> that they cannot control this revolution.[3]

Sihanouk accepted Chou's offer of reconciliation, although he theorized that the Chinese "did not want to exacerbate the situation because the Cambodian fruit is not yet ripe."[4]

For several years Sihanouk's policies had been based upon the assumption that Cambodia's integrity and independence could best be protected by a close association with Peking, which hopefully would restrain Vietnamese ambitions toward Cambodia. But after the events of 1967, Sihanouk seemed to be less sure of his major premise, and he began to inch back toward a neutral position between the United States and the Peking-backed communists in Indochina.

The communist insurgency in Battambang died down near the end of the year but surged forward with increased vigor in January 1968. By midyear, clashes had occurred in practically all of the provinces of the country, and government control was virtually nonexistent in the North, where large North Vietnamese and Viet Cong units were sheltered. Sihanouk declared that this insurgency was stimulated by China and North Vietnam, both of whom, he said, were dissatisfied with his efforts in December 1968 and January 1969 to insulate Cambodia from the Vietnam War.* Sihanouk said that the

---

*Although politically and logistically giving support to the North Vietnamese in the war, Sihanouk had attempted to avoid actual physical involvement by (1) informally acknowledging the right of U.S. troops to engage North Vietnamese in Cambodia so long as no Cambodians were killed, and (2) obtaining from the United States a formal pledge

communists hoped that he would have to hand power over to someone who would call for U.S. aid and that "when the Americans gave Cambodia arms and money," the communists "would have a pretext for having their Vietnamese and Chinese masters come and invade Cambodia."[5]

The Khmer Rouge was an obscure organization, which, according to Sihanouk, originally consisted of partisan "cells" that were formed by the Vietnamese communists during their partial occupation of Cambodian territory between the years 1949-54 and that were reactivated in 1966. The Khmer Rouge was the fighting arm of the small communist organization in Cambodia, the People's Revolutionary Party, which had operated through an organization called the Pracheachon, which claimed to have been in existence since 1955. By 1969, there were an estimated 3,000 Khmer Rouge operating independently as well as with North Vietnamese and Viet Cong units.[6]

In March 1969 Sihanouk, for the first time, openly admitted that large Vietnamese communist units were encamped on Cambodian soil; he gave their location and indicated that he might not care if U.S. war planes bombed them.[7] Actually, as far back as January 1968, Sihanouk indicated to Ambassador Chester Bowles that he would not object to U.S. bombing of the sanctuaries so long as it was kept secret. (When the secret finally came out in 1973, Sihanouk naturally denied that he had given approval.) Sihanouk in early 1969 also admitted that many areas, including all of Rattanakiri province, were "in the hands

---

to respect Cambodian territorial neutrality. In this way, Sihanouk hoped to discourage both North Vietnamese and American violation of Cambodian borders. But Sihanouk has disclosed that China "was not happy" about this development, and shortly after the U.S.-Cambodian agreement, the Cambodian communists unleashed their campaign of violence.

Sihanouk charged that "the Maoist camp" had threatened Cambodia but that "when verbal threats failed, they decided to foment war in our country. . . . They said, if you do not break right away with the Americans, if you do not return to your former policy—that is, pro-Chinese and pro-Viet Minh sattelizers [sic], . . . you will have war." (Phnom Penh Domestic Service in Cambodia, 1000 GMT, Jan. 27, 1968.)

The evidence cited by Sihanouk included the capture of a junk ("a Viet Cong launch") loaded with "Chinese-made weapons," including mortars and rockets, which was allegedly intercepted as it attempted to resupply "Khmer Reds" in Cambodia. Five other junks reportedly escaped. (See Sihanouk's speeches of March 6 and 7, 1968, carried by Phnom Penh Domestic Radio Service.)

of the Vietnamese."[8] In June it was reported that Rattanakiri and Stung Treng provinces were both militarily and administratively controlled by the North Vietnamese.[9] (One year later Sihanouk would claim these provinces as part of his own "liberated area.") Later in 1969 the new prime minister and concurrent defense minister, General Lon Nol, reported that 35,000 to 40,000 "foreign troops" were stationed on Cambodian territory.[10] Sihanouk also began to talk of resuming relations with the United States, a move that he said would "combat Communist maneuvers against the country."[11]

In March 1969 U.S. B-52 bombers for the first time raided several Viet Cong and North Vietnamese base camps in Cambodia. There was no protest from Phnom Penh, and several thousand sorties were flown during the next year. Moreover, authorities in Cambodia were said to be increasingly cooperative with U.S. and South Vietnamese military men at the border, often giving them information on Viet Cong and North Vietnamese movements. Several encounters also took place between Cambodian troops and Vietnamese communist forces.

At the same time, however, Vietnamese communist units continued to receive an increasing amount of supplies and equipment through the port of Sihanoukville with the approval and facilitation of the Cambodian authorities. On September 25, 1969, Sihanouk reportedly concluded a trade and payments agreement with the DRV and the National Liberation Front (NLF) covering supplies forwarded through Cambodia.[12] Moreover, he continued to release communist Vietnamese troops captured by the Cambodian Army.

Thus, Sihanouk maintained his balancing act; politically and logistically supporting the Vietnamese communists but attempting to keep down their presence in Cambodia and their ability to aid the Khmer Rouge by allowing the United States freedom to bomb the communist sanctuaries. He was also banking on playing off the Chinese and the Americans; but perhaps most important, he still hoped that Peking would have some interest in discouraging Vietnamese hegemony in Indochina.

After the strains of 1967, Chou En-lai and his harassed foreign minister, Chen Yi, had moved to restore a friendly relationship with Cambodia. Early in 1968, according to Sihanouk, Chen told the Cambodian Ambassador that the PRC was considering additional economic aid for Cambodia. Chen also assured the ambassador that China "knew only the Cambodian legal government under the sole leadership of Prince Sihanouk and that China did not want and will never want to intervene in the internal affairs of Cambodia."[13]

Very likely the primary Chinese interest in Cambodia at this point was to see that the country continued to act as a safe supply point and sanctuary for the Vietnamese communists, a service that

Cambodia was performing on an increasing scale. Although Peking was presumably irritated at the prince's occasional barbed remarks about China's hegemonic ambitions, it was probably basically satisfied with the existing state of affairs in Cambodia. Sihanouk's government was avowedly neutralist, but it supported the communist line in Indochina, and while it continued to build what balance it could into its foreign relations, it still gave most weight to its relations with China.

Nevertheless, Sihanouk still expressed skepticism about the long-term intentions of Peking. In November 1969 he wrote:

> The People's Republic of China presently conducts itself in a very correct manner towards us . . . [but] whatever may be its respect and friendship for Cambodia of the Sangkum,* Communist and Maoist China will be unable to renounce its "sacred mission" which is to stand by the so-called movements "of liberation of oppressed peoples by bourgeois and reactionary governments and regimes"—and to support, more or less discreetly, these movements.
>
> Whatever may be the popularity of the Sangkum in Cambodia, this great patriotic movement and I will always be classified amongst the leaders and regimes as "reactionary enemies of the people" which must be crushed.
>
> With respect to this, the new China, just like socialist Vietnam or the other Communist powers, neither could nor would help us in any way to resolve the problem of the "Red Khmer" rebellion, nor especially that of the infiltration and occupation by the Viet Cong and the Viet Minh of our territory. It is in effect, as all know, the aim of the Communists to assist by all possible means the communisation of countries not yet "brothers" in ideology, if they be officially called "friends."
>
> When the Communist powers and movements become indignant over the aggressions committed against us by the United States, when they condemn this "imperialist" power and categorically take our side, they do not have as an end to assist Cambodia to survive, they but work to win the sympathy of the Khmers in order to communize them more easily.
>
> . . . Under these conditions, the Sangkumian Cambodia . . . knows in advance that it will not be able to count on

---

*Sangkumian Cambodia refers to Sihanouk's conception of the country as neutral, independent, and Buddhist-socialist.

the "friendly" Communist countries in case of difficulties with its socialist neighbors and with their "Red Khmer" valets.

All of this comes back to the fact that however well seen and anti-imperialist it may be, the Sangkumian Cambodia will see its lot depend upon the position which will occupy in our region, after the Vietnam War, the US on the one hand, and, in a parallel manner, the position of the Soviets, and on the evolution of relations of the USSR with the People's Republic of China.[14]

It is possible that the radicals in Peking who still were in control of relations with foreign communist movements, supported the Khmer Rouge insurgency beginning in 1967. It is unlikely, however, that Chou En-lai and the pragmatic faction, or many military leaders for that matter, would have seen any advantage in such a course. Given the close historical and political relationship between the communists of Cambodia and those of North Vietnam, a victory for the Khmer Rouge might, at least for the short run, actually have reduced China's influence in the country. Chou was clearly prejudiced in favor of retaining the status quo in Cambodia, whether under Sihanouk or someone else.

Events, however, were out of Peking's control. The number of North Vietnamese and Viet Cong troops in Cambodian base camps increased as did DRV support for the Khmer Rouge and the Cambodian montagnard (Khmer Loeu) dissidents in Rattanakiri and Stung Treng provinces. One Hanoi objective in expanding its support for these insurgents was apparently to assure its administrative control of the critical base areas in Cambodia. But probably more important, it was preparing an alternative to the existing arrangements with Sihanouk in case they broke down, arrangements that were already being stretched to the breaking point.

In January 1970, after a setback in his criticism of the Lon Nol government in the National Assembly on domestic issues, Sihanouk departed for France, leaving Cheng Heng as acting chief of state. In early March, anti-Vietnamese demonstrations broke out in Phnom Penh, reportedly sanctioned by the authorities, and the Viet Cong and DRV embassies were sacked. On March 6, negotiations between the Lon Nol government and the Vietnamese communists began on the subject of the Viet Cong and DRV presence in Cambodia. As expected, no concessions were made by the Vietnamese communists.

On March 13, Sihanouk left Paris for Moscow and Peking, avowedly to seek their assistance in persuading the communist forces to leave Cambodia. Shortly before his departure from the French capital, Sihanouk published an article in the Paris monthly, Preuves, in which he said "all Asia remains persuaded of the domino theory," and if the United States retired completely from Southeast Asia, the balance of power would break down. In this eventuality, Sihanouk said, "we would be obliged, despite ourselves, to become satellites of China. That is, if the Vietnamese Communists permit it, because it seems that they consider Cambodia, just like Laos, their own game preserve."15

Despite this anticommunist and nationalist attitude, Sihanouk had created a widening gulf between himself and the other Cambodian elite. Sihanouk still believed that it was necessary not to push Cambodia's protest with the Vietnamese communists to the breaking point. His colleagues, however, felt that the DRV and Viet Cong occupation of extensive areas of Cambodia, their support of local insurgents, and their effective denial of administrative control in two provinces to the Phnom Penh government had become intolerable. In addition, there was increasing dissatisfaction among the elite and intellectual groups with economic stagnation and Sihanouk's high-handed personal rule.

On March 18, the Cambodian National Assembly, by unanimous vote, declared Sihanouk was no longer chief of state. Cheng Heng remained acting chief of state and Lon Nol continued as prime minister. Sihanouk apparently learned of his ouster on the way to the airport in Moscow en route to Peking.

CHINA'S REACTION

In the Chinese capital, Sihanouk was met by Chou En-lai, who, according to the prince's later account, "did not have any hesitation or delay . . . [but gave me] formal assurance of complete support in all fields . . . multifarious aid, militant solidarity, and de facto recognition."16

Chinese statements continued to refer to Sihanouk as head of state, and NCNA reported that he and Chou had held "sincere and friendly" talks. NCNA immediately began to publish Sihanouk's messages, including the March 23 announcement of his intention to form a Royal Government of National Union in exile, a liberation army, and a National United Front of Kampuchea (Cambodia; NUFK). However, Peking itself made no comment on the affair. High-level Chinese officials missed several opportunities in public speeches to refer to Cambodian events and no People's Daily editorial appeared. On March 24, Peking papers published an extensive article on the events in Cambodia based on selected foreign news agency and newspaper reports, but there was no direct Chinese comment.

In contrast, Hanoi, on March 21, directly condemned the ousting of Sihanouk as "part of the U.S. plan to invade the Indo-chinese countries . . . turn Cambodia into a U.S. neocolony and military base . . . and to oppose the Vietnamese People's resistance. . . ."[17]

The DRV officially pledged its support to Sihanouk and the NUFK on March 25, but it was not until April 7 that Chou En-lai endorsed Sihanouk's proclamation.[18] According to the Cambodian Ambassador to Peking at the time, Nay Valentin, Sihanouk was at first undecided whether to return to Paris or to stay in Peking and lend his name to a revolutionary movement that was bound to be dominated by Vietnamese and Cambodian communists. DRV Premier Pham Van Dong flew to Peking to persuade Sihanouk to accept the latter course. Supported by Sihanouk's wife, Monique, Pham Van Dong apparently won the prince over by solemnly assuring him "that when the peoples of the three Indochinese countries defeat their common enemies—the imperialists and their leaders—Vietnam will fully and continually respect Cambodia's independence, sovereignty, and territorial integrity within the present frontiers, and regime."[19]

Sihanouk, we may surmise, decided to throw in with the communists for two reasons. First, always a great egotist, he must have felt himself to be the indispensable man for the task of preserving Cambodia's future integrity. Second, he had previously calculated that the communists, backed by Hanoi, would eventually triumph in South Vietnam and in Laos. He had hoped that his policies of benign neutrality in favor of the communist Vietnamese, his pursuit of Chinese favor, and some patching up with the United States would provide continuing freedom of action for Cambodia. But without himself at the helm, he probably believed, the Cambodian communists, again directly backed by Hanoi, would also eventually win in Cambodia. Therefore, he concluded that the best hope for his country was for himself to accept leadership of the movement against Lon Nol, nominal though it might be, and to strengthen the movement's ties to China.

But, as mentioned, compared to Hanoi, China was slow in throwing its support to Sihanouk. This restraint may have been a subtle attempt not to appear to be promoting Sihanouk's actions, but, according to Lon Nol, Peking

> waited a long time to let its representatives see me and ask if our government would continue aiding North Vietnam as it had done in the past. China said it would consider Sihanouk's ousting an internal affair of Cambodia, forget about Sihanouk, and continue to respect our authority provided: we continued to permit the supply of arms and medicine from China to North Vietnamese and Viet Cong troops—as we had done in the past—so they could continue the war against South Vietnam; we continued to allow North Vietnamese and Viet Cong troops to rest in Khmer territory; and we continued to use our propaganda to support our friends.[20]

Lon Nol stated that after trying to contact him several times up to May 5, China decided it would not gain satisfaction, and it simultaneously broke relations with Phnom Penh and granted formal recognition to Sihanouk.

While it is possible that Lon Nol exaggerated the Chinese position in order to embarrass Sihanouk, it seems likely that Peking was initially disturbed that the extension of the conflict into Cambodia would open up all sorts of uncertainties and problems, and that even if these were overcome, it would provide Hanoi with a commanding position in postwar Cambodia. In addition Chou was probably concerned that the widening of the war would trample underfoot the budding Sino-U.S. détente. Therefore, Chou probably did favor an effort to explore the possibilities of retaining the status quo, with or without Sihanouk.

The Chinese hesitation may also have been affected by indications from Washington that it too preferred the status quo in Cambodia. According to one informed Washington reporter, President Nixon sent word secretly to Hanoi through several channels that he would respect its Cambodian sanctuaries if it would make no effort to move out of its base areas in Cambodia and threaten the Phnom Penh government. If the communist forces did move out, Nixon reportedly threatened that he would have to take serious action.[21]

According to the same source, the United States "went to the extraordinary length of subtly, but unmistakably, encouraging Lon Nol to negotiate an agreement with Hanoi" for preservation of the sanctuaries. Washington reportedly ordered a halt to clandestine raids into the sanctuaries by U.S. and Saigon forces and a cessation of the U.S. bombing of the sanctuaries, which had been implicitly approved by Sihanouk a year previously. Statements by high U.S. officials indicated no intention to exploit the situation in Cambodia in order to weaken the communists.

Finally, on April 20, Nixon proceeded with his announcement of the withdrawal of another 150,000 U.S. troops from Vietnam within the next 12 months.

While the United States apparently sought to keep alive the abused neutrality of Cambodia, the Lon Nol government also attempted to preserve a nonalignment posture, presumably hoping to retain the tolerance of Peking. On March 21, Lon Nol appealed to the International Control Commission (ICC) to return to Cambodia, but this effort was rebuffed by the Soviet Union, which clearly did not wish to offend Hanoi. The Cambodian Government informed the United Nations of its appeal to the ICC, but soundings at the UN indicated that there was little hope of getting Security Council action—again because of the obstruction of the USSR.

Attempting to demonstrate impartiality, the Cambodian Government in March protested U.S. and South Vietnamese border violations, announced it had no intention of joining SEATO, and at one point even indicated that it did not intend to return a U.S. munitions ship that had been hijacked to Cambodia a few days before the coup.

But Lon Nol and his colleagues, despite U.S. efforts, insisted on ending the agreements with the Vietnamese communists and trying to force their departure from Cambodia. This question, after all, had been what the ousting of Sihanouk had been all about. Six days before Sihanouk was deposed, the government had canceled the agreement under which arms and supplies were unloaded at Sihanoukville port from Chinese ships and carried to the Vietnamese border. On March 23 Cambodia officially proclaimed the border with Vietnam closed, and on March 25 it announced that Sihanoukville was closed to any ship bearing arms for communist forces.

The same day, the Cambodian Ministry of Foreign Affairs notified the DRV and NLF representatives in Phnom Penh of the Government's desire to resume negotiations (which had been initiated without effect on March 6) on the presence of their forces in Cambodia. The Vietnamese communists rejected the invitation and announced the withdrawal of their embassy staffs.

The first open military moves by the communist Vietnamese within Cambodia began on March 29 and again on April 3. Attacks were launched against Cambodian forces in Svay Rieng province. The slaughter of Vietnamese civilians in Cambodia and continued raids by South Vietnamese forces across the border further aggravated the situation. In addition, the movement of the Vietnamese communist troops could have been planned in expectation of a large-scale allied attack across the frontier. Hanoi's political decisions, however, made it clear that it had rejected any attempt to negotiate a modus vivendi with Phnom Penh, not only because it distrusted its implementation but also because it was prepared, perhaps eager, to risk the short-term security of its sanctuaries in return for bringing Cambodia into the struggle against the United States.

China retained its flexibility somewhat longer than did North Vietnam; but like the United States it was boxed in by the decisions and actions of the Vietnamese and Cambodian contenders. By early April the Chinese had probably decided to support the attempt to over-throw the Lon Nol government and to turn the situation to the best possible advantage. Keeping to proper protocol and to its own record of never having broken diplomatic relations with any country, China waited until Sihanouk's Royal Government of National Union had been formally established on May 5 before it broke its ties with the Lon Nol regime.

THE SOVIET VIEW

The Soviets saw nothing good in the whole Cambodian affair.
They again found themselves with no appreciable leverage in an escalating situation. Sihanouk, they believed, had thrown in completely
with the Chinese, and they were not prepared to encourage him. In
April, a joint editorial in Peking on the occasion of the 100th anniversary of Lenin's birth made a vitriolic personal attack on Brezhnev and
Kosygin.[22] It was apparent that there was to be no compromise in the
Chinese goal of undermining the political position of the Soviet leaders
at home and abroad.

Moscow attempted to solve its dilemma by renewing its pledges
of support for Hanoi, backing the new Cambodian revolutionary movement in principle but not officially, and once again floating the idea of
a conference to end the Indochina war. On April 16, Soviet UN Ambassador Yakob Malik excited heartbeats in Washington when he expressed interest in convening such a conference. However, three days
later, Le Duan, Hanoi's Lao Dong party chief, arrived in Moscow for
the Lenin centenary, and the Soviets shortly thereafter shot down their
own trial balloon.

We may guess that in addition to raising the conference proposal,
the Soviets may also have urged Le Duan to explore the avowed American willingness to see the status quo on the sanctuaries continue under
Lon Nol. On the latter issue, Moscow and Peking were thus possibly
in agreement. But again this was clearly Hanoi's decision, and, in
any event, it was too late for this course even if Le Duan had been
convinced. The day before he arrived in Moscow, North Vietnamese
forces captured Saang, 18 miles from Phnom Penh. Preparations
were also probably already well under way to hold the April 24-25
summit conference of the three Indochinese peoples, which would
symbolize the unity of the revolutionary movements in Indochina.

A UNITED FRONT

The conference met someplace in South China, and Chou En-lai
hovered discreetly in the background as the patron saint of the movement. Chou's attendance was not even reported by the Chinese press
until May 2 and then only after the text of his speech had been broadcast by Radio Hanoi. The DRV also assumed a modest role, and
Sihanouk was allowed to chair the meeting.

Chou promised the conference delegates that the "700 million
Chinese people" now provided a "powerful backing" and a "reliable

rear area" for the "three Indochinese countries."[23] A Chinese Government statement of April 28 also officially pledged that China would provide a "powerful backing" for the three Indochinese peoples in their "war against U.S. aggression."[24]

In their joint communiqué, the four leaders, Sihanouk, Pham Van Dong, Souphanouvong (chairman of the Laotian Patriotic Front), and Nguyen Huu Tho (president of the South Vietnam National Liberation Front), affirmed their solidarity and "their determination to . . . give mutual support" to one another.[25]

The pledges of unity and coordinated action among the four movements were important for China. Sihanouk had become a major Chinese political asset in Indochina. Perhaps it was because of Hanoi's awareness of this factor that no permanent body or formal united front was established to coordinate the activities of "the Indochinese peoples." Sihanouk in fact showed considerable sensitivity over the failure of the conference to establish an "organ of cooperation." He explained that such an organ was "unnecessary because our four parties are in constant touch. . . ."[26]

Hanoi intended that the conference should serve only propaganda purposes and not get involved in planning operations. As we will see later, neither Peking nor Sihanouk would have direct influence over the actual "revolutionary forces" in Cambodia, which would remain under North Vietnamese leadership for the next two years.

Five days after Chou pledged the support of the Chinese Government in bringing about the overthrow of the Lon Nol government, Nixon announced the incursion of U.S. and South Vietnamese forces across the border to attack the sanctuaries. The president was presumably influenced by the bellicose statements from Hanoi and Peking against the new government in Phnom Penh as well as by fresh reports of further movements by the North Vietnamese forces in Cambodia. In addition, Nixon was reportedly influenced by the concurrent appearance of Soviet pilots in Egypt and by intelligence reports that the Indochinese communists were counting upon U.S. weakness and indecision.

THE CAMBODIAN FRONT

On May 5, Sihanouk announced the political program of the NUFK and the list of members of the Politburo of the Central Committee of the Front, and at the same time he proclaimed the formation of the Royal Government of National Union (RGNU). The front's program was "national democratic"—that is, a noncommunist one, in the manner of Mao's "New Democracy." Instead of class struggle, it sought to mobilize all social classes and strata and all political parties "to overthrow the fascist, racist dictatorship of the American imperialists' flunkeys headed by Lon Nol-Sirik Matak." Power under the RGNU was said to be in the hands of the "genuine working peoples," but Buddhism was to remain the state religion and property protected. The NUFK's foreign policy was likewise to be one of peace and neutrality but also of support for the peoples of the world against U.S. "imperialism."[27]

Three of the most important members of Sihanouk's cabinet and of the Politburo of the NUFK were the former leftist members of the National Assembly who had been purged by the prince in 1967: Khieu Samphan, minister of National Defense; Hu Nim, minister of Information and Propaganda; and Hou Yuon, minister of Interior.

In May 1970, these men donned new hats and continued with their work—now greatly facilitated by the use of the prince's name and by direct military support from the Vietnamese communist forces. Khieu Samphan was later named deputy prime minister, and in 1971 he became commander of the NUFK's Liberation Army.

Sihanouk, as he admitted in press interviews, had no direct control over the situation inside Cambodia itself, and Peking's influence in the spring of 1970 was largely limited to its leverage with him. The small Cambodian communist organizations—the Khmer Rouge and the Prachaechon—with their historical links to the Viet Minh and their physical reliance upon the North Vietnamese Army, were probably responsive to Hanoi's desires. The DRV was undoubtedly in command of military operations in Cambodia from 1970 to 1972 and probably continued during those years to administer most of the areas it had cleared of Cambodian Government control. The mission of Hou Yuon, a highly respected intellectual, as minister of Interior in Sihanouk's new regime was to build up local governmental and party structures in the "liberated areas."

In May 1970, Hanoi very briefly surfaced the Pracheachon when it released a statement from the group voicing support for Sihanouk's proclamation of March 23. The Pracheachon message revealed no socialist bias but emphasized the united-front effort needed to overthrow Lon Nol and set up a peaceful and "truly neutral government" that would "defend democratic liberties."[28] In June, NCNA reported that Sihanouk had received another message from a Cambodian named Keo Meas sent in the name of the executive committee of Pracheachon. This message, which revealed that Pracheachon was a member of the NUFK, pledged the party's support for the front's political program and wished the prince "brilliant success" in his forthcoming visit to the DRV.[29] Keo Meas was named as Sihanouk's RGNU Ambassador to Peking but subsequently was replaced and dropped out of sight. The Prachaechon itself returned to the shadows and by 1973 had not reemerged. Nevertheless, it seemed likely that Prachaechon represented the core party group in the NUFK and that its military arm, the Khmer Rouge, had become the "Cambodian Liberation Army."

From the spring of 1970, a continuing objective for Peking was to build up independent lines to these Cambodian communists, while Hanoi naturally tried to maintain this area as its exclusive preserve. Meanwhile, China continued to do everything possible to enhance Sihanouk's status. During the next year, it provided him intense publicity coverage and catered to him on matters of protocol. In August 1970 the Chinese People's Republic and Sihanouk's Government of National Union signed an agreement for military and economic aid, and in December the prince claimed that China had shipped equipment and arms for 30,000 men in 1970.[30] This aid, however, was no doubt channeled through the DRV and probably included assistance to DRV and Viet Cong forces inside Cambodia.

In summary, while Chou was not enthusiastic about the turn of events in Cambodia in 1970, he was able to extract short-term advantage from them by subtle diplomacy. As a result of the Cambodian events, China had recovered some of the influence in Hanoi it had lost in the 1968-69 period, while Soviet influence diminished slightly because of its failure to back the RGNU. Hanoi's pledge of solidarity with Sihanouk had also provided Peking with some additional indirect leverage over the DRV's future decisions regarding Cambodia.

DIFFERENCES OVER CAMBODIA

There is virtually no documentary evidence of a dispute within the Peking hierarchy about the Cambodian affair. But we now know that tension and conflict between the top leaders below Mao was boiling away furiously. Within 16 months of the U.S. incursion into Cambodia, the Chinese Politburo was rent apart. First came the purge of the radical chieftain Chen Po-ta in September 1970 and then, a year later, the spectacular fall of Lin Piao and the four top Chinese military leaders. More likely than not, the question of China's security interests in the Cambodian affair was dragged into the Peking power struggle.

The Cambodian episode came at a time when Sino-U.S. détente was taking its first faltering step forward in many years. Ambassadorial talks between the two countries were held in Warsaw in January and February. For the first time the talks were conducted in the U.S. and Chinese embassies, safe from Polish eavesdropping. The conversations reportedly were businesslike. As Chou practiced restraint in reacting to developments the next month in Cambodia, his political enemies in Peking very likely argued that U.S. actions in Cambodia proved that the Americans still represented the major threat to China and that appeasement would encourage further aggression. Lin Piao was apparently able to regain the initiative.

Mao's statement of May 20, 1970 responding to Cambodian developments was read out by Lin Piao at a mass rally in Peking. The statement, which urged the people of the world to unite against "U.S. imperialism," seemed to signal a turning point in Peking's foreign policy, entailing the dampening of Sino-Soviet antagonisms after the hostilities of the previous year and a return to a strong anti-U.S. posture.

But it was also a typically Delphic Mao quote, open to various interpretations. Lin and his clique probably interpreted the key phrase, "the danger of a new world war still exists . . . but revolution is the main trend in the world today," as meaning that the Soviet threat of war had receded and primary emphasis should be placed on opposing "U.S. imperialism." Lin had long been identified with Mao's anti-Soviet line, but he had consistently given primacy to the struggle against the United States. It was on this fundamental question of defining China's "main enemy" that Lin probably chose to attack Chou, very likely pointing to the U.S. incursion into Cambodia to prove his point.

Chou, however, probably chose to interpret Mao's statement as aimed at both of China's major adversaries and as sanctioning a flexible peaceful coexistence strategy. The Cambodian development, Chou probably insisted, did not warrant throwing away the advantages to be gained by détente with the United States. Chou could also point to the widespread disapproval in America and elsewhere of the U.S. incursion into Cambodia and argue that the U.S. adventure was a temporary one doomed to failure and that it did not signal any aggressive threat to either China or North Vietnam.

THE CRITICAL SECOND PLENUM

Throughout the summer of 1970 there were contradictory indications in Chinese statements of the priority of the U.S. and Soviet threats. Peking propaganda still focused on the United States as the main enemy, and Chief of Staff Huang Yung-sheng said in June that "relaxation of Sino-U.S. tension is, of course, out of the question."[31] But on July 10, Chou signaled his interest in proceeding with the search for détente by the release of Bishop Walsh, the American former bishop of Shanghai who in 1958 had been sentenced to 20 years' imprisonment.

Three months after the U.S. military action inside Cambodia, a major turning point in Peking's factional struggle took place at the Second Plenum of the Ninth Central Committee, which met in August and September 1970. Very likely the meeting discussed Mao's May 20 dictum and China's relations with the United States, the USSR, Japan, the Third World, and the international communist movement.

Lin Piao apparently sought to rally the left and the military against Chou En-lai by attacking the prime minister's intention to accept the U.S. overture. Mao himself later confirmed that Lin attempting to build up his clique within the state organs broke rank with the leadership on a number of domestic and foreign issues including the decision to seek a normalization of relations with the United States.[32]

Very likely Lin objected to the emphasis and the style of Chou's policies. Probably he did not oppose negotiations with the Americans in principle but only the manner in which Chou was proposing to go about them, in particular the proposed invitation to President Nixon. Such a move, Lin probably argued, would be a shock to China's friends and undermine its credibility as well as the war effort in Vietnam. Moreover, Lin very likely stressed that the Nixon invitation would provoke the Soviet Union and represent a crossing of the Rubicon in relations with Moscow. For Lin, the United States remained the number-one enemy.

But as indicated by Mao's invitation to the American author Edgar Snow to stand beside him during the October 1, 1970 National Day parade, and also by subsequent events, the plenum endorsed Chou En-lai's foreign policy line of active diplomacy between China's major adversaries including acceptance of the U.S. offer of détente; peaceful coexistence and championship of the Third World against the superpowers, requiring the downplaying of revolutionary and ideological considerations; and abandonment of the attempt to polarize the communist camp and concentration on its atomization in order to weaken Moscow's control of the movement.

According to President Nixon, sometime in the fall of 1970—that is, sometime after the second plenum—the Chinese responded to his overtures, and both sides began "working to launch a process."[33] The decision to accept the U.S. approach was probably a serious setback not only for the civilian radicals but for Lin Piao's clique as well.

On home affairs the civilian radicals were also defeated on most major issues, and Chen Po-ta was accused of excesses during the Cultural Revolution and was soon purged from the Politburo.

The plenum also apparently approved a new draft constitution, which embodied no radical change in the economic or political system except for institutionalization of a military role in political and administrative organs. The dismantling of the Mao cult as well as the new expanded aid program for the Third World were also very likely endorsed by the plenum with Mao's blessing.

Lin Piao had compiled the Little Red Book of Mao's thought and had played the major role in building up the Mao cult. Nevertheless, despite the plenum's apparent decision to dismantle Mao worship and to accept Chou's foreign policy line, Lin's personal position seemed at the time strengthened by the plenum, which endorsed the draft constitution's explicit provision for his succession to the leadership. In addition, about this time Peking issued another "little red book" of Important Documents on the Great Proletarian Cultural Revolution in China, which was dominated by Lin's speeches and reports.

However, in retrospect, it seems likely that Lin recognized that the policy decisions of the plenum in foreign affairs, on the economy, and on the Mao cult, represented a turning of the tide—and of Mao—against him. Mao also apparently rebuffed Lin's attempt to be named chairman of the People's Republic. Lin could see that with the purge of Chen Po-ta, he now faced a strong coalition led by his many enemies among the provincial and regional military leaders and Chou En-lai and other veteran cadres. Moreover, with Mao increasingly bestowing his favor on this group, the surviving civilian radicals in the Politburo, including Mao's wife, Chiang Ching, began to trim their sails accordingly.

The struggle between Lin and Chou now centered on the selection of new party committees in the provinces and secondarily on the naming of ministers in the central government, which was being reconstituted. The second plenum apparently gave approval for the power-holders in the provincial Revolutionary Committees—who were largely military men—to override the demands of radicals and Cultural Revolution activists for positions in the new party organs and to proceed with party-building. Responsibility at the top for this process was taken away from Kang Sheng and given to Chou En-lai.

As the new provincial party committees were announced, beginning in December, it became clear that coalitions of professional military leaders and veteran officials were consolidating political authority on the local level, rehabilitating some Cultural Revolution victims, and dropping most upstarts who had "seized power" in the provinces in the name of radicalism. In the 29 provincial-level Revolutionary Committees that had replaced the provincial governments during the Cultural Revolution, the power balance was as follows: military 38 percent, old cadre 38 percent, and radical 24 percent. On the other hand, in the 29 provincial-level party committees formed in 1970-71, the makeup was military 58 percent, old cadre 33 percent, and radicals 9 percent. Twenty-four out of the 58 new first and second party secretaries were only alternates or not on the Central Committee elected in 1969, when Lin Piao was at his peak.

The military were also divided between Lin Piao and anti-Lin groups, with the latter in the majority in the regional and provincial commands. The power struggle that took place in the first nine months of 1971 centered around Lin's increasingly desperate efforts to push his clique's representation in the new party and government structures. Lin was, of course, alert for opportunities to undermine Chou En-lai, and since foreign affairs was Chou's principal domain, the vice chairman remained eager to find a weakness or a failure in this field to exploit. Just as he probably tried to use the Cambodian events of 1970 to disprove the assumptions behind Chou's U.S. policy, Lin was provided one final opportunity in 1971 to challenge the premier's line. This time, the events centered on Laos.

THE CHINESE ROAD

The Chinese throughout 1970 were still saying that the U.S. troop withdrawal program was a "trick" and a "fraud", but the pullback of U.S. forces from Cambodia as promised and the continued removal of U.S. troops stationed in Vietnam had probably reinforced Chou En-lai's assessment that the Nixon Administration was disengaging from Indochina. However, last-minute "desperation" efforts by the United States were not discounted even by Chou.

One battlefield in particular continued to worry the Chinese as well as the North Vietnamese. By the end of 1970 the communists began to fear that the Allies would attempt to duplicate their tactical success in Cambodia by cutting off the Ho Chi Minh Trail through Laos.

With the loss of Sihanoukville as a Viet Cong supply point, the road and waterway network of more than 1,500 miles in the Laos panhandle became even more important for the communists. The shuttling of supplies into the panhandle began with the dry season in late October or early November and reached its peak during the months of February through April.

Signs of a South Vietnamese-U.S. incursion against this important trail complex were evident by late 1970. People's Daily on December 31 warned that a U.S.-backed invasion of Laos or even North Vietnam was possible. This contingency and possible counterstrategies were probably discussed by Chinese and North Vietnamese officials at several meetings in early 1971. In addition, Laos was no doubt discussed by the Lao Dong Central Committee, which met in plenum session in January.

As Chinese support troops withdrew from North Vietnam in late 1968 and early 1969, the PRC had expanded its involvement in Laos. Beginning in 1965, Chinese engineers began preliminary surveys to extend a road from the Chinese border town of Botene 50 miles across the northern Lao province of Phong Saly to the Pathet Lao town of Muong Sai. Construction of this road by the Chinese

Government had been tentatively agreed to by the Laotian Government in January 1962. The protocol was never ratified by the Laotian Government, but when in late 1968 several thousand Chinese Army engineer, support, and security troops began actual construction of the road, the government of Souvanna Phouma chose to raise no objection.

The Chinese Army road-builders reached Muong Sai in May and eventually linked up with Route 19, which extended eastward across the North Vietnamese border to Dien Bien Phu. But one branch of the road unexpectedly took a turn to the southwest along the Beng River valley. The intended terminal for the road was the village of Pak Beng at the confluence of the Beng and Mekong Rivers only 20 miles from the Laotian border with Thailand. It was estimated that when the road was completed, trucks would be able to make a run either from China's Yünnan province or from North Vietnam to the Mekong River in one day. By the end of 1969, Chinese forces in Northern Laos had risen to between 6,000 and 8,000. One year later, these figures had soared to approximately 14,000, of which about 2,000 were based along the section of the road leading to Thailand.

A staff report of a Senate Foreign Relations subcommittee, released in early August 1971 reported in detail on the Chinese activity in Laos:

> In recent months the Chinese Communists have increased their air defenses along the road they are building in northern Laos, making the "area one of the most heavily defended in the world." The Chinese have moved in "a heavy new increment" of radar-directed anti-aircraft guns raising the total to 395, including for the first time 85 mm and 100 mm guns that are effective up to 68,000 feet.
>
> The area around the Chinese-built road is "off limits" to American planes, but on at least two occasions the road had been attacked by unmarked Royal Laos Air Force T-28's furnished by the US.
>
> The Chinese build-up of anti-aircraft defenses began after an attack by two Laotian planes in January 1970.
>
> In the last two years the size of the Chinese forces along the road has increased from 6000 to between 14,000 and 20,000. Since November, 1970 the Chinese, in addition to "upgrading earlier road constructions," have constructed eight small-arms firing ranges of a kind normally associated with garrisons of ground troops as well as a large headquarters building and 66 basketball courts.[34]

163

The purpose of the road was unclear, but the report observed that in terms of "areas of influence," the "practical effect of the Chinese road is that the Chinese border has already been shifted southward to encompass a substantial portion of northern Laos."

Presumably the road linking up with Route 19 and Dien Bien Phu was meant to supply communist forces in northeast Laos, but the road southwest from Muong Sai promised to cut off the remote northwest area of Laos, where the Lao Government had previously maintained some semblance of authority. Control of this area by the communists would complete the last link in a chain of Chinese-influenced communist zones stretching across the southern border of China from North Vietnam's western border to India.

The Thai Government was, of course, worried about the possibility that the road would be used to step up infiltration of Thai communists and arms into Thailand. On the other hand, the Chinese may have believed that the construction of the road would deter greater Thai involvement in the Laos conflict. Peking frequently denounced the construction of strategic roads within Thailand as an offensive threat to Laos.

However, the Chinese roads were probably built primarily to counter U.S. involvement in Laos.[35] The road served as a logistical contingency in the event of massive U.S. ground intervention in Laos, a subsequent threat to northern Laos or North Vietnam, and a Chinese decision to counterintervene. The Chinese presence also gave the PRC a stronger voice in the eventual political settlement in Laos.

FEAR OF INVASION AND
NUCLEAR WEAPONS

The possibility of a U.S. invasion of North Vietnam or of northern Laos did not seem seriously to worry Hanoi until 1967, and perhaps at no time until the Lamson operation in 1971 were the communists concerned that such a drastic step was possibly imminent.

The contingency of a U.S. movement either into northern Laos or North Vietnam, however, loomed on the horizon with the launching of "Operation Lamson 719" in early February 1971. With U.S. forces backstopping them in northern South Vietnam and with full U.S. air support, the South Vietnamese Army began to move across the Lao border on February 4 and headed up "Route 9" of the Ho Chi Minh trail toward the road and supply center of Tchepone.

Shortly before and immediately after Lamson 719 began, Chinese media made a flurry of references to possible U.S. use of tactical nuclear weapons.

In keeping with their vigorous opposition in 1968-69 to Hanoi's general offensive strategy and their own political and security interests, it is virtually certain that Mao and Chou favored a response of "active defense" to the Lamson Operation. In this strategy, the North Vietnamese would roll with the punch and, backed by greater Chinese material assistance, would employ intense guerrilla, antiaircraft, and small-unit tactics to harass and drive back the invaders–the protracted war of attrition would then continue. Chou feared that a massive counteroffensive by the DRV would risk provoking the United States into some drastic step such as the use of tactical nuclear weapons or an invasion of the North.

On February 8, NCNA discussed an article in the January issue of Foreign Affairs analyzing the implications of the "Nixon doctrine." NCNA, however, omitted any mention of this article's central theme, which related U.S. nuclear strategy to the "containment of China." Likewise, Peking media failed to pick up an article by C. L. Sulzberger in the New York Times on February 3, which described another writer's scenario of a U.S. nuclear war against China.[36] The Chinese report of February 8 focused on Earl C. Ravenal's thesis that under the Nixon doctrine the United States in certain extremities might be forced to a final choice among unlimited conventional escalation, defeat of U.S. forces, or use of nuclear weapons.

It was apparent from the flurry of attention in Peking to the nuclear weapons issue that the context in which the United States was seen as being tempted to use such weapons was when and if it became the only way "to stave off defeat." The nuclear threat was portrayed not as an imminent one and not aimed at China, but as a consideration that might arise in Indochina if and when the U.S. side was faced with a catastrophic defeat.

LIN AND LAOS

China's reaction to the new crisis in Laos was probably affected by the power struggle within the Chinese leadership and by the question of China's relations with the United States and the USSR, which was now a hot issue between Lin Piao and Chou.

The future course of Sino-U.S. relations was symbolized on Mao's birthday, December 26, 1970, when a picture of the chairman and Edgar Snow appeared on the front page of People's Daily. It was about this time that Mao was telling Snow that the Ministry of Foreign Affairs was "thinking of allowing American people of the left, of the middle-of-the-road and of the right to visit China." In an obvious reference to the secret overtures from Washington, Mao said that

Nixon would also be welcome because "the present questions between China and the US must be solved with Nixon."[37]

Snow said he had learned from foreign diplomats that in January 1971 the White House again transmitted a message "inquiring how a private representative sent by the President to hold talks with leaders of the highest ranks in China would be received in the capital of China."[38] At this time, according to Nixon, the U.S. Government had reason to believe that its moves were being evaluated by the Chinese.[39] A favorable evaluation was greatly influenced by the fact that there were now one-third more Soviet divisions in the Far East than there had been in 1969.[40]

Chou's diplomatic strategy, however, seemed threatened by the U.S. side's operation in Laos just as it had been by the U.S. incursions into Cambodia the previous year.

The now dominant anti-Lin Piao group in Peking was probably distressed that the incursion into Laos might get out of hand and eventually force China into more direct participation in the fighting. Lamson 719 threatened once again to delay Chou's diplomatic gambit, particularly if the operation enjoyed some tactical success or if its defeat required an expanded Chinese involvement.

Looking for weapons with which to attack Chou's foreign policies, Lin possibly argued that the Allied operation into Laos again disproved Chou's assumptions that the United States was in fact withdrawing from Indochina, and that the U.S. threat to China was diminishing. We may wonder whether the strange and sudden flush of attention in Peking media to the possibility of U.S. use of tactical nuclear weapons was not a reflection of this contentious issue within the Peking leadership. In addition, Chou's citation in Hanoi in early March of a Mao instruction that it would be betrayal "if any among us" opposed assistance to the Vietnamese cause may have been a rejoinder to charges by Lin that Chou was backing off from support for the DRV.

In early February, Lin and his generals made exceptionally strong statements about the fighting in Laos and unusually direct warnings about possible Chinese reaction. Lin said that the Chinese people and the Chinese People's Liberation Army would "definitely not allow the U.S. aggressors to run amuck in the area of Indochina."[41] Li Tso-peng, deputy chief of staff and political commissar of the navy, said that the United States was "plotting to attack North Vietnam by surprise in a military adventure" and that the Nixon Administration's expansion of the war was also a "provocation against the people of China."[42] The navy commissar, a close associate of Lin's, also warned that "we will never allow U.S. imperialism to do as it pleases in Indochina."[43] Air Force Chief Wu Fa-hsien, another Lin man, proclaimed that "the Chinese people and the Chinese People's Liberation Army have long made up their minds to . . . go all out to support and assist you for the complete defeat of the U.S. aggressors."[44] Lin was apparently hoping that Lamson would substantiate his thesis that the United States remained the number-one enemy.

Subsequent Soviet as well as Chinese statements also raise the possibility that Lin, at this time searching for an alternative policy, attempted to promote a partial Sino-Soviet rapprochement or that he argued for an even-handed treatment of both major adversaries. As suggested, Lin may have approved of negotiations with the United States on the question of Taiwan, but evidence indicates that he was opposed to the drama of a visit to China by Nixon, as this was bound to suggest more than a general détente in Sino-U.S. relations. To counter Chou's move with the United States, Lin may have attempted to promote over Chou's head a settlement of the Sino-Soviet border dispute.

Moscow, perhaps made aware of the developments in Sino-U.S. relations by Lin Piao, may have moved to enhance the option of a Sino-Soviet rapprochement. We know that sometime in the first half of the year Moscow made a significant concession by agreeing to conclude a new border treaty rather than simply to amend the existing accords.[45] Subsequent Soviet commentaries claimed that Moscow had made other important concessions during the year on the border issue. Brezhnev one year later revealed that Moscow had offered to conclude non-aggression and non-use-of-force agreements with Peking.[46]

According to a Western journalist, the Soviets in 1971 had also offered to accept the principle that the main navigable channels of the Amur and Ussuri Rivers should be considered as the international boundary with the exception of Big Ussuri Island opposite the important Siberian city of Khabarovsk.* The Chinese allegedly rejected this offer.[47] Later in the year, Izvestia charged that "constructive proposals" suggested by the Soviet Union for settlement of the border problem had been rebuffed by the Chinese because in their view a settlement "would tie their hands, prevent them from playing on international differences and from making China into a central power in the world."[48]

The new Soviet offers may have been put forward at a meeting in March between Chou, the Soviet Ambassador, and the chief Soviet negotiator. But as Moscow continued to refuse to withdraw its troops from disputed areas, Chou was not moved by the Soviet proposals, probably because he believed that a settlement under the existing conditions would have seemed to be negotiated under Soviet duress.

---

*Pravda journalist Yuri Zhukov told a Soviet television audience on October 20, 1973 that the Soviet Union had agreed to accept the main channel as the boundary in the Ussuri and Amur Rivers.

China would be in a better bargaining position once it had ended its hostile relations with the United States and Japan. Chou's response very likely was challenged by Lin, who may have seized upon the Soviet concessions to argue for a counter-concession from the Chinese side.[49]

Hints of a Soviet angle to Lin Piao's fall first appeared in the July 1 Chinese party anniversary editorial, which warned of "enemy agents" in the party and "hidden traitors" who have "illicit relations with foreign countries." This charge was heralded as early as April 1971 in a Red Flag (No. 4) article, which quoted Mao's criticism of "imperial envoys" who rushed about "causing a hullabaloo and brought disaster to the country."

After Lin's fall, People's Daily (September 25) also implied that there was a Soviet aspect to Lin's disgrace when it charged that Moscow was threatening nuclear blackmail and conniving with party dissidents inside China. After describing how the Japanese had won over traitors to a "capitulationist 'peace movement'," the article charged that today the Soviets are "following in the footsteps of Japanese imperialism . . . indulging in nuclear blackmail on the one hand, while hypocritically preaching and extolling the 'kingly way' and benevolent administration."

The charges leveled against Lin by Peking media at the end of the year (although still not directly naming him as the culprit) included the most serious crime of being a "conspirator" who had betrayed the party.[50] The charge of "illicit relations with foreign countries" became a recurrent theme in the condemnations of Lin.[51] Provincial broadcasts obviously referring to the Lin Piao affair also charged that "counterrevolutionary revisionists at home always attempt in vain to collude with international revisionism [meaning the Soviet Union] to plot counterrevolutionary restoration."[52] One revealing broadcast said that in international affairs Lin's group "wanted to surrender to social-imperialism [again meaning the Soviet Union] and turn China into a colony of social-imperialism."[53]

Official documents of the Central Committee that circulated on the mainland in the fall of 1971 as background briefings for cadres, explained that Lin and his cohorts had plotted to assassinate Mao after they had discovered that the chairman intended to replace Lin as his successor because of the latter's past connection with the radical Chen Po-ta.

According to the party documents, when the plot failed, Lin and some of his colleagues on September 13 attempted to flee to Mongolia or the Soviet Union in a Trident jet airliner but were killed when the plane crashed.[54] This explanation of Lin's flight was obviously intended to suggest that the vice chairman was leaning toward, if not working for, at least partial reconciliation with the Soviets.

In the summer of 1972 Mao himself confirmed this version of the Lin affair[55] and Chinese embassies abroad issued official statements describing Lin's alleged plot and charging that he opposed Mao's "revolutionary foreign policy."[56]

Moscow also implied that Lin's fall was due to his conciliatory approach to the USSR. Moscow Radio charged that the purge of high-ranking PLA officers was proof that "healthy forces" within the Chinese military had opposed Mao's policy of terminating "cooperation with the fraternal armies of the Socialist countries—primarily, the USSR army."[57] Moscow also quoted East European journals as saying that "Lin Piao and his group were opposed to open collusion with U.S. imperialism,"[58] and Pravda claimed that the purge of Lin meant the ascendancy of extreme anti-Sovietism in Peking.[59]

HANOI'S VIEW

While Chou and Lin fought over the broader implications of Operation Lamson 719, the North Vietnamese leaders apparently saw the U.S. side's operation into Laos as providing an opportunity to strike a decisive blow at the South Vietnamese Army and at the policy of "Vietnamization." Again, we have little evidence of the discussion of strategy within Hanoi, but some North Vietnamese leaders were probably worrying that the revolution was marking time. There is reason to believe that General Giap felt that the withdrawal of U.S. troops had reached the point where another sudden constriction of the protracted struggle was in order.

In December an article by the Viet Cong defense minister and commander of the People's Liberation Armed Forces, Tran Nam Trung, had stressed the importance of "big-unit fighting." Trung suggested that the area for new offensives had expanded and that the communist forces possessed "new abilities for large-scale offensives" throughout Indochina.[60] The call for more big-unit operations was not immediately repeated, but the February 3 communiqué of the Lao Dong Central Committee indicated that greater sacrifices would be required of the North Vietnamese people than had been necessary during the previous two years of small-unit warfare.

With the Allied forces concentrating for their attack into Laos, Giap, the man who devised the strategies for Dien Bien Phu and the Tet offensive, was attracted by a bold scheme to lure in the South Vietnamese Army by not resisting its advance into Laos and then to launch a massive counterattack to trap and destroy it. Eventually the DRV threw dozens of battalions into the fighting around Route 9; in so doing it stripped its garrisons in the southern part of North Vietnam and left itself vulnerable to attack across the DMZ.

Peking probably warned that Hanoi's bold plan might fail because of U.S. air power and that it might be dangerous even if it succeeded. The Chinese—perhaps with Lin Piao dissenting—probably argued that a serious defeat for the Saigon forces might halt the U.S. withdrawal program, and furthermore, if faced with such a catastrophe, the United States might possibly employ tactical nuclear weapons or strike into the southern part of North Vietnam to relieve pressure of the Saigon forces in Laos. The motivation for Peking media's unusual attention to the possibility of nuclear weapons being used in Indochina was perhaps intended as an argument against those who advocated a major counteroffensive. Interestingly, Hanoi during this crisis never referred to the nuclear danger.

A divergence of views on strategy may also account for the failure to hold another Indochina Summit. Sihanouk was in Hanoi from January 26 to February 9 and met separately with President Ton Duc Thang of the DRV and Prince Souphanouvong of the Lao Patriotic Front (the latter meeting was said by VNA and NCNA to have taken place on the Lao frontier, but from the photographs it is clear that both meetings took place in the same room).[61] Hanoi may have felt that it had more freedom to pursue its own policies and strategies outside the confines of a summit meeting in which Peking would be hovering in the background. In addition, by seeming to vest decisions within the Chinese-backed Indochinese summit, Hanoi would have gravely irritated the USSR. Therefore, in order to retain their freedom of maneuver, the North Vietnamese made the decision to deal separately with their Indochinese allies.

As at the time of the Cambodian incursion, the Chinese on February 15 signed a supplementary economic and military aid agreement with the DRV. But as in 1970, Peking was again hoping to discourage drastic expansion of U.S. involvement. The Saigon forces inside Laos began to get bogged down about this time, and contrary to the worst fears of the Chinese, U.S. ground troops did not intervene to save the operation nor were nuclear weapons or an invasion of the North even threatened.

Unexpectedly, U.S. leaders took pains to rule out the threat of nuclear weapons as a deterrent to Chinese intervention. Secretary of State William Rogers, in a press briefing on February 10, described allegations about possible U.S. use of nuclear weapons as "bunk." President Nixon on February 17 said that allied actions in Laos presented no threat to the PRC and he scoffed at the idea of employing nuclear weapons. People's Daily of February 20, however, brushed off this "explanation" by the Nixon Administration and charged that the president's words "reeked of gunpowder."

Nevertheless, shortly afterward, the Chinese became visibly more relaxed and confident. A high-level meeting apparently took place in Peking about this time, and its relatively cool assessment of the Laos crisis was reflected in speeches by Politburo members Chang Chun-chao and Hsu Hsih-yu on Februay 22 and March 1, respectively, which described the situation in Indochina as "excellent" and made no reference of a menace to China.

One month after Lamson 719 had begun, the Chinese were relatively confident that the situation would be controlled, although some danger of a dramatic U.S. reaction still remained. Chou En-lai visited Hanoi March 5 to 8 in order to dramatize Chinese support for the DRV and also to discuss possible contingencies in the final stages of the North Vietnamese counteroffensive. The North Vietnamese desired stronger expressions of Chinese backing in order to secure their rear. Chou responded by again directly linking China's security to developments in Indochina but retained full flexibility for the future. Citing Mao, Chou said that failure to assist the Vietnamese would be "betrayal of the revolution," and he promised that if necessary the Chinese were prepared to make the "greatest national sacrifice" to honor their commitment to Hanoi. Chou avoided specifying the conditions under which Peking would consider such sacrifices necessary, but it was apparent that he was referring to a U.S. invasion either of North Vietnam or of northern Laos.[62]

By the end of March, the South Vietnamese troops in Laos seemed to be in a precarious position, and they suddenly withdrew, saved from entrapment by a massive U.S. helicopter airlift. In coordination with Hanoi, Peking launched an intensive campaign to portray operation Lamson 719 as a debacle for the U.S. side and as a victory of "great strategic" importance for their side. This interpretation was expounded by Chou En-lai at a "victory" banquet in Peking on March 26, in the Chinese leaders' March 29 message of congratulations to their Indochinese allies, and in the flood of Chinese news reports of the "disastrous defeat" of the U.S. and South Vietnamese forces. In their propaganda drive, Peking media made extensive use of Western press reports to convince its readers that the communist side had won a decisive battle.

As a result of Lamson 719, the PRC had been able to identify itself more intimately with the cause of the DRV and again to overshadow temporarily the role of the Soviets—all with some risk but little cost to China. Chou's dramatic visit to Hanoi and the attention focused on the Chinese reaction to events tended to portray Peking as the main supporter of the North Vietnamese and of their Indochinese allies.

Peking charged that the Nixon Administration had hoped to win political capital out of an "early victory" in Laos but had in fact created a "political crisis" and increased both the "credibility gap" and antiwar sentiment in the United States. Chou En-lai probably

171

believed that the "defeat" of Lamson 719 and increasing opposition
to the war in the United States, combined with China's own policies
of peaceful coexistence, would add momentum to his diplomatic
strategy. Perhaps most important of all, the outcome of Lamson 719
in contrast to the Cambodian incursion in 1970 permitted China to be
seen as dealing from a strong hand in its relations with the United
States.

Moreover, the failure of the United States to intervene in order
to save the Lamson operation seemed to confirm the assumptions
behind Chou's planned moves with the Americans. Chinese statements
began to describe the situation in Indochina as "unprecedentedly fine,"
a description that would eventually be interpreted to mean that the
time was ripe for U.S.-Chinese as well as U.S.-DRV negotiations.
Thus in April, the Chinese could move confidently ahead with "ping
pong diplomacy," the first step toward pursuing high-level exchanges
with the U.S. Government.

The Chinese also indicated that the campaign in Laos had
demonstrated that "people's war" tactics of close-quarter fighting and
night operations could overcome massive use of air power by the
enemy.[63] The Chinese preference for applying a gradual squeeze on
the forces of the U.S. side was evident in an NCNA statement of March
12 that the Indochinese were "chewing up U.S. imperialism little by
little" and its admonition that the opening of a new well after one dig-
ging is impossible, as is "killing a big tiger with a single blow."[64]

In contrast, Hanoi described the "defeat" of Lamson 719 as a
decisive and "total" victory, which demonstrated the efficacy of "big
campaigns of annihilation," and DRV statements called for more of
the same. The North Vietnamese Army newspaper Quan Doi Nhan
Dan and other Hanoi press comment indicated that the communist
forces had deliberately sought the confrontation between main-force
units in a departure from their tactics of the previous two years.
The Allied forces were said to have fallen into a trap by advancing
rapidly to Ban Dong and there being cut off.[65] Hanoi claimed that
15,400 enemy troops had been "put out of action" and 496 aircraft
(mostly helicopters) had been destroyed.[66]

The continued withdrawal of U.S. forces and the retreat of
the South Vietnamese troops from Laos convinced the DRV leaders,
and General Giap in particular, that the war was entering a new stage.
Hanoi believed that it was now possible and necessary to annihilate
South Vietnamese military forces "by big chunks."[67] "After the
withdrawal of 200,000 U.S. troops, the balance of power on the battlefield has undergone an important change. . . . The test of Vietnamization has entered its fiercest phase."[68]

Giap's success in defeating Operation Lamson 719 encouraged
him to push forward with plans for the largest offensive ever: the

full-scale invasion of South Vietnam in the spring of 1972 by virtually the entire North Vietnamese Army. It also gave Hanoi confidence to engage in new talks with the United States.

PEKING ENDORSES PEACEFUL
SETTLEMENT

In June 1971 at a secret U.S.-DRV meeting in Paris, the North Vietnamese proposed a nine-point plan for a settlement of the war. Interestingly, the Chinese and Sihanouk were not informed of this secret proposal.[69] The North Vietnamese plan covered all of Indochina and provided for a ceasefire in Laos and Cambodia but without requiring that specific political conditions in regard to these states be met first, as was demanded in the case of South Vietnam. This seemed to suggest Hanoi's readiness to negotiate over the heads of its Lao and Cambodian allies.

On July 4, 1971, People's Daily officially endorsed the July 1 seven-point proposal made public by the Viet Cong delegation in Paris,* which omitted the sections in the secret proposal dealing with the other states of Indochina. For the first time since 1965 the Chinese approved of a plan for a "peaceful settlement" of the Vietnam war.

The PRC's first endorsement of a Viet Cong peace plan had appeared in a December 13, 1970 joint party-government statement and subsequently in the joint communiqué of March 10 released after Chou's visit to Hanoi. The July 4, 1971 editorial, however, was the first time a "peaceful settlement" as such had been approved by the Chinese in six years.

In another People's Daily editorial of July 20, Peking spoke favorably of the 1954 Geneva agreements for the first time in five years. Since 1966, Peking had described the Geneva accords as "already nonexistent," "cast into oblivion," and "torn to shreds." Although the 1971 editorial also denounced the United States for tearing up the 1954 agreement, it praised the accords as an "important success" for the Indochinese peoples.

The circumstances of Peking's favorable comments on the Geneva agreements plus an earlier misinterpreted report from an Australian visitor to China that the PRC favored a new international conference seemed to suggest that as part of its new diplomacy, the

---

*This proposal was similar in most respects to previous solutions raised by the Viet Cong side. However the seven points indicated that U.S. troop withdrawal and prisoner release by both sides would begin and end on the same date.

173

PRC intended to push for a broad multination meeting to deal with the Indochina problem.[70]

HANOI AND MOSCOW REACTION

Hanoi reacted to the July 15 news of President Nixon's invitation to Peking and China's sudden enthusiasm for a "peaceful settlement" with ill-disguised suspicion and bitterness. The North Vietnamese leaders were irritated because the Sino-U.S. announcement had taken the spotlight away from the seven-point proposal in Paris and had at least temporarily relieved Washington of antiwar pressure at home. But more important, Hanoi feared that the Chinese might now push for a broad settlement of the Indochina conflict and that Peking and the Soviet Union would again pursue their wider interests at the expense of the DRV's objectives in Vietnam.

A subsequent flurry of statements from Hanoi stressed the independent foreign policy of the DRV and its refusal to succumb to pressure from the big powers.[71]

It would be "sheer ignorance," the Viet Cong Liberation Radio said, for "Nixon to think that by courting and attracting one person or another and borrowing or relying on the strength and pressure of other people, he can ease his present difficulties."[72] The DRV felt that its position was much stronger than at the time of the 1954 Geneva conference, and it warned the "imperialists" that their practice of "replying on the strength of big powers to bully smaller countries will no longer work."

Moreover, as Peking dropped its personal abuse of Nixon, Hanoi intensified its own attacks, describing him as the "worst anti-Communist bellicose and reactionary element."[73]

The change in Peking's attitude on a negotiated settlement reflected Peking's new orientation toward both the Indochina conflict and the United States. By 1971 it was apparent that continuation of the Indochina war could not bring about any substantial improvement in China's position vis-à-vis the Soviet Union. On the contrary, as the U.S. position in Asia weakened, the major beneficiary seemed to be the Soviet Union, which was eager to fill any vacuum and shoulder the burden of "containing" China. Moscow stepped up efforts to expand its ties to the governments of Southeast Asia, and Soviet propaganda harped on China's alleged aggressive attentions, its support for Maoist insurgents in the area, and the danger posed by the overseas Chinese. The USSR since June 1969 had advocated a "collective security" system for Asia, which was generally interpreted to mean containment of these Chinese threats.

MAKING UP WITH HANOI

Peking still had a large stake in its relations with Hanoi deriving from its competition with the USSR as well as from China's basic political and security interests in Indochina. Peking could not threaten to abandon its Vietnamese ally. Thus prior to Henry Kissinger's visit to Peking, China attempted to reassure Hanoi of its support. On July 4, the PRC and the DRV signed a new supplementary military aid agreement for the "gratuitous" supply of military equipment and materials.

This transpired a few days after the July 1 joint Peking editorial on the CCP's anniversary, which condemned "hidden traitors" in the party who had "illicit relations with foreign countries." We now know that this was aimed at Lin Piao and his alleged contact with the Soviet Union. Clearly Lin by this time was on the skids, and he must have known that his purge was inevitable.

After the announcement of the presidential visit to Peking, Hanoi employed opportunities as they arose to demonstrate its independent foreign policy and its own support for the vital interests of fraternal parties. A Japanese Communist Party delegation was received in Hanoi (as in 1966, the delegation was led by Miyamoto); friendly messages were exchanged with the French Communist Party; DRV delegates attended party congresses in the satellite countries; and North Vietnam condemned the suppression of the pro-Moscow Sudan Communist Party (Peking on the other hand provided support to the Sudanese Government). These actions were an implied criticism of China's foreign policy, dominated as it now was by its fear of and feud with the Soviet Union.

For some time following the July 15 announcement, the DRV even refused to characterize Chinese assistance to its cause as based on the "spirit of proletarian internationalism."[74]

Moscow moved to take advantage of the opportunity to exploit Hanoi's suspicions. TASS, Pravda, and Radio Moscow fulsomely reported DRV comment, which expressed, in veiled terms, anxiety over Sino-U.S. relations. The USSR took up the charge that the United States was attempting to split the socialist countries and that its "perfidious diplomatic activity" was aimed at making North Vietnam accept a solution to the conflict on U.S. terms.

The Soviets contrasted their own "unshakable" solidarity with Hanoi and their support for united action by the socialist camp in aiding the Vietnamese people with the "splittist" policies of the PRC. Moscow at this time was also beating its propaganda drums over the "Pentagon Papers", which it claimed proved that U.S. "aggression" in Indochina had been promoted by Peking's refusal to join in united action with the Soviets. (Chinese media made only occasional passing reference to the secret papers.)

To highlight its fraternal attachment to the cause of the DRV, Moscow dispatched President N. V. Podgorny to Hanoi in early October. In the communiqué at the end of the visit, the USSR pledged itself to support the Vietnamese cause until total victory on the three fronts: military, political, and diplomatic. In return, the DRV endorsed Soviet policies in Europe, specifically Moscow's treaty with West Germany and the recently initialed draft agreement on West Berlin. This North Vietnamese endorsement of Soviet policies in Europe was reminiscent of Ho Chi Minh's 1953 effort to link his own goals in Vietnam to Soviet interest in heading off establishment of a European Defense Community.

Assaulted by Soviet polemics, by Hanoi's veiled criticisms, and possibly by last-minute opposition from the now desperate Lin Piao group, the Chinese leadership moved to assure the North Vietnamese that while it had good reasons for negotiations with the United States, it had no intention of getting out ahead of the DRV on the question of a Vietnam settlement. Peking reiterated its support for the seven-point proposal, and in interviews with visiting Americans Chou En-lai took a tough stand on the question of Indochina; he emphasized that the PRC would not attempt to mediate the conflict and that it was not pushing for a new Geneva-type conference. Chou even indicated that China would refuse to take part in an international agreement guaranteeing the postwar frontiers of Vietnam.[75]

On August 3, People's Daily maintained that in the face of defeat on the Indochina battlefield, the United States was "vainly trying to turn the tide and seek a way out by calling a new Geneva Conference." This can never be done, the editorial said, quoting Sihanouk's assertion that "we three Indochinese peoples are not in need of a new Geneva Conference at all."

The Chinese premier also has the opportunity to explain Peking's policy to Le Duc Tho, who stopped off in Peking at the end of July, and to the Viet Cong foreign minister, Mme. Nguyen Thi Binh, in early September.

Peking further attempted to quiet Hanoi's anxieties with generous flood relief aid in late August; and in September, after the dramatic death of Lin Piao, the PRC dispatched Vice Premier Li Hsien-nien to Hanoi to sign the economic and military aid agreement for 1972. Li also very possibly briefed the North Vietnamese on the Lin affair.

Shortly after, Soviet charges of Sino-U.S. collusion were made to sound somewhat hollow by the announcement that Nixon would be visiting Moscow in May, after his trip to Peking. This announcement brought home to DRV leaders the fact that both the PRC and the USSR intended to pursue their own interests in regard to the United States

and that the dynamics of the triangular relationship between the three
major powers transcended the issue of Indochina.

In November, the North Vietnamese received more high-level
assurances from Peking of material backing and of noninterference
in the political issues of the war. When Premier Pham Van Dong
visited Peking that month, Chou En-lai was careful simply to echo
the DRV's hard-line position on the war and to leave all references
to negotiations, coalition governments, and so on to his Vietnamese
guest. Differences were submerged in mutual expressions of friendship and admiration while sensitive subjects such as Sino-U.S. and
Sino-Soviet relations were virtually ignored in public statements
during the visit.

When President Nixon on January 25, 1972 revealed the secret
eight-point peace proposal made by the United States the previous
October, Peking was also quick to follow Hanoi's lead in denouncing
it. People's Daily termed the proposal a "new stratagem of U.S.
imperialism in its aggression against Vietnam."[76]

But despite Chinese efforts to reassure the North Vietnamese,
Hanoi naturally remained greatly disturbed by the turn in Sino-U.S.
relations and apprehensive about the consequences on its negotiating
position. On the eve of the Nixon visit to Peking, the North Vietnamese
protested to their allies that the Americans were exploiting the contradictions between them and that Nixon's intention in negotiating
with the Soviet Union and China was to sow discord between them
while furthering U.S. détente with each of the communist powers. In
this way, the North Vietnamese warned, Nixon hoped to gain advantage
in the military, political, and diplomatic contest over Vietnam.[77]
Their fears were well-founded.

Only when Moscow and Peking, as in 1954, both possessed separate and overriding interests in a compromise end of the Indochina war
could either back off from its support for Hanoi without fear, that the
other would exploit the situation to gain the advantage. The circumstances in 1971 were different from those of 1954; not only were the
Chinese and the Soviets locked in ideological and national enmity and
unable to cooperate on policy, but in 1972 the alternative to a compromise settlement in Indochina was not, as 10 years before, a much-
feared U.S. intervention in the conflict, but simply indefinite protrac-
tion of the fighting with a continued drain on the economies of all
three powers.

Nevertheless, by 1972 as in 1954, the Chinese as well as the
Soviets had goals toward the United States, which were more important
than the gains provided by winning a leg up either in Hanoi or in the
ideological contest. Moscow was seeking a conference on European
security and more concrete moves toward stability in Europe. In
particular, it sought acceptance of the status quo in Eastern Europe—

the division of Germany and Soviet dominance of the bloc. In addition the Soviets had a large stake in the completion of strategic arms limitation and other disarmament agreements with the United States that would formalize the Soviet position of strategic parity. Moreover, the Soviets sought expanded economic relations with the United States. In 1972 it became apparent to the Soviet leaders that Russia faced a disastrous wheat harvest. As a result the USSR that year purchased 28 million tons of grain from the West, three-quarters of the total amount from the United States—the latter negotiated at low prices.

But most important of all was the dynamics of the new triangular relationship between the USSR, China, and the United States brought about by the Peking-Washington détente. The Chinese and the Americans had both gained important new leverage against the Soviets. Moscow henceforth found itself with a competitor for U.S. favor, and it was certainly not going to pick up the strategy the Chinese had dropped of staking their world position on militant opposition to "U.S. imperialism."

By extending détente to China as well as the Soviet Union, the United States had not only turned Sino-Soviet rivalry to its benefit in getting out of the Indochina war but had changed the complexion of world politics and gained an unofficial partner in the containment of Soviet world power.

The Chinese acceptance of U.S. overtures represented abandonment of the basic strategy that China had pursued in the 1960s—opposition to "U.S. imperialism." We have already suggested some of the reasons for the move: the Soviet threat, changes in U.S. policies, and the failure of the polarization strategy within the communist and Third Worlds. But the new strategy also represented a fundamental shift in the Chinese view of world politics.

MAO'S EXPLANATION OF THE CHANGE

In July and August 1971 Lin Piao and his military group within the Politburo probably pointed to the strong North Vietnamese reaction as evidence of the high cost of the invitation to Nixon. In addition, they may have warned that the Soviet diplomatic reaction as seen in the West Berlin agreement and the Indian-Soviet treaty was predictable—boxing and encircling China. Peking, Lin very likely argued, had now persuaded Moscow that the PRC was intransigently hostile to the USSR; on the other hand, by its agreement to high-level dealings with the United States, the Chinese party had thrown away the main issue with which it had challenged Moscow for leadership of the communist camp—Soviet collusion with the "U.S. imperialists." Whereas

Liu Shao-chi six years before had advocated a partial détente with the USSR out of fear of a U.S. attack on China, Lin Piao and his military backers in 1971 rejected détente with the United States for ideological reasons and for fear it would provoke the Soviet Union.

Mao's position, however, was consistent. The lines were once again drawn between Maoism and revisionism, between boldness and caution, and between pragmatism and adherence to the long-range goal. Mao continued to give priority to his struggle with the heretical revisionists, and the events of 1969-70 convinced Mao (and Chou) that the Soviets were now the number-one national as well as ideological enemy of China.

An important article appeared in the August 2, 1971 issue of the theoretical journal Red Flag, which gave Mao's justification of China's new diplomatic line.[78] The article, which discussed the current relevance of a 1940 Mao piece entitled "On Policy," stressed the importance of flexibility and of distinguishing between the enemy camps, "between the primary enemy and the secondary enemy and between the temporary allies and the indirect allies." It was apparent from the context of the article that the main enemy on the present world stage was the Soviet Union.

Those cadres that did not understand or approve of the new tactic in regard to the United States were admonished to correct their "lopsided views," to overcome "absoluteness in thinking," and not to base revolutionary tactics on "revolutionary sentiment."

Lin Piao apparently did not take this advice to heart. The next month he and his colleagues made a desperate attempt to salvage their positions. Whether, as the regime charged, this act involved an attempt to kill Mao or whether it was aimed instead at simply overthrowing Chou, we do not know. But in any event, in September, Lin fell from the most exalted place in China—next to Mao—to the lowest rank of traitor and renegade.

Mao's world view of the 1970s was expressed in the joint New Year's editorial for 1972, which emphasized that the characteristic feature of the present world situation could be summed up as "global upheaval." The main development in this upheaval was the rapid decay of America as a world power and the concurrent rise of Soviet "social imperialism" following "in the footsteps of U.S. imperialism." The United States was described as "enormously weakened" and in its worst plight in history.

As noted earlier, the same theme of upheaval and reorganization had figured in major Chinese policy statements seven years before, signaling rejection of any accommodation with the USSR or united action with Moscow against the United States in Vietnam.[79] At that time, the upheaval referred particularly to the communist camp and to Mao's determination to polarize the movement primarily on the issue of relations with the United States, "the most ferocious common enemy of the peoples of the whole world."[80] "Opposition to or alliance with the U.S." was then said to be the "sharpest difference of theory and line" between Moscow and Peking as well as the standard by which the Third World and the socialist camp would choose between the two antiimperialist centers.

Mao and Chou En-lai now believed that for a variety of reasons, mostly related to U.S. economic and social crises and to the Vietnam war, the United States was retrenching, in its international activities. Likewise, the "failure" of the U.S. "containment" policy in Indochina, the rise of militant economic nationalism, U.S. support for Israel, and the equivocal U.S. stand on the black liberation struggles in Africa were said to have weakened the U.S. position throughout the Third World.

At the same time, the Chinese suggested, the United States had lost or was losing its absolute military superiority over the Soviet Union. The 1960s, according to Peking, was an era of transition in the U.S.-Soviet struggle for world hegemony, and it was apparent that the 1970s would be the period of "rapid decay" in the U.S. position. Although not publicly discussed by the Chinese, U.S.-Soviet "nuclear parity" was obviously a major element in their view of the shifting balance of forces. The Chinese also suggested that the United States was simply losing its taste for the role of "overlord" while Soviet appetites had been whetted.

Meanwhile, two other independent power blocs in the "second intermediate zone" were seen by Peking as in the process of emerging in the 1970s—West Europe and Japan. "A profound change has taken place in the balance of forces" between these emerging blocs and the United States, the joint editorial said, and contradictions with the United States had intensified over economic problems. These areas were no longer auxiliaries of the United States but were now independent medium powers vulnerable to Soviet intimidation.

China's embryonic nuclear shield and its sudden bursting upon the diplomatic stage in the 1970s added another element to the multi-polar scene. In keeping with its antisuperpower theme, China muted comment on its own modest contribution to the world balance of power, and Chou agreed with Nixon that China's "potential" rather than its actual power was the fifth force in the world. Yet Peking knew that it was the major factor in Asia, and it was fond of quoting others who proclaimed that no world problem could be solved without China's participation.

The Soviets in 1972 were pictured as seizing opportunities to expand their power and influence at both U.S. and Chinese expense. As evidence of Soviet aggressiveness, the Chinese cited the USSR's military buildup on the Sino-Soviet border, its role in the 1971 Indo-

Pakistani war, its invasion of Czechoslovakia and intimidation of the
Balkans, the Brezhnev doctrine, the expansion of the Soviet fleet into
the Mediterranean and the Indian Ocean, Moscow's promotion of "collective security" in Asia, and its alleged subversion in the Sudan and
other places. But, in the Chinese view, Moscow had increasingly
come to focus on the objective of weakening and if possible eliminating
the Chinese challenge to its leadership. The Soviets had become primarily concerned, Peking believed, with "encircling" China and containing its influence.

The Chinese implied that U.S. policies in Asia were now defensive and not anti-China-oriented as before and were increasingly
aimed at countering Soviet influence. The likelihood of continued U.S.
presence in Asia appeared to be fully appreciated by the Chinese leaders.
What was changing in their view was the purpose of this power.

This new Chinese Weltanshauung provided the rationale for the
PRC's increased maneuverability on the world stage, particularly its
active diplomacy between the two superpowers. The claim to be more
opposed than Moscow to the United States was no longer Peking's
sharpest difference with Moscow; now the charge that the Soviet Union
itself was threatening the sovereignty of the nations of the world was
the primary issue.

Therefore, the effort to polarize both the communist camp and
the Third World on the basis of opposition to the United States was
abandoned. The result was a more broad-based effort to exploit
existing conflicts of interest with both superpowers and to maximize
acceptance, sympathy, and support for China wherever possible.
More than ever, Peking would now be vigorously discriminating in
supporting only those national liberation wars, secession movements,
and rebellions that served China's foreign policy interests. Power
politics more than ever would characterize China's competition with
the Soviet Union and the United States as well as its policies in Indo-
China.

Sino-Soviet rivalry, which heretofore had taken the form of
an ideological competition for leadership of both the communist and
the antiimperialist movements in the world, now more clearly assumed
the shape of a power struggle between two nation-states whose differences were accentuated by a territorial dispute and an ideological
schism. The Indo-Pakistani war of 1971 signaled this new stage in
the Moscow-Peking conflict. For the first time, they found themselves
clearly on opposite sides of a war within the Third World.

So it came about that, in the eyes of the present Chinese leaders,
the Soviet Union was the number-one national as well as ideological
enemy of China, and the main goal of Chinese policy henceforth was
to reduce Moscow's freedom of action vis-à-vis China. This new
united front policy in 1971 was still directed at eroding U.S. prestige,

181

influence, and leadership in the Third World, but this objective now had secondary priority. The Chinese leaders appreciated above all the coincidence of Chinese and U.S. interests in containing Soviet power. The Chinese concept of the balance of power continued to evolve until by the end of 1972 it was apparent that Peking saw U.S. power as the only deterrent to Soviet dominance of Europe and Japan and thus ultimately as a guarantor against Soviet hegemony of the Eurasian landmass and Japan.

Mao and Chou now believed that the USSR was following a long-term policy of neutralizing and isolating the United States while Soviet power achieved a dominant world position. Once this was achieved, Moscow would then be able to bring China to heel. Thus Peking began to make clear that it favored strong U.S. forces in Europe, the retention of the U.S.-Japan Mutual Security Treaty, and even the maintenance of some U.S. bases elsewhere in Asia.

1972—THE VISIT AND THE OFFENSIVE

The world view of the North Vietnamese leaders naturally did not change. Shortly before Nixon flew into Peking, Hanoi released a speech by Politburo member Truong Chinh that reiterated the view that the basic contradictions in human society were between the socialist and the imperialist camps, between the working class and the bourgeoisie, between the oppressed peoples and imperialism, and between the imperialists. U.S. imperialism was changing its tactics, Truong Chinh said, but it still had one central objective: world hegemony.[81] After Nixon had returned from his successful visit to China, Nhan Dan indirectly attacked the Sino-U.S. communiqué and Nixon's statements in Peking about peace in Asia. Like Truong Chinh, Nhan Dan proclaimed that the United States was still seeking dominance in Asia, that it had "not changed a bit," and that it was still "the most dangerous enemy, the enemy number one of all nations in the world."[82]

China did not agree. In the communiqué signed by Nixon and Chou in Shanghai on February 27, 1972, China expressed its firm support for the struggle of the Indochinese people in attaining their goal but did not directly condemn the United States in this regard. Both sides agreed that their relations should be conducted on the basis of peaceful coexistence and that international disputes should be settled without resort to the use of threat of force. Both sides also agreed that neither should seek hegemony in the Asian Pacific region and that each was opposed to efforts by any other country or group of countries to establish hegemony.

Thus, the United States and China formalized their mutual re-assessment of the other's intentions; each no longer saw the other as the major threat in Asia but instead as an important counter to the expansionism of others.

China's reaction to the North Vietnamese spring offensive of 1972 and the U.S. blockade of the DRV reflected the changes that had been wrought by the U.S.-Chinese rapprochement.

During 1971, Hanoi had continued to stress the importance of offensives by main-force units and the decisive impact of "battles of annihilation." With the withdrawal of U.S. ground combat forces, the ground war once again became essentially a battle between the two Vietnamese armies. The North began to claim that its main-force army could now "completely defeat the southern puppet army" even if the latter received U.S. logistics and air support. On March 26 the DRV military commentator, "Chien Thang," in an article in Nhan Dan reiterated the view that only with large attacks by regular forces could one side bring about a "clear change in the balance of forces on the battlefield."

"Chien Thang" was apparently reflecting the decisions of the Lao Dong Central Committee meeting earlier in the year for the launching of the all-out conventional warfare offensive against the South. On March 31 all but 4 of the 15 divisions of the North Vietnamese Army smashed into South Vietnam on three major fronts. The DRV was intent on maximizing its military position before responding to Nixon's eight-point proposal, which had been given secretly in Paris in October 1971. In addition, Hanoi probably felt that before it could agree to a ceasefire and a political settlement it had to occupy territory within the South and to deal a blow to "pacification."

The United States responded with intensified bombing of North Vietnam and in May with extensive mining of DRV harbors. Peking's reaction to the sharpening of the conflict was shaped to minimize the effect on Sino-U.S. relations while secondarily protecting China's stake in its relations with Hanoi. The Soviet reaction was balanced in the same manner. In June another Sino-DRV supplementary aid agreement was concluded, and by September the Chinese had given in to pressure from Hanoi for increased facilitation of Soviet supplies through China. Soviet and East European ships began to unload aid shipments for Hanoi in Chinese ports, which were then transported overland to the Vietnamese border. The Chinese also reportedly agreed to increase rail shipments of Soviet aid across China.

But in contrast to Peking's categorical point-by-point rejection of Nixon's eight-point proposal, which was made public on January 25, 1972, the Chinese after the Shanghai communiqué made no direct criticism of U.S. peace plans. At the same time Peking gave only limited support to the People's Revolutionary Government's (Viet Cong) seven-point proposal, referring to it as providing a basis for settlement but not, as stated before, the "only" basis. The implication was that Nixon's new proposals of May also provided a basis for a compromise agreement.

The PRC's support in the summer and fall of 1972 for an early U.S.-DRV compromise was suggested by Hanoi's continued criticism of "none too agreeable" outside pressures for compromise. In addition, Peking indicated that there was no alternative to dealing with Nixon and that the U.S. elections were unlikely to result in an administration willing to capitulate. Unlike Hanoi, Peking ignored the U.S. election campaign as well as criticism of the president's Vietnam policy by his political opponents or even by U.S. newspapers. In the Chinese outlook, McGovern's Vietnam proposals and indeed the senator himself hardly seemed to exist.

Peking reacted with composure to the breakdown of the Vietnam negotiations in October and then in December 1972. China's controlled reaction was seen in its restrained treatment of the alleged bombing of a Chinese ship in Haiphong harbor and in various official statements on Vietnam. Most striking was the calm reaction of both Peking and Moscow to the intense U.S. bombing of Hanoi during Christmas week.

It is uncertain what direct pressure the Chinese or the Soviets brought upon the North Vietnamese. But it is clear that their attitude contributed to a sense of isolation in Hanoi and greatly strengthened the position of those in North Vietnam who argued for a settlement. Finally the agreement on ending the war was signed in Paris on January 23.

The Chinese called the agreement a "great victory" ending the involvement of foreign forces and allowing the South Vietnamese people to solve their political problems free of outside interference. Like Hanoi, Peking referred to the struggle as entering a "new stage." But it was clear that the Chinese foresaw a protracted political stalemate in South Vietnam and that they favored communist acquiescence in this situation for some indefinite time.

The North Vietnam assessment was similar to that of 1954. In light of the attitude of their allies and the balance of forces, another temporary settlement short of total victory was necessary.

The party journal Hoc Tap spelled this out in its March 1973 issue in an article by alternate Central Committee member Hoang Tung. The author pointed out that the settlement did not represent a "complete" victory but only "the greatest victory we could win considering the actual balance of forces between us and the enemy." Hoang Tung noted that the failure of the earlier wars in Korea and Vietnam to unify their respective countries had also been due to the "stalemate" between the international "revolutionary and counter-revolutionary forces."

184

In Cambodia the communist forces had steadily grown and by the end of 1972 no longer needed to rely upon Vietnamese communist troops. The Lon Nol government in Phnom Penh, beset by corruption and efficiency and atrophied by reliance on U.S. air power, was tottering on the brink of defeat. At the beginning of 1973, it was evident that Peking favored a settlement that would maximize Sihanouk's role but that it was also working to keep its fences mended with the communist forces led by Khieu Samphan and with Hanoi.

As in its policies toward Vietnam, China's primary interest in Cambodia was now to limit the impact of events there on its broader interests with the United States and in particular to avoid escalation. So long as the conflict could be contained, the Chinese seemed confident that whatever the outcome it would not be unfavorable to their limited interests in Cambodia.

COST AND BENEFITS

The long-term consequences of the Indochina wars await the future historian's judgment. Certainly the social and human costs for the United States for both Vietnams, and for Laos and Cambodia were enormous. The political benefits for the United States were, at best, intangible, and the consequences for the two Vietnamese regimes remain uncertain.

A 36-page statistical report by a Library of Congress team released on July 10, 1971 detailed the "Impact of the Vietnam War."[83] The cost of the war for the United States from fiscal year 1965 to 1971 came to about $120 billion, or about $600 for every American man, woman, and child. Using past wars as a guide, the researchers noted that one economist had estimated that veterans' benefits would eventually add another 50 percent to the military cost of the war.

In the 10 years from January 1, 1961, through February, 1971, the United States lost a total of 44,610 men killed in action, and 149,154 were wounded serious enough to require hospitalization. By official count, the United States lost 4,318 helicopters and 3,284 fixed-wing aircraft in Southeast Asia, about half of which were lost to hostile action and the others to accidents. In World War II, the United States lost 45,806 aircraft to all causes and during the Korean conflict 3,314.

South Vietnamese troops and militia suffered a total of 135,970 battle deaths through 1970. The United States claimed 714,984 North Vietnamese and Viet Cong had been killed through February 1971. The United States expended some 5.5 million tons of "aviation munitions," about twice the total of U.S. bombs dropped in World War II.

On the other hand, the material cost to both the Soviet Union and China was minimal. Extrapolating from State Department figures, one may estimate Soviet and Chinese costs for the period 1965 to 1971 is approximately $3.5 billion and $1.5 billion, respectively. Combined, their economic cost was equivalent to 1/24th that of the United States. In lives, both communist powers lost only a handful of citizens caught inadvertently in U.S. bombing raids on North Vietnam.

On the positive side, the United States at the time of the peace agreement could claim to have shown its willingness to back up its international commitments, to have prevented the North Vietnamese with Soviet and Chinese backing from having achieved their final goals, and to have given the Saigon government the opportunity to defend itself. Critics, however, could point out that the experience had made the American people less willing to back up other less ambiguous and more realistic commitments and that the long-term viability of the Siagon government was questionable. Hanoi had not been forced to give up its long-term objectives in the South.

The U.S. effort to contain China by forcing Hanoi to abandon its goals in Vietnam failed in part because of the American fear of provoking China. This frustrating episode of containment of a supposed Chinese proxy forced a reassessment of the policy and the beginning of its political opposite—a search for accommodation with China itself.

Although Hanoi's bold strategies during the Tet offensive, the Cambodian incursions of 1970, and the Lamson operation of 1971 had given Mao some bad moments, he could claim that some of his views of 1964-65 had been vindicated. As he had predicted, the "local war" of national liberation in Vietnam had been contained and nuclear war had been avoided, and at the same time Peking had made no concession to its "revisionist" rival in Moscow. Mao had continued to give priority to his own internal goals and to his challenge of Moscow's ideological leadership.

Liu Shao-chi had been purged in 1966 when the United States was threatening and he urged reconciliation with the USSR. Lin Piao was purged in 1971 when the Soviets were threatening and he opposed reconciliation with the United States. Mao felt he could handle the capitalist Americans whether they were threatening or entreating, but he was determined never to make up with the heretical Soviets until they accorded equality to China within the international communist movement.

In addition, although the intensification of the Vietnam war heightened the military encirclement of China for several years, the inconclusive results actually enhanced interest among anticommunist Asian governments in accommodation with China and in military neutralization.

On the other hand, the Soviet policy of reengagement in the Vietnam conflict and its offer of united action in support of Hanoi effectively destroyed Mao's budding communist front in Asia. By 1971, China's interest in Vietnam and Indochina no longer focused on its contest with the USSR for leadership of the international movement but rather on the strategic goal of discouraging the expansion of Soviet and potentially Japanese power into the partial vacuum created by U.S. retrenchment.

Security and ideology had been reconciled. The Indochina wars no longer posed a threat to China, and the ideological goals of 1965 in regard to the United States were no longer relevant.

NOTES

1. Here, for example, is Sihanouk on Chau Seng (Phnom Penh Domestic Radio, September 18, 1967): ". . . Well, you see, the fact is that through Chau Seng, they tried to infect all of Cambodia by means of a well-planned maneuver. Now, in Peking they regret their failure. Of course, it is now necessary to move back a little in order to move forward better, to overcome a new obstacle. However, I come to the conclusion that no matter what may happen and even though China and Cambodia remain very friendly, I will never give it such a free hand here in my house, ha, ha. Naturally, China is free to do as it pleases in its house or even in the houses of others, ha, ha, if the others gladly allow themselves to be swallowed by China. This is their own affair and not the affair of Cambodia."

2. Phnom Penh Domestic Service, September 18, 1967.
3. Ibid.
4. Ibid.
5. Phnom Penh Domestic Radio, March 6, 1968.
6. Far Eastern Economic Review, September 4, 1969.
7. Phnom Penh Domestic Service, March 6, 1969.
8. Ibid., April 23, 1969.
9. Sangkum, June 1969.
10. Ibid., October 1969, p. 95.
11. Straits Times, April 17, 1969.
12. Documents on Viet Cong and North Vietnamese Aggression Against Cambodia (1970), Ministry of Information, Phnom Penh.
13. Phnom Penh Domestic Radio, March 18, 1968.
14. Sangkum, November, 1969.
15. Washington Post, February 28, 1970.
16. Sihanouk speech on the first anniversary of his arrival in China, NCNA (English), March 19, 1970.

17. Hanoi Domestic Service, March 21, 1970.

18. In a speech in Pyongyang, NCNA April 8.

19. Quoted by Sihanouk in his message of thanks to Pham Van Dong, March 26, 1970. Hanoi Radio in Vietnamese, March 31, 1970.

20. Phnom Penh Domestic Radio, May 11, 1970.

21. Stuart H. Loory, Washington dispatch, May 8, International Herald-Tribune, May 9, 1970.

22. People's Daily, April 21, 1970.

23. Peking Review, Special Issue, May 8, 1970.

24. Ibid.

25. Ibid.

26. Sihanouk statement, April 30 NCNA, April 30, 1970.

27. NCNA, May 6, 1970.

28. VNA, May 3, 1970.

29. L'Espresso, Interview with Alessandro Casello, Rome, December 27, 1970.

30. Ibid.

31. NCNA, June 27, 1970.

32. Report by John Burns of Toronto Globe and Mail in International Herald-Tribune, July 29, 30, 1972.

33. The President's "Annual Foreign Policy Report," February 9, 1972. United States Information Service, "Documentation" (Hong Kong: February 1972).

34. New York Times, August 3, 1971. The staff report was written by James G. Lowenstein and Richard M. Moose.

35. According to the Foreign Relations Committee Staff report cited earlier, in fiscal year 1970, which ended on July 1, a "partial total" of U.S. expenditures in Laos came to $284.2 million, of which $162.2 million was for military aid, $52 million for economic aid, and $70 million was spent by the CIA exclusive of the amount spent on Thai forces in the country. For fiscal year 1971 the military and economic aid plus the CIA programs—including a 30,000-man irregular force—was expected to come to $374 million. Not included in these estimates were the costs of U.S. bombing operations in northern Laos in support of the Royal Laotian forces and in southern Laos against the Ho Chi Minh supply trail. U.S. air sorties in Laos were 340 in April 1970 compared to 440 in the first part of 1969.

36. Sulzberger was citing an article by Edmund Stillman of the Hudson Institute published in the Annals of the American Academy of Political and Social Science. Stillman set up the theoretical circumstances of a U.S. invasion of North Vietnam, the DRV's disintegration, Chinese intervention, and U.S. nuclear attacks on China.

37. Edgar Snow, "A Conversation with Mao Tse-tung," Life, April 30, 1971.

38. Ibid.

39. "Foreign Policy Report," 1972, op. cit.

40. Soviet Divisions in the Far East: 1968-15, 1969-21, 1970-30, 1971-33, "The Shadow of Peking in the Pages of Pravda," Radio Free Europe Research, September 7, 1971.

41. Lin Piao message to Minister Tran Nam Trung on 10th anniversary of Vietnam People's Liberation Armed Forces. NCNA February 14, 1972.

42. NCNA, February 13, 1971.

43. Ibid., February 15, 1971.

44. PRC Government Statement, February 12, NCNA February 12, 1971, editorial.

45. Pravda. This offer was revealed in a July 1 article by Alexandrov.

46. Revealed by Brezhnev in a speech to the Trade Union Congress, March 20, 1972, Radio Moscow, March 21.

47. Henry Bradsher in Washington Star, November 2, 1971.

48. Bernard Gwertzman in New York Times, August 25, 1971.

49. Red Star in an article by V. Vasilyev on December 29, 1971, suggested that the Sino-Soviet border question was an issue in the Chinese leadership struggle.

50. Red Flag, People's Daily, Liberation Army Daily, Joint Editorial, December 1, 1971.

51. For example, in the 1972 New Year's joint editorial.

52. Hunan Provincial Radio, November 5, 1971.

53. Szechwan Provincial Service, April 13, 1972.

54. Hong Kong Standard, December 2, 1971.

55. International Herald-Tribune, July 29, 30, 1972.

56. Asian, August 6-12, 1972.

57. Radio Moscow, November 30, 1971.

58. Ibid.

59. Pravda, December 5, 1971.

60. Tuyen Huan (Party Study Journal), January-February Issue.

61. Peking Review; see pictures in February 19, 1971 issue.

62. NCNA, March 5-8, 1971.

63. People's Daily, March 21, 1971.

64. NCNA, March 12, "Worker-Peasant-Soldier Battlefield Special Column."

65. Quan Doi Nhan Dan, March 24, 1971.

66. Nhan Dan, March 25, 1971.

67. Quan Doi Nhan Dan, April 2, 1971.

68. Ibid.

69. South China Morning Post, February 5, 1972. Chou told this to a visiting delegation of U.S. scholars.

70. This view was given by Gough Whitlam, leader of Australia's opposition Labor Party, upon leaving China in early July. However,

later, Whitlam indicated that no Chinese official had told him this was the PRC's policy.

71. See Nhan Dan editorials July 19, 20, and 22, and Foreign Ministry statement July 21.

72. Liberation Radio, July 19, 1971.

73. Nhan Dan, July 22, 1971.

74. General Giap in his congratulatory message to Lin Piao on the anniversary of the PLA neglected to apply this term to Chinese aid for the first time in seven years.

75. Chou told this to a French parliamentary mission. South China Morning Post, February 11, 1972.

76. People's Daily, January 29, 1972.

77. Troung Chinh, "Apropos of the US Global Strategy," Vietnam Courier, February 14, 1972.

78. "A Powerful Weapon to Unite the People and Defeat the Enemy," Red Flag, no. 9, August 2, 1971.

79. People's Daily, November 11, 1965.

80. "Decision of the Central Committee of the Chinese Communist Party Concerning the Great Proletarian Cultural Revolution," August 12, 1966 (Peking: Foreign Languages Press, 1970).

81. Truong Chinh, op. cit.

82. Nhan Dan, March 3, 1972.

83. Washington Post, July 11, 1971.

4

CHINA AND BURMA:
A LESSON IN PEACEFUL
COEXISTENCE

Burmese neutrality was based on the assumption that the non-communist neighbors of China could reach a satisfactory and permanent accommodation with the communist regime in Peking without surrendering their own neutrality or integrity. The essence of this relationship was a recognition on each side of the other's sovereign interests. As a "bourgeois nationalist" regime not tied to "imperialism," Burma had pledged nonparticipation in any military bloc or alliance aimed defensively or otherwise at China. In addition, to earn peaceful coexistence, such regimes were expected to support China on those international issues that touched upon the basic legality and sovereignty of the communist regime—namely the questions of Taiwan, Tibet, and Chinese representation in the United Nations. In return, China was expected to refrain from interference in the internal affairs of these states, in particular by abstaining from material support to indigenous communist parties and by adopting a cooperative attitude toward the question of overseas Chinese nationals.

Initially, this policy did not seem promising. The young regime in Peking adopted a hostile and ideologically oriented attitude toward the bourgeois government of U Nu, as it did toward the regimes of Jawaharlal Nehru, Sukarno, and others. But the Burmese leaders displayed extraordinary restraint, and by 1954 their hope that a non-hostile posture on Burma's part would evoke a live-and-let-live response in the Chinese seemed to have been realized. Nevertheless in the summer of 1967, the PRC reversed its policy and publicly called for the overthrow of the Burmese Government. It once again pledged support for the Burmese Communist Party (BCP) in its revolutionary war against the "reactionary" Rangoon regime and demanded that it allow the overseas Chinese in Burma to demonstrate their loyalty to the motherland. By early 1968 there were reports of substantial Chinese material help to Burmese communists and tribal insurgents along the Sino-Burmese border. During the Cultural Revolution, fears that China's ultimate intentions might go beyond the establishment of friendly and neutral neighbors appeared to be confirmed. At this time, clashes over traditional and parochial interests were exacerbated by China's ideological position and by the radicalization of China's internal politics.

CHINA AND THE BURMESE COMMUNISTS

For several years prior to the Cultural Revolution, various elements within the Chinese leadership had worked at cross-purposes in regard to the Burmese communists and the Burmese Government. This duality in approach to Burma had gradually evolved from different evaluations of how best to promote China's ideological and strategic interests in Burma.

The ambivalent approach within the CCP is reflected in the history of the relationship between the BCP and CCP. The BCP was established on August 15, 1939, and until the end of World War II it was theoretically the ward of the British Communist Party. In the postwar years, however, there was a natural reorientation of the Burmese party to the increasingly powerful CCP to the north.

The two major BCP leaders, Thakin Than Tun and Ba Thien Tin,* attended the communist conferences in Calcutta in February 1949, where the new militant Cominform line dominated the discussions.[1] Inspired by this experience, by the example of the Chinese and Vietnamese communists, and by conditions in Burma, the BCP denounced the "sham independence" achieved by U Nu and the Anti-Fascist People's Freedom League (AFPFL) and launched its own violent insurrection. One of the BCP leaders who supported the revolutionary line was an Indian Burmese named Goshal, of whom we will hear more later.

The communist uprising combined with rebellions of the various minority groups, especially the Karens, came close to toppling the

---

*In 1946 one BCP leader, Thakin Soe, broke away from the main organization, formed a splinter group known as the Red Flags, and immediately launched a campaign of violence. Personal animosity maintained the split within the Communist Party, but the Red Flags were always a much smaller force than the BCP (known as the White Flags). China apparently maintained ties only with the BCP. Thakin Soe was killed by the Burmese Army in November 1970.

AFPFL government, which at one point held only the capital city. But despite several efforts, the enemies of the government were unable to create any effective unity. By July 1950, the tide had turned, and at the end of that year it seemed the worst was over.[2]

In late 1949 or early 1950, the BCP sent two Central Committee members to Peking for consultation.[3] From this time on, the BCP was increasingly tied to the Chinese party.

The Chinese Marxists, carried away with their own astounding victory, were in full accord with the assertive Cominform line of 1947. The new People's Republic of China felt that Burma, India, Pakistan, Ceylon, Indonesia, and the Philippines were still under the "imperialist yolk." At the meeting of World Federation of Trade Unions in Peking in November 1949, speakers directly attacked U Nu, Nehru, and Sukarno. Liu Shao-chi stressed the need in Asia "to create, wherever and whenever possible, people's armies . . . and supporting bases" under the leadership of local communist parties. He twice mentioned the Burmese rebellion immediately after that of the Vietnamese and before those of Malaya, the Philippines, Indonesia, and other areas, a priority that would be repeated in Peking's propaganda 18 years later. The various organs of Chinese propaganda denounced the "reactionary" government in Rangoon, praised the revolutionary struggle of the Burmese communists, and urged the overseas Chinese in Burma to lend this struggle their support.

U Nu and the other Burmese leaders, however, chose to overlook China's propaganda and political support for the BCP and to demonstrate an accommodating posture toward Peking in the hope that correct, if not friendly, relations could be established.[4] Consequently on December 16, 1949, Burma became the first noncommunist government to recognize the People's Republic of China. The Chinese however delayed the full establishment of diplomatic relations until August 1950, after the Korean War had begun and after the main communist threat in Burma had passed.

During this early period, the government of Burma was most concerned about the prospect of direct Chinese assistance to the BCP insurgents—often referred to as the White Flags. Rangoon hoped that China's internal problems together with the Korean War, Taiwan, and Indochina would occupy its resources and prevent flagrant intervention in Burma. This hope seemed to bear fruit, for Peking began to talk less of the "liberation of Burma" and more of friendship.[5] Nevertheless during the next few years radio broadcasts from Peking continued to carry subversive messages and propaganda in the name of the Burmese Communist Party.[6]

By 1950 several thousand remnants of the Chinese Nationalist Army had taken refuge across the border in Burma. During the Korean War, the U.S. Government allegedly supplied these troops in the hope that they could be used somehow to divert the Chinese communists. This development embittered Burmese-U.S. relations for many years. At the same time Peking was still furnishing the BCP with arms, training, and even some military advisers, but it made no significant effort during these early years to assist the BCP to overthrow the Rangoon government.[7] As suggested, this was because of the weakening position of the BCP insurgents after 1950, their failure to establish a base on the Sino-Burmese border,[8] China's preoccupation with other serious external problems, and its interest in retaining the political support of the Burmese Government on such issues as UN representation and UN condemnation of China as an aggressor. In addition, Burma's consistently friendly posture, its efforts to drive out the Chinese Nationalist remnants, the obvious reality of its independence, and its Marxist orientation served to change the perceptions of at least some of the Chinese leadership as to the nature of the "bourgeois-nationalist" government in Rangoon. Some leaders, such as Liu Shao-chi and Chou En-lai, apparently began to see promising opportunities for China in the development of a "united front from above" with such "national-democratic" regimes as U Nu's. In fact, one of the earliest signs that Asian communist parties outside of Indochina were preparing a major reversal in strategy occurred in Burma.

In the course of 1951 the Burmese Army cleared the communist insurgents from the frontier region, and subsequently the Chinese began to advise the BCP to promote a negotiated settlement.[9] That same year Liu Shao-chi reportedly criticized the Burmese Communist Party for following an ultra-leftist line and urged it to adopt a moderate stance toward the AFPFL government, to declare its desire for peace, and to restrict its military activity to defensive actions.[10] Accordingly, the BCP, in October 1951, adopted a new line, which called for an end to the fighting and the formation of a coalition government. In May 1951 the Chinese Ambassador to Burma publicly denied that there was any contact between China and the BCP in Burma,[11] and in December the party once again called for a coalition government under a broad united front.[12] For the next two and a half years the BCP held to this line, but the Burmese Government rejected a coalition and refused to legalize the party. Instead it continued to offer amnesty only if the communists laid down their arms.

THE FIVE PRINCIPLES ARE IMPLEMENTED

Friendly, as distinct from correct, relations with the PRC were initiated in June 1954. Chinese Premier Chou En-lai visited Rangoon and joined with U Nu in declaring adherence to the "five principles of peaceful coexistence." These principles, which Chou and Nehru had previously formalized as the guiding precepts in Sino-Indian relations, were (1) mutual respect for territory and sovereignty, (2) nonaggression, (3) noninterference in internal affairs, (4) equality in mutual benefit, and (5) peaceful coexistence.

In a joint communiqué issued at the close of this visit, Chou affirmed that "the people of each nation should have the right to choose their own state system and way of life without interference from other nations." Chou seemed to pronounce an embargo on the export of revolution by proclaiming that "outside interference with the common will expressed by the people of any nation should not be permitted."[13] During his visit, Chou advised U Nu not to join the Manila pact or engage in any military agreements with the United States.[14] And in return for the Chinese pledge of noninterference, the Burmese leaders reaffirmed their neutralist course. U Nu also may have received a direct Chinese pledge of a hands-off policy toward the Burmese insurrection during his trip to Peking in November 1954. Upon his return to Rangoon, U Nu, in reply to a press conference question, implied that the Chinese Government had categorically denied any connection with the BCP.[15]

Shortly before Chou's visit in June, however, the Burmese Communist Party had fallen out of step with the Chinese Government and deviated from the peace-and-unity line with a new campaign of violence. But this departure did not last, and in 1955 the BCP, apparently under Chinese pressure, again adopted a line that called for negotiation and coalition.[16] This line however was reinstituted only after a serious struggle within the party—a struggle that continued for the next 12 years and that culminated in a bloody intraparty purge in 1967.

In 1954 most of the BCP cadres who had been sent to China between 1951-53 to receive political and ideological training were assigned jobs elsewhere in China. Many took Chinese wives and settled down for an indefinite exile. A few of the Burmese communists led by Ba Thien Tin and Than Myaing remained in the Chinese capital and set up a small office of the BCP. This liaison group was kept discreetly in the background until the Cultural Revolution.

THE UNITED-FRONT-FROM-ABOVE

The effect of China's united-front-from-above with the Burmese Government called for a temporary abandonment of the BCP's hopes for the seizure of power by force. Emphasis was given to the legal struggle of the above-ground communist-front groups in Burma, the most important of which was the Burmese Workers' Party (BWP). Soviet comment on the BWP indicated that it was eventually to be regarded as the official communist party. The BCP later charged that at this time the "revisionist renegades" were "putting into practice their so-called road of peaceful development . . . and even attempted to foster another party to counter the Communist Party of Burma."[17]

For the next two years the united-front strategy seemed to be making headway. The BWP formed a National United Front (NUF) with several other organizations for the 1956 elections. The NUF campaigned on the promise that it would negotiate on equal terms with the communists and form a coalition with them for a national-unity government.[18] The possibility of a parliamentary path to power for the Burmese communists seemed confirmed when the NUF, which allegedly received financial assistance from the PRC Embassy,[19] won 30 percent of the votes in the 1956 elections. Presumably, if the NUF had actually won the election, it would have allowed the BCP to join the government and still retain its independent armed force. (The AFPFL, on the other hand, still insisted that the communists surrender their arms.) This situation would have constituted a united front on the Maoist model in which communist elements participated in a coalition (or a national democratic united front) but retained an independent program and an independent power base until such time as they were effectively in control. Later, Liu Shao-chi allegedly advised the BCP to disband its people's army and take up what was essentially a revisionist united front.

Before this occurred, however, the communists were provided increased room for political maneuver by the factional breakup of the AFPFL in mid-1958 caused by a conflict between U Nu and two of his deputy prime ministers. As a result, U Nu was forced to rely upon the parliamentary support of the NUF to retain his premiership.[20] In August the U Nu government offered full amnesty to all surrendering rebels. A large group of communists thereupon "came out into the light" and almost immediately established a new legal party, the People's Comrades Party, to contest the November elections with a procommunist international and domestic program.[21] At the same time the BCP stepped up its campaign for a negotiated settlement.

The armed forces, however, under General Ne Win, opposed U Nu's sweeping amnesty terms, rejected suggestions to incorporate the surrendering rebels into the military, and cautioned U Nu not to accept parliamentary support from the communists.[22]

Political stability declined rapidly, and in the autumn of 1958, Ne Win, commander of the army, took over the premiership at U Nu's request and established a caretaker government. The November elections were called off.

During the next two years, Ne Win moved vigorously against the estimated 8,000 communist guerrillas and tribal insurgents and reduced the total to approximately 5,000.[23] By the time of the 1960 elections the NUF was unable to win a single seat in parliament and polled only 5 percent of the total vote.[24] Thus, for the time being, the hopes of the BCP of achieving power through a united-front-from-above were over. In 1959 the BCP established another "illegal" united-front-from-below with some of the minority insurgents; this organization was called the National Democratic United Front (NDUF).

Despite the suppression of the "proletarian forces in Burma," China soon began to make an even larger investment in its relations with the government in Rangoon. In 1960 China concluded a preliminary boundary agreement with the Ne Win government on terms favorable to the Burmese.[25] It reversed its previous position on the boundary and accepted terms that were essentially those proposed by U Nu in 1956. The PRC also concluded with Burma its first treaty of friendship and nonagression with a noncommunist state. Shortly afterward, the two governments cooperated in the ousting of the "remnant KMT troops" in Burma* (although Rangoon denied that Chinese troops were involved in the campaign), and in January 1961, with U Nu temporarily back as premier, China officially extended a 30 million pound, interest-free loan to Burma, the largest China had ever made to a noncommunist country.

General Ne Win assumed power a second time on March 2, 1962 (this time in a coup), and his military Revolutionary Council attempted to implement a new, more Marxist "Burmese way to socialism." At the same time, the Revolutionary Council relentlessly pursued the communist guerrillas and followed a more isolationist-type neutrality. U.S. activity was particularly restricted. The Ford and Asia Foundations were closed by the government. Fulbright exchanges were ended, and it even became difficult for American students and scholars to travel to Burma for field study. To some Western observers, it appeared that despite its vigorous suppression of its domestic communists, the military government was leaning dangerously close to Communist China.[26] China continued to treat its relations with the Ne Win government as a model of Peking-style peaceful coexistence. The two top government officials in Peking, Liu Shao-chi, who was now the chief of state, and Premier Chou En-Lai, as well as Foreign Minister Chen Yi, all appeared to have a personal role in this policy.

The BCP and China, however, were both faced with the question of what strategy the communist forces in Burma should adopt in the

---

*Approximately 4,300 Nationalist irregulars and their dependents evacuated Burma in 1961, and the majority returned to Taiwan.

face of Ne Win's suppression of the communist front groups. Should the BCP continue to keep the bedraggled insurrection scratching along as best it could, or should it give up its independent power base— that is, disband its armed force? If it continued the armed struggle, it had little prospect of success without major Chinese assistance, and such assistance would surely have compromised China's large investment in its relations with Rangoon. However, if it followed the latter course, it would have had to abandon the thought of seizing power and content itself with exerting political influence on the radical but still "bourgeois" government. In effect, it would have been pursuing the path of peaceful transition to power.

Liu Shao-chi apparently did not consider the 1960 Moscow declaration on the existence of "national-democratic" states and peaceful transition so profoundly revisionist as did Mao Tse-tung. The fact that the CCP in 1964 declared that it was wrong in having made concessions on this point in the 1960 declaration and the deluge of charges made beginning in 1967 that Liu always had been a recalcitrant revisionist and that he had sold out the Burmese Communist Party tend to support this supposition.

At this time, ideologues in the Chinese party placed more emphasis than did Liu and Chou on the interests of the Burmese Communist Party and on maintenance by the BCP of its independent power base. They were prepared for the BCP to engage in a Maoist strategy of coalition and cooperation with a "national-democratic" government so long as the BCP retained its people's army—the issue on which past negotiations had always foundered and on which the Ne Win regime seemed even more adamant than its predecessor. The pragmatic Chinese leaders concerned with foreign affairs, however, tended to stress the importance of maintaining a friendly and accommodating government in Rangoon, even if an anticommunist one. From about 1960 to 1963, a moderate line was generally followed by the Burmese communists. The BCP itself attended the December 1960 Moscow conference, and its Politburo adopted a number of resolutions, including a eulogy of the conference and a statement that "peace through negotiations" remained the party's policy.

In the early 1960s, intensification of the conflicts in Indochina, China's growing dispute with India, and the PRC's own serious internal problems gave the moderates in China increased incentive to strengthen government-to-government relations with Burma. The development of the Sino-Soviet dispute and China's related determination to expand its diplomatic activity in Africa and Asia also provided additional motivation for cordial relations with the Burmese Government. A friendly Sino-Burmese relationship could be pointed to as a model and as a refutation of Indian, Soviet, and Western charges of alleged Chinese aggressiveness. It also provided China with a communications gateway to South Asia and Africa. In addition, as a result of the collapse of the Great Leap Forward, pragmatism and liberalism were in relative ascendancy in China during the first two years of the 1960s; and the reorganization of internal policies provided scope for a similar approach abroad.

Thus Peking's policy toward Burma at this time was "revisionist" or classic rightist in that it emphasized a united-front-from-above with the government of Burma on the international as well as the national level. For the BCP in early 1963 the Sino-Soviet dispute was strictly theoretical without practical consequences. Both Moscow and Peking at this time were emphasizing state-to-state relations with the Government of the Union of Burma (GUB), and although China still provided sanctuary to the BCP cadres who had come over in the early 1950s, there is no evidence of any new movement of Burmese recruits or cadres into China during the late 1950s or the early 1960s.

Consequently, there was no basis for a split in the BCP at this time between pro-China and pro-Soviet positions.[27] The Burmese communists were probably in general agreement on supporting Peking, with whom they had been closely tied since 1950, as against Moscow. However, a division gradually developed within the BCP that paralleled and was stimulated by the evolving division of the Chinese party along Liu-ist and Maoist lines.

The Indian-Burmese Goshal (who was one of the founders of the party), Yebaw (Comrade) Htay, and others were apparently convinced by the end of 1962 that Liu's assessment of Ne Win's new Revolutionary Council was substantially correct; that is, it was an antiimperialist "national-democratic" government whose goal was socialism. Therefore, it was a regime with which the BCP as well as Peking could collaborate.[28]

Than Tun, on the other hand, adamantly opposed any fundamental concession to the Burmese Government, but at this time he was in a difficult position because the Chinese as well as the Soviets supported collaboration with the Rangoon government, and both praised its "Burmese way to socialism."

In April 1963, Liu Shao-chi paid an unusually long visit to Burma and discussed the Sino-Indian border dispute. But probably the main point of discussions during this 20-day visit was the question of negotiations between the Burmese Government and the BCP. Only a few weeks before Liu's arrival, the Rangoon government had, in fact, made a new amnesty offer to the rebels, and a number of prominent communist leaders had accepted.

According to later charges in the Chinese press, Liu Shao-chi, during this visit, "advised the BCP to 'consider the position of Ne Win' and to 'bury their weapons underground and to reorganize their army into national defense units and to surrender to Ne Win's reactionary government.'"[29] In another article, Liu was accused of advising the BCP at this time to follow the "path of India," meaning the path of peaceful transition to power.[30] At this time, according to Peking, another sharp struggle between the two lines was going on in the Burmese Communist Party, "to persist in the revolutionary road of seizing political power by armed force or to go for peaceful transition."[31]

The BCP later publicly charged Liu with disrupting the Burmese revolution in the early 1960s and harboring a "soft spot" for Ne Win but not for the BCP.[32] At the same time Liu was accused of lauding Ne Win's "so-called socialist program" and proclaiming that "should the Burmese form of socialism prove effective, China may have to learn from Burma."[33]

Liu and Chou were in effect treating Burma as a "national-democratic" state—that is, one that could make the transition to socialism without a revolutionary proletarian (Marxist-Leninist) leadership, or one that could attain such a leadership by evolution.

Apparently as a result of the talks between Liu and Ne Win, the Revolutionary Council in Rangoon on June 11 offered "unconditional negotiations," an offer that all previous Burmese governments had refused to make.[34] According to later defectors, Than Tun asked Peking for instructions and was told to proceed.[35] Goshal and Htay were reportedly anxious for the talks to begin, and they were pleased when Ba Thien Tin in Peking informed them of the "green light."[36]

In July and August, some 32 Burmese and Kachin returned from China to join the local BCP delegation led by Htay, which had arrived in Rangoon to negotiate with the Revolutionary Council about an amnesty and legal recognition for the BCP. The hard-line position of the BCP officials who had come from China and who often spoke Chinese among themselves was soon apparent. This group of "Peking returnees" generally supported Than Tun's hard line in the negotiations, a line that actually contradicted the policy of Peking. Than Tun reportedly told the "Peking returnees" that their arrival had been a "dose of strength" for him and had saved the party and the revolution.[37]

This was the time of "struggle between the two lines" in the BCP. If, as seems likely, Liu and Chou were urging the BCP to accommodate the Revolutionary Council and at least superficially disband its revolutionary forces in return for a legal role in the government, the BCP militant faction headed by Chairman Thakin Than Tun successfully resisted any such move.

As suggested, Than Tun had no option in the early spring of 1963 but to go along with the negotiations. But events during the summer began to bring into focus the significance for the BCP of the Maoist line in the international movement and within the CCP itself. The Sino-Soviet bloc was split asunder in July with the agreement on a nuclear test ban treaty between the United States and the USSR, and Peking began openly to challenge Moscow for leadership on the basis of Mao's opposition to the policy of détente with the West and by extension, the BCP could reason, with such "bourgeois nationalists" as Ne Win. The Rangoon talks broke down over the issue of disbanding the insurgent communist forces and over the BCP demand for the retention of "liberated areas." Goshal and Htay were reportedly "most disappointed,"[38] as most likely were Liu Shao-chi and Chou. According to later defectors from the BCP, the party asked Peking for its views on the breakdown of the negotiations. The Chinese party allegedly replied that the BCP should avoid paying too much attention to the past and should concentrate on building unity within the party. The Chinese, however, also allegedly said that the breakdown of the talks had exposed "Ne Win's bogus peace move and his bogus socialism," but that it was wrong to conclude that there were no possibilities for peace in the future. The Chinese allegedly urged the Burmese communists to call for peace "whenever an occasion arises."[39]

A few of the BCP officials returned to China, but 27 of the "Peking returnees" went underground.

In November, Ne Win again moved against the leftists with the arrest of over 300 persons, mostly members of the National United Front.[40] And in January 1964, hostilities between the communist guerrillas and government forces resumed, with the Revolutionary Council proclaiming another all-out war against the insurgents.[41]

At the same time, the Revolutionary Council adopted further measures to isolate the country from the intensifying conflicts in Southeast Asia. Unlike earlier measures, some of these were directed equally against China as against the Western powers. In early 1964, for example, the GUB banned all foreign propaganda, and the cultural and information services of all foreign embassies were placed under tight control. Distribution of unapproved Chinese communist propaganda was declared illegal for the first time since independence. Two hundred Chinese schools were nationalized in 1965 together with all other private schools, and four Chinese newspapers with a combined readership of 200,000 were closed down.[42] In March 1964, the Revolutionary Council passed a law setting up a one-party system, the Burma Socialist Program Party, thereby ruling out any possibility of legal status for the BCP.

These internal actions of the Burmese Government in no way affected its relations with Peking. Chou En-lai visited Rangoon in February, and in July Chou and Chen Yi paid a surprise visit, apparently to counter an earlier visit by Soviet Deputy Premier Anastas Mikoyan. The communiqué issued at the end of the July meeting expressed concern over the situation in Southeast Asia and reaffirmed the validity of Article 3 of the Sino-Burmese treaty, which precluded Burma's joining any military alliance.

While Peking-Rangoon relations seemed to continue on an increasingly warm and cordial basis, the Burmese Communist Party under the control of Than Tun now decided on a new offensive. The Central Committee of the BCP held a series of meetings from June to September 1964 during which the party formulated the line of "winning the war and seizing political power," and it "thoroughly smashed the 1955 bourgeois reactionary line," which had advocated legal struggle.[43]

This meeting was dominated by Thakin Than Tun and the "Peking returnees" led by Ko Aung Gyi, Bo Zeya, and Thakin Pu.[44] The increasingly radical Maoist orientation of this group was reflected in the decision that year to launch an "unprecedented campaign of studying and applying Mao Tse-tung's thoughts"[45] and in the establishment in March 1965 of a new Central Marxism-Leninism School for the party.[46]

The BCP's new line of intensified armed struggle did not fit in with the policy of the Chinese Government toward Rangoon, nor was it apparently compatible with the personal views of Liu and Chou. The Chinese Government leaders were, however, unable or unwilling to pressure the BCP into line. This situation was probably due to the fact that the BCP's policy of intensified struggle appealed to the ideologues in Peking who were directing the conflict with Moscow over just this type question of revolutionary strategy.

Here, then, was a most complex political situation. BCP officials were ensconced in Peking itself, and they were no doubt active lobbyists against the Liu Shao-chi line and for more Chinese assistance to the revolutionary struggle in Burma. They probably found encouragement and support from the radical elements who were gathering strength to challenge Liu Shao-chi. A dichotomy already existed within the Chinese leadership between the ideologists and the relative pragmatists and between the pro- and anti-Liu groups, but unity was maintained through this period, as the latter group, consisting of the major government and party officials, paid lip service to Mao's dictums while apparently attempting to maintain pragmatic and relatively conservative internal and external policies. Peking's ambivalence toward the BCP and the Burmese Government began to come into the open.

This was demonstrated when the BCP sent an anniversary message to the Chinese Communist Party on the occasion of China's National Day on October 1, 1964; the message was broadcast by Peking Radio in both English and Burmese,[47] probably to the consternation of officials in the Chinese Foreign Ministry. The message asserted that the BCP would continue to strive for establishment of "a new Burma of real independence, politically and economically," and it blamed the collapse of the 1963 talks on "sabotage by imperialism, internal reaction and revisionism."[48] The Rangoon press reacted angrily to this incident, but the Burmese Government made no public protest.[49] Rangoon, however, may have made a private protest to the Chinese, possibly at the time of Chen Yi's visit in December of that year, for in 1965 and 1966 no similar statements were carried by Chinese media.

During 1965 the situation remained superficially much the same: Cordial relations were maintained on a state-to-state basis; the BCP continued its armed struggle with no apparent major assistance and little or no political support from China;[50] and the Burmese Government continued its suppression efforts against the communist insurgents. The implicit understanding between Ne Win and the PRC was dramatized when the Burmese Government launched yet another massive drive against the communist insurgents in May 1965[51] and when two months later Ne Win was warmly received by Liu and Chou on an official visit to Peking. In September, Ne Win made a balancing trip to Moscow, which had begun to praise the Revolutionary Council and the "Burmese way to socialism" as following the "noncapitalist" path of development.

DISTURBING SIGNS

While Sino-Burmese relations remained calm on the surface, there were several developments that disturbed the Burmese government. These were the escalation of the war in Vietnam, Peking's assistance to and apparent guidance of the new armed struggle in neighboring Thailand, the increased revolutionary militancy in Peking's propaganda, China's bullying behavior in connection with the Afro-Asian conference, reports of Chinese involvement in the attempted coup against the Indonesian Army on September 30, 1965, and China's role in the Indo-Pakistani war of August and September.

The contradiction between the application of a Maoist revolutionary model in Burma and China's interest in cordial state relations with the Burmese Government, or in any noncommunist country with a significant communist insurgency, was implicit in the September 3, 1965 article by Lin Piao commemorating the V-J Day anniversary. Lin's article, which came only two months after Ne Win's warm reception in Peking, described how Mao's combination of a political strategy of national-democratic united front combined with the self-reliant military tactics of a people's war brought victory against the Japanese imperialists and set the stage for the CCP's eventual seizure of power on the Chinese mainland. Lin emphasized the importance of going through the stage of the national-democratic united front, the "universal truth of Marxism-Leninism" that "without a people's army, the people have nothing," and the "universal practical importance" of Mao's theory of the establishment of rural revolutionary base areas.[52]

This was the exact model the BCP was attempting to follow in Burma. Unlike the Indonesian Communist Party, the BCP possessed a "people's army," but the difficulty was that the country lacked a common enemy against which the party could achieve a true national-democratic united front. Lin Piao had reiterated that a national-democratic revolution must precede the socialist revolution and that in the national-democratic stage, "imperialism and its lackeys are the principal enemies." In Burma, however, there was no imperialist enemy. And while there was always the hope of uniting the tribal insurgents with the social revolutionaries in Burma, it was difficult indeed for the BCP to rally the nation against a "reactionary" government that was accorded high honors by both Moscow and Peking. To complete the Maoist revolutionary model, what the BCP needed was some good old imperialist oppressors and a "Chiang Kai-shek government" in Rangoon.

By the spring of 1966, it was probably apparent to Ne Win that a serious power struggle was under way within the CCP, with the strong prospect that the radical, ideologically oriented faction would come to the top.

In mid-April Liu Shao-chi visited Burma, at which time he may have hinted at the developing struggle on the mainland. In any event, a very warm communiqué and an editorial in the People's Daily again hailed the close ties between Burma and China, based on the principles of peaceful coexistence.[53] These close ties were of course a product of Liu's and Chou's policies. After Liu's visit in April and as the Cultural Revolution was getting into swing in China, Ne Win expressed some concern over China's intentions. In a June interview with a U.S. correspondent, itself an unprecedented act, Ne Win reiterated that neutralism was the only viable policy for Burma, but he declared that he was staunchly anticommunist and aware of China's threat to Burma.[54] In another article, the same correspondent reported that the Burmese Government was reluctant to improve communications along the China-Burma border because of "abundant evidence of Chinese intrigue." According to this article, Ne Win perceived that the nature of Chinese proposals for aid projects would have improved facilities along the Rangoon-Irrawaddy-Burma Road line. As a result there was a careful reduction in projects that might further the Chinese objective.[55]

Although there was no essential modification of Burma's policy of neutrality, a warming in relations with the United States also became manifest in 1966.* In September, when Ne Win made his first official visit to the United States, President Johnson lauded Burma's "independent foreign policy," and in a joint communiqué the United States expressed "understanding" of Burma's neutrality. Almost one year later, after the reversal of its policy in Burma, China charged that, following this visit, the Burmese Government "embarked on the path of opposing China in an all-around way."[56] There were, however, no agreements signed during Ne Win's U.S. visit, which seemed only to reflect a more relaxed view on both sides.[57] Far from threatening Burma's policy of neutrality, the visit indicated U.S. recognition that such a policy was beneficial to its own interests.

China itself continued to issue official praise of Ne Win and his regime long after his trip to Washington. In January 1967, for example, on the occasion of Burma's Independence Day, Foreign Minister Chen Yi praised the great achievements of Burma under Ne Win's leadership:

> Under the leadership of Chairman Ne Win, the Burmese Government and people have waged unremitting struggles toward the road of independent development in order to safeguard State sovereignty and independence and to develop the natural economy and culture, and have scored great successes. In its international relations, the Union of Burma has steadfastly followed a policy of independence, peace and neutrality, and has made valuable contributions to the promotion of Afro-Asian solidarity and the defense of world peace.[58]

But by this time, it was apparent that Liu Shao-chi had been effectively purged from the Chinese leadership. Subsequently, the Chinese press charged that after the overthrow of "Ne Win's good friend" (that is, Liu), the Burmese Government stepped up its "anti-China drive" and that Rangoon papers began to publish articles "viciously attacking the Chinese people's great leader Mao Tse-tung and the Cultural Revolution."[59] In fact, Rangoon papers carried only wire service reports of the Cultural Revolution, which were based on the only sources available, the official Peking press and Red Guard posters. These were sensational enough portrayals but were no more covered in the Burmese press than in any other noncommunist country. Rangoon papers generally avoided editorializing on the subject.[60]

---

*Senator Mike Mansfield visited Burma in December 1965 and proposed that Ne Win accept an invitation to visit the United States.

THE BCP AND THE CULTURAL REVOLUTION

The effects of the Cultural Revolution did however begin to spill over into Burma during the first part of the year. In February, the Burmese foreign minister privately protested against demonstrations outside the Soviet Embassy by Chinese personnel and attacks on the Soviet Union in the Chinese Embassy's photo display case. These protests were later cited as proof of the Burmese Government's "anti-China policy."[61] At the same time, press stories began to appear in Rangoon of numbers of Chinese fleeing Red Guard persecution across the border into Burma. Hundreds of these illegal immigrants were rounded up by Burmese authorities and returned to China.[62]

But most important, as far as the Burmese Government was concerned, were the effects of the Cultural Revolution on the Burmese Communist Party and the overseas Chinese in Burma and eventually upon the institution and psychology of Chinese foreign policy.

In November 1966, a BCP message to the Albanian party congress denounced "peaceful evolution" and the effort of the Communist Party of the Soviet Union "to turn Burma into a country which applied their view." The party was fighting, the BCP declared, "to overthrow the Ne Win government," and this would be achieved "under international conditions and chiefly in accordance with internal conditions."[63]

As 1967 began, the "international conditions" referred to must have seemed promising to the BCP: Liu Shao-chi and his closest colleagues, except for Chou En-lai, were ousted from power, and a violent political campaign with the major theme that "revolution is always right" swept across China. Mao's internal and external enemies were denounced for, among other things, selling out the revolutionary forces, compromising with imperialism and reactionism, and failing to grasp the elemental truth that "the seizure of power by force, the settlement of the issue by war is the highest form of revolutionary struggle." Liu was accused specifically of "reducing assistance and support to the revolutionary struggle of other people."[64]

There was thus created in China the right psychological climate and a political requirement for the Chinese Government to demonstrate with a militant stance its credentials as the bastion of antiimperialism. This need was partially satisfied by the abuse of diplomats in Peking, but it was also manifest in a tough and successful stance against the Portuguese authorities in Macao in January 1967 and the initiation of a similar but unsuccessful effort in Hong Kong in May that same year. The effect was also soon noted in China's propaganda stance toward the various communist parties of Southeast Asia. In May Peking Radio carried the text of a statement by a pro-Peking faction of the Philippine Communist Party, which proclaimed a new armed struggle against the Manila government.[65] In April an official PRC Foreign Ministry statement proclaimed an approaching "new revolutionary high tide" in Indonesia to "overthrow the reactionary rule," and it promised that the Chinese people were determined to provide "firm support" to this revolutionary struggle.[66] During the spring, Chinese propaganda became ecstatic over the alleged "revolutionary armed struggle raging in India," with particular reference to the rebellions of the Nagas and the Mizos and to peasant disturbances in the Darjeeling area of West Bengal.[67] The Communist Party of Thailand, with most of its officials in Peking, also began to surface in 1967, first identifying itself as "supporting" the Thai Patriotic Front (TPF) in its armed struggle to overthrow the Bangkok government[68] and later proclaiming itself as the directing force of the movement.[69]

Certainly this rejection of the Bandung principles nourished by Liu and Chou must have encouraged the BCP. And its leaders in Peking presumably moved to exploit the militant and radical atmosphere in China to their own ends—that is, to convince the Cultural Revolution group to alter the Liu-Chou policy toward the Burmese Government and to put primary stress on the promotion of the BCP revolution.

Perhaps the best evidence that the BCP did attempt to jump on the Cultural Revolution bandwagon and steer it its own way is the report that the propaganda department of its Central Committee in April 1967 launched another intensive campaign to study the thought of Mao Tse-tung. The department also reportedly translated and published Chairman Mao's "brilliant works" in order "to enhance the revolutionization" of the ideology of the Burmese "liberation fighters," and aping the Chinese example, a "Revolutionary Young Red Guard" organization was formed.[70] The party also was said to have organized the "broad masses of Party members" to repudiate the writings of Liu Shao-chi.[71]

The repudiation of Liu Shao-chi may have dumfounded the Burmese "broad masses," but it presumably appealed to the radical Chinese leaders in Peking who were also looking for ways to discredit Liu and indirectly Chou. An optimistic reassessment of revolutionary prospects in Burma was also fostered by reports from the NCNA correspondent in Rangoon and probably by confidential dispatches from the embassy.[72] The NCNA reports served not only to strengthen the Burmese Communist Party's position in Peking but also to create suspicion and resentment within the Burmese Government.

In March, the Chinese Ambassador in Rangoon together with many of his staff departed for home and indoctrination in the Cultural Revolution. The ambassador was replaced by a chargé d'affaires fresh from the ferment of Peking.

But the obsequious adoption by the BCP of the full Maoist line, Red Guards and all, created a serious new division within the ranks of the BCP. This new internal struggle came to a head at a party meeting in April 1967. At this meeting Than Tun and the "Peking returnees" disregarded party organizational rules and packed the meeting with young members in much the same way as Mao had packed the eleventh plenum of the CCP's Central Committee the previous August.[73] Goshal presented a memorandum that again took the view that the goal of the Ne Win regime was indeed socialism and that the view of the BCP was dogmatic and unrealistic.[74]

Goshal and Htay were not only dismissed from the party; they were executed by Than Tun on June 18, 1967. Three other Central Committee supporters of Goshal were also killed—one of them reportedly in Peking (Thakin Than Myaing). This split was later referred to by the BCP vice chairman in Peking as a "fierce battle" in which the thought of Mao Tse-tung had "again triumphed" within the party and the army.[75]

It is of course not known to what extent the BCP, in return for its expressions of loyalty to Mao, was able to win formal commitments from the Cultural Revolution group for a new Chinese policy toward Burma before the events of June. But its lobbying activities in Peking probably had an important influence on the handling of the June incident. It is perhaps significant that the first public Peking broadcast of a BCP message since the report in October 1964 occurred on June 23,[76] the day after Chinese students in Rangoon protested a government ban on Mao buttons.

OVERSEAS CHINESE COME TO LOVE MAO

Also inherent in the polemics of the Cultural Revolution was a strong ethnocentric impulse, which was of direct concern to all Southeast Asian countries. If China was now the "bastion," "the citadel," and the hope of a world socialist state, it naturally followed that the leader of China was the leader of all the world's people. This phenomenon was expressed in the effusive claims of the radicals that people the world over revered Mao Tse-tung as the "most red, red sun in their hearts." Ultimately this ended in the explicit claim that Mao was the spiritual leader of 90 percent of the world's population, obstinately opposed by only 10 percent, the recalcitrant imperialists, revisionists, and reactionaries.

Not surprisingly, this view of the world gave free rein to Chinese chauvinism. As Stalin's propagandists in the 1930s and 1940s credited the Russian people with near superhuman qualities, so Peking's new political campaign resulted in a heightened ethnocentricism among the Chinese and a new focus on the mutual obligations between China and the overseas Chinese.

This view ran counter to the philosophy of Chou En-lai and his colleague Liao Cheng-chih, who was in charge of overseas Chinese affairs. An early hint of a conflict over the question of overseas Chinese between Chou and Liao, on the one hand, and Lin Piao and the radical civilian group, on the other, occurred in October 1966, when Liao went to Kwangtung to greet a group of overseas Chinese returning from Indonesia. The official China News Service quoted Liao as telling the refugees that Mao and Chou were much concerned over them and extended their regards.[77] However, the other official organ, the New China News Agency, reported, without direct quotation, that Liao said he was sent by Lin Piao as well as Mao and Chou. China News Service issued a correction the next day inserting Lin's name between that of Mao and Chou wherever they were mentioned in its previous news item. Red Guards later accused Liao of having deliberately ignored Lin Piao on this occasion.

Beginning in early 1967 a small but activist element among overseas Chinese in many parts of Southeast Asia took to wearing Mao badges and conducting study courses in the thoughts of Mao Tse-tung. Ironically, this nationalistic activity among some of the overseas Chinese was most pronounced in those countries that had friendly relations with the PRC and thus where the Chinese Embassy could encourage it. The promotion of Chinese chauvinism as well as Chinese harassment of Soviet missions in Cambodia, North Vietnam, and Burma provoked all of these governments. Again ironically, the only really serious trouble was generated in Burma, where the overseas Chinese seemed to present less of a social and political problem than perhaps anywhere else in Southeast Asia.[78]

Peking's policy toward the overseas Chinese in Burma by the summer of 1967 seemed to have come full circle. During the early years of Burma's independence, Peking propaganda coupled support for the communist insurgents with attacks on the Rangoon government for its alleged persecution of the overseas Chinese, and at the same time overseas Chinese businessmen were pressured into supporting the BCP.[79] In 1954, however, Chou En-lai announced the principle that overseas Chinese should either become citizens of their host country or disassociate themselves from local political activity. During his visits to Burma in 1955 and 1956, Chou held conversations with leaders of the overseas Chinese community, and he urged them to forgo their Chinese loyalties.[80] This policy continued well into the second Ne Win regime, with Peking failing publicly to protest Burmese Government measures such as nationalization of Chinese schools, newspapers, and businesses or the closing of the Chinese consulate in Mandalay.

In 1967 however, the chauvinism generated by the Cultural Revolution began to manifest itself not only in China's approach to the question of overseas Chinese but also in the attitudes of the pro-Peking Chinese residents in Southeast Asia. In Burma, as in other countries, the reaction of the Chinese population to the Cultural Revolution was mixed. Most of the overseas Chinese in Burma preferred to remain nonpolitical, but many, if not a majority, were probably repelled by the extremism of events on the mainland (this of course is an impressionistic assertion). However, a small but active communist minority, which many years before had won political control of the community, was emboldened to copy the activity of the Red Guards. This activity took the form of organized study sessions of the thoughts of Mao Tse-tung and the wearing of lapel or collar buttons emblazoned with the portrait of Mao. In both these activities, they were encouraged by officials of the Chinese embassy, many of whom by the summer of 1967 had returned to their posts after several months of being dipped into the Cultural Revolution and instructed on the new, more activist proletarian diplomacy.[81] It was at this time that the ultra-leftists in Peking were intensifying their attacks on Liao Cheng-chih's Overseas Chinese Affairs Commission as well as the Foreign Ministry for having curbed the overseas Chinese and having prevented them from "making revolution."[82] The cultural officer of the Chinese Embassy in Rangoon was one of those who after his period of indoctrination returned to his post with new zeal for his job. Certainly he and the other diplomats in the embassy could conclude that it was difficult to err on the side of militancy.

Special night classes were begun on May 12 among overseas Chinese in Rangoon, presumably arranged by the Chinese Embassy. These classes were ostensibly for the study of "Chinese language and culture" but were actually focused on political subjects such as Mao's thought and the Cultural Revolution. According to later Chinese charges, the government of Burma suspended these classes, but the Chinese residents carried on with them as usual.[83]

THE GREAT BUTTON INCIDENT

The stage had now been set for the chain of events that would turn Sino-Burmese relations back to 1949. Institutional, political, and psychological changes associated with the radical political campaign on the mainland would generate a series of actions and decisions by Chinese personnel in Rangoon, which would provoke an unexpected reaction from the Burmese. This incident in turn would provide the BCP and its radical supporters in Peking the opportunity to recommit China to the revolutionary struggle in Burma.

Following the institution by the overseas Chinese in Rangoon of classes in the thoughts of Mao Tse-tung and the sprouting of numerous Mao buttons, the Burmese Government reissued a regulation banning the wearing of badges or buttons other than those authorized by the government. This order was ignored by many Chinese students. The continued confident and even arrogant attitude of some of the activists in the Chinese community was expressed in a rally on June 18 in front of the Chinese Embassy in Rangoon, the occasion of which was to celebrate the explosion of China's first hydrogen bomb. The Burmese Government had supported the nuclear test ban treaty and had played an active role in promoting the nonproliferation agreement. Nevertheless a message drafted by this rally of overseas Chinese hailed the explosion of China's H-bomb in ecstatic terms and proclaimed that "we shall be ever victorious in the whole world."[84] Moreover, as noted earlier, on June 23, before the major crisis in Rangoon, NCNA carried a congratulatory message from the BCP on the H-bomb success.

On June 22, the principal at a "former Chinese middle school"[85] collected Mao buttons from his Chinese students. The students demonstrated in protest at this affront and reportedly molested teachers and photographers. The next day Rangoon newspapers carried pictures of a Chinese Embassy staff car that had arrived on the scene with a fresh supply of buttons and words of encouragement for the students. The protest movement by the militant Chinese students spread to other schools during the next few days. The young Chinese shouted Mao slogans, sang patriotic Chinese songs, and reportedly confined some headmasters to their offices.[86]

News coverage of these incidents and distorted rumors of even worse outrages inflamed anti-Chinese sentiment among the Burmese population in Rangoon. Rangoon schools were closed temporarily by the government, and counterdemonstrations against the Chinese by indignant Burmese began to develop. After the June 22 incident, the Chinese chargé d'affaires protested to the Burmese Government that "it is the legitimate right of overseas Chinese to wear badges with the profile of Chairman Mao, great leader of the Chinese people, and that no one must deprive them of that right."[87]

If the Burmese Government was not irritated at the assertion of this "right," many Burmese had become aroused, and the anti-Chinese demonstrations in Rangoon began to turn ugly. It is conceivable that after the long series of chauvinist exercises in the Chinese community the authorities wished to teach the Chinese a lesson and that cadres of the Burmese Socialist Program Party or others were encouraged to stir up popular feeling. This speculation can be neither proved nor disproved, but in any event on June 26 a Burmese mob assaulted the Chinese Embassy and official PRC agencies in the city.[88]

Peking's immediate reaction was an official protest note, which was strongly worded but no more than might be expected in the circumstances.89 The note demanded that the Burmese Government take emergency measures to prevent further aggravation of the situation and stated that China reserved the right to demand compensation. The strongest portion of this note claimed that the attacks were "instigated and undertaken with the connivance of the Burmese government," but no adjectives such as "reactionary" or "imperialist" were applied to the government. Those in Peking who drafted and approved this note apparently expected relations with the government of Burma to survive this storm and to continue much as before.

But just at the time the note was handed over in Peking, the Chinese Foreign Ministry was made aware of the killing of one Chinese "expert" within the Rangoon Embassy, an event that occurred at about 1 p.m. that same day (June 27). The Chinese Foreign Ministry official made a verbal reference to this incident when the written note was handed over, and he indicated that a new protest would be forthcoming.90 An NCNA report describing the death of the "expert" came out in the early morning of June 28. This report was the first indication that the incident would be treated as more than a passing storm and that it heralded an official reversal of Peking's policy toward the Burmese Government, the Burmese Communist Party, and the overseas Chinese in Burma. Significantly, this NCNA report was written and presumably approved before the news of the bloody attacks by mobs in the Chinese section of Rangoon about 4 p.m. on June 27.

NCNA's report, which referred only to the murder of the one "expert," contained a startling and comprehensive denunciation of the Ne Win government:

> Since its assumption of power the Ne Win government has all along pursued anticommunist and anti-people's policies. Its economic policy of harsh exploitation and plundering of the people has created extreme difficulties and chaos in the domestic economy. At present class contradictions in the country have become acute and the people's discontent with the government has been growing. The armed struggle waged persistently by the Burmese National Democratic United Front formed by the Burmese Communist Party and other revolutionary organizations has been steadily developing. In this situation the Burmese government is carrying out frantic anti-China and anti-Chinese activities with the obvious aim of fanning up class contradictions inside the government which are caused by its economic policy of exploiting the people. It wants to use these actions to attack

212

and weaken the forces and influence the Burmese Communist Party and to stabilize its own rule.91

Again it should be noted that this reaction was provoked by the news
of the murder of the one Chinese communist official (or technician)
within the Rangoon embassy. Burmese troops had kept the mob from
entering the embassy, but a lone assailant had sneaked into the com-
pound.

On learning of the numerous other deaths, put at over 50, in
the Chinese community, the PRC chargé on June 28 demanded that
the culprits be punished, families and losses be compensated, the
PRC Embassy be permitted to inspect the corpses of the slain, and
the 600 detained overseas Chinese be immediately released.

On June 29 the Chinese Foreign Ministry issued its second note
on the affair, which followed the line taken by NCNA in charging that
the Burmese Government had "over a long time" followed a reactionary policy against the Burmese Communist Party and the people. It
added that the government of Burma was "catering to the needs of
the U.S. imperialists and the Soviet revisionists," and it tacked on an
additional demand that the Burmese Government must "publicly offer
apologies." This Foreign Ministry note did not directly support the
BCP struggle to overthrow the Ne Win regime, but an editorial on
June 30 in People's Daily denounced the Ne Win government as reactionary and fascist and praised the revolutionary successes of the
BCP against the "oppressive government of Burma" and declared
that "Burma's national democratic revolution has taken a new and
important step forward."

What caused the change in China's official response between
its first note and the NCNA article on the morning of June 28? Apparently the news of the killing of the Chinese "expert" was sufficient
provocation or pretext to carry the day for those elements within the
leadership that were disposed to a more revolutionary policy and
that, perhaps most importantly, were eager to eliminate Chou En-lai,
along with his policies.

The news of the "massacres" of their compatriots in the Chinese
sections of Rangoon probably only served to confirm the views of the
radicals. In addition, at this point the BCP officials in Peking were
very likely excited into intense lobbying activity. In the political
atmosphere then prevailing, the moderate and pragmatic elements,
including Foreign Minister Chen Yi and Chou En-lai, were both unable
as well as unwilling to assert themselves on this issue, and 13 years
of peaceful coexistence came tumbling down.

The Chinese Foreign Ministry was in the midst of a great upheaval just at this time. Members of the Cultural Revolution group
using as a front man the former Chinese chargé d'affaires in Jakarta,

Yao Teng-shan, were attempting to oust Chen Yi and Chou En-lai from control of China's foreign affairs. Chen had come under three successive waves of Red Guard poster attacks, and it was not unusual to see the ministry plastered with slogans calling for his overthrow.

In April, following the suspension of Sino-Indonesian relations, Yao Teng-shan had returned to Peking and a hero's welcome by the Chinese leadership. China Pictorial the next month carried a picture of Yao with his arms around both Mao and Mao's wife, Chiang Ching. Such a display of intimacy with the chairman was unusual, to say the least. The ambitious Yao immediately became involved in Red Guard affairs and linked up with the Cultural Revolution Group headed by Mao's confidante, Party theoretician and Red Flag editor Chen Po-ta, and Chiang Ching. The party's old intelligence boss, Kang Sheng, was "adviser" to the group.

Within the Cultural Revolution group two of Chen's deputy editors of Red Flag, Ch'i Pen-yu and Wang Li, took the lead in attacks on the Foreign Ministry. Together with Yao Teng-shan, they encouraged such radical student organizations as the 516 Group (named after the May 16, 1968 Central Committee directive on the Cultural Revolution) to press for an overthrow of the Foreign Affairs leadership. According to later charges, they even plotted assassination attempts and aimed at the ousting of Chou En-lai.[92] The man behind the scenes in this struggle for power within the Foreign Ministry was Chen Po-ta, who apparently operated with the support of Lin Piao. Lin probably saw that the attacks on Chen Yi would undermine Chou En-lai. Chairman Mao was later to claim that the seizure of the Foreign Ministry by "ultra-leftists" had been made without his approval.[93]

The incidents of late June in Burma provided Ch'i Pen-yu and Yao Teng-shan an opportunity to denounce the "weak" foreign policy line of Chen Yi and Chou En-lai and similarly to attack the "traitorous" policies of the Overseas Chinese Affairs Commission, headed by Chou's man, Liao Cheng-chih. Ch'i was not satisfied with the vehement Foreign Ministry note to Rangoon of June 29, presumably preferring the even more bellicose June 30 editorial in People's Daily, which as previously noted was then under the full control of the Cultural Revolution Group.

The following is from a Red Guard publication friendly to Chou En-lai written in March 1968:

> On June 29 and 30, 1967 [sic], our government and the Ministry of Foreign Affairs issued a statement and a note on the frantic anti-Chinese incidents perpetrated by the reactionary Ne Win government of Burma. Ch'i Pen-yu at once availed himself of the opportunity thus offered.

The plan having been mapped out, Ch'i's underlings, big and small, began to run here and there, kindling the fire at the basic level. Some were engaged in inviting foreign guests; others in inviting notables. Some were contacting photographers and reporters; others were drafting documents for the rally.

In the forenoon of July 2, Chin and Lu called at the Central Committee's propaganda department a mobilization meeting of various units and organizations of literary and art circles. Chin Ching-mai said in an instigative vein: "The statement of our government and the note of our Ministry of Foreign Affairs are not high enough in tone. They fall far short of expressing the great spirit of the Chinese people." "Let our literary and art circles take the lead and whip up a high tide. The tone must be high and strong."

. . . After the meeting Chin Ching-mai made an arrangement with Lu Kung-ta and told him: "You proceed to organize some Red Guards. When the rally is over, we'll bombard the Deputy Minister and query him about the statement." Lu Kung-ta at once started running hither and thither. On the one hand, he went to invite the Deputy Minister; on the other, he assigned a task to the Central Conservatory of Music . . . to organize the Red Gurads, after the rally was over, "to call the Deputy Minister of Foreign Affairs and others to gather together against whom we shall rebel and on whom we shall apply some pressure!"

. . . After instigating the "storming of the Foreign Ministry," Ch'i Pen-yu, who had allowed his underlings to spread the word everwhere that "he was fit to be Minister of Foreign Affairs," hastened to give on August 4 a talk which was reeking of poison. He wildly clamored that storming the Foreign Ministry was "perfectly correct in orientation and the question of the method employed was only secondary in importance."

He continued: "Ideologically the leadership of the Foreign Ministry is unduly apprehensive. They are afraid of this and afraid of that. Even when subjected to abusive cursing, they still carry on with talking about friendly relations between two countries."

In conclusion he said with an ulterior motive: "It seems that in future the hope of our diplomatic front will have to rest with our small young generals!" This was a direct confession of his aggressive design to seize the leadership power of the Foreign Ministry.[94]

China's sudden declaration of subversion against the Burmese Government thus was sparked by an incident that was not deliberately planned but that was exploited by elements in the leadership to serve their own purposes. The other decision-makers felt constrained to react in the way they did by the political climate of the day. This type of foreign policy development is nothing new. Many modern conflicts have been brought on by domestic reactions to unplanned or unwanted events. The Japanese attack on China in 1937 is the most apt historical example. As is well known, the Marco Polo Bridge incident was initiated by Japanese officers on the scene, and its consequences were contrary to the policies of the Tokyo government. Although the Konoye cabinet in 1937 did not want a war with China, there were those in Japan, particularly in the military, who quite fervently did wish for such a course. The unplanned incident in China in 1937 provided the pretext and the justification for a radical departure in Japanese policy. Something parallel to this type of situation existed in China on the question of relations with Burma and indeed on the general orientation of foreign policy.

The militants in the Chinese case were the Lin Piao military group and the civilian radicals, both of which Mao later disowned. Although Lin's position may have been essentially opportunistic, he had also established himself as an authority on "people's wars" in Asia, and he was outspoken during the Cultural Revolution in proclaiming China's support and identity with the communist revolutionaries of the area. Lin gave high priority to China's role as the model, the supporter, and by implication the leader of genuine proletarian revolutions.

As we saw in the chapter on Vietnam the intensification of the war in that country in 1965 seemed to present the leadership in Peking with a critical choice between a compromise of ideological principles (that is, rapprochement with the Soviets for "united action" in Vietnam and thus acknowledgment that Moscow was not so revisionist after all) or a serious exposure of China's security (that is, support for North Vietnam while remaining outside the Soviet nuclear umbrella). The posing of this dilemma aggravated the evolving differences within the CCP, and it became a major issue in the power struggle. Related disputes developed over the determination of Mao, Lin Piao, and Chen Po-ta to pursue a divisive political campaign at home despite the threatening external situation and over their drive to polarize both the Afro-Asian and the communist worlds at a time when their opponents believed that broad international support was required to deter U.S. "aggression" against China. The aggravation of this internal conflict throughout 1965 and its apparent manifestation in the September-October 1965 Central Committee meeting in Peking gave Lin Piao the issue for which he was waiting, and it resulted in Mao's determination to purge the ideological deviants and to launch his most radical and revolutionary campaign ever.

The element in these disputes, which involved Burma's future relations with China, was the question of the polarization of the Afro-Asian world and the related strategy in dealing with foreign governments that were opposed by significant internal communist forces. It also involved the goal of polarizing the communist world, for if this was to be done by contrasting China's fraternal behavior with the "collusion" of the Soviet Union, consistency required Peking to give priority to its relations with the BCP and not to the Burmese Government.

The Chinese radicals may also have believed that Burma was ripe for revolution. The country's economic situation was deteriorating; armed bases were possible; and perhaps most important of all, China—the self-professed "new center of world revolution"—was in a position to provide "rear base" support. Lin Piao and his group were thus prepared to give up the political and security benefits of a neutral and accommodating government in Rangoon in the interest of pursuing a long-range and more ambitious revolutionary power strategy in Asia. In effect, they were in favor of abandoning the "classic right" strategy toward Burma that had been followed since the early 1950s.

The implications were far-reaching. To portray the Burmese Government as reactionary and thus possibly to drive it into the arms of the imperialists would require the surrender of China's short-term interest in a neutral area with a 1,300-mile border with China. The radicals, however, could argue that the immediate loss and the potential danger would be less than believed by Chou En-lai and his fellow pragmatists and would be worth the long-term gains—that is, a communist Burma under China's influence. For the radicals, the Burmese Government's type of neutrality and nonalignment, like that of India's, served to undermine Chinese great power interests in that it sought to promote détente between the two world camps.

The Chinese had made the rejection of détente with the United States a central issue in their split with the Soviet Union, and they had sought to polarize the communist and Afro-Asian worlds on this issue, attempting to reorient neutralist governments to identification with and accommodation to China's struggle against the U.S. "imperialists." The Government of Burma, although supporting China's position on issues of sovereignty and security, made no distinction between the "imperialist aggressors" and revolutionary forces on vital questions such as the struggles in Southeast Asia. This pristine neutrality was interpreted by the Chinese radicals as serving the interests of the "imperialists." Because of the intensification within China of the political struggle against revisionism and the showdown nature of the struggle in Vietnam, the friendship of a noncommunist and strictly neutralist Burmese Government did not seem to the Cultural Revolution group as useful as before.

The Maoist extremists must have anticipated that a protracted internal conflict in Burma might eventually lead to U.S.-Soviet assistance to the Rangoon government. This development, while involving risks to China, would provide the unifying nationalist issue that the BCP lacked and upon which it might build a viable united front.

While a prolonged and uncertain struggle was no doubt expected, the fruits of victory in Burma were certainly tempting to the Chinese radicals and to Lin Piao as a confirmation of their theories of people's war. If the Burmese Communist Party had succeeded in seizing power, the psychological and strategic benefits for China would have been staggering. The "wave of the future" psychology, so undermined by the destruction in 1965 of the Peking-Jakarta axis, would have been reinvigorated, and the militant Maoist approach to furthering the goals of the communist camp would have seemed confirmed.

Evidence that the radicals in Peking related the new revolutionary policy in Burma to other areas of Southeast Asia is suggested by propaganda emanating from Peking. The BCP pledged "to unite and support" the Thai movement,[95] and the Thai Communist Party in turn charged that U.S. weapons allegedly destined for Burma were being stored in Thailand.[96] The Malayan Communist Party (MCP) also praised the struggle of the Thai communists as a powerful support to the Malayan "liberation war" and promised to cooperate with "all brotherly parties to fight the imperialists, revisionists and reactionaries."[97]

CHINA OPENS ITS VERBAL ASSAULT

Whatever its motivations, Peking, following its statement of June 28, 1967, began an orgy of denunciations of the Ne Win government. People's Daily alleged that the Rangoon regime had colluded with the United States and the Soviets, thrown off its "mask of positive neutrality" in foreign affairs, and "viciously turned upon China and the overseas Chinese." In taking this course, it warned, the Burmese Government was "only accelerating its doom."[98] On June 29, 200,000 people demonstrated in front of the Burmese Embassy in Peking, and the next day twice that number turned out shouting such slogans as "Resolutely support the revolutionary struggle of the Burmese people" and "The days of the Burmese reactionaries are numbered."[99] These demonstrations, which were organized by the radicals Ch'i Pen-yu and Yao Teng-shan, continued for several days, and at a July 5 rally the main speaker was the Burmese Communist Party first vice chairman, Ba Thien Tin, who accused the Burmese Government of colluding, not only with the United States and the USSR, but also with the Chiang Kai-shek KMT "bandit gang" and "China's Khrushchev" (Liu Shao-chi).100 Chinese speakers at the rally promised the full backing of the "700 million Chinese" to the struggle of the BCP.101

This pledge of support was made official in an August 14 message of the Central Committee of the Chinese Party to the Central Committee of the BCP on the 28th anniversary of the founding of the Burmese party: "The Chinese Communist Party and the Chinese people firmly support the people's revolutionary armed struggle led by the Burmese Communist Party. We regard such support as our bounden proletarian internationalist duty."102

Such an official message from the Party Central Committee required the approval of the party inner core group, specifically of Mao and Lin Piao.

The first evidence of new Chinese support for the BCP was characteristically in the field of propaganda. On July 21, Radio Peking announced an increase of seven hours in its Burmese-language service to a weekly total of 24 hours and 30 minutes.103 These broadcasts informed the Burmese people of the vilification being heaped upon their government,104 and the officially controlled Rangoon press also reported the demands and protests of China. The Burmese Government, however, continued to respond to the provocative Chinese protests in low key, informing the PRC that order was being restored and that the matter concerning the Chinese community was an internal one.105 The Burmese Government talked of "preserving friendly relations,"106 and on August 29, it informed China that it did not consider that the recent unfortunate incidents should in any way "disrupt effective implementation of projects under the agreement on economic and technical cooperation." In early September, the Rangoon government, fulfilling "its duty to uphold and protect its national sovereignty," rejected a PRC demand that it be allowed to send an "investigation and comforting delegation to Burma to express sympathy and concern for the broad masses of the overseas Chinese there."107

The official equanimity of the Burmese Government apparently infuriated the radical Chinese leaders even more, and first place was accorded the revolutionary struggle in Burma in various Peking public statements on the "rising tide of world revolution." On October 1 for example the BCP delegation headed by Ba Thien Tin was listed first among the "fraternal party delegates" attending the PRC's October 1 National Day celebration. Peking informed Rangoon on October 4 that pending a satisfactory reply to its demands, "there exists no condition whatsoever for Chinese experts to continue their work." The Burmese Government replied that in view of this position, it would be best if all Chinese experts and technicians were withdrawn. On October 28

China issued a statement announcing that it was bringing back all Chinese aid personnel from Burma.

The most ominous threat from Peking came in August 1967, when the PRC publicly protested against alleged Burmese Government "military provocations" along the Sino-Burmese border. Burmese troops and aircraft were said to have continually intruded into China's Yünnan province for purposes of harassment and sabotage, and a number of Chinese border inhabitants were said to have been killed by Burmese forces.108 The Burmese Government was charged with being "bent on creating tension along the border," and it was warned that it "would surely meet with severe punishment from the Chinese people and the Chinese PLA."109

While charging provocative Burmese military actions along the border, China also raised the specter of the border issue itself . . . a problem that seemed to have been solved for good in 1960. In November 1967, Peking charged that the Burmese Government had "connived with the government of India to forcibly occupy a large tract of Chinese territory."110 In November the PRC again accused the Burmese of ruthlessly carrying out a campaign of "killing, burning and looting against Chinese residents of the border area." An ominous threat concluded this authoritative message: "Because the Ne Win clique has fired the first shot in opposing China, the Chinese people have obtained the right to counterattack."111

Since the prospect of the Burmese military in 1967 or at any time conducting provocative actions against China appeared remote, these charges seemed to create the specter of a casus belli, and the threats connected with them were part of China's psychological war against the Ne Win government. One objective was apparently to reinforce those elements within the Revolutionary Council in Rangoon that might have favored greater accommodation with the Chinese colossus.

It is also possible that these threats were related to the subsequent crossing of the border into Burma of a sizable force of Kachin communists—an incident described below.

China accused the Ne Win regime of being "like Nehru" a lackey of both the United States and the Soviets, and it charged the Burmese Government with accepting large amounts of military assistance from both Moscow and Washington. Quoting Western press stories, Peking claimed that the United States was rushing "Vietnam-tried weapons especially designed for anti-guerrilla action in the border tribal area" to Burma. It is not clear what weapons might be designed for "border tribal areas," but the object of Peking's propaganda seemed apparent.112 By the same token, the Soviets were said by Peking to have diverted one shipload of arms to Rangoon, and Kosygin was charged with personally pledging full support for the "national liberation" struggle in Burma, that is, with being on the side of the "reactionaries."113

BLOOD IS THICKER THAN WATER

Concurrent with Peking's dramatic change in attitude toward the Burmese Communist Party, there was a further marked alteration in its policy toward the overseas Chinese in Burma. Following the attacks on the Chinese Rangoon community in June, China made a number of demands on the Burmese Government that would have effectively extended extraterritoriality to Chinese in Burma and sanctioned nationalist political activity by the Chinese community. In addition, official Chinese propaganda urged the overseas Chinese to oppose the Ne Win regime with the assurance that "the great motherland is their powerful backing."[114]

The Chinese Foreign Ministry demanded that the Burmese Government not only compensate the victims of the June riots and punish the guilty but also at once release detained Chinese, lift "the armed siege of the Chinese residential quarters," and make a public apology to China and the overseas Chinese in Burma.[115] In addition, Peking officially insisted that the overseas Chinese have the right to study Mao Tse-tung's thought, wear his badges, and engage in "patriotic activities."[116] The Commission on Overseas Chinese Affairs in Peking also sent a message to the Chinese community in Burma, which proclaimed a special position for that community:

> You have displayed the heroism characteristic of the great
> Chinese people. You deserve to be called the fine sons
> and daughters of the motherland, armed with the thought
> of Mao Tse-tung. . . . Your struggle is just; you are
> struggling correctly and well. The great socialist
> motherland firmly supports you! The 700 million people
> of the motherland stand by you! . . . We are convinced
> that the masses of patriotic overseas Chinese in Burma
> will hold even higher the great red banner of the invincible
> thought of Mao Tse-tung. Make a living study in applica-
> tion of Chairman Mao's works in the course of their
> struggle. Close ranks with all forces which can be united
> excluding the enemy. Form the broadest united front in
> the anti-persecution struggle. Dare to struggle and be
> good at struggling and resolutely smash all the criminal
> anti-China anti-Chinese activities carried out by the Bur-
> mese reactionaries.[117]

This line represented a considerable change from the position taken by Chou En-lai in his visits to Rangoon in 1954, 1955, and 1956. In fact it represented, as in the case of China's attitude toward the

Burmese Communist Party, a return to the 1949 position, when Peking claimed and expected allegiance from the overseas Chinese. As in the earlier period, the overseas Chinese of Burma were called upon to support China in its policy toward the Rangoon government. As in the Foreign Ministry, radicals with the support of the Cultural Revolution group had taken over control of the Overseas Chinese Affairs Commission (OCAC) and had ousted the commission chairman, Liao Cheng-chih. Liao was accused of having failed to protect the interests of the overseas Chinese. According to the Red Guards, Liao "asked the Overseas Chinese 'to mind their own business,' and 'to stick to their own port,' and 'not to criticise the internal affairs of the local government.'"[118] Those who took over the OCAC enthusiastically embraced the idea that China and the overseas Chinese should vigorously defend one another.

But the faithful in the Chinese community of Rangoon must have had some second thoughts about the applicability of the chairman's thoughts to the situation in Burma. A long history of tolerant relations between the Chinese and Burmese communities had been broken, with much suffering on the Chinese side. Despite all its promises, the "powerful motherland" provided no support to the overseas Chinese in Burma except to fly back to China those who wished to go.[119] The PRC's influence in the community was thus greatly weakened as the most militant Chinese left the country, and of those who remained behind many blamed their troubles on Peking. Anticommunist elements in the Chinese community who had fallen silent in the early 1960s also began to exert their influence.

THE BCP AND THE PATH OF MAO

The Maoist purges of April 1967 within the BCP failed to consolidate the party's leadership; instead it intensified the BCP's internal conflict. After the executions of Goshal and Htay in the spring of 1967 and China's subsequent declaration in July of support for the revolution in Burma, the party was rent by a series of other executions and murders. One year later, the need for party consolidation was recognized. In August 1968, First Vice Chairman Ba Thien Tin, in another statement issued from Peking, reiterated that the party had fought still another successful internal struggle against revisionism, and he proclaimed that the "chief task," which took precedence over armed struggle and united-front work, was that of "party construction." Nevertheless ultimate victory for the party, he said, still depended upon the struggle against revisionism. Shortly afterwards, conflict broke out within the party again.

One clique within the group of "Peking returnees," who had promoted the Maoist line and who reportedly had personally executed
some of the non-Maoists in April, were themselves brutally eliminated
in 1968. Than Tun became suspicious of "Peking returnee" Bo Tun
Nyein, who led the party's Delta division and who was director of the
party's Marxist-Leninist Training School. According to documents
captured at the BCP's headquarters, Tun Nyein advocated a temporary
truce with the government in order to build up the party's military
and political organization while Than Tun still opposed even a tactical
deal with the government.120

After a revolutionary trial in August, Tun Nyein and six of his
young followers from the Delta division, described as university
students, were executed.121 By the end of the year it was reported
that of the 27 "Peking returnees" who had attended the 1963 peace
talks and had remained behind in Burma, five had been killed by the
army, two had been captured, two surrendered, and two were executed
by their fellow communists.122

The August executions in turn led to Than Tun's own assassination. On September 24, 1968, a 22-year-old Chin, Maung Mya, reported that he had killed Than Tun (while the latter was relieving
himself in the forest) in revenge for Tun Nyein's execution.123 This
report was confirmed when the Burmese Army was led to Than Tun's
grave by another defector.124 Six months later in an unprecedented
public display of personal support, Chou En-lai—perhaps biting his
tongue—and Kang Sheng met with the BCP leaders in Peking to express
condolences on Than Tun's death on behalf of Mao, the Chinese party,
and the Cultural Revolution group.125 One of the party's deputy vice-
chairmen, Thakin Zin, who apparently had never been to China, became
the new chairman, but Ba Thien Tin, who, with about 90 other Burmese,126 remained in China, took over "responsibility of leading the
armed revolution."127

Increasing numbers of defections and defeats however followed
the death of Than Tun. The party's internal troubles reduced its
ability to hold the positions it had clung to for 20 years, and the armed
forces of the BCP suffered a string of reverses throughout 1968 and
into 1969. In April 1968 the party's military headquarters in the Pegu
Yoma Hills was captured and its military commander, Bo Zeya, was
killed. Of the 20-member Central Committee of 1967 only nine remained free and alive two years later, leaving only 12 of the 27 "Peking returnees" at large.128

"Peking returnee" Ko Aung Gyi, in April 1969, began to lead
about one-half of the surviving BCP guerrillas on a long march out
of the Pegu Yoma foothills region north of Rangoon. Aung Gyi's
group, however was intercepted, and he was killed along with two
other China-trained comrades. About 730 remnants set up a new

headquarters on the eastern bank of the Sittang River not far from Thailand. Eventually some of these reached the Chinese border. Another estimated 1,000 BCP guerrillas remained dispersed throughout the Delta area and along the Irrawaddy River.

The BCP had not suffered such losses of prestige and morale since 1950. Nevertheless, the party faithfully adhered to the Maoist line, echoing Peking media on the Soviet invasion of Czechoslovakia, the formal ousting of Liu Shao-chi, the 12th Plenum of the CCP, the PRC's hydrogen-bomb test of December 1968, and the Sino-Soviet border clash of March 1969. In its anniversary statement in August the BCP Central Committee reiterated that today was "the era of Mao Tse-tung" and that the BCP was still determined to follow the road of armed revolution "blazed by the Great Leader of the oppressed people of the world."[129]

STUCK WITH A POLICY

The disappointment in Peking over the difficulties of the BCP must have been considerable, and to some extent it was now possible for the pragmatists to turn the tables and criticize the radicals for their Burma policy, which had been counterproductive both externally for China and internally for the BCP. The moderates could claim that their views had been confirmed, but they were not yet in a position to restore their policies.

The situation in Burma had become an important issue within the leadership in Peking; Lin Piao could not back down without seeming to confirm the policies of his domestic opponents. The subject also became involved in the Sino-Soviet dispute. Moscow continued to praise the policies of the Ne Win government as laying the "foundation . . . for the construction of Socialism"[130] and to blame the BCP's defeats on the fact that the party's leadership had blindly followed the Maoist line: "The Maoist experiment in Burma has again confirmed the point that the Peking line will bring only destruction to those on whom it is imposed."[131]

The amateur extremists in the Chinese Foreign Ministry, including Ch'i Pen-yu and Yao Teng-shan, were purged by early 1968, and the ministry itself appeared to be back in the hands of Chou En-lai and the moderates. The Overseas Chinese Affairs Commission, which had sent out such fervent statements in the summer of 1967, ceased operations. However, the freedom of action of the moderates in making foreign policy remained tightly constricted. The Lin Piao military group and the civilian radicals still occupied the most powerful positions in the Chinese leadership. It was possibly Lin, as minister of Defense, who authorized the arming and training of a large communist force in China to fight under the flag of the BCP (see below).

Although some of Chen Po-ta's subeditors at <u>Red Flag</u> lost their positions in 1968, the radicals also remained particularly strong in the media and propaganda field and in the party's International Liaison Office, which dealt with other communist parties, including the BCP. The high point for the radicals was April 1969, when Chen Po-ta and Kang Sheng were elected to the five-man standing committee of the Politburo along with Lin Piao, who was officially proclaimed successor to Mao.

TRIBAL KEY

After the BCP's setbacks of 1967-68, the Chinese began increasing their support for the rebellious minority tribes in Burma and renewing efforts to promote the tribes' membership in the united-front-from-below. The greatest potential in this regard lay with the Kachin tribesmen, of which there were about 450,000 in Burma and 1.5 million in Yünnan province in China. The Kachin, along with the Shan, Karen, and several other tribes, had been in a state of sporadic insurrection against the Rangoon government for 22 years.

Once before, the communists had attempted to promote tribal participation in the BCP's National Democratic United Front but with only limited success. In the earlier revolutionary period of China's policy toward Burma, 1949-53, there were reports that China had provided arms and training to Kachin insurrectionists[132] and dubious charges that it had developed plans for a "Greater Kachin" to extend over the Kachin areas of both China and Burma.[133]

In 1952 a left-wing group of the Karen tribe led by Mahn Ba Zan formed a Karen National United Party, which in 1959 joined the BCP-dominated National Democratic United Front. Communist influence subsequently spread to most wings of the Karen movement.

Generally, however, efforts by the BCP to unite with the tribal insurgents broke down because of divisions among the tribal groups as well as the fact that until now the Burmese communists, as a basically Burmese organization, had not been prepared to promise full autonomy to the minority areas. In addition, Christianized tribes tended to be suspicious of the atheistic communists and of their ties to the Chinese. Nevertheless, after 1967, Peking saw the minority tribes as the key to victory in the Burmese revolution:

> In Burma, there are more than 100 minority nationalities,
> many of whom are carrying out armed struggles. The

Communist Party of Burma holds that the question of the minority nationalities is a special problem of the revolution in Burma. The correct handling of this question is the key to seizing victory in the revolution. The Communist Party of Burma has carried out a correct national policy, and, on the common political basis of the national-democratic revolution, has formed a national-democratic united front with political parties of the Karen, Mon Kayah, Chin, and other nationalities. The Communist Party of Burma is also actively working for cooperative relations with the progressive armed forces of other nationalities.[134]

In early 1968, a BCP delegation reportedly met with a group of noncommunist Kachin insurgents in the Kachin Independence Army (KIA) and appealed for a joint effort.[135] But the BCP warned that it could not permit the establishment of a Kachin republic. On at least one occassion, however, the party called for a "Federal Republic"[136] and for autonomy for the minority peoples; but the BCP clearly intended to retain a unified country under a communist government in Rangoon:

> The Communist Party of Burma stresses that the national question in Burma is in essence a question of the peasantry. The armed struggle of the nationalities is an armed struggle of the peasants against feudal oppression. The correct settlement of the national question is the realization of the worker-peasant alliance under the leadership of the working class.[137]

In subsequent broadcasts the BCP dropped the "federal" suggestion and simply promised a People's Democratic Republic of Burma. Some Kachins were prepared to join the BCP on this basis.

THE BCP GAINS A BASE

In 1967 the BCP with Chinese assistance created the "Northeast Command," a group of Chinese-based Kachin communists led by a Burmese Kachin named Naw Seng. Naw Seng and some of his followers had reportedly been in China for several years in camps located at Teng Chung and Lung Ling just over the eastern Sino-Burmese border.[138] In 1968, Naw Seng's group, which included a large percentage of Kachins who were Chinese nationals, and also many PLA officers crossed over into Burma. His subsequent successes contrasted with the disasters encountered by the BCP's regular forces in central Burma. Naw Seng, who had defected to the communists from the Burmese Army in 1948 and reportedly won a seat on the Central Committee of the BCP in January 1968, was variously reported to have under his command several hundred to 2,000 well-trained forces fully equipped and supplied by China. These forces were apparently joined by remnants of the defeated BCP guerrillas from the Pegu Yoma area. Naw Seng's intention reputedly was to establish an impregnable "revolutionary base" contiguous with the Yünnan salient of China.139 For the first time the BCP was to gain a substantial "liberated" area on the Chinese border.

General Ne Win reported "quite heavy fighting" between the Burmese Army and this group beginning in late 1967 and early 1968 along the Chinese frontier.140 The movement of organized guerrilla units across the border followed shortly after Peking's warnings to Rangoon about its alleged provocations on the frontier—warnings, as we suggested, which may have been intended to discourage the Burmese Army from engaging the communist units coming across the line. Ne Win in fact decreed that no bullet should land across the border.141

It is interesting to note that at this time Kang Sheng, who was then responsible for relations with foreign communist parties, reportedly warned vaguely of enemy activities in Burma:

> Yunnan is a border region. The enemies are on the other side of the boundary. We have learned that Chiang Kai-shek secret agents have carried out activities on both sides of the boundary in Yunnan. In particular, the prestige of the Liberation Army must be upheld.142

Naw Seng's forces apparently had little difficulty in occupying a strip of territory 2 to 10 miles deep into Burma. By late 1969 Naw Seng's army had staged battalion-sized attacks against the old Burma Road as far south as the town of Kut Kai in the northern Shan state.143 According to communist claims, the Burmese People's Armed Forces "annihilated" four battalions of Burmese troops in 1968 and three battalions in the first six months of 1969.144

In addition to Chinese military officers serving with the insurgents, Chinese civilian cadres, according to some press reports in 1969, were helping to administer the new "liberated" areas along the border.145 Peking was apparently referring to these areas when it claimed that "people's political power" was established in some rural areas of Burma in 1969 by the BCP.

The Rangoon government gave out little news on the fighting in this area, but in November 1969, Ne Win told a party conference that Burmese troops, in a series of skirmishes with "communist forces" on the Chinese border, had suffered 425 casualties, including 133 deaths.[146] According to Ne Win's report there had been 18 clashes in the first eight months of the year, eight of them major. In addition to the Burmese casualties cited by Ne Win, there were said to have been 355 dead and 217 wounded on the other side.[147]

In 1970, however, the BCP's Northeast Command suffered some setbacks. Units of the KIA that had cooperated with the BCP largely deserted the cause. According to Ian Ward, who at the time was with Karen rebel forces in eastern Burma, the Kachin and other tribal insurgents had become increasingly anti-Chinese, apparently fearing the escalating Chinese involvement in northern Burma. In March, according to Ward, Naw Seng's headquarters near Lashio was attacked by the KIA, with heavy casualties on both sides. Naw Seng reportedly moved his headquarters to Bhamo, closer to the border.[148]

Also in March, the Burmese Government abandoned the border town of Kuyhkok, and from May through August three battles were fought between the Northeast Command and the Burmese Army. After September 1970, the Northeast Command appeared to drop its offensive tactics and assumed a largely defensive posture in the areas it controlled. This sudden quieting of the war was related to developments both on the diplomatic front and in the internal politics of China.

Before examining the next stage in the evolution of China's policy toward Burma, it is worthwhile to turn briefly to another Burmese event and Peking's reaction to it.

A NEW DEVELOPMENT

While the BCP was being harassed in the Pegu Yoma Hills and Naw Seng was moving across the border, important political developments were taking place within Burma.

Ne Win moved to unite the nation behind him, and to this end he seemed prepared to consider some modification of his military rule. The Revolutionary Council had released U Nu and several other political prisoners in 1966, and during the early months of 1968 a total of 225 other "detainees" were given their freedom. In November, Ne Win invited 33 former political leaders to form a National Unity Advisory Board to offer suggestions for a new constitution for Burma. At the end of the year, U Nu submitted a memorandum urging the immediate formation of a national government headed by himself as prime minister as the first step toward free elections. The majority of the advisory board in their later report also urged the restoration of democratic institutions.

In the fall, U Nu sneaked out of Burma and traveled around the world announcing his intention to overthrow the Ne Win government by force of arms. In Tokyo the former premier said he could not reveal where he would procure arms, but in Hong Kong he announced that he would soon go to Peking to try to enlist aid for his fight. Furthermore, U Nu charged that the Rangoon government had provoked the incidents of June 1967, and he promised to restore friendship with China.

In a later clandestine broadcast by the U Nu organization, Ne Win was charged with having "created the foreign aggression on the Sino-Burmese border in order to divert the growing anger of the people similar to the case of the Sino-Burmese riots he himself created."[149]

After a year's exile in Bangkok, in October 1970, U Nu formed a new United National Liberation Front, which included some Karen and Mon rebels, and launched his military campaign against Ne Win.

But despite U Nu's friendly gestures toward Peking, the Chinese failed to show any interest and apparently rejected his application to visit China. According to the former prime minister himself, during his travels in 1970, "when the time came to go to Peking, the consul would not even see us."[150] By this time, relations between Rangoon and Peking had already begun to improve.

RETURN TO NORMALCY

In his November 1969 speech, Ne Win said he wanted to establish friendly relations with China, and he asked the Burmese people not to be angry over his disclosure of the border clashes because he did not want to see a repetition of the anti-Chinese incidents of 1967, which he thought best forgotten.

Ne Win's response to China's new phase of hostility was to be like U Nu's passive response to a similar situation 20 years before. The general emphasized that Burma could not and would not retaliate and that it would "not permit any foreign or local elements to use Burmese soil as a base to provoke or cause trouble to our neighbors." Burma, he promised, would not seek assistance from others, as this was a "short-sighted approach." About the same time, the Rangoon government demonstrated its wish for conciliation by releasing all Chinese nationals jailed after the 1967 disturbances.

In 1970, Burmese representatives began to return to the Canton trade fairs, and in April press reports speculated that Ne Win had

asked Nepal's King Mahendra to use his good offices to improve Bur-
mese-PRC relations. Sometime in August, Ne Win apparently asked
for Peking's agreement for the appointment of a new Burmese Ambassador to China.

The Chinese also probably took note when Burma did not seek
to renew its small military sales agreement with the United States.
The last contingent of the U.S. military equipment delivery team,
which had been attached to the U.S. Embassy in Rangoon, left Burma
on June 30, 1971. In addition, the Burmese Government also rejected
a U.S. offer to sell Burma at low prices surplus military equipment
and machinery left over from the Vietnam war.[151]

China's response on the governmental level to Ne Win's conciliatory measures was gradual but positive. Throughout 1969 and
up until mid-1970, however, it was apparent that on the party level
and in Peking media priority was still doggedly being accorded to the
revolutionary interests of the BCP.

NCNA reports on Burma in early 1970 were still abusive of the
Burmese Government although much less so than in 1967, and there
were no more threats of violent "punishment" for Burma.[152] Not
surprisingly, Peking's reports of the insurgency concentrated on events
in the Delta and the Pegu Yoma Mountains and made only rare references to the Kachin and Shan states across the Sino-Burmese border
where Naw Seng was operating. Still under the strong influence of
Chen Po-ta, Chinese media at this time stressed the difficult and
"protracted" struggle that lay ahead for the BCP but insisted that
victories were still being won.[153]

In April 1969, Lin Piao in his report to the Ninth National Congress of the Chinese Party listed Burma as one of the countries where
armed struggle was progressing. In an apparent reference, among
other things, to Peking's past policies toward the Burmese revolution,
Lin said that Mao had led the party in criticizing Liu Shao-chi's
alleged revisionist line of "suppression of revolutionary movements
in various countries." The most explicit condemnations of Liu Shao-
chi in this context had been in regard to Burma.

Mao's acquiescence was presumably once again required when
the Central Committee of the Chinese party on August 16, 1969 sent
anniversary congratulations to the BCP for the third time in a row.
However, the tone of this message was considerably less optimistic
than similar pieces in 1967 and 1968 in its proclamation of faith that
the BCP "will certainly be able to overcome all difficulties on the
road of advance." Nevertheless, the Chinese party again pledged
that it would "resolutely support the revolutionary armed struggle
of the Burmese people."[154] The BCP's own anniversary statement
stressed that "the present era is the era of Mao Tse-tung," and in
October, NCNA carried a BCP message marking China's National

Day (October 1), which stated that China is "doing her utmost to perform her proletarian internationalist duties."155

But while Peking continued to issue propaganda against the Burmese Government and Chinese-backed guerrilla war continued in Burma, there were small signs that the Chinese Foreign Ministry, now fully under Chou En-lai's control, was attempting to improve diplomatic relations with Rangoon. Expressions of good will actually appeared as early as 1968, when Peking made a Red Cross donation to assist Burmese hurricane victims and the Chinese Embassy began attending some official Burmese functions and giving receptions of its own, including an October 1 National Day fete.

This mixed pattern, which continued throughout 1969, reflected the evolving political struggle within Peking, briefly reviewed in the chapter on Vietnam, and the increasing resurgence of the broad united-front policy in foreign affairs. In 1969, Chou En-lai and his moderate colleagues, faced with the threat of a Soviet attack and worried over the resurgence of Japanese power, speeded up the return to the united-front tactics of the mid-1950s and early 1960s, which sought to maximize China's international support. If China was to end its dangerous state of isolation among the world's powers and if peaceful coexistence was again to be the main theme of China's foreign policy, it was necessary to make credible Peking's professions of noninterference in the internal affairs of other states. The most glaring contradiction to the principle of peaceful coexistence was China's post-1967 policy toward the government of Burma.

In an early 1970 review of the progress of revolutionary struggles in Asia, NCNA claimed that "people's political power had been set up in some rural areas" of Burma. However, in 1970, Peking's reports of BCP "victories" were sanitized of attacks on Ne Win, and the frequency of the reports themselves fell off. From January through July NCNA carried only three such stories. In April and May there was a flurry of four statements from the BCP reported by NCNA on the subjects of China's earth satellite, Cambodia, Lenin's birthday, and Mao's May 20 statement.

Like the PKI, the spirits of the BCP were revived by the Cambodian events of 1970 and the Chinese-sponsored summit conference of the three Indochinese peoples in April. The Burmese communist leaders hoped that the BCP could join an expanded anti-U.S. united front in Asia and thereby tie their fortunes to that of the Indochinese communists. The BCP proclaimed, "We must follow the teaching of Chairman Mao and strive for the further unity of the people of Burma and the three Indochinese countries." Ne Win, the BCP pointed out, "does not support the war against U.S. aggression waged by the Vietnamese people."156

231

The Burmese communist leaders also apparently hoped that Mao's much-publicized May 20 statement, which concluded that "revolution is the main trend in the world today," heralded a new emphasis in Peking on struggles such as that of the BCP. Mao's statement, according to the BCP Central Committee, "will certainly give further impetus to the struggle against U.S. imperialism and its lackey, the Ne Win military government," and "we will do our utmost to make due contribution to the formation of the international united front against U.S. imperialism."

The BCP, however, soon came to understand that Mao's statement, at least as interpreted by the increasingly dominant moderate coalition led by Chou En-lai, did not embrace strictly internal social revolutions in countries willing to accommodate China's vital interests. To Chou, Mao's statement meant that the war threat to China posed by both the Soviet Union and the United States had decreased and that the present task was to consolidate this trend and to stress the common cause of nationalism against both the United States and the USSR—the latter, however, being increasingly seen as the main enemy.

As observed in an earlier chapter, this united-front-peaceful-coexistence foreign policy line was apparently endorsed by the Second Plenum of the Ninth Central Committee of the CCP, which met from August to September 1970. In addition, the chief radicals in the Politburo, including Chen Po-ta and Kang Sheng, were apparently criticized at the plenum for the excesses of the Cultural Revolution, including acts injurious to China's foreign relations. Significantly, for the first time since 1967, no mention was made in Peking media of the August 15 anniversary of the BCP, and the last NCNA article devoted exclusively to the cause of the BCP appeared on September 4, two days before the ending of the plenum. The plenum communiqué section on international relations stressed China's adherence to the principle of peaceful coexistence, noted the expansion of Peking's diplomatic relations, and said nothing about the revolution in Burma. It is very likely that the plenum specifically approved the decision to accept Ne Win's overtures and improve governmental relations with Burma. This decision was a serious setback for the radicals and Lin's military clique and was the first step in the vindication of Liu Shao-chi and Chou En-lai's policy toward Rangoon.

Changes in the working staff in the International Liaison Department of the CCP perhaps were equally significant for the Burmese. The PRC Ambassador to Rangoon during the hey-day of the Liu Shao-chi and Ne Win friendship, Keng Piao, was named head of this department in the Central Committee in late 1970. Keng was also a long-time associate of Chou En-lai.

Ba Thien Tin attended the October 1, 1970 National Day affair in Peking, as he had since 1967, but no message was publicly reported from the BCP. Instead, a message of congratulations to Chou En-lai from Ne Win was recorded by NCNA for the first time in five years.[157] Events now moved rapidly. In October the People's Republic gave its agreement for the appointment of a new Burmese Ambassador, who arrived in Peking in late November and was received by Chou on December 5. When the new ambassador gave his January 4, 1971, independence anniversary reception, Kuo Mo-jo, vice chairman of the National People's Congress, attended. Chou En-lai sent a message of greeting to Ne Win, but it was indicative of the continuing sensitiveness of the issue in Peking that NCNA did not report it. Peking, however, announced the appointment of its new ambassador to Rangoon in March.

In January the PRC also returned to its pre-1967 practice of purchasing Burmese rice to fulfill part of its commitment to Ceylon in a rubber-for-rice barter agreement. This purchase marked the return to normalcy of trade affairs between Burma and China.

The Chinese stand on the question of overseas Chinese in Burma also began to work its way back to the reasonable posture of the Bandung days. In 1968, there were several Chinese Government notes to Rangoon on the subject of the Burmese Government's treatment of its Chinese residents. In September, for example, Peking protested the sentencing of eight local Chinese for the 1967 riots. Yet the wording of this note was mild, and it was reminiscent of the earlier Chinese position in stressing the loyalty of the overseas Chinese to the local society rather than to China. After this, the People's Republic did not again mention in public the alleged plight of the Chinese in Burma. Also, by 1968, the PRC had stopped repatriating overseas Chinese from Burma back to China.

Peking's attitude toward the problems of the Chinese in Burma indicated that the PRC leaders intended to reestablish the previous policy, which did not claim the loyalty of Southeast Asians of Chinese origin but rather encouraged their assimilation. Chou would later state this directly to Ne Win. Chinese leaders like Chou did not wish to saddle the PRC with responsibility for protecting the interests of bourgeois Chinese communities abroad whose actions Peking could not control. The 1967 chauvinist aberration in China's policy toward the overseas Chinese in Burma simply confirmed the assumptions behind the previous policy—that is, that the Chinese community abroad, while a valuable source of foreign exchange remittances, was more a political liability for China than an asset; China had no effective way to protect their interests, and as evident in the case of Burma, efforts to do so were counterproductive.

233

Although the NCNA no longer carried BCP statements attacking the Burmese Government, on ambivalence remained in China's policy. In March 1971, a clandestine radio station calling itself the Voice of the People of Burma began broadcasting anti-Ne Win articles and statements by the BCP in Burmese and two minority languages spoken in the northeast, Jingpaw and Shan. The Voice of the People of Burma, like the clandestine radio stations of the Malayan and Thai Communist Parties, was also apparently located in China.

But in addition to the establishment of the new clandestine radio in Burma, other signs of a sharp contradiction in Chinese policy toward Rangoon were evident in 1971. The Shanghai radical and Politburo member, Yao Wen-yuan, accompanied Ba Thien Tin to the May 1 celebrations in Peking, and an NCNA article on the anniversary of Mao's May 20th statement hailed the progress of revolutionary struggles in Asia, including that of the BCP against the "reactionary authorities of Burma." This was the first such provocative comment on Burmese affairs since the preceding September, and it is worth quoting in full:

> Fighting in unity, assisting and closely coordinating with each other, the people's armed forces led by the Communist Party of Burma and the armed forces of various national minorities in Burma have in recent years smashed more than ten large-scale counter-revolutionary military encirclement and suppression operations, expanded their operations areas and tied down large numbers of enemy troops, bringing about a new situation in the revolutionary armed struggle in Burma.
>
> In the past year the Burmese people's armed forces unfolded guerrilla warfare widely in different parts of the country, fought more than 40 battles and wiped out large numbers of enemy men. Since the beginning of the year, the people's armed forces of Burma have launched many attacks on the reactionary troops and police in Pegu, the Irrawaddy Delta and other places. They blew up enemy trains and intercepted enemy trucks and ships, causing the reactionary troops and police to run hither and thither in terrible plight.158

Despite such statements, the triumph of the Peking moderates in foreign and domestic affairs became increasingly apparent in late 1970 and early 1971. This was expressed, for example, in Chou

En-lai's apology to the U.K. chargé d'affaires for the burning of the British Mission in Peking in the summer of 1967 and in the regime's campaign to denounce the ultraleftist Red Guard organization, the 516 group, for most of the extremist acts of the period. The Chou moderates seemed intent on restoring the country's reputation and punishing those who were responsible for the events of 1967, including Chen Po-ta and Lin Piao.[159] Retribution for those directly involved in the takeover of the Foreign Ministry in 1967 and in the verbal onslaught of the time against the Burmese Government came in June, when Yao Teng-shan, the ex-chargé in Jakarta, was publicly tried for his offenses and reportedly sentenced either to death or to a long prison term.[160]

As we have suggested, Lin Piao was also at least indirectly involved in the radical attack on Chou En-lai's and Liu Shao-chi's Burma policy. While relations with the United States and the USSR very likely constituted the most contentious foreign policy question between the two groups, policy toward Burma was probably another issue over which the two rivals fought. On this issue, Lin probably found himself being forced to defend the unadulterated application of the theory of "people's war" in a situation where, it was increasingly obvious, this theory was not beneficial to China's foreign policy interests. Lin, as minister of Defense, may have been responsible for providing the BCP with broadcasting equipment and with friendly publicity on May Day 1971.

By midyear, however, Lin was in sharp decline and the joint Peking editorial on the 50th anniversary of the CCP on July 1 implicitly warned against interventionist policies against neutralist states. The concluding section on proletarian internationalism contrasted with Lin Piao's April 1969 report to the Party Congress. Chinese readers were now reminded that "Chairman Mao has always educated the whole party and the whole people . . . so that they can overcome both 'left' and right opportunist interferences and correctly handle the relation between the revolution in China and her support and aid to the world revolution."

As in the united front of the 1930s, China had now to appeal to the broader proletarian internationalist loyalties of the Southeast Asian communist parties to win their cooperation in or at least their understanding of a diplomatic strategy of united front from above in a period of "great upheaval" in world politics. An article in the August issue of Red Flag, entitled "A Powerful Weapon to Unite the People and Defeat the Enemy," was clearly meant to enlighten foreign friends as well as the Chinese public about the new line. The semiofficial communist organ in Hong Kong, the Ta Kung Pao, on September 2 said that the article should be of interest to China's "friends abroad who are eager to appraise these policies [of China] and their ramifications."

In a passage that could be interpreted as relevant to the South-east Asian revolutionary scene, the Red Flag article proclaimed that the contradiction between the proletariat and the bourgeoisie in capitalist and revisionist countries will inevitably lead to revolution. But "while regarding armed struggle as the principal form of struggle, we must wage struggles of various forms against the enemy in many fields." The article advocated that, in both internal and external policy, united front is the main form of struggle because it "is neither all alliance and no struggle nor all struggle and no alliance, but combines alliance and struggle." Thus, the writers seemed to suggest that the previous emphasis on armed struggle as the path to power should be shifted where possible to united-front efforts.

As in the late 1930s, the primary task, as explained by Red Flag, was to pursue policies that would support China in the present great upheaval and in its struggle with the imperialist and social-imperialist enemies. In other words, governments like those in Rangoon and Kuala Lumpur, which indicated a willingness to accommodate China's vital interests, might qualify as indirect, secondary, or temporary allies. It followed that if Peking was to seek a modus vivendi with such governments on the international level, a similar united-front line by the Maoist parties on the national level would be consistent with China's interests. Continued pursuit of a militant policy of armed struggle by Maoist parties in countries willing to accommodate China was an unwelcome complication.

Another article in the same issue of Red Flag seemed implicitly to modify Peking's unequivocal support of the 1960s for the policy of armed struggle (although the article did not say so directly, it appeared to be addressing itself particularly to the situation of some Southeast Asian communist parties). The article, entitled "Taking the Initiative Is an Important Guarantee to Winning Victory in the Revolution," castigated Liu Shao-chi and other "political swindlers" (a term that referred to both the purged radical Politburo member Chen Po-ta and to Lin Piao) for having made an "idealist, . . . over-optimistic . . . and erroneous appraisal of the revolutionary situation." This attitude, according to the article, led to "opportunism or putsch-ism," which "brought heavy losses to the revolutionary cause."

NE WIN RETURNS TO PEKING

On August 1, 1971, Ba Thien Tin was listed among the "distin-guished guests" at the Army Day reception in Peking given the previous evening by Chief of Staff Huang Yung-sheng, who would soon fall from power along with Lin. But on the same day NCNA made the startling announcement that Ne Win would make an "informal" visit to China.

On August 6, Ne Win, who had now assumed the position of prime minister of Burma, was greeted by Chou En-lai in the Chinese capital, where four years before he had been the most vilified individual in the Cultural Revolution's pantheon of foreign demons.

Restraint was evident in the regime's failure to turn out a large crowd to greet the Burmese leader, but Chou En-lai seemed intent on exploiting Ne Win's visit in order to dramatize to both external and internal audiences the reversal of China's hostile policy toward neutral Burma. Chou met Ne Win and his wife at the airport and hosted a banquet for them. People's Daily carried on the front page a picture of Mao greeting Ne Win; Lin Piao was notably absent from the photograph. Interestingly, Madame Mao, along with the other members of the Cultural Revolution group, also made themselves scarce during the visit.

Chou paid the Burmese leader the unusual honor of escorting him to Canton in Southern China. On August 9, the signing of the Indo-Soviet defense treaty was announced, and a few days later NCNA reported that Ne Win and Chou En-lai had resumed their talks. The implications of the new Soviet treaty with India was probably among the subjects discussed.

For Peking, the Soviet pact with India was a serious development. While the Indo-Soviet accord was obviously intended to deal with the Indo-Pakistan problem—specifically to deter Chinese backing of Pakistan—the Chinese interpreted the treaty as aimed in the long term at the "containment" of China and as the first materialization of the Soviet version of "collective security." As the Soviets clearly desired to conclude similar accords with other Asian states, Burma was a possibility, even if only a remote one.

For several months, in fact, Moscow propaganda had been playing up the allegedly continuing Chinese interest in overthrowing the government of Burma. Thus, it was now even more essential than before for the Chinese to relieve the fears of Southeast Asian nations about China's intentions. Ne Win's hand was thus strengthened by this last-minute development.

Burmese satisfaction with the results of the visit was indicated by Ne Win, who at a farewell reception in Canton expressed "joy and deep satisfaction for having reached an understanding in the discussion on the various matters concerning the two countries and on international problems."[161]

Back in Rangoon the general revealed that in his meetings with Chou it was agreed that the Chinese aid program to Burma would be resumed. Chou also took the occasion to proclaim the return of the pre-Cultural Revolution policy toward overseas Chinese in Burma and elsewhere. Ne Win asked for advice as to what the Burmese Government should do for the Chinese nationals in Burma who had suffered in the disturbance of 1967.

> To this, the Chinese Prime Minister replied that the Union of Burma being a sovereign independent state, we could do whatever we thought appropriate in this matter. He added that we should not be concerned over the death of a Chinese technician; this matter would be attended to by the Chinese Government, he said.
>
> The Chinese Prime Minister then explained the policy of the Chinese Government. He said they did not accept exploitation being done by capitalist overseas Chinese in foreign countries. He would not allow overseas Chinese to retain dual citizenship. Either they keep Chinese citizenship or become citizens of the country of residence; they must be citizens of only one nation.
>
> He then said he would like citizenship to be given to pure Chinese or half-castes who have been in foreign countries for one or two generations, should they so desire, according to the law of the land. I said that was quite fair and, since we had been doing the same thing, we accepted that point.
>
> He said it was the policy of the People's Republic of China to ask its citizens living abroad to obey the law of the nation they reside in. He also said the Overseas Chinese Bureau has been dissolved, told us many things we formerly did not know. When foreigners were ruling China, Dr. Sun Yat-sen was active in the freedom struggle and the help of overseas Chinese was enlisted in this struggle to overthrow the imperialists and thus the Overseas Chinese Bureau emerged. But now it is no longer needed and has been dissolved.[162]

Ne Win declared that Sino-Burmese friendship had been successfully reestablished.

The showdown between the Lin Piao and Chou En-lai groups was only a few weeks away during Ne Win's visit to China, and Chou was not yet willing or able to go as far as Ne Win in publicly proclaiming the restored friendship.

Chinese media did not report Ne Win's remarks made either in Canton or Rangoon on the success of the visit. Moreover, despite the high-level treatment given the prime minister, the Chinese press did not report any praise of the achievements of the Burmese Government or make any reference to peaceful coexistence or to the Sino-Burmese treaty of friendship and nonalliance.

Broadcasts of the BCP radio attacking Ne Win also continued throughout the visit. A few days after his return to Rangoon on the occasion of the Burmese Party's 32d anniversary, the BCP raised the subject of the China visit:

At present Ne Win's military clique is confronting difficulties in the political, economic, military and other fields. They could not get as much help as they wanted from their masters, and U.S. and British imperialists and social imperialists. Their masters could not help because they themselves are facing difficulties. Ne Win is trying to use sly tricks to get out of these difficulties. He is cheating the people with all kinds of tricks such as transformation of the cadre party into the people's party, return of power to the people and visiting the People's Republic of China.[163]

Nevertheless, the broadcast said, the BCP, with the help of Mao Tse-tung's thought, had exposed these tricks and had made clear that "the policy of armed revolution, military victory, and seizure of political power is the only policy for Burma." The broadcast ended as usual with the exclamation "Long Live Great Chairman Mao Tse-tung "

Peking continued to ignore this as well as other BCP broadcasts, and as in 1970, the Chinese did not note the anniversary of the Burmese party. After the fall of Lin Piao, Chou's freedom of action increased. On October 8, NCNA reported renegotiation of the terms of the 1961 agreement on economic and technical cooperation, and in November a Burmese trade delegation in Peking signed a new trade accord and commodity loan agreement with the Chinese. In January, Chou again sent greetings to Ne Win on Burma's National Day, and unlike the previous year NCNA reported the text of this message.[164]

Finally in the spring of 1972 a Burmese Government economic delegation was given a rousing welcome in Peking reminiscent of the best days of Sino-Burmese friendship. While there had been no crowds to greet Ne Win the previous August, a large group was turned out for the economic delegation.

Meanwhile, the BCP insurgents had renewed their offensive in the Northeast, launching an attack on the key town of Kunlong. The guerrillas were still apparently being supplied by China and using China as an active sanctuary.[165] The continuation of this subversive activity showed that Chou was still unable or unwilling effectively to force the BCP into a policy that would be consistent with the PRC's diplomacy.

The BCP's aggressive strategy along the border in late 1971 was probably its own decision, perhaps taken in the face of Peking's opposition. But the Chinese regime, probably at the instigation of Chen Po-ta and Lin Piao, had made previous commitments to supply the BCP guerrillas and Chou was not ready to pay the political price— internal and external—of totally reneging on this agreement.

China is not the first nation that has found it difficult to control the policies of a weak ally or to make a parasitic guerrilla organization that was once fostered behave according to the will of the host. Other governments have also unenthusiastically followed through on a foreign adventure because of inertia and domestic political constraints. China's wish to show consistency and credibility within the international communist movement—while in fact substantially altering its ideological positions—strengthened the force of inertia in Peking's backing of the BCP.

In addition, at the end of 1971 the political situation in China was still marked with tension as Chou En-lai sought to come to terms or deal with the former associates of fallen Vice Chairman Lin Piao. Deeper down there were other rifts in the Chinese leadership—between radicals and moderates, and civilians and military—which complicated a clear resolution of controversial issues like China's relations with the BCP. Although he was now more powerful than ever before, Chou very likely feared that internal enemies could still make use of this issue against him, charging that he held back the BCP just as victory was near.

Chou thus sought to retain China's moral commitment to the BCP by providing limited and clandestine backing to the party's revolution. The Premier could also calculate that his restoration of friendly governmental relations with Rangoon had minimized the diplomatic cost of China's support for the BCP. The Burmese Government was not making an issue of this affair. Nevertheless it seemed clear that Chou's ultimate objective was to make Sino-Burmese relations once more a model of peaceful coexistence.

CONCLUSIONS

The return of the peaceful coexistence line in Chinese policy toward Burma was due in large part to the tact, patience, and firmness of the Burmese Government. Without making any concession to the communists, the Rangoon government nevertheless satisfied the Chinese sense of rectitude by the release of the Chinese residents arrested in connection with the riots in 1967 and by taking the initiative in normalizing diplomatic relations. Moreover, as noted previously, Burma did not respond in kind to Peking's verbal abuse, nor did it compromise its neutral foreign policy. At the same time, the Burmese Army, with no foreign advisers and with little use of artillery or air power, decimated the communist guerrilla forces in their traditional strongholds in central Burma, and after a tactical pullback from the Sino-Burmese border, the army appeared to be holding the line against new encroachments by Chinese-backed insurgents coming across the border.

Meanwhile, external developments, which posed new threats to the People's Republic of China, and the fall of Lin Piao's clique in Peking were essential ingredients in the fusion of events that promised the return of peaceful coexistence as the central theme in Sino-Burmese relations.

Both sides, however, had learned a lesson. The Burmese would not easily forget the experience of 1967-70 or the continuing aspects of Chinese subversion, and they would know that despite Burma's best intentions, events beyond Rangoon's control could conceivably turn China once again to an openly interventionist policy. But the Chinese would also probably remember for some time the costs of their interventionist period in Burma to their international prestige.

NOTES

1. J. H. Brimmel, Communism in Southeast Asia (London: Oxford University Press, 1959), pp. 193-194. See also Ruth McVey, The Calcutta Conference and Southeast Asian Uprisings, Southeast Asian Program (Ithaca, N.Y.: Cornell University Press, 1958); and Charles B. McLane, Soviet Strategies in Southeast Asia (Princeton, N.J.: Princeton University Press, 1966), pp. 359-361.

2. Richard Butwell, U Nu of Burma (Stanford, Cal.: Stanford University Press, 1963), p. 106. Also Frank Trager, From Kingdom to Empire (New York, 1966), p. 113.

3. Brimmel, op. cit., p. 311.

4. Frank N. Trager argues convincingly that Burma's early foreign policy was in two stages. In the immediate period after its independence Burma's security was tied to a defense treaty with Britain. After the insurrections began in 1948 Burma attempted unsuccessfully to obtain Western military aid. Only after this failure did it turn toward complete neutralism. See Trager, op. cit.

5. William C. Johnstone, Burma's Foreign Policy (Cambridge, Mass.: Harvard University Press, 1963), p. 161.

6. New York Times, July 8, 1951.

7. Information on this subject remains inconclusive, but Johnstone, op. cit., pp. 180-182, gives details on reports of Chinese aid

to the BCP and of the travel to China of BCP guerrillas. McLane, op. cit., p. 384, also quotes declassified Malayan Government files that refer to interrogations of captured Burmese guerrillas who testified to the presence of Chinese officers in North Burma. A BCP official captured in December 1968, Bo Ba Nyun, reported that with 27 other BCP cadres he was sent to the PRC in November 1950. From 1951 to 1955 he studied at the Peking Marxism-Leninism School and later attended the military staff college at Chungking. As one of the "Peking returnees," he returned to Burma for the 1963 peace talks and went underground when the talks broke down (Rangoon Domestic Service, December 16, 1968).

8. Several sources report that the establishment of such a base was a principal objective of the Chinese communists. See the report of the former Soviet diplomat in Rangoon, Aleksandr Kaznacheev, Inside a Soviet Embassy: Experiences of a Russian Diplomat in Burma (Philadelphia: Lippincott, 1962), pp. 139, 215. A former member of the BCP during 1949-59, U Than Maung, has also testified to the importance of this strategy; see series in Mandalay Sun of 1959 by Than Maung cited in Johnstone, op. cit., p. 181. McLane also reports his interview with Than Maung on this subject: McLane, op. cit., pp. 384-385.

9. Brimmel, op. cit., p. 312.

10. Ibid., pp. 312-313. Unfortunately Brimmel gives no citation for this assertion and the previous one. But as we will see the BCP later confirmed that Liu's advice was as stated.

11. Johnstone, op. cit., p. 183.

12. Brimmel, op. cit., p. 313.

13. Quoted by Johnstone, op. cit., p. 168.

14. Ibid., p. 169.

15. Ibid.; also see Butwell, op. cit., p. 177.

16. Brimmel, op. cit., p. 318.

17. NCNA (English), May 13, 1970; Statement of the Central Committee of the BCP on the centenary of the birth of Lenin.

18. Brimmel, op. cit., p. 319.

19. Robert Elegant, The Dragon's Seed (New York: St. Martin's Press, 1959), p. 252.

20. A. Doak Barnett, Communist China and Asia (New York: Harper, 1960), p. 497.

21. Trager, op. cit., pp. 178-179.

22. Ibid.

23. Trager, op. cit., pp. 182-183. In 1968 Trager reported that estimates of communist insurgents in the various fronts ranged between 1,400 and 2,800. "Burma 1967: A Better Ending Than Beginning," Asian Survey, February 1968, p. 115.

24. Ibid., p. 187.

25 Harold C. Hinton, Communist China in World Politics (Boston: Houghton Mifflin, 1966), p. 315.

26. Lucien Pye, Burma: Opening on the Left in the Military Manner (Cambridge: MIT Press, 1963).

27. A report in the Nation, December 20, 1962, claimed that such a split had taken place, with Goshal taking a pro-Soviet position and Than Tun a pro-Peking position. Persons interviewed by the author, who worked on the Nation at the time, however, believed that the story was a misconstrued and elaborated report of a rumored policy dispute in the BCP. This dispute was along Liuist and Maoist lines, not Moscow versus Peking.

28. As will be noted below, Goshal made these points about the Revolutionary Council in a memo to the party in 1967.

29. An article by the Shantung Military District carried on Tsinan, Shantung Provincial Service Radio in Mandarin, 1200 GMT, January 11, 1968. This charge against Liu was also repeated in a speech by the first vice chairman of the BCP, Thakin Ba Thien Tin, on July 5, 1967, at a Peking mass rally. See NCNA, July 5, 1967.

30. Article in People's Daily, September 1, by a BCP member, quoted in NCNA, September 1, 1967.

31. NCNA correspondent's "Report on Progress of the BCP." NCNA, December 29, 1967.

32. Speech by the first vice chairman of the BCP, note 29 above.

33. Tsinan, Shantung Provincial Service in Mandarin, op. cit., January 11, 1968.

34. Botatung, September 17, 18, 1967.

35. Reuters report of May 26, 1969 on Burmese-language book The Last Days of Thakin Than Tun by former BCP officials: Mya, Bo Tin Shein, Ba Khet, and Saw Mla.

36. Botatung, September 17, 18, 1967.

37. Last Days of Thakin Than Tun, op. cit.

38. Botatung, September 17, 18, 1967.

39. New York Times, November 17, 18, 1963.

40. Last Days of Thakin Than Tun, op. cit.

41. New York Times, January 28, 1964. At the beginning of the year Ne Win also charged that opposition elements backed by "a foreign country" were plotting to seize power. It was not clear if he was referring to China.

42. Current Scene, October 17, 1967.

43. NCNA article of December 29, 1967, op. cit., and resolution of the Central Committee of the Burmese Communist Party's journal, People's Power 2, 2 (1967), quoted by NCNA, December 15, 1968.

44. Article by Aung Moe, Guardian, December 15, 1968.

45. NCNA, December 29, 1967, op. cit.

46. Aung Moe, op. cit.

47. Hinton, op. cit., p. 415.

48. NCNA, September 30, 1964.

49. New York Times, November 1, 1964.

50. However, a People's Daily/Red Flag article of March 23, 1965, attacking the new Soviet leaders included charges of "carrying on all kinds of disruption and subversion against the Burmese Communist Party."

51. Ibid., May 22, 1965.

52. Lin Piao, "Long Live the Victory of the People's War," Peking, NCNA, September 2, 1965.

53. People's Daily, January 28, 1965.

54. Harrison Salisbury in New York Times, June 20, 1966.

55. New York Times, June 22, 1966. Nevertheless, the two most strategic bridges in the Shan states were later completed by the Burmese.

56. NCNA, November 1, 1967.

57. The United States had made a small $35 million allocation for the cut-rate sale of certain military equipment and spare parts over a 10-year period to the Burmese Government. As this agreement was due to expire in 1967, its renewal may have been discussed during Ne Win's visit. If so, it represented no departure in U.S.-Burmese relations.

According to later reports this program was extended after 1967 on a year-to-year basis and eventually totaled $88 million by 1970, at which time it was ended. See Robert A. Holmes, "China-Burma Relations Since the Rift," Asian Survey, August 1972.

58. NCNA (English), January 4, 1967.

59. Ibid., November 2, 1967.

60. The Rangoon Daily, however, on January 23, 1967, predicted civil war in China and warned that "neighboring countries may have to exercise great caution."

61. Ibid.

62. Reuters, April 12, 1967.

63. Radio Tirana, November 6, 1966.

64. NCNA, April 3, 1967, "PLA Fighters Attack Liu-Shap-chi"; and NCNA, April 5, 1967, "Historians' Attack on Liu Shao-chi."

65. NCNA, May 21, Peking Radio in Tagalog, May 23, 1967.

66. NCNA, April 26. See also Red Flag, issue no. 11, July 1967, which states, "the people of Indonesia are determined to make revolution and the Chinese people are determined to support their revolution."

67. See for example People's Daily; May 19, NCNA, June 27, 1967.

68. Broadcast January 7, 1967, by the clandestine radio Voice of the People of Thailand (VPT), believed to originate from China.

69. VPT broadcast, November 21, 1967.

70. Guardian, June 15, 1967, report of BCP defector, Yebaw Thein Myint.

71. NCNA correspondent article on BCP, December 29, 1967.

72. NCNA story from Rangoon on February 12, for example reported the good news that "Burmese workers love Chairman Mao who is not only the great leader of the Chinese people, but also the great leader of the proletariat in the whole world." And on May 19 Burmese workers and youth were reported by NCNA to have pledged to follow the chairman's teachings and to oppose "counter-revolution-aries and pseudo-revolutionaries."

73. The story of this meeting was revealed by a BCP leader, Thein Myint, who surrendered to the government in June 1967. For a good summary of these events see Frank N. Trager, "Burma: 1968— A New Beginning?" Asian Survey, February 1969.

74. Botatung, September 17, 18, 1967; Guardian, June 5, 11, 26, 1968.

75. Ba Thien Tun's August 14, 1967 speech, op. cit.

76. NCNA, June 23, 1967, BCP congratulatory message on the explosion of China's H-bomb.

77. Ta Kung Pao, Hong Kong, October 18, 1966.

78. Lea A. Williams, The Future of Overseas Chinese in South-east Asia (New York: McGraw-Hill, 1966). For one thing, there are relatively few Chinese in Burma—about 400,000, or 1.6 percent of the population. The small numbers are due to the British policy in colonial days of encouraging Indians to emigrate to Burma to fill the commercial and trading jobs that in most of the other societies of Southeast Asia were held by Chinese. Thus popular resentment as well as the Ne Win's government's war against "economic insurgents" fell most heavily upon the Indians, and not upon the Chinese.

79. John H. Badgly "Burma's China Crisis: The Choices Ahead," Asian Survey (November 1967).

80. Ibid.

81. In admonishing the Burmese Government, People's Daily on July 10 also proclaimed that "to propagate Mao Tse-tung's thought is the sacred and inviolable right of Chinese personnel working abroad."

82. Pi' Liao Chan Pao (Criticize Liao Combat Newspaper), Peking June 18, 1967, translated in JPRS, Communist China Digest, no. 42, 977, October 16, 1967, cited by Melvin Gurtov, "The Foreign Ministry and Foreign Affairs in China's Cultural Revolution," Santa Monica, Cal., RAND Corporation, Memorandum RM-5934-PR, March 1969, p. 34.

83. NCNA, August 2, 1967. The Burmese Government at this time (May 1967) was still attempting to play down any possible difficulty with China. Foreign Minister Thi Han, for example, told a U.S. reporter in May that there had been "no pressure on Burma from China before or during the Cultural Revolution." New York Times, May 2, 1967.

84. NCNA, June 22, 1967.

85. The Burmese Government nationalized most private schools, including some 200 Chinese schools, in 1965. One thousand Chinese teachers had returned to China by the end of 1966 (Current Scene, October 17, 1967).

86. Guardian, June 23-26, 1967.

87. This was revealed in the PRC's note of June 28, NCNA, June 28, 1967.

88. It was reported that 37 shots were fired at the crowd by officials inside the embassy. This seems unlikely but was perhaps believed by the mob. See Guardian, June 27, 1967.

89. Ibid.

90. NCNA, June 27.

91. Ibid., June 28, 1967. It is interesting to compare Peking's treatment of the Rangoon anti-Chinese riots to similar disturbances in Indonesia in March and April of 1963. In the latter instance 13 Chinese were killed and hundreds wounded. Peking and Sukarno both blamed the incident on "counterrevolutionaries" and China did not pursue the matter. Justus van der Kroef, The Communist Party of Indonesia (Vancouver: University of British Columbia Press, 1965), pp. 290-291.

92. Wilfred Burchett, "A New Road for Communist China," Yomiuri Shinbun, May 9, 1971. Burchett is a well-known communist writer who has frequently visited China.

93. Edgar Snow, "A Conversation with Mao Tse-tung," Life, April 30, 1971.

94. "Wei Tung Chieh-Hua-pi" (Tearing off the mask) in the Peking Wei Tung, March 28, 1968; Supplement to SCMP, no. 225, January-June 1968, pp. 30-32. The dates given in this article are often inaccurate. Foreign Ministry statements were issued on June 28 and 29. It also quotes Ch'i as lamenting that on July 1 no rally was apparently to be held, although a protest rally of 200,000 against the Burmese Government was actually held in Peking on June 29.

95. VPT, December 5, 1967.

96. Ibid., December 4, 1967.

97. Ibid., January 5, 1968.

98. People's Daily, June 30, 1967, carried by NCNA (English) June 30.

99. NCNA, June 30, 1967.

100. Ibid., July 5.

101. Ibid.

102. Ibid, August 14, 1967.

103. Radio Peking, July 21, 1967.

104. People's Daily, on July 10, for example, set some kind of a record when in a single editorial it called the Ne Win government a dictatorship, a pack of reactionary warlords, fascist hangmen, insatiable blood suckers, imperialist agents, and colluders with U.S. and British imperialism, Japanese militarism, Soviet revisionism, the Tito clique, India, Israel, Malaya, and Indonesian reactionism.

105. The Burmese Government apparently did not release the text of its replies to Peking's protests. But the gist of their content can be deduced from several references to them by the Peking press.

106. NCNA, July 1.

107. Ibid., September 7, 1967.

108. Ibid., August 10 and 11. The killing incidents that were listed were said to have occurred over the previous six months. The alleged intrusions went back over two years.

109. PRC Foreign Ministry note, August 11, NCNA, August 11, 1967. Emphasis added.

110. People's Daily "Commentator" article, November 2, 1967. The PRC was referring to the map attached to the March 1967 Burma-India boundary agreement, which reflected the Indian version of the Sino-Indian boundary in that area. This consideration of course did not affect in any way the Sino-Burmese boundary. The Burmese Government was maintaining its neutrality in handling the situation in this way, for in its 1960 boundary agreement with China it had allowed the attached map to reflect the Chinese version of the Sino-Indian border. At that time, India also protested to the Burmese Government. See Butwell, op. cit., pp. 233-236. For text of Indian protest note, see G. V. Ambekar and V. D. Divekar, Documents on China's Relations with South and Southeast Asia (Bombay: Allied Publishers Private Ltd., 1964), pp. 166-167. In the 1960 boundary treaty with Burma, China accepted the traditional (McMahon line) Sino-Burmese boundary with the exception of the Diphuk Pass area, which links China with Assam (See "Diphuk-ult Impasse," Far Eastern Economic Review, January 9, 1969).

111. People's Daily "Commentator" article, November 2, 1967. Emphasis added. "Commentator" articles are believed to represent considered and official policy statements.

112. NCNA, November 29, 1967. The article quoted reports in the Sunday Times, London, November 19, and the Christian Science Monitor, November 22. The American Embassy in Rangoon was quoted in the New York Times, January 30, 1968, as denying any "major" American arms shipments to Burma. U.S. military equipment, however, was provided until 1970. See note 57.

113. Ibid.

114. People's Daily, June 30, NCNA, June 30, 1967.

115. NCNA, July 1, 1967.

116. Ibid., September 12, 1967.

117. Ibid., July 2, 1967.

118. Pi' Liao Chan Pao, op. cit.

119. After the June incident a large number of pro-Peking overseas Chinese in Burma returned to China. As of May 20, 1968, 15,000 were reported to have departed (Working People's Daily, Rangoon, May 23, 1968). By 1969 the PRC was refusing to repatriate other Chinese residents.

120. Working People's Daily and Guardian, September 24, 1968. Also see BCP reference to these purges in its statement carried by NCNA, March 20, 1969.

121. This information comes from several BCP defectors: Bo Tin Shein (Press Conference, Rangoon Radio, October 20, 1968); U Mya (Press Conference, Rangoon Radio, November 28, 1968); and Maung Mya (Press Conference, Rangoon Radio, September 27, 1968). Among those executed was the son of Than Tun's "best friend," Hla and his wife Ahmar, editors of the now-suppressed pro-Peking Ludu, a Mandalay newspaper.

122. Rangoon Radio, December 16, 1968. Report on capture of "Peking returnee" Bo Ba Nyun.

123. Ibid., September 27, 1968; Straits Times, September 28, 1968.

124. Ibid., November 28, 1968.

125. International Herald-Tribune, March 21, 1969, NCNA (English) March 20, 1969. The Central Committee of the CCP also sent a message of condolence, which expressed the thought that the BCP would turn its "grief into strength."

126. The figure of 90 was given by captured "Peking returnee" Bo Tin Shein. Guardian, October 21, 1968.

127. Speech by Ba Thien Tin, Peking Radio, NCNA, March 20, 1969.

128. Botatung, April 12, 1969.

129. NCNA, August 14, 1969.

130. Radio Moscow (Burmese), June 30, 1969, commentator, Valeri Salamov.

131. "Practical Experiment in Burma," Literaturnaya Gazeta, Radio Moscow (Burmese), June 27, 1969.

132. Hinton, op. cit., p. 311.

133. Johnstone, op. cit., p. 183.

134. NCNA, April 27, 1969.

135. Report of a BCP defector, Botatung (Rangoon), May 18, 1968.

136. BCP statement, NCNA, March 20, 1969.

137. NCNA, April 27, 1969.

138. Working People's Daily (Rangoon), February 8, 1968.

139. Anthony Polsky, "Threatening Command," Far Eastern Economic Review, September 26, 1968.

140. Rangoon Domestic Service (Burmese), March 1, 1968; New York Times, March 20, 1968.

141. Ibid., March 1, 1968.

142. Canton Wen-ko Feng-lei (Cultural Revolution Storm), no. 3, March 1968.

143. Stanley Karnow in Washington Post, dateline Hong Kong, November 2, 1969.

144. NCNA, April 29, 1969. Peking Radio in Burmese, August 15, 1969, address by Ba Thien Tin.

145. Karnow report cited in note 143.

146. Straits Times, November 8, 1969.

147. Far Eastern Economic Review, November 13, 1969, p. 346.

148. Ian Ward, London Daily Telegraph, April 15, 1970.

149. Patriotic Youth Front Radio clandestine broadcast, May 1, 1970.

150. Interview by Sterling Seagraves, "U Nu Underground," Far Eastern Economic Review, December 12, 1970.

151. SCMP, New York Times Service, Malcolm Browne, August 19, 1971.

152. According to one report, when Ne Win visited Pakistan in January 1969, he met with members of the Chinese diplomatic mission there to discuss Sino-Burmese relations (Far Eastern Economic Review, February 16, 1969). In Rangoon, however, this report was described as without foundation.

153. Liberation Army Daily article, March 27, 1969, and NCNA, March 28, 1969.

154. NCNA, August 15, 1969.

155. Ibid., August 14, Oct. 9, 1968.

156. Ibid., May 12, 1970.

157. Ibid., October 3, 1970.

158. Ibid., May 19, 1971.

159. For an excellent review of the "516" group, see Current Scene, August 7, 1971.

160. Ibid.

161. Botatung, August 13, 1971.

162. Working People's Daily, September 27, 1971. The restoration of the liberal line on overseas Chinese was reflected in the concurrent reappearance of Liao Cheng-chih, the former head of the Overseas Chinese Affairs Commission.

163. Voice of the People of Burma (Burmese), 1200 GMT, August 15, 1971.

164. NCNA, January 3, 1972.

165. Naw Seng was reportedly killed in a fall on March 9, 1972. Voice of the People of Burma Radio broadcast, April 25, 1972.

5

In the international politics of Southeast Asia the four states of Thailand, Malaysia, Singapore, and the Philippines, dissimilar in history and culture, find themselves bound together by a common fear of China and a common orientation to the West. In the same way, the communist parties of these states have common as well as distinctive features.

The distinguishing characteristic of the Malayan and Thai communist parties (the former including Singapore) has been the dominating influence of ethnic Chinese and their relative political orientation to China. The bonds of ideology have been strengthened by the more persistent ties of Chinese nationalism. In the Philippine Communist Party (PKP), however, the influence of the Chinese party and the role of ethnic Chinese has fluctuated but always remained marginal.

In this final chapter, we will investigate the relationship of these parties to China and the concurrent development of China's relations with the governments of Thailand, Malaysia, Singapore, and the Philippines.

THE FOUNDING OF THE MALAYSIAN AND THAI COMMUNIST PARTIES

The history of the Malayan Communist Party (MCP) is unique in Southeast Asia. Basically ethnically Chinese, the MCP came near to a successful seizure of power. The communists in China at an early date became interested in the revolutionary possibilities in the Chinese city of Singapore. Only four years after its own founding, the Chinese Communist Party (CCP) reportedly sent an agent to the

British Crown Colony to begin organizational work for the construction of a new party. After the break with the Nationalist Party in China, a South Seas Communist Party (South Seas or Nan Yang is the Chinese word for Southeast Asia) was established in Singapore. In April 1930, this organization created a Malayan Communist Party with responsibility for Malaya, Singapore, and Thailand. Although the MCP attempted to recruit among all the races, it remained largely a Chinese movement pledging to establish a republic, thus doing away with the Malay sultans. A major appeal of the MCP was to Chinese nationalism, and it contained a strong anti-Japanese strain, a strain that had no particular appeal for the Malays, who resented the industrious Chinese. The party also remained obedient to the Communist International, switching to the united-front line in 1935 and back to opposing the British war effort after the Nazi-Soviet Pact of 1939. It revealed its ties with the CCP, however, by dropping the anti-British line in September 1940 upon the instruction of the Chinese party.

As in the MCP, Chinese were instrumental in the founding of the Thai Communist Party (TCP). In fact, until recent years, communism in Thailand was, as David Wilson has said, "almost a complete monopoly of Chinese and Vietnamese."[1] Consequently successive Thai governments have always been able to link real and alleged threats of the TCP to the two-edged national fear of Chinese internal economic dominance and of China's external power. Because of the unproductive social-political climate in Thailand, particularly the absence of a colonial past and a major peasant problem, the TCP, until the 1960s, was the frailest of the Southeast Asian parties. The Thai communists were late blooming into a formal organization, and they were positive laggards with regard to armed struggle. The Thai party's early history is therefore lost in a fog of insignificance. Until 1935, Thailand was apparently under the jurisdiction of the MCP and its parent organization in Singapore, the South Seas Communist Party. In 1935, J. H. Brimmel reports, a TCP group was represented at the Seventh Comintern Congress.[2] However, if there was such a formal communist group in Thailand at that time, it was presumably a branch of the Chinese Communist Party or perhaps of Ho Chi Minh's Indochina Communist Party,* for the TCP in 1967 revealed that it was not established until December 2, 1942.[3]

---

*Ho was in Bangkok in 1928 as the Comintern agent for Southeast Asia mostly concerned with the revolutionary movement in Indochina, including the 30,000 Vietnamese in Thailand.

THE WAR YEARS

We know nothing of the Thai Communist Party's activities, if any, during World War II. Thailand of course, was not at war, having allied itself with Japan after a desultory resistance. Thailand not only escaped destruction and occupation but as a reward for coming to an agreement with the Japanese acquired two of the Burma Shan states, four states of northern Malaya previously ceded to the British, and a slice of Cambodia. Although the former premier, Pridi Phanamyong, organized an underground movement, no actual fighting took place against the Japanese, and it was not until Japan seemed a sure loser that many Thais were attracted to a line of resistance to Japan. According to its own testimony, the TCP was formally organized during this time (1942), and presumably it succeeded in stimulating some support from the Chinese community by means of its anti-Japanese appeal to Chinese nationalism. The TCP's only important benefit from the war came after it was concluded and the Royal Thai Government in an expiation of its sins of collaboration legalized the party.

In contrast to Malaya and Thailand, the development of the Communist Party in the Philippines had only tenuous connections with China and the Chinese community in the islands. In 1924, five Filipinos attended a communist-sponsored conference of Transport Workers of the Pacific in Canton, and in 1927, the leftist Filipino union leader, Crisanto Evangelista, reportedly attended another such conference in Hankow.[4] Evangelista's peasant organization established a communist party in November 1930, and elected a Central Committee of 35 members including three Filipino Chinese.[5] The Politburo of seven members included one "Chinese representative."[6] According to another source, a small branch of the Chinese Communist Party was also set up about the same time within the Chinese community in Manila.[7] Others, however, report that this was merely a "Chinese branch" of the PKP.

Government sources frequently refer to the establishment in 1938 of a "Chinese Bureau," which in the past operated under various names and which allegedly still exists in the shadows of Manila. The organizational relationship of the "Chinese Bureau" and the PKP is unknown, but presumably the bureau, if it in fact existed, channeled funds from the Chinese business community into the PKP.[8]

At the First Congress of the PKP held in May 1931, a resolution was passed that proclaimed solidarity with the communist forces in China whose achievements were said to have been a "mighty inspiration."[9] During the next decade, the PKP remained a disciplined party that followed directions on strategy and political line as laid down by Moscow. But what contact the PKP had with international communism was largely through the Communist Party of the United States. There is no record of any further communication or connection between the PKP and the CCP until the Japanese attack on the Philippines.

For both the Malayan and the Philippine communist parties, the war presented a golden opportunity. The Malay and the Filipino elite, in contrast to their Burmese and Indonesian counterparts, felt that they possessed a stake in the colonial regimes; the British in most of Malaya were a "protecting power" only governing by indirect rule, and the Americans had solemnly promised to surrender full power and independence to the Philippines. Nevertheless, the Filipino and the Malay elites, with important exceptions in the former case, either were passive in the face of the Japanese occupation or else expediently collaborated.[10] But at the same time, there were important segments of the population in Malaya and in the Philippines that were susceptible to appeals to resist the Japanese. In Malaya, this segment was, of course, the large Chinese population, whose anti-Japanese nationalism was immediately heightened by the brutalities inflicted upon it by the occupying Japanese. In the Philippines, thanks to the U.S. policy of fostering Filipino nationalism, there was a genuine loyalty to the United States among a large percentage of the people. In addition the already downtrodden Filipino peasantry suffered further under the Japanese and thus became even more sympathetic to resistance.

It was then that the communist parties in Malaya and the Philippines, with their experience in clandestine and revolutionary violence, seized leading roles in the anti-Japanese campaigns. The Malayan People's Anti-Japanese Army (MPAJA) and the PKP thus became in many areas of their respective countries the only authority in opposition to the Japanese. These two forces constituted the largest resistance movements in Southeast Asia.* It is interesting to note, however, that both the Malayan and the Filipino communists, in Maoist fashion (although perhaps not necessarily in accordance with Mao's wishes at that time), concentrated on strengthening their own positions rather than on attacking the Japanese. The MPAJA initiated few engagements with the Japanese, and like the Huks, it reportedly killed more of its own compatriots than Japanese.[11]

Many years later, a Maoist faction in the PKP denounced the 1943-44 "retreat for defense policy" as having lost the opportunity of expanding the party's armed potential.[12]

---

*The Huks of course also competed with and sometimes fought with guerrilla units organized by United States Armed Forces Far East (USAFE).

254

There was obviously little that Mao could do directly to help the military efforts of these two parties, but he did make a token contribution by providing a few "military advisers." Luis Taruc, one of the major Huk leaders (released from prison in 1968) has recounted that there were four CCP officials who joined the PKP Politburo as advisers and as liaison officers shortly after the war began. Two of these, he said, were from the mainland.[13] But Taruc relates that their advice often seemed related mainly to the interests of the Chinese war effort rather than to those of the Philippines. For example, he reports that the Chinese recommended an aggressive policy against the Japanese, which brought down upon the Huks a vicious and costly Japanese counterattack.[14] At a PKP meeting in September 1944, a number of Filipinos were reportedly dropped from leading organs in the party on charges that they had followed too mechanistically the Chinese communist experience.[15] However, a pro-Peking PKP history in 1971 stated that the "retreat for defense" policy was dropped at this meeting.[16]

In addition to these few advisers, a squadron of guerrillas recruited from the Chinese community in Manila served with the Huks during most of the war. Some of these guerrillas were said to have served with the Chinese Red Armies on the mainland. If so, it is not known under what circumstances they had come or returned to the Philippines, but the group was professional enough so that it trained other Huk squadrons.[17]

In Malaya the entire MPAJA was parallel to the ethnic-Chinese "Hwa Chiao" squadron of the Huks—that is, its members came almost entirely from the Chinese community. The Communist Party of China apparently retained a liaison officer with the MPAJA, but contact with Yenan, as in the case of the Philippines, was probably no more than sporadic. Nevertheless, although specific evidence is lacking, the record of the MCP up to that time suggests that it was under the loose guidance of the CCP.[18]

But in the case of the Philippines, it seems highly unlikely that a similar organizational relationship with the CCP existed. There probably was no more than a rather nebulous community of kindred spirits between Yenan and the communist guerrillas in central Luzon. The only important influence of the CCP on the Huks was an inspirational and ideological one.[19]

THE POSTWAR ADJUSTMENTS

After the end of the fighting against the Japanese, the MCP, the PKP, and the TCP all faced distinctly different situations. The PKP had emerged from the war with a strong guerrilla organization and with the fundamental issue of the land problem in a more critical stage than ever. But as Filipino independence was obviously to proceed on schedule, the PKP lacked the more emotional and class-transcending issue of a national liberation struggle. The MCP also retained a fighting organization that could readily be revived, but under the Labour government in Britain, self-government and independence for Malaya also seemed assured. Even more important, however, the MCP remained a communal organization with no base among the Malay population. The TCP, on the other hand, was without any armed resources, with virtually no mass base, and with few issues in an independent and relatively unscarred and prosperous Thailand.

All of these situations suggested that a violent attempt at the seizure of power was not in order. Consequently in the early postwar years, all three parties launched upon periods of legal struggle and upon attempts at forming united fronts with leading noncommunist elements in their respective countries.

This was also the period referred to previously in which Stalin hoped to achieve a further extension of communist influence in Western Europe, especially in France and Italy, through continuation of the united-front-from-above. During the same period the CCP was also gaining tactical and political advantage by espousing a coalition with its KMT enemy in China. Likewise, the Viet Minh were pursuing a moderate policy, hoping to win acceptable political terms from the French popular front government (and to rid the country of the Chinese Nationalist forces).

Some elements in the MCP and the PKP urged the continuation of armed struggle immediately after the war, but the local situations we have reviewed as well as the international climate of the time dictated lines of peace and unity in all these countries.

The extent of Chinese communist influence on these decisions varied widely between the parties. The MCP kept in close touch with the CCP during this period and was apparently directly advised by the Chinese in 1946 to refrain from insurrection and rely on united-front tactics as long as the Labour Party was in power in Britain.[20] But the CCP advisers to the Huks, according to Luis Taruc, returned to China soon after the war ended, and there were no such advisers thereafter.[21] Nor is there any evidence of high-level liaison between the PKP and the CCP during this period.[22] The PKP's policies therefore were largely, if not entirely, products of the pressure of events in the Philippines and the party's own analysis of alternative courses of action.

Presumably the TCP in its emergent and uncertain state and with its ethnic Chinese orientation established some form of contact with the CCP and accepted a measure of organizational subordination to Mao's headquarters—to the limited extent that the headquarters had time for such matters. A close relationship was suggested when a principal leader of the TCP, Prasert Sapsunthorn, fled to China after the coup in Thailand in 1947. The Second Session of the Thai party's Central Committee was apparently held in China in 1953.[23]

Thus the three parties proclaimed similar political programs of united front with their respective national bourgeois political organs.

In the Philippines in February 1946, a PKP-controlled "democratic alliance" promoted an electoral bloc with the Osmena Nationalistas for the 1946 elections on the basis of the PKP's five-point program. This program called for independence as promised, punishment of collaborators, democracy, and social and agrarian reform.[24] The MCP in 1945 also released its own program, which likewise stressed democratic and moderate social goals. At the Eighth Plenum of the MCP's Central Committee the secretary general, Loi Tek, affirmed that conditions were not favorable for a bloody revolutionary struggle but required liberation through a national democratic front.[25] The MCP thereupon devoted its efforts to obtaining a united front between Malaya's Chinese population and left-wing Malays in opposition to the British and the conservative United Malay National Association.[26] Likewise, in Thailand the Communist Party in 1946 released a 10-point program, which emphasized democracy, equal rights for national minorities (that is, Chinese), higher living standards, and so on.[27]

TWO TURN TO VIOLENCE

But by the end of 1947, world events as well as the domestic circumstances of the communist parties had changed significantly. In China, the People's Liberation Army was sweeping the KMT before it, and the Cold War had clearly commenced in Europe, where popular-front coalition governments had broken down. This situation and an aggressive response from the international communist movement was affirmed by Andrei Zhadanov in his famous speech of September 27, 1947, which explicitly encouraged militancy upon the communist parties of the world. This view was also promulgated to the various Asian communist parties at the Calcutta meetings, which we referred to earlier in regard to the Burmese Communist Party. Shortly after the Zhadanov speech, the new secretary general of the Malayan Communist Party, Chin Peng, and a group of his colleagues reportedly traveled to Hong Kong and China to seek advice from the CCP.[28] Two delegates from the MCP attended the Calcutta conferences. Following the Calcutta meetings, the MCP in March 1948 renounced the policy of peaceful struggle and proclaimed that a "people's revolution" was the ultimate aim. By June 1948, armed struggle had begun in Malaya.

The MCP decision to move to guerrilla war and terrorism was, of course, influenced by its physical capabilities in this regard as well as by the poor performance of its united-front efforts. But perhaps more than any other party of Southeast Asia the Malayan Communist Party was swayed by the advice it received from the international communist movement, including the British, Australian, Soviet, and Chinese communist parties. In the end, however, it was probably Mao's military successes of the time that had the greatest impact upon the decision of the Chinese in Malaya to "pick up the gun." This inspirational link was revealed in the MCP's analysis of the civil war, which the party produced six months after the "emergency" was proclaimed. This document, entitled "Strategic Problems of the Malayan Revolutionary War" (in the manner of Mao's 1936 "Strategic Problems of China's Revolutionary War"), quoted Mao extensively and reflected the Maoist doctrine of a protracted war. The party's 1949 program for a Malayan People's Democratic Republic also was a straight copy of the Maoist model of the "New Democracy."

A Filipino delegation also attended the Calcutta conferences.[29] But in contrast to the MCP, the PKP apparently was little influenced by the international communist movement in its decision to move to full-scale insurrection. Although intermittent fighting had begun in 1947, the Philippine Party did not turn to a policy of insurrection until the beginning of 1950. PKP officials, in fact, lived unmolested in Manila until October 1950. Following the rigged Liberal victory in the November 1949 elections, in which the PKP had supported the Nationalistas, the party in January 1950 called for the armed overthrow of the government. José Lava reportedly believed that victory was possible within two years because of three external factors: the certainty of a third world war, an economic recession in the United States, and the victory of the Chinese communists.[30]

The relative delay of the Huk rebellion was the result of divisions and confusions within the PKP and the hope among some elements in the party that an acceptable united-front-from-above could still be arranged. José Lava, however, has described this period of negotiations with the government as a "tactical maneuver" designed to capture the political initiative.[31]

Thailand meanwhile remained a revolutionary backwater. The liberal regime of Pridi Phanamyong was ousted in 1947, and Pridi fled the country, turning up in China in 1954. His successor, Phibun Songgram, launched a campaign against the Chinese community as well as against the leftist organizations that had mushroomed under Pridi. Nevertheless, the Thai Communist Party, which had scurried underground, continued its peace and unity line. According to a later TCP statement, the party in January 1948 issued a communiqué that called for a "coalition government consisting of patriotic political parties and nation-loving people."[32] In 1952 the party held a secret congress, where allegedly Prasert Sapsunthorn pushed a "revisionist" line that advocated peaceful struggle.[33]

Thus, while communist parties in most of the rest of Southeast Asia were engaged in armed struggle, the small TCP limited itself to the occasional issuing of pamphlets and organizational work. The party did, however, set up a paper united front called the Thai National Liberation Organization.

What assistance or supervision did the Chinese Communist Party provide to the Malayan and Filipino insurrections? Evidence is obviously inconclusive on this subject, but direct Chinese assistance was probably marginal in the case of the former and less than that in the latter instance. There are reports of Chinese communists smuggling both people and goods into the Philippines and assistance to the Huks by the Filipino branch of the Chinese Communist Party.[34] These reports however, are difficult to substantiate. Of the several thousand illegal Chinese immigrants who came into the Philippines from Hong Kong after the fall of the mainland, the overwhelming majority were simply refugees from the communists. A few agents may also have slipped into the country, and some funds from the Chinese community in Manila may have been provided to the PKP. No final judgment can be given as to the role such assistance may have played in the Huk rebellion in the early 1950s, but it probably was not significant.

The Filipino branch of the Chinese Communist Party, according to Luis Taruc, took its instructions from Peking and in practice maintained an almost independent existence and kept the PKP only vaguely informed of its connections with the CCP.[35] According to another source, the Filipino branch of the CCP in 1952 had about 3,000 members among the overseas Chinese in the Philippines and over several years received approximately $200,000 (U.S.) from mainland China.[36]

In contrast, in Malaya, there was a relatively close relationship between the MCP and the CCP, a relationship that probably provided the latter with a voice on important policy questions. The strong ideological influence of the Chinese party upon the MCP probably grew during the years of the "emergency," but it was still very likely exercised in a very informal way—with the MCP leaders interpreting Peking's views by their reading of official Chinese statements and articles.[37] During these years clandestine MCP newspapers gave much attention to developments in China, and world news usually consisted of monitored NCNA dispatches.[38] While the MCP maintained no public headquarters in Communist China, liaison officers were very likely exchanged between Peking and the MCP.[39] But as the MCP became consumed in fighting its life or death struggle, there was probably an increasing tendency to disregard tactical and strategic advice from China. Later events suggest that this was so.

During this revolutionary period in the international communist movement, Chinese hegemony over the Asian revolution was acknowledged by Moscow. The Chinese experience was explicitly held up as a model to the communist parties of Southeast Asia not only by Peking but by Moscow as well. Nevertheless it is interesting to note that during this time the Chinese communist press had relatively little to say about the revolutionary movement in Malaya or in the Philippines. In part, this inattention was due to China's preoccupation with other more pressing affairs and in part may have been a deliberate tactic intended to avoid embarrassment to local communist parties. More reports on these national liberation struggles seem to have been carried in the Soviet and Cominform press than in Chinese media.[40]

Both the MCP and the PKP had reason to play down their ties with China. While the MCP was undeniably an ethnic-Chinese organization and while a principal political weapon of the party was Chinese chauvinism, it still tried to assume a multiracial complexion and to rebut charges that it was an instrument of Communist China. Although the PKP and the Huks operated in a society in which there were only a few hundred thousand Chinese, anti-Chinese feeling was easily exploited in the Philippines.[41]

THE END OF VIOLENCE

By 1952, the rebellions of the Huks and the MCP as well as those in the rest of Southeast Asia outside of Indochina had clearly been beaten. The communist defeat in Malaya was achieved by a critical use of Commonwealth troops and in the Philippines by an important but less critical supply of military materials and economic assistance from the United States. In both areas, however, the major political factor was the inability of the communists to undermine the nationalist prestige of the noncommunist leaders and to make credible the threat of Western imperialism.

Subsequently all of the insurgent parties of Southeast Asia began to call for negotiations and to adopt policy lines that again stressed legal struggle and peace and unity with their respective bourgeois governments. Concurrently, the communist governments in Moscow and Peking began to emphasize peaceful coexistence with the nationalist governments of Asia and Africa. Tentative moves toward rapprochement were first initiated in 1951 and were directed at those nationalist regimes that appeared to be the most receptive to such overtures: India, Burma, and Indonesia. The nationalist leaderships in these countries were distinguished from those in Malaya, Thailand, and the Philippines by their more anti-Western as well as more Marxist orientation. Although India, Burma, and Indonesia had also experienced violent communist attempts to seize power—attempts that also received moral and political encouragement from the communist bloc—they were intellectually, emotionally, and politically receptive to a foreign policy of neutralism and to friendly relations with the communist camp.

Because of the historical and political reasons that we described earlier, the Thai, Malay, and Filipino elites embraced neither an extreme nationalism nor an extreme anti-Westernism. Nor were they at all inclined to Marxism by their social and economic status. In addition, the Malay and the Thai leadership were faced with Southeast Asia's largest proportion of ethnic Chinese among their populations, and thus their respective nationalisms tended to be more concerned with the threat of Chinese dominance, both internal as well as external and cultural as well as economic, than was the case in India, Burma, or Indonesia. Moreover, the communist attack in South Korea and Peking's political support for insurrections in Southeast Asia had seemed to confirm the reality of a Chinese communist threat. Later in 1953-54, the Viet Minh invasion of Laos and Cambodia and the establishment of a Pathet Lao government raised fears in Bangkok of a conventional attack upon Thailand, as well as of subversion among Lao-related Thais and the 40,000-50,000 Vietnamese in Thailand, both living mainly in the Northeast.

Finally the geopolitical positions of India and Indonesia reduced what fears they had of aggressive Chinese behavior. Burma's sheer exposure, on the other hand, also made a policy of isolation appear unrealistic. But Thailand, Malaya, and, to a lesser extent, the Philippines were situated somewhere between these two extremes. The possibility of physical and political isolation from China seemed feasible as well as desirable, particularly when backed up by a commitment of Western military assistance.

By 1954, the Moscow-Peking strategy of peaceful coexistence was in full swing. The immediate objective of this strategy in Asia was to forestall the creation of a U.S.-centered collective defense organization that would have arrayed all the noncommunist governments of Asia in a NATO-like bloc of containment against the communist powers. The intention of Moscow and Peking was to make neutralism an attractive alternative and to promote the concept of a "zone of peace" in Asia as well as in Europe. At the Geneva conference of 1954, China hinted at a formal system of "collective peace" in which the Asian nations would "make joint effort to safeguard the peace and security of Asia by assuming obligations mutually and respectively."[42] Chou En-lai also stated that his proposals did not envisage the exclusion of any country. Indeed the hope was to include the Western-oriented nations in this system of "collective peace," whatever its form might take. While the neutralist countries were being wooed, however, a two-edged approach was necessary in regard to the Philippines, Thailand, and Malaya, which were moving in the opposite direction to what was desired. This ambivalent diplomatic approach to the allied countries involved an effort to make credible the benefits of following the path of peaceful coexistence as well as the political and security cost of formal alignment with the United States and the United Kingdom.

But from 1950 to 1952, before the full blossoming of the peaceful coexistence line, Peking still paid surprisingly little attention to the foreign policies of these countries. Significantly, Peking comment on these three states before 1953 was in large part related to alleged persecution of overseas Chinese. The most dramatic pressure against the overseas Chinese was taking place in Malaya, where the authorities had instituted the "Briggs plan" for the controlled settlement of Chinese villagers and also had begun to deport thousands of Chinese nationals suspected of complicity in the communist insurgency. Because of this situation as well as Peking's closer relationship with the MCP, the People's Republic from 1950 to 1953 directed more attention toward Malaya than upon events in Thailand or the Philippines. Beginning in 1950, Peking lodged numerous official and unofficial protests of alleged British persecution of overseas Chinese in Malaya. An early Foreign Ministry protest, for example, demanded that a delegation from Peking be admitted to Malaya to inspect the condition of the Chinese there.[43] No reply was given to this demand, and subsequent messages gave the British the standard warning that they would "bear the full consequences." Nevertheless, deportations continued, and by the end of 1952, China stated that she had received almost 15,000 overseas Chinese deported from Malaya.[44]

There was apparently no official Chinese comment on the separate Thai and Philippine defense agreements with the United States signed in 1950 and 1951, respectively. What public attention Peking did award to Thailand and the Philippines was again primarily in regard to alleged persecution of overseas Chinese in those countries. The Philippine and Thai governments were referred to as "reactionary," but as stated before, little or no public reference was made in these years to the insurrection in either country. All this would suggest that Peking at this time really had little interest and even less faith in the communist movements in these two countries.

But in 1954, there was an upsurge in China's interest in both Thailand and the Philippines. This interest was occasioned, first, by fear that the Thai Government might cooperate with a possible U.S. effort to intervene in the war in Indochina, which was approaching its climax, and, second, by increasing indications that the United States would push for a collective defense treaty in Southeast Asia.[45]

In early 1954, Peking charged that the United States was working out a war plan for Thailand.[46] And the government in Bangkok was accused of making war preparations.[47] After the fall of Dien Bien Phu (May 7) and the commencement of the Geneva conference, Peking accused the United States of turning Thailand into a base for aggression.[48] In mid-July, a few days before the conclusion of the Geneva conference, editorials in two Chinese papers, which for several months had been extolling the choices of India, Burma, Indonesia, and Ceylon for neutralism, spelled out the alternatives for Thailand. For the first time Peking specifically proposed a relationship of peaceful coexistence with the Royal Thai Government.

> The five principles laid down by the Chinese, Indian, and
> Burmese Prime Ministers are perfectly applicable to
> relations between Thailand and other countries. . . .
> There is no doubt Thailand can save itself from being
> dragged by the United States to disaster if it adopts an
> independent policy.[49]

The consequences of rejecting the neutralist path, it was clearly suggested, would be felt internally as well as externally.

> No single government in Asia could escape the fate of
> being disowned by its own people and the people of the
> whole of Asia if it willingly sides with imperialists and
> colonialists and betrays its own people and national in-
> dependence.[50]

These editorials were followed by a more dramatic, and to the Thai leaders a more unsettling, article by Pridi Phanamyong, who, we will recall, had fled the country in 1947. The article not only confirmed Pridi's presence in China (which was announced a few days previously) but also represented the first explicit call emanating from China for the people of Thailand to "wage a struggle" against their rulers, who were deemed puppets of U.S. imperialism.[51] Pridi charged that Thailand was being used as an "aggressive base" and that the independence and liberty of Thailand were being lost. The former premier urged the alternative of acceptance of the "five principles" of peaceful coexistence. The Thai leaders interpreted Pridi's appearance in China and his article as confirming their fears that Peking was preparing to support the former premier in an effort to establish a pro-Chinese government in Bangkok, possibly, they feared, through some sort of subversion in connection with the Thai autonomous region, which was set up in 1953 in China's Yünnan province.[52]

The same general line was explicit in Peking's sudden attention in 1954 to affairs in the Philippines. Warnings of the dangers of following the United States were coupled with blandishments of a new peaceful order in Asia in which the Philippines could take part. Whereas China held up the implied threat to the Thai Government of support for a Pridi-backed movement against it, in the case of the Philippines it held up the specter of renewed activity by the People's Liberation Army, or the HMB, as the Huks were now called. Peking had referred only infrequently to the activities of the Huks since 1950, but in the summer of 1954, interest was suddenly renewed, and reports of insurgent activity that appeared in the Manila press were eagerly picked up by Peking.[53] At the same time, NCNA articles reported alleged expansion of U.S. military facilities on the islands.

The focus of Chinese attention toward Thailand and the Philippines in 1954 was clearly in regard to their imminent participation in the Southeast Asia Treaty Organization (SEATO), a fact that seemed manifest in Peking's silence on affairs in Malaya, which, although not yet independent, had indicated it did not wish to join the U.S.-sponsored military pact in Southeast Asia. At the time of the conclusion of the SEATO pact, China made clear its interpretation of the pact as "aimed at China" and as "intended to force the countries in Southeast Asia into a position of permanent antagonism to China."[54] Peking pointed with satisfaction to the fact that only three Asian governments were willing to join the military alliance, and their decision to do so, it warned, ran counter to the desires of the people of their own countries.[55]

These warnings had little effect on the Manila meetings of September 1954. Thailand in fact played an energetic but unsuccessful role in attempting to achieve a military alliance as strong as that of NATO. In addition, the Thai delegation was most concerned over the security of the three states of Indochina—Laos, Cambodia, and South Vietnam—and it led the way in bringing these countries under the protection of the treaty. However, the Thai Government failed to achieve as airtight an alliance in the final SEATO agreement as it had desired and thus opened itself up to internal criticism that its security policy had served to provoke Chinese hostility but had failed to provide conclusive and binding protection by the SEATO powers. Thai disappointment over this issue together with the full development of peaceful coexistence by China led in the next few years to a reevaluation in Bangkok.

After the conclusion of the SEATO agreement, Peking's charges of war preparations by the United States in Thailand and in the Philippines continued well into the next year. In the case of the Philippines, Peking reports of expanding activities by the People's Liberation Army also continued throughout the last half of 1954, but there is no evidence that Peking actually attempted to stir up the Huks to renewed activity. Nor did public Chinese reports on the Huk movement take any account of the new dissension within the ranks of the PKP in 1954. (Luis Taruc and his followers surrendered in May 1954). China's influence on the PKP in fact continued at a minimal, almost insignificant, level.

THE BANDUNG LINE

In 1955, China made its major effort to promote a peaceful coexistence strategy and to convince Thailand and the Philippines that the policy of alignment with the United States was less desirable than Indian-type neutrality. China's first direct approach to these two governments took place during the April 18-24, 1955 Asian-African Conference in Bandung, Indonesia.

In his opening remarks to the conference, the Thai delegate, Prince Wan Waithayakon, foreign minister, expressed in detail the fears of Chinese aggressiveness that lay behind the security policy of his own government.

> Though it is a fact, which in all responsibility I have to take into account, that Pridi Phanomyong, a Thai politician, is organizing the training of Thai-speaking Chinese and persons of Thai race in Yunnan for purposes of infiltration and subversion in Thailand, I have also to know for certain the attitude adopted by the Chinese People's Republic in regard to the so-called persons of dual nationality in Thailand or in other words to the Chinese community of 3,000,000 in Thailand out of a population of 18,000,000. I might also mention the presence of 50,000 Vietnamese refugees in Northeast Thailand on the border of the Mekong, the vast majority of whom chose to be repatriated to North Vietnam. In view of this situation as well as the invasion of Laos by Viet Minh forces in 1953 and also in 1954, Thailand has had clearly to face a threat of infiltration and subversion, if not of aggression itself.[56]

Chou En-lai, who headed the Chinese delegation, had come prepared to be conciliatory on all questions, and this attitude was strik-
ingly reflected in his reply to the issues raised by Thailand (and
less directly also by Cambodia). On the question of dual nationality,
Chou said this was a problem "left behind by old China" and that the
People's Republic was ready to solve this problem. In testimony
to this attitude, during the course of the conference, Chou negotiated
a treaty with Indonesia for the ending of dual nationality.

Chou also dismissed the idea that the Thai autonomous region
in Yünnan was a threat to Thailand, insisting that it was no different
from the other autonomous minority regions in China.[57] Chou insisted that China had no intention whatever of subverting the governments of its neighboring countries.

Later, Chou held private conversations with both Prince Wan
and the Philippine chief delegate, General Carlos P. Romulo. Chou
assured the Thai representative that Pridi was not in Yünnan organizing local Thais but was in Peking as a political exile. Chou
invited the Thai government to send a delegation to visit the Thai
autonomous region and see for itself. In addition, Chou offered to
conclude a treaty with Thailand on the Chinese nationality problem,
as was being concluded with Indonesia.[58]

Chou made the same offer of a nationality treaty to Romulo and
volunteered the same assurances that China would not resort to aggression or indirect threats against the Philippine Government. Likewise, Chou invited the Philippine Government to visit China's coastal
regions ("particularly Kwantung and Fukien") to see if there were
any activities constituting a threat to the Philippines.[59] Finally,
Chou arranged separate talks between Prince Wan and DRV Foreign
Minister Pham Van Dong, which resulted in an agreement for the
repatriation of the procommunist Vietnamese settled in northeast
Thailand back to North Vietnam.[60]

While Prince Wan and General Romulo (as well as the Pakistan
delegate) insisted that SEATO was a defensive organization only,
Chou, as expected, was unconvinced, and he insisted on the need to
eliminate all such "antagonistic military treaties." In his report on
the conference to the Standing Committee of the National People's
Congress, on May 13, 1955, Chou pursued the point that since China
had given full assurances, and there was no threat of armed attack,
SEATO had been established for "the sole purpose of obtaining manpower and insuring the setting up of new military springboards and
bases as well as to place the small countries in a subordinate position
politically and economically." Chou reiterated that Peking was "willing to establish normal relations and live together . . . with all countries on the basis of the five principles for peaceful coexistence."[61]

Thus, despite the formalization of SEATO, the Chinese People's Republic in 1955 was still hopeful of promoting a major reorientation of the organization's Asian members toward neutralism.

PURSUING PEACEFUL COEXISTENCE

The operational program with which China hoped to achieve its political goals in Southeast Asia operated as usual on three levels: people, state, and party. Programs and propaganda were directed at various classes, mostly the bourgeois, in order to gain support for a policy of accommodation with China. Business groups in particular were wooed with visions of profitable trade. Cultural exchanges were promoted, and front groups, political parties, and newspapers were encouraged and in some cases perhaps financially assisted in a concerted effort to generate pressure toward the same end. On the state level, a conciliatory attitude became the dominant theme in China's treatment of the pro-Western national bourgeois governments. While potential trade advantages of relations with China were driven home, the disadvantages—political, economic, and social—of close ties with the United States were vividly spelled out.

China's foreign policy stand was in essence designed to undermine the credibility of a threat from China and thus to destroy the rationale of the SEATO relationship. Concurrently the communist parties in these three countries were constrained by Peking as well as by their own circumstances to adopt postures compatible with China's state policy.

In China's propaganda, the element of threat became much more muted in drawing the alternatives for the pro-Western countries. This change, of course, was not mere cynicism; China itself was now more confident and less apprehensive than it had been a year earlier. The danger of massive U.S. intervention in Vietnam had passed for the moment with the carrying out of the first stages of the Geneva agreement. The emphasis of Chinese propaganda switched from the assertion that SEATO and its member states constituted an aggressive threat to China to the general theme that the United States was controlling and exploiting the allied states in a "new-type colonialism."

This period of China's diplomacy also reflected the different degrees of control Peking exerted over the three communist parties. The Thai Communist Party still seemed more shadow than substance, while the MCP, despite its defeat, remained a going organization; both, however, seemed to respond to Peking's political guidance during this period. The PKP on the other hand, remained more distant, and Peking's influence remained slight.

Let us now turn to a more detailed review of China's relations on the levels we have mentioned with these three nations from 1955 until the end of the Bandung period in 1959.

INITIAL SUCCESS IN THAILAND

Chou En-lai's performance at Bandung together with a general thaw in the Cold War had an important impact in Thailand. The relaxation of Thai fears and the general reduction of world tensions facilitated Premier Phibun Songgram's decision in June 1955 to launch an internal liberalization program. Phibun had just returned from a world tour and was full of enthusiasm for democratic ways, and to some degree he was apparently sincere in wishing to establish a similar system in Thailand. In addition, such a policy was probably also intended to provide Phibun a base of popular support to strengthen his own hand against the other two important political factions in Thailand, the police and the army.

While China's peaceful coexistence strategy provided the proper context in which internal relaxations could be made in Thailand, the policy of liberalization within Thailand at the same time greatly facilitated China's diplomatic offensive. Political freedoms that had existed all along in the Philippines were now instituted in Thailand— most importantly, freedom to oppose the government's foreign policy. Restrictions on newspapers were removed, political parties that had been suppressed sprang up again, and pressure on the Chinese community was relaxed. A 1952 ban on the Communist Party, however, remained.

The result over the next three years was increased expression of opposition to the government's SEATO policy and its nonrecognition of China. Businessmen, opposition newspapers, and opposition politicians began a campaign for relaxation of controls on trade with China and for a new orientation in foreign policy.[62] Several of the new parties were established by Pridi's former associates, a number of whom returned at this time from exile.[63]

In the summer of 1955, Peking began to blame its bad relations with the Thai Government strictly on the United States, and it ceased referring to the Thai rulers in uncomplimentary terms.[64] From this point on, China concentrated on the advantages to be gained by trade and political relations with China and on the cost and inequities of Thailand's ties to the United States.

In early 1956, a Thai "good will mission" led by a leader of one of the neutralist parties, at the invitation of the Chinese People's Institute of Foreign Affairs, paid an important visit to China, where it was received by Mao and Chou. Mao in his interview appealed for friendly relations between Thailand and China, and he made a special point of attacking SEATO.

> Even though America is strong militarily, still one day
> the people will not fear it. America has gone around
> making pacts to prepare aggression such as SEATO and
> the Baghdad Pact. I would like to compare SEATO with
> a brick to make a wall. Such bricks make a big noise
> but one day they will tumble down, because they are divi-
> ded against themselves. . . . SEATO is a wall . . . which
> does not allow men to look at each other. It is not the
> mistake of you who make those pacts but the mistake of
> the imperialists. Beloved friends, is it mistaken if I say
> that these military pacts are tools which prevent under-
> standing between men and nations? . . . These pacts are
> also anti-Asian.[65]

Mao also said that Thailand could sell its rice and rubber to China and that if the two countries had diplomatic relations, China could help Thailand in building industries such as glass, paper, and textiles. Chou En-lai in his talk with the Thai delegates reportedly addressed himself to the same question of peace in Asia:

> It is our opinion that the Asian nations ought to have a
> treaty of peace and live together in peace without any
> aggression. We do not support military treaties; there-
> fore we are happy to receive you who come in friend-
> ship and peace. We will be friends and live in peace.[66]

Upon their return to Thailand the members of this mission were arrested for violation of the Act Against Communism, but the charges were soon dropped. Despite the initial unfriendly home reception for this mission, further "good will" toward China began to be expressed in Bangkok—this time by Thai Government leaders. In the spring and summer of 1956, Peking happily reported remarks by the Thai foreign minister and by Premier Phibun that Thai mer-chants would be permitted to visit China and that normal trade rela-tions except in strategic goods could be resumed.[67] (David Wilson comments that at the time the potential for trade was important for neither party and that the decision was, therefore, a political one.)[68] In addition, the Thai foreign minister was quoted as saying that "the government of Thailand has begun to change its original stand on the recognition of China in the light of the change in the present inter-national situation; it will accord recognition the moment China enters the United Nations.[69]

Although Communist Chinese goods had been imported to Thailand through Hong Kong for some time, after the lifting of official trade restrictions, Chinese consumer goods were soon much more in evidence in the Bangkok markets. The People's Daily interpreted the appearance of these goods as a sure sign that spring had arrived in Sino-Thai relations. Some overseas Chinese were said to have been moved to tears at the sudden sight of merchandise from the homeland including "shining bicycles, exquisite sewing machines, beautifully designed radios, . . . etc."70

The role of the Thai Communist Party in the anti-U.S. and pro-Peking campaign being waged in Bangkok is impossible to assess. Although the party remained outlawed under the 1952 act, occasional pamphlets and circulars were mailed to newspaper offices or to students. The theme of these statements was simply anti-U.S. and expressed no clear domestic program. Except for perfunctory references to feudalism, the party carefully avoided attacks on the government. A message of greetings from the Thai Communist Party was read at the Eighth Congress of the Chinese Communist Party on September 22, 1956. This message, which was carried by NCNA, was again devoted almost entirely to nationalist and antiimperialist themes.

In January 1957, as the united front seemed to be developing, the TCP published as a mailed mimeograph flyer a "new year's message to the Thai people." This message which was discussed in the NCNA broadcast over Radio Peking on January 25, spelled out in detail the program for a broad patriotic front against U.S. imperialism, which would consist of "every nationalist class and every nationalist party."71

The year 1957 was the high tide of China's first peaceful co-existence offensive in Thailand, Malaya, and Singapore. Activity was intense and promising on both the levels of "people's diplomacy" and informal state relations. Peking's operations on the party level, at least in its public aspect, accordingly all but disappeared.

Delegations of Thai basketball players, artists, journalists, and trade union leaders paraded into China, all at the expense of the Chinese Government. And while there were fewer such cultural exchanges in Malaya, numerous businessmen from Kuala Lumpur and Singapore were also invited to China. Various local newspapers continued to call for the strengthening of Sino-Thai and Sino-Malayan relations, and attacks on the United States and against SEATO grew in intensity within Thailand.

On the domestic political scene, developments were also most promising in Thailand. A number of leftist politicians were released from jail, and in January 1957, the same month the TCP issued its call for a "broader patriotic front," a number of the neutralist and leftist political parties formed a Socialist Front built primarily around the Economist Party and its leader, Thep Chotinuchit.* The foreign policy of this front called for a neutralist stance on the basis of peaceful coexistence, denounced the United States and SEATO, and called for diplomatic relations with China.

For our purposes there are two questions that arise in connection with the establishment of the Socialist Front and the contemporary political scene in which it operated. First, to what extent was the Socialist Front actually an instrument of the TCP and to what extent were its activities inspired or supported by Peking? Second, what were the objectives of the Thai Government in permitting the political campaign against its policies to develop, and why did the government itself show signs of moving toward friendly relations with China?

Clearly the program espoused by the Socialist Front was identical both with the program proposed by the TCP and also with the policy objectives of Peking. This similarity of views, of course, does not prove that there was any coordination of strategy. Most of the leaders in organizations associated with the front were apparently non-Marxist and were united only in their opposition to the government and in support of various social and political reforms that at least on the verbal level ranged from Fabian to "clean government."[72] Some of these parties were identified with Pridi, but others were independent of the exiled premier. Unlike other political organizations in Thailand, the Socialist Front was not based on personal and factional ties but actually had a ideological foundation—anti-Western nationalism.

China and its ally, the TCP, were no doubt pleased with the development of this national democratic front, which, in the Maoist model, took U.S. imperialism as its principal enemy. The Peking and TCP strategy was to promote the infiltration of the front by communist party members and eventually establish "communist hegemony" over the movement. But at some point disagreement began as to whether or not concurrent preparation for armed struggle should proceed.

The TCP was at this time, for all practical purposes, headquartered in Peking, where Prasert Sapsunthorn, one of the party leaders and the Thai figurehead in the TCP, had fled in 1949. Prasert was later accused of having advocated in 1957-58 that the party "should help another party [that is, the Socialist Front] seize state power so that we could gain partial access to the democratic process and enjoy

---

*Chotinuchit was a member of Parliament from the Northeast who had served briefly as a deputy minister of communications. He was the leader of the goodwill mission that visited China in January 1956 and was briefly jailed following his return.

limited rights." "Once we have achieved this," he allegedly said, "we could make our move openly and topple the party later when revolutionary conditions were ripe and more favorable."[73] The TCP in 1968 claimed that the party "strongly opposed the suggestion made by Prasert and criticized his revisionism and defeatism."[74]

It seems doubtful, however, that there was actually any serious dispute within the TCP in 1956-57 over the correctness of the united-front-from-above strategy. The low-key, virtually invisible posture of the Thai Communist Party and the concentration upon the national-democratic Socialist Front during this period was consistent with Peking's own peaceful coexistence policy toward the Bangkok government.

Despite the present claims of the TCP, opposition to Prasert and the policy of united-front-from-above without a concurrent development of revolutionary potential very likely did not arise until early 1958, when the consequences of Sarit's takeover had become apparent and after the Socialist Front had not done well in the December 1957 elections.

Sometime in the first few months of 1958, Prasert apparently defended his line of legal struggle before the TCP Central Committee (presumably meeting in Peking):

> He still opposed armed struggle, again attacked the party's policy, and tried to cajole us into shifting to a peaceful struggle in the National Assembly in accordance with his revisionist ideology. He claimed it was not necessary to wage a national liberation war in Thailand, said that none of the favorable conditions for such a war existed here, and suggested that our party continue to struggle under the existing undemocratic conditions and atmosphere.
>
> Dealing with the state power, he suggested that our party continue to struggle for a democratic government. When the Soviet revisionist clique began to reveal its "peaceful coexistence," Prasert Sapsunthorn began acting more arrogantly, thinking that the Soviet policy would be a strong prop for his theory. He boldly stated that if our party openly stated its platform to acquire state power through peaceful struggle, it would be most beneficial for us.[75]

Later in the year Prasert apparently broke with the TCP, or perhaps he was made the scapegoat for the failure of a policy that had been endorsed, if not directed by Peking.*

In any event it is clear that Peking and the TCP from 1957 to 1958 were banking heavily upon the success of the Socialist Front to consummate their united-front-from-above strategies in Thailand on both the international and national levels. To this end, China may have financed through indirect channels—probably Chinese-Thai businessmen—certain individuals concerned and possibly some of the newspapers and political organizations in Thailand.

The anti-Western nationalism to which the new parties gave vent in 1957 ran counter to the pro-Western alliance policy of the Thai Government. Therefore, it is important to try to understand the motivation of the Thai authorities in permitting fairly free rein to the expression of these sentiments and their own unmistakable movement toward a détente with China.

As stated earlier, Phibun to some extent had become enamored of the democratic process, and perhaps unconsciously he was motivated by a desire to erase his image as a ruthless dictator and a one-time collaborator with the Japanese. In terms of domestic politics, a relaxation of restraints on the opposition was one way to release internal pressures, and, Phibun, as noted, also sought to construct some base of popular support through a mass party and trade union organizations.

The opposition, which for a variety of reasons was thus allowed to bloom and contend in Thailand (this period, coincidentally, was contemporany with the "Hundred Flowers" campaign in China), took as a main target the government's foreign policy. Consequently, the Thai Government's concurrent movement toward a détente with China was in part a defensive reaction to this opposition—democracy was working its way. For example, shortly before the February 1957 election, encouraging words were heard from the highest Thai authorities on the prospect of relations with China. In January, Phibun emphasized the principle of maintaining friendly relations with all nations, and a Thai Government spokesman declared that "Thailand has never thought of not being friends with Communist China.[76]

The most important criteria for the shift in the Thai Government's attitude, however, was a reassessment after the Bandung conference in 1955 of China's intentions. China's effective peaceful

---

*Prasert, together with an associate of Pridi's Sanguan Tularak, returned to Bangkok the month before Sarit's coup of October 1958. He was imprisoned, but after denouncing communism he was released. On August 17, 1964 he was officially purged from the TCP.

coexistence offensive and the general relaxation in world tensions to a large extent mollified the fears of the Thai elite concerning China's possible aggressive behavior. The main effect of this development was to seem to confirm the view that Thailand had nothing to gain and possibly much to lose by attempting to isolate a powerful but apparently friendly China. At the same time, the Thai Government had been disappointed in the limited nature of the security commitment it had received through its association with SEATO and also in the refusal of the U.S. Government to support some of Thailand's more ambitious economic development projects.[77]

The uneasy triumvirate of three men who then ruled Thailand, Premier Phibun, Police Commander Phao, and the military commander, Field Marshal Sarit Thanarat, in varing degrees all apparently supported this assessment and they not only permitted but also to some extent encouraged the public campaign for accommodation with China. Sarit was reportedly the most active of the three, and he assumed an increasingly nationalistic stance apparently as part of his power struggle with Phibun. Newspapers he owned or controlled adopted a neutralist and anti-U.S. line. Sometime during this period, Sarit allegedly held a private meeting in Hong Kong with a Chinese communist general.[78] Several other unpublicized but official contacts were also made with the Chinese Government, and an understanding was reportedly reached on the eventual establishment of relations.[79] It was reportedly agreed, however, that advancement to this goal would be in stages so as to accustom the Thai people as well as the U.S. Government to the idea.

Meanwhile, important political developments were taking place inside Thailand. There were reported last-minute attempts by the government to rig the February 1957 elections, and leftist members ended up occupying about 21 of the 160 seats.[80] A period of confusion and popular dissatisfaction ensued in Thailand, and opposition forces as well as papers controlled by Sarit continued as before to rail at the government's foreign policy. The Phibun regime reacted by making more explicit its willingness to adjust relations with Peking. In July, the Thai foreign minister said that Taiwan was an integral part of China and that the Taiwan question was an internal affair of China. NCNA quoted the foreign minister as saying that "according to international principles the Chinese Communist government was the real legal government of China." The foreign minister reiterated that Thailand would recognize the PRC only after its admission to the United Nations.[81] In August the foreign minister was again quoted in Peking as saying that Thailand's mutual contacts with China were friendly.

BANDUNG ENDS IN BANGKOK

Before anything could come of this evolving policy in Phibun's administration, his government was suddenly brought down. In September 1957, Field Marshal Sarit, claiming that the government had lost popular support, carried out a sudden coup. Sarit's seizure of power went unreported in Peking, as it was far from clear that he intended to reverse Thailand's development of friendly relations with China. For the next year the domestic situation remained in some respects the same as it had been in 1957. Neutralist political parties and newspapers continued to enjoy full freedom to attack the United States and SEATO and to urge relations with China. Meanwhile, people's diplomacy went its way unhindered. However, no more official statements on Thailand's friendship with China or on possible recognition were heard. Although several weeks elapsed before Sarit made a firm commitment that Thailand would remain in SEATO, his caretaker government was headed by Pote Sarasin, the secretary general of SEATO, who announced that Thailand would continue to support the organization. U.S. economic aid for Thailand subsequently increased substantially in 1958 (from $24 million in 1957 to $46.5 million in 1958).

After new elections in December 1957, the parliamentary situation and the political scene in general remained in an uncertain condition. The results of these elections—generally agreed to have been conducted fairly—indicated that fears of a radical shift to anything like communism in Thailand were greatly exaggerated. The extreme leftists despite their wide press support failed to win even one seat in Bangkok.[82]

Despite the basic loyalty and conservatism of most of the population, Sarit in October 1958 launched a new coup—more or less against himself—and established a military dictatorship. Basing his actions on an alleged communist plot to carry out an Iraqi-style coup, Sarit initiated a crackdown that eliminated all sources of opposition. Leftist politicians were arrested, and neutralist newspapers were closed down. A total ban of Chinese imports was soon instituted. Thus did China's Bandung policy as applied to Thailand end in failure—although the failure was not fully to be acknowledged by Peking until some six months later.

Why did the seeds of peaceful coexistence, which Chou En-lai had planted at Bandung and thereafter carefully nurtured, bear no fruit in Thailand? Contrary to some interpretations, internal politics in Thailand probably was not the main dynamic in Thailand's rejection of neutrality; rather it was primarily the interaction of a complex of external events. To denounce all internal opposition as communist was, of course, useful for Sarit, but it did not require a parallel rejection of tolerably friendly relations with Peking.

Perhaps the principal element in the wilting of the Bandung line in Thailand was the fact that a similar policy was flowering in neighboring Cambodia, where diplomatic relations with China were established in July 1958. This event took place against the background of a historic antagonism between Thailand and Cambodia and most immediately in the context of a small but bitter border dispute between the two countries. Prince Norodom Sihanouk's choice of neutrality and his intention of using Chinese support to balance Thailand's and South Vietnam's ties to the United States tended to polarize the issue of relations with China. Just as Cambodia's suspicions of the United States multiplied because of Washington's close relations with Thailand and South Vietnam, so the Thai Government's mistrust of China spiraled as Peking grew closer to Phnom Penh.

The Thai leadership again became concerned that China represented a threat to Thailand's integrity, this time by subversion through Cambodia as well as Laos. To some, this fear was confirmed by the joint communiqué signed by Chou En-lai and Sihanouk in July, which was interpreted as containing implied threats to Thailand. Also by 1958, communist activity in Laos and South Vietnam, backed in both cases by Hanoi, raised apprehension concerning the designs of the North Vietnamese and the Lao communists on Northeast Thailand, where the bulk of the population was not only related to the Lao but where 30,000 to 40,000 Vietnamese refugees continued to live (20,000 having been repatriated under the agreement reached at Bandung).

Sarit's decision to abandon his policy of promoting relations with China was taken in the context of these developments, but also it was very likely significantly influenced by arguments and new commitments made to him by the U.S. Government. Sarit visited the United States in 1958 for medical treatment, and while there he reportedly sent back a cable to his editor instructing him to drop the paper's pro-China line.[83]

A SEARCH FOR RELATIONS WITH MALAYA

At almost the same time as trade was opened between Thailand and China in 1956, an intensive campaign by Peking and interested economic groups in Malaya gained a significant victory that had political as well as economic implications. The embargo on rubber sales to China was lifted by both the Malayan and the Singapore governments in June 1956. This success for peaceful coexistence diplomacy followed not only a year's campaign on economic grounds but also a major change in Peking's political posture toward Malaya.

As mentioned earlier, in 1953-54, Peking was concerned with
the possible cooperation by Thailand and the Philippines in a U.S.
intervention in Vietnam and later with their participation in SEATO.
In these years, China paid little public attention to events in colonial
Malaya and to the waning struggles of the MCP. The Soviets in 1954
also grew silent on developments in Malaya.[84]

In 1955, however, there was a renewal of Peking's attention to
Malaya and a decided shift in its treatment of the Malayan insurgency.
In the early part of that year, Peking media reported that the Malayan
National Liberation Army was keeping up its attacks and persisting
in the struggle.[85] But shortly after the Bandung meetings in April,
the Chinese line changed and thereafter emphasized the need for
a negotiated end to the fighting, for peace and unity, and for recognition of the MCP as a legal party. During the latter part of the year,
NCNA reports on the fighting stressed that the government forces
were persisting in attacking the Malayan National Liberation Army,
which was now pictured as merely defending itself.[86]

The switch to the peace and unity line in Malaya was in fact
highlighted at the Bandung conference, where two "Malayan representatives" appeared as observers. These apparently uninvited communist Malayans urged the conference "to seek an end to the war in
Malaya through the repeal of the emergency regulations" and "to
establish a provisional government in Malaya under responsible
international supervision until free and democratic elections are
held. . . .[87]

In June, the MCP indicated a desire to negotiate, and in September the newly elected alliance government in Kuala Lumpur offered the communists an amnesty.[88] In November, NCNA quoted Lim
Chin-siong, a procommunist member of the People's Action Party
(PAP) in Singapore, as calling for recognition of legal status for the
MCP as the "most realistic way to end the war in Malaya." And on
November 17, 1955 the MCP secretary general, Chin Peng, formally
offered to negotiate with the "national bourgeois" political leaders
in Kuala Lumpur. Before the meeting took place, the central committee of the MCP on December 22 issued a communiqué putting forth
a new eight-point program for the communist party. This program,
like that put forward by the TCP the next year, was entirely nationalistic and scarcely Marxist. It called for an end to the fighting "on
just and reasonable terms by negotiations and independence as soon
as possible and a fully elected Malayan Assembly to adopt a new constitution." The nonrevolutionary posture was evident in the proposed
constitution, which would have provided "respect for the position of
the Sultans," thereby reversing the party's previous line toward the
institution of the Malay royalty. Point eight of the program called
for diplomatic relations with all countries on the basis of the five

principles of peaceful coexistence, and it also enjoined "development of cultural and economic relations with all countries but on the basis of equality and mutual benefit."[89]

The communiqué concluded that this was not a program for "people's democracy nor socialism" but was a common program for "independence, democracy and peace in Malaya." Nevertheless it was stated that the communists had "never concealed their long-term goal of struggling for the achievement of people's democracy and socialism."[90]

On December 28, Tunku Abdul Rahman, with David Marshall, chief minister of Singapore, met in the small town of Baling in Northern Malaya with Chin Peng. On the same day a People's Daily article blamed past failures to end the war in Malaya on the British and not on the noncommunist Malayans. The article urged agreement on a "fair and reasonable basis," which, it said, meant the legalization of the Malayan Communist Party.[91] This was, of course, the exact position taken by Chin Peng in his negotiations with the Malayan officials at Baling. Chin insisted on legalization of the party, and he refused to disarm until the elected government of the Malayan Federation had taken over complete control of internal security and the local armed forces. The Tunku insisted that the party surrender on the basis of his government's amnesty offer, and he refused to legalize the MCP. Chin rejected these terms and went back into the jungle.

In commenting on the failure of the talks, Peking continued to excuse the Malayan officials and thus to keep the door open for its own relations with them. It put all the blame instead on the machinations of the British colonialists. People's Daily suggested that Rahman went to the talks "with his hands tied" and was unable to carry out his desires.[92]

As in Burma, the Chinese Government under Liu Shao-chi and Chou En-lai was urging a new line of peaceful transition upon the Malaya Communist Party consistent with China's own Bandung diplomacy and its interest in a settlement in Indochina. According to later MCP statements, the decision to accept within limits the revisionist line with the result of Soviet as well as Chinese pressure:

> Therefore, beginning in 1954, British imperialism intensified its efforts to push the political fraud of so-called elections, peaceful negotiations, self-rule, and independence, while continuing the encirclement and suppression in a vain attempt to attain its objective of wiping out our party and army. This was a manifestation of the enemy's isolation politically and of the impasse it had fallen into militarily.

On the other hand, our party and army also encountered great difficulties under the prolonged attacks of the
enemy. But it was a temporary difficulty on the road of
advance. At this crucial juncture, our party should have
exposed the political fraud of the enemy, fought with
greater determination, overcome difficulties, and developed the favorable situation.

However, precisely at this juncture [1954], the renegade cliques of Khrushchev and Liu Shao-chi ganged up
together and, in coordination with British imperialism's
military and political offensive, put pressure on our party
and caused it to carry out once more the right capitulationist and revisionist line. The result of the implementation of this line caused the armed struggle of our
country to suffer a serious setback.[93]

The 1954 revisionist line, the MCP later charged, was promoted
by Liu Shao-chi (and most likely by Chou En-lai as well) on the basis
of a "theory of conditions for armed struggle." This theory argued
that armed struggle in Malaya was not practicable because the country was not adjacent to socialist countries and its territory was small,
with well-developed communications. In addition, it was allegedly
argued by the Chinese leaders that armed struggle in Malaya could
not be continued so long as the revolutionary forces were composed
primarily of Malaya's "foreign nationalities," that is, the ethnic
Chinese. Therefore, it was maintained, armed struggle could not
be continued before "national unity with Malays as the core" was
achieved; otherwise the imperialists would be able to turn the revolutionary war into a racial conflict.[94] But, as in the case of the Burmese
Party, the MCP leaders only partly accepted the Peking-advocated
policy of cooperation with the national bourgeoisie.

Nevertheless, because our party Central Committee to
a certain degree resisted this line, it was not implemented smoothly or without resistance. Under extremely
difficult conditions, our party and army persisted in
fighting on, thus keeping the enemy's strategic plans to
wipe out our party and army from succeeding.

Although the MCP was a separate movement with interests and
viewpoints of its own, it accepted Chinese guidance at the time partly
because of the party's explicit acknowledgment of Peking's ideological
and political supremacy within the Asian area of international communism. But there was a practical as well as a political relationship that made for consistency between its policies and those of Peking.

Whenever the armed struggle was going well in Malaya, Peking as well as the MCP had little interest in conciliation with the government; when things were going badly, however, they were inclined respectively to coexistence and constitutional struggle. If legality was denied the party, it could choose a period of retrenchment and reorganization; at the same time, Peking could pursue as far as possible government-to-government conciliation.

Consequently, despite the failure of the Baling talks, in early 1956 Peking began to concentrate on winning over the national bourgeois government in Malaya, and in keeping with this policy it dropped virtually all public references to the MCP. The party's tactics at the time facilitated this policy; MCP remnants pulled back into the jungle on the Thai side of the border and adopted a purely defensive stance.

The MCP itself now concentrated on the creation of front groups and the infiltration of other political organizations and parties while Peking emphasized people's diplomacy and efforts to make credible its political posture.[95]

MALAYAN INDEPENDENCE
AND ISOLATION FROM CHINA

From the time of the London conference in January 1956, the Federation of Malaya advanced steadily toward complete independence, and its government persisted in refusing any accommodation with the MCP. Nevertheless, Peking was hopeful that the new government would offer diplomatic recognition. As in Thailand the Malayan leaders indicated at least an open mind on this question. In January 1956, NCNA reported that Tunku Abdul Rahman had told newsmen that after national independence was achieved, the "Malayan people's wish to recognize the PRC" (NCNA's phrase) would be given due consideration.[96] As in Thailand, but to a lesser extent, in Malaya opposition political leaders and businessmen were quoted as calling for closer contacts and normal relations with China.

When full independence was granted to the Federation of Malaya on August 28, 1957, both Mao and Chou cabled messages of congratulations. Addressing Rahman as "your highness," Mao extended "warm congratulations," while Chou informed the new government that "the Chinese People's Republic has decided to give recognition to the Federation of Malaya."[97] In its more detailed analysis on this event, Peking hailed Malayan independence as the product of the long struggle of the Malayan people against British colonialism. However, national independence, it was explained, was not complete, as British troops

280

were still stationed in Malaya and the economy was allegedly still in the hands of British monopolists.[98]

In these editorials, no mention was made of the MCP, but in a longer analysis in a Chinese journal the winning of independence was attributed to the armed struggle "led by the MCP." The article concluded that if "real independence" was to be achieved, the people must continue their struggle. The implication, however, was that the struggle was to be in the political arena, for "the testing stone" of the alliance government would be its attitude on "national unity and domestic political peace"—that is, the right to a legal existence for the MCP.[99] The MCP took precisely the same line when in September it issued a manifesto that again refused surrender but promised to work "not by means of armed struggle or violence, but by democratic means within constitutional limits."[100] It did not, however, offer to disband its remnant Liberation Army.

It soon became clear, however, that the new Malayan Government did not intend to conciliate either the MCP or its mentor, the People's Republic of China. The Federal Government of Malaya shunned membership in SEATO but concluded a military treaty in October 1957 with the United Kingdom that provided joint action to resist any armed attack on Malaya or on British territories within the Far East. British bases would be maintained in Malaya, but any military action taken from these bases would be done only by agreement of the Federation of Malaya. Despite Mao's polite approach, the alliance government refused to accord either Chinese government recognition, and it continued to take actions to isolate the country from the influence of the People's Republic of China. Publications from the mainland for example were banned, and the Bank of China Branch in Kuala Lumpur was closed. Although it avoided a broader entangling alliance, the federation's orientation was evident in the fact that Tunku Abdul Rahman's first visits abroad after independence were to South Vietnam, Thailand, and the Philippines. And in February 1961, Kuala Lumpur was a leading force in bringing the three allied states together in an Association of Southeast Asia (ASA) in order "to promote economic and cultural development" among themselves.

Malaya's policy of relying upon Commonwealth ties for security and of attempting to isolate itself from China sprang not only from the brutal experience of the communist insurgency but also from the main fact of political life in Malaya—the large number of ethnic Chinese in the population (2,500,000 out of a total of 6,900,000 in 1960). Official PRC representation in Malaya, it was feared, would provide the Chinese Government an instrument to stimulate Chinese chauvinism and also clandestinely to assist a comeback for the Malayan Communist Party. It was not realized that enmity with Peking was more likely to spark these activities than was accommodation. Nevertheless, fear and resentment of China in Malaya, unlike in Thailand, was related primarily to the internal situation, while the prospect of direct or even indirect Chinese aggression seemed relatively remote.

SINGAPORE—A NEAR MISS FOR A
UNITED-FRONT STRATEGY

The Malayan communists always looked upon Singapore as an integral part of Malaya, and they insisted upon that attitude until about 1971. Although China made few references on the status of Singapore after the latter broke away from Malaysia in August 1965, it likewise treated the island city as a part of Malaya until 1971.

Commenting on the independence of the Federation of Malaya in 1957, Peking denounced the separation of Singapore from the federation as a British device "to create national and regional disintegration" so as to continue its rule.[101] At this time both communist and noncommunist political groups in the city called for a merger of Singapore and Malaya. Among these groups was the democratic-socialist People's Action Party (PAP) of Lee Kuan-yew, established in 1954.

Support for the merger among noncommunists was inspired by the assessment at the time that Singapore had to be at least economically integrated with Malaya if it was to survive. But for the communists, probably more important was the political fact that Singapore when joined with Malaya provided a heavy Chinese plurality. Furthermore, the Chinese-dominated MCP naturally found a large following in Singapore. During the Cong guerilla war Singapore had been a principal source of supplies for the Malayan People's Liberation Army operations in Malaya.

Within the crown colony, the MCP had concentrated on organization and infiltration, but following the defeat of the guerrillas in Malaya, the main focus of communist political activity shifted temporarily to Singapore, where it soon appeared that the MCP was in fact close to seizing power via a Maoist united front. The communist strategy was to infiltrate the leftist PAP. One wing of the PAP was led by Peking-oriented associates of the MCP head by Lim Chin-siong. For the next six years, the MCP strove to gain control of the PAP.[102] By the mid-1950s, the communists had also established a strong position in Singapore's trade unions and Chinese schools, and during the first years of the elected local government communist front organizations in the left wing of the PAP staged a series of violent strikes and student riots. These disturbances were approvingly reported in the Peking press as being of an anti-British nature, but at the same time Peking began to apply its Bandung diplomacy to Singapore as well as to Malaya. David Marshall, who was chief minister at the time of the 1955 riots, was, for example, royally received in Peking on a visit at the end of 1956.

Marshall had led the Singapore delegation to the London constitutional talks in April and May 1956. These talks broke down when the British Government insisted on control over internal security. In his opening address Lennox Boyd, secretary of State for the colonies, declared that "we do not intend that Singapore should become an outpost of Communist China and in fact a colony of Peking."[103] The communists attempted to exploit the failure to attain full self-government, and a new round of civil disorders in the city broke out. Following this outbreak, a group of communist leaders were arrested, including some of the extremists of the PAP. The peaceful coexistence line was at this time in full swing, and there was little attention in Peking media either to the disturbances in Singapore or to the arrests. The emphasis in China's propaganda line toward Singapore as toward Malaya and Thailand was clearly on potentials for trade. In August 1956, for example, Chou En-lai told visiting Malayan and Singapore businessmen that China was directing her main efforts to over-all construction and production, and therefore "She not only has large quantities of goods available for export but at the same time needs all kinds of essential raw materials to speed her industrial production and projects."[104]

In April 1957, new talks in London resulted in agreement on the creation of a new self-governing State of Singapore with a compromise arrangement on internal security. Peking reported this development in a straightforward manner, while emphasizing that the British would be able "to take over all powers external and internal from the Singapore government at any time."[105]

In August 1957, the communists in the PAP failed in an attempt to overthrow Lee Kuan-yew, and at the same time the Singapore government again ordered the detention of a number of communists, including five members of the newly elected executive committee of the PAP.[106] This event occurred the same month as independence was achieved in Malaya, and China, anxious not to spoil its chances with Kuala Lumpur, kept silent on the arrests.

But during 1958 China's hopes in regard to Singapore and Malaya made no significant advance. In fact, both governments in 1958 banned publications from China.

In August 1958, the military significance of Singapore was highlighted by the "visit" of a U.S. marine contingent to the city at the time of the Middle East crisis that year. This incident occasioned the charge from Peking that "Singapore has always been an important

U.S. and British base for interference in and threats against the Southeast Asian countries."[107] In the May 1959 elections in Singapore, the PAP swept 43 out of 51 seats on the platform of "independence through merger" (with the Federation of Malaya). At Lee Kuan-yew's insistence, the leading communist members of the PAP, including Lim Chin-siong, were released from jail. But these elements were given appointments in the new government in positions where they could be contained and "do the least harm." The People's Daily greeted the new self-governing state of Singapore as a "victory of protracted struggle," but it denounced the British for continuing to prevent the merger of Singapore with Malaya; the two areas, it still asserted, constituted an "inseparable entity, geographically and historically."[108]

NO SUCCESS IN THE PHILIPPINES

The Bandung strategy was pursued by the PRC in its policy toward the Philippines in the mid- and late 1950s, but in contrast to the early promising signs in Thailand and Malaya, there was no tangible success in Manila. Through the first half of 1955, NCNA occasionally quoted Manila reports as a basis for the claim that the Philippine People's Liberation Army was active in Luzon. Nevertheless, China's attention at this time was focused on opposition in the Philippines to the U.S. military presence and to alleged U.S. economic exploitation. NCNA approvingly quoted Filippine Senators as calling for trade relations with and recognition of Communist China. But, unlike in Thailand and Malaya, these themes were not significantly picked up by Manila newspapers or political or business organizations.

This lack of response was probably due to several factors, the first of which was Peking's relatively small interest in the remote Philippines as compared to Thailand and Malaya. Moreover, the Philippine economy did not produce an important primary product such as rubber or tin, the prospect of the sale of which to China was appealing to significant vested interest groups.

People's diplomacy in the Philippines also failed to get off the ground at this time because of travel controls to China instituted by the Manila government. In October 1955, however, a group of Philippine reporters from the Manila Chronicle visited China and talked with Chou En-lai. Chou took the occasion to reiterate his Bandung position that China hoped for peaceful and friendly relations with the Philippines.[109] This interview was followed by an editorial in the Tientsin Ta Kung Pao, which discounted "the notion of some people in the Philippines that China's liberation of Taiwan would menace the security of the Philippines." The editorial called for more frequent contact, and it concluded with the promise that all questions including dual nationality of Chinese nationals in the Philippines could be settled in a peaceful and friendly way. But few significant contacts materialized during the 1950s.[110]

The Philippine Communist Party (PKP) continued in organizational disarray during the mid-1950s and was generally ignored in Peking's public comments. There was, for example, no Chinese comment on the Philippine party's efforts in 1954 to negotiate with the Manila government; these efforts came a year earlier than those of the MCP, whose own negotiating position was well covered in Peking media.

It is clear that Peking's role in the decisions of the PKP existed only to the extent that Mao's tenacity provided a guiding inspiration. China itself did not again turn its attention to the Philippines and the PKP for almost another 10 years.

THE TURNING POINT

By the end of 1959 the Bandung approach to the aligned nations of Southeast Asia had come to an end. Bangkok's relations with Peking were increasingly confrontational, while Malaya's attitude was one of strained detachment. In January 1959, Thailand banned the import of all products from the mainland; trade was allowed to continue in Singapore and Malaya, but restrictions were put on cement and textile imports from China in late 1958.[111] Also in January the Malayan Government closed the Bank of China Branch in Kuala Lumpur.

At first Peking responded in early 1959 to both these actions in terms of the Bandung spirit. A spokesman of the China council for the promotion of international trade told Thailand that:

> China is always willing to develop equal and mutually
> beneficial trade relations with Thailand on the basis
> of peaceful coexistence. Sino-Thai trade was suggested
> by the Thai side and it is now being destroyed by the
> Thai government; it therefore has no influence whatever
> on China. On the contrary this action of the Thai gov-
> ernment of returning evil for good will only harm its
> own interests.[112]

In a similarly pained expression, People's Daily "Commentator", on February 5, lamented the Malayan government action in closing the Bank of China.

China has all along esteemed the development of friendly relations with Malaya whose relations with China date back to the early 14th century. China has also consistently esteemed the restoration and development of trade relations with Malaya on the basis of equality and mutual benefits. . . . But the Malayan authorities have not supported the consistent and positive attitude of China by promoting friendly trade relations between the two countries, on the contrary they have time and again obstructed the development of such relations.[113]

But in April the tone of China's comments on Thailand changed. The phrase "Thai ruling circles" was resurrected in connection with the charge that Thailand was intervening in China's internal affairs by its statements on the Tibetan revolution.[114] In May the "Thai reactionaries" were charged with instigating the "Lao reactionaries" to launch a civil war and they were warned that "those who play with fire get themselves burnt."[115] Finally, in and by June, Sino-Thai relations seemed to have come full circle back to 1953. A People's Daily editorial in response to the Thai government expression of support for the government of Laos issued a clear warning:

If the Thailand authorities persist in this wrong task by acting contrary to the interest of peace and independence of their people serving as accomplices of the U.S. imperialism and being hostile to the Indo-Chinese and Asian peoples they will certainly stand convicted before history.[116]

Although Malaya had sponsored the UN condemnation of China's actions in Tibet, the federation was not directly involved in the Laotian crisis, and its relations with China did not at this time reach such an openly hostile state as did Sino-Thai relations. In 1960, for example, Malaya switched to the "two Chinas" policy in the United Nations on the question of Chinese representation. (Although this was a more flexible approach, it did not, of course, please Peking.) A high level of hostility would not be evidenced in regard to Malaya until another broader issue arose—that is, the formation of Malaysia and China's relations with Indonesia. Yet it was clear to Peking by the end of 1959 that the attitude of the new Singapore government and the government of the federation of Malaya had stymied for the time being the Bandung approach—neither Peking's state-to-state relations nor the interests of the MCP had been furthered.

A new priority of interests and a new strategy were soon indicated. On March 1, 1959, Radio Peking began language broadcasts in Malay as well as in Hindi. And in September, the MCP, which had not been referred to by Peking in 1958, was reported by NCNA as having sent greetings to the Chinese Communist Party on the occasion of China's National Day (October 1). This message was the first evidence that the MCP would follow Peking in its dispute with Moscow, for it pointedly praised the already controversial Great Leap Forward. The message did not refer to armed struggle in Malaya nor did it denounce the government in harsh terms. It only promised to try to "change the policy hostile to socialist countries especially adopted by the government of the Federation of Malaya."[117]

A complex of factors was now at work reshaping China's strategy in Southeast Asia. First of all, the failure of the Bandung line in one aspect seemed confirmed by the policies of the allied governments, which continued to isolate themselves from China, and by the fact that U.S. power presence in Southeast Asia was now greater than ever. The United States was succeeding in its effort to isolate China. These were the basic reasons for the collapse of China's short-lived Bandung policy, which had seemed to emphasize national or sovereign interests and which had sought to promote independent neutrality among the allied states. But at the same time there was an interaction of events in China, in the Soviet camp, and in Indochina that shaped evolving views in Peking as well as in the three pro-Western capitals.

Internally, a period of rational, self-confident growth and intellectual liberalization in China came to an end and the Great Leap Forward campaign began in 1958. This internal radicalization was concurrent with and partly related to the developing Sino-Soviet dispute. Central to the crisis in the socialist camp was Mao's view that a new world balance favorable to the communist world had begun in 1957 and thus that a more forward posture was possible. Out of all this, there evolved a heated dispute between Peking and Moscow over the questions of strategy for the communist camp as a whole and strategy for individual communist parties.

At the root of the conflict, however, was the fact that after the death of Stalin, China began to insist on an equal voice within the international communist movement. The Soviets refused, for to do so would threaten their control of Eastern Europe and Mongolia. Consequently, the Chinese began to challenge Moscow's leadership, at first in the ideological sphere and then in the realm of international policy. The Soviets responded by trying to undermine the Chinese party, and an ever widening ring of hostility began to emerge.

In April 1959, Chinese forces put down the Tibetan revolt, an action that not only led to the undermining of Sino-Indian relations but also brought forth condemnation from Thailand, Malaya, and the Philippines. This event was followed by the crisis in Laos of 1959, which directly involved Thailand. The gradual escalation of the fighting in South Vietnam also widened the gulf as Thailand, the Philippines, and Malaya provided political and moral as well as some material support to the Saigon government.

Nevertheless, despite the failure of the Bandung policy and the conflict of interest over events in Indochina, China still paid relatively little public attention to the pro-Western states from 1959 until about 1961. At the same time the communist parties in these countries continued their low postures, and Peking's comment on their activities remained virtually nonexistent.

China's interest in Thailand, Malaya, and the Philippines did not revive until the early 1960s, and in each case it was directly related to broader strategic events.

PREPARATION FOR SUBVERSION IN THAILAND

Because of the continuing Laotian crisis and Bangkok's increasing involvement with the U.S. containment policy, China's attention was turned increasingly to Thailand. In fact, of all the allied countries the one that received the bulk of China's interest in the 1960s was significantly the one most directly involved in the Vietnam war— Thailand. Moreover after 1965, outside Indochina, the threat of armed struggle was most serious in Thailand, although the communist organization there was historically the weakest of any in Southeast Asia.

There were several positive circumstances that worked against a communist movement in Thailand. Perhaps most important was the fact that Thailand had no serious land problem, the great bulk of its tilled land being held by small holders. But despite the disadvantages for a revolutionary movement, a major and well-planned effort was made to promote insurrection in Thailand. Organizational planning for armed struggle in Thailand was probably begun in the very early 1960s. In 1961, the TCP held a meeting of representatives of the party at which it was decided that the people should "form their own groups to fight the enemy."[118] This meeting, which may have been held in Peking, marked the first call ever of the TCP for armed struggle. The message was not made public at that time, and in fact the TCP was not formally to identify itself with armed struggle in Thailand until 1966.

In April 1962, after the U.S. guarantee to Thailand that if necessary it would defend Thailand unilaterally, Peking charged that Thailand was following a dangerous road because of its involvement with "intensified U.S. military adventures" in Southeast Asia.

"This runs directly counter to the interest of the people of Thailand and is arousing growing dissatisfaction and resistance. The actions of the Thai reactionaries will boomerang sooner or later."[119] For the first time, it was clearly suggested that the pro-Western-alliance policy of the Thai Government would result in an internal uprising.

In coordination with North Vietnam, preparations were in fact under way for the long and difficult task of creating a guerrilla structure in the Northeast and ultimately in other parts of Thailand. In the pattern that developed, political and leadership cadres, were generally trained in China, while a military training camp for Thai insurgents was set up at Hoa Binh, 50 miles southeast of Hanoi. Staffed with Thai and Vietnamese instructors, the camp graduated 62 Thai recruits in 1962. This number rose to about 130 graduates in 1965.[120] A press conference was given in Bangkok on March 9, 1967 by a number of Thais who had attended this school. In China, a special school had reportedly been established as far back as the early 1950s in Chungking for political training of Thai communists, and recruitment for this school was expanded in the early 1960s.[121]

The propaganda apparatus was also tuned up. In 1962, the China-based clandestine radio Voice of the People of Thailand (VPT) began broadcasting.*

The increase in tension in Indochina and the signs of a developing confrontation with the United States thus provided the tactical justification for Peking's promotion of armed struggle in a country that had rejected neutrality. To what extent Peking's motivation was tactical pressure on Thailand and to what extent it was part of a strategic design to bring pro-Peking communist governments to power in Southeast Asia is a moot question. But our analysis of the evolving bifurcation of the Chinese leadership in these years suggests that one group tended to look upon the policy toward Thailand as a tactic, whereas others, probably including Mao and Lin Piao, saw it primarily in terms of the ideal design for Southeast Asia. In any event, once a full commitment has been made to such a revolutionary movement, the policy develops a momentum of its own, and its success becomes, or threatens to become, an end in itself. In the case of Thailand, international events in 1965 as well as the policies. of the Bangkok government probably justified the policy in the eyes of almost all opinion in Peking.

_____

*VPT was first thought to be operating in Laos but is now located as operating out of China. Its strongly anti-Soviet line suggests that Hanoi has no relationship with the station.

The Thai Government, after all, had rejected friendship with the PRC, continued relations with the regime in Taipei, allowed KMT elements to run operations from Thailand into China and to maintain a Chinese-language radio station in Thailand, committed itself to the U.S. policies of containment and isolation, and opposed the PRC on every issue vital to China in the international arena.

While training of Thai cadres in North Vietnam and China proceeded and a revolutionary structure was being created throughout Thailand, the political framework was being evolved in accordance with the Maoist model of a national-democratic revolution. An ostensibly noncommunist united front would appear that would take as its principal issue opposition to alleged U.S. domination of Thailand and to what it would claim was Thailand's subjugation as a "new-type colony."

In April 1962, Peking warned that resistance would appear among the Thai people, and in July 1964 (before the August Tonkin gulf incident) an article in Ta Kung Pao sounded the call for the creation of a "broader united front" and for a resolute struggle by the Thai people to oppose the turning of their country into "a new-type colony."[122]

During the first part of 1964, several clandestinely distributed TCP leaflets appeared in Bangkok. But in October the Thai Communist Party received its first official attention from China in many years. NCNA carried a message from the TCP to the Chinese party on the occasion of China's National Day. The message appealed for the cooperation of all antigovernment elements in a "patriotic democratic united front."[123] Also in October it was announced that the new Peking School of Foreign Languages, which opened in September, would teach, in addition to English and Japanese, a three-year course in Thai. On November 1, the formation of a new organization was announced from Peking—the Thai Independence Movement (TIM). Mongkhon Na Nakhorn, who in March would be introduced in Peking as the TIM liaison representative, reportedly left Thailand quietly about October or November 1964. In January 1965, there were reports that the Bank of China in Hong Kong had made large purchases of Thai currency,[124] and according to later press reports Chen Yi in the early part of January informed a Western diplomat that "a war of national liberation might start in Thailand by the end of this year."

The organizational structure for this national liberation war was soon formalized. On January 22, the VPT broadcast a January 1 statement inaugurating a new all-embracing front organization, the Thai Patriotic Front (TPF). On February 5, People's Daily reported the formation of the TPF and its six-point program. The program was antiimperialist and in no way hinted at a Marxist orientation. It called for national independence and the ousting of all U.S. troops; granting of democratic rights; overthrow of the fascist dictatorship; establishment of a foreign policy of peace and neutrality and withdrawal from SEATO; development of the national economy, restriction of foreign capital, and improvement of the people's livelihood; and development of education.

These events in Peking and Thailand took place before the U.S. bombing of North Vietnam began on February 7. But the build-up of airbases and strategic roads in Thailand had been going on for some time prior to the actual bombing of North Vietnam. It is not known when operating U.S. squadrons actually began staging into Thailand or when they began to take part in raids on the north. The New York Times first reported that U.S. jets were operating out of Korat in central Thailand in April 9, 1965.[125]

The important question that is raised at this juncture is whether or not China's and North Vietnam's subversive activities in Thailand would have continued if the United States in early 1965 had opted for a withdrawal from South Vietnam. This question of course can never be conclusively answered, but the history of the creation of the revolutionary organization in Thailand suggests that China's objectives in promoting a communist revolution in Thailand were mainly a product of the Vietnam war and the policies of the Thai Government. The revolutionary objective was an ideal explicit in the Chinese communist ideology, but forceful attempts to achieve it were adopted only when the Bandung policy toward Thailand failed, leaving no other channel for the assertion of Chinese state influence.

The decision to encourage an insurgency in Thailand came before the radicals and the Lin Piao clique had seized control of China's foreign affairs institutions. China's orientation to this question, however, was affected by the posture it had taken in attempting to show that it was more militant than the USSR in opposing "U.S. imperialism" and in supporting fraternal parties. Tactical objectives of diverting U.S. resources and punishing the Thai Government in connection with the war in Vietnam certainly made the adoption of the policy of subversion a natural choice. Had the Vietnam and Laotian wars been resolved on terms favorable to the communist side in 1965, the nature of Peking's relationship with the communist insurgency in Thailand would have depended primarily upon the willingness of the Thai Government to establish some minimum accommodation with the PRC. Nevertheless, the nature of the leadership in Peking would have had some influence on the question.

With the commencement of the regular bombing of North Vietnam (February 28) and the introduction of large numbers of North Vietnamese and U.S. troops into South Vietnam in the spring and summer, respectively, incidents of assassination of local officials in Northeast Thailand began to increase. Warnings and threats from Hanoi and Peking directed at the Thai Government also gained in intensity. In April, Phayom Chulanont was identified as the "representative abroad of the Thai Patriotic Front," which had not yet referred to any connection with the Thai Communist Party. The TCP was, however, mentioned publicly by Peking again on April 16, 1965 when NCNA acknowledged a message of condolence from the Central Committee of the TCP on the death of a Chinese party Politburo member.[126] Through the mouthpiece of the Thai Independence Movement, China in March 1965 issued a clear threat that the flames of war would spread to Thailand. "The other party has every right to fight beyond its border in order to defend itself," it warned.[127] In authoritative editorials and statements, Peking backed up official North Vietnamese protests to the Thai Government, and it warned of the "self-destruction" and "terrible consequences" that would result from the U.S. use of Thailand as a base for the war in Vietnam.[128]

More immediately relevant, however, was the statement that the "antiimperialist patriotic struggle" of the people of Thailand was "the inevitable outcome" of the Thai Government's policies. The more the Thai Government collaborates with the United States, the editorial warned, "the more widespread and intensified will be the patriotic struggle" in Thailand.[129]

Armed struggle in Thailand was, in fact, continuing to rise. The Thai Patriotic Front now dates the beginning of such struggle in Thailand as August 7, 1965.[130] Again, according to a later TCP communiqué, the first "people's armed unit, under the leadership of the Communist Party of Thailand" was "publicly set up" on November 19, 1965 in the northeast province of Ubon Ratchanthani.[131] As noted earlier, about 130 Thai recruits returned from military cadre training in Hoa Binh, North Vietnam, during 1965—the fourth group to return since the school began in 1962.

On September 1, the TPF, in Maoist fashion putting the struggle in defensive terms, denounced the Bangkok government's antiguerrilla activities in the Northeast and called for a "just struggle in self-defense." In December, guerrillas in the Northeast launched their first raid on a police station, and the TPF announced, again from Peking, that armed struggle had begun in several parts of the country.

In its 1966 New Year's message, the TPF formally proclaimed that armed struggle was under way in the Northeast and in the central and the southern provinces, and it proclaimed itself as "the center which unites all patriotic forces."[132] Throughout 1966 subversive activity grew steadily in intensity. Assassinations, ambushes, and armed propaganda campaigns in the villages all increased throughout the Northeast. The VPT began broadcasting in Lao to the northeast provinces, and the Chinese press and radio enthusiastically reported on the progress of the "raging people's war."[133] In August, as the Cultural Revolution in China was just getting under way, People's Daily waxed enthusiastic about the revolutionary flames of armed struggle that were burning even higher on the soil of Thailand.[134]

An important step to complete the Maoist model was the recognition of the communist party's hegemony over the united front and the formal establishment of a liberation army. The TCP, which we will recall momentarily resurfaced in October 1964, now came forward in a series of deliberate stages to reveal its leadership. The first step was the message of the Central Committee of the TCP to the Albanian Workers (Communist) Party Congress on November 6, 1966, which stated that

> The Thai people guided by the Thai Communist Party
> and oriented by Marxism-Leninism have taken up arms
> and are defending themselves by heroically demolishing
> the enemy encirclement. . . . We shall fight with all
> our forces for our final aim: the achievement of the
> social revolution and the building of Communism in
> Thailand.[135]

In November, the Thai Independence Movement announced that it was joining the Thai Patriotic Front, and in December the Thai Communist Party praised the TPF and stated that the party would continue to support it.[136] It was not until August, however, that Phayom Chulanont referred to "TCP leadership" of the armed struggle, which, he claimed, in the previous two years had spread to 23 of the country's 71 provinces.[137] In November 1967, Phayom Chulanont endorsed a TCP statement of policy of November 9, and thereafter it was openly proclaimed that the TPF was under the leadership of the Thai Communist Party and was guided by Mao Tse-tung's thought.

CHANGES IN THE THAI ARMED STRUGGLE, 1967-69: A SHIFT TO THE TRIBES

Throughout 1967 the focus of guerrilla activity was in the Northeast, and government efforts at suppression as well as economic and social progress were stepped up in this area. But beginning in early 1968 the center of struggle shifted to the northern provinces, and, as in Burma, dissident hill tribesmen seemed increasingly to play a major, if not the dominant, role in the liberation struggle. The temporary stalling of the movement in the Northeast was an encouraging sign for Bangkok, but as the demographic and social nature of the Thai insurrection changed, the intensity of the liberation war increased.

A serious threat developed near the end of 1968 from the approximately 66,000 Meo tribesmen in North Thailand, whose cousins live in neighboring Laos and in China's Yünnan province. According to Thai Government claims, several hundred Meos from Thailand trained in Yünnan and Laos infiltrated into the northernmost provinces of Thailand (Loei, Petchabun, Phitsanulok, and Chiang Rai) to incite the local Meos to rebel on the promise of establishing an autonomous Meo state in the region.

In November 1968 the VPT began broadcasting in Mung (a White Meo dialect) and called upon the tribesmen to unite under the leadership of the TCP to overthrow the government. Near the end of November, the Meos launched a series of attacks on resettlement villages, and in January, in the first such incident, they ambushed a government convoy.[138] Chinese-made weapons also began to turn up in increasing numbers.

As will be described in the next section on Malaysia, another important political change noted during 1968 was the open pledges of support between the TCP and the MCP. In July 1968, the Central Committee of the TCP sent its first public greeting to the MCP. The Thai party promised to study the lessons of the MCP's armed struggle, and it declared, "The Thai and Malayan peoples must be more closely united, supporting and coordinating with one another to more strongly and violently attack our enemy."[139] For the MCP, cooperation with the TCP implied warring on the Thai as well as on the Malaysian Government, a policy that inevitably stimulated greater cooperation between the Thai and Malaysian security authorities.

The consequences of the open alliance between the two parties were less clear for the TCP. Nevertheless, by the end of the 1969, guerrilla units of the TCP had moved down into at least one of Thailand's four border provinces inhabited by the MCP forces. In conjunction with increased attacks at this time by Chin Peng's guerrillas against the Malaysians, and simultaneously with intensified activity by Moslem separatists and bandits in the border provinces, the Thai Communists launched a series of successful ambushes against government security forces.[140]

In late 1968 the TCP issued a new "policy" of 10 points, which with Bolshevik candor was called the "short-term policy."[141] In comparison with the six-point program of the Thai Patriotic Front issued in February 1965, the 10 points paid slightly more attention to social reform. For example, the new policy called for the confiscation of all land and property of "reactionary landowners" and for "land reform in accordance with local traditions." While state-owned industry was to be developed, private industry was to be "controlled." This short-term" policy, which was another version of the Maoist "New Democracy," was endorsed by the TCP.[142]

One of the most interesting "points" of the policy promised "to permit all ethnic minorities to govern themselves as one of the members of the big Thai family."[143] As in the case of Burma, the Thai communists hoped to win cooperation of the minorities by promises of autonomy.

The Thai armed struggle reached a new stage in January 1969 with the announcement of the creation of the Thai People's Liberation Armed Forces (TPLAF), thus capping the Maoist model with a people's liberation army. The "Supreme Command" of the TPLAF (which was stated to be "under the leadership of the TCP") explained that because guerrilla operations had expanded to areas covering the entire country and the scope of operations had intensified, it was necessary to establish the TPLAF and its Supreme Command in order to make operations more "efficient and unified."[144]

According to the TPF the armed struggle had now spread to 110 districts and 30 out of the 71 provinces. "The revolutionary situation of Thailand had advanced to a new historical period," the Thai Patriotic Front leader, Phayom Chulanon, declared in January 1969, "and the people's war would take the offensive in attacking the enemy."[145]

The first order of the Supreme Command of the TPLAF was an injunction to its forces "to study and firmly grasp" the thoughts of Mao Tse-tung.[146] The second order was "to expand the people's war; to attack the enemy with well-planned tactics and take more offensives against him. . . ."[147]

In the 1969-70 period, terrorist activity again increased in the northeast region, while still expanding among the Meos in the North and the Moslem areas of the South. On the sixth anniversary of the armed struggle in August 1971, Peking claimed that "relatively consolidated revolutionary base areas" had been established in certain regions in northern Thailand. The communists were said to possess not only a regular force, but regional forces, guerrillas, and militiamen.[148] Six thousand "U.S.-Thai troops and policemen" were said to have been wiped out.

The expansion of the communist guerrilla wars in the North and the Northeast of Thailand corresponded with the extension of the Indochina conflict into Cambodia, the allied incursions into Laos, and the increased involvement of Thai troops in Laos.

PEKING'S COVERAGE OF THE THAI INSURRECTION

During the Cultural Revolution, China's support for the Thai communists assumed an important ideological function. The radicals in Peking apparently saw the revolution in Thailand not only as a verification of their own militancy but also as leading eventually to the establishment of a Peking-oriented communist regime in Bangkok. From 1967 to 1969, their view predominated over those Chinese leaders who took a more jaundiced and opportunistic approach to the communist movement in Thailand.

In the 1967-69 period China's coverage of the Thai "national liberation war" intensified in volume and language. The role of Thailand in the Vietnam war and the U.S. buildup in Thailand were of course major themes. In 1967, Peking warned that the Vietnamese people had earned "the right to hit back" at the Thai authorities.[149] This type of comment, however, was not repeated in 1968, possibly due to China's strained relations with the North Vietnamese at that time. As differences between Hanoi and Peking increased over the Paris negotiations, Chinese media virtually dropped attention to the war in South Vietnam and instead concentrated on the Maoist-led struggle going on in Thailand.

Throughout 1967 and 1968, Peking Radio and the VPT occasionally emphasized the theme of Thailand's alleged potential role as a U.S. "aggressive base" aimed at "the underbelly of China"[150] and as a "strategic stronghold to encircle China from the South".[151] The VPT accused Thailand of launching "provocative and criminal action" against China, and at one point it even warned that the "Chinese people will retaliate."[152]

NCNA and People's Daily commentaries regularly praised the Thai armed revolution, which was said to be led by the TCP and inspired and guided by Mao Tse-tung's thoughts. During the Cultural Revolution period, of all the wars in Southeast Asia, including the one in Vietnam, the Thai struggle was most often referred to by Peking as the model and the verification of Mao's revolutionary doctrine. Peking Radio and the VPT also referred to China's resolute support in much the same terms as in the case of the Burmese party. But official government and party pronouncements from Peking still avoided any direct commitment of assistance.

At the beginning of 1969, verbal support from Peking for the TCP-led revolution rose to a new level. The People's Daily, commenting on the establishment of the Supreme Command of the TPLAF, described the situation as "excellent and getting better still." The Chinese people, it said, "take the Thai people's just struggle as their own struggle and the Thai people's victory as their own victory. We

firmly support the Thai people's liberation struggle."[153] Peking
spokesman Kuo Mo-jo explained that "the Chinese people, now steeled
in the Cultural Revolution, would . . . provide more powerful backing
to the revolutionary people of Thailand. . . ."[154]

During the 1967-69 period, the Chinese were also strengthening
their influence over the Thai movement by purging the Thai exile
group in Peking of those who had refused to accept the communist
party's dominant role. In early 1967 a group of Thai liberal politicians
who had taken refuge in Peking in the late 1950s were expelled by the
Chinese because they refused to cooperate with the communist party
and had wanted the TPF to be independent of both China and the communists.

In May, Peking Radio broadcast a speech by a Miss Phatthanothai
in which she accused her father, Sang Phatthanothai, a left-wing Thai
who had visited China in February 1967, of trying to persuade the
Thai exiles to leave China and to move the TPF headquarters to
Laos.[155] In June, Peking said that a "reactionary clique" of Thai
exiles who had been guilty of "anti-China activities had been driven
from the country.[156]

Divisions within the TPF and resistance to Chinese control
apparently continued as the TPC took more of the limelight. Finally,
the united-front organization disappeared. The last Chinese or VPT
reference to the TPF was in April 1969. The previously active front
men, Phayom Chulanont and Mongkon Na Nakorn, also disappeared
at this time. Thus, the Thai Patriotic Front suffered the same fate
as the Malayan National Liberation League at more or less the same
time.

Interestingly, Hanoi continued to refer to the TPF as leading
the struggle in Thailand (see for example Vietnam Courier, February
14, 1972) but took little note of the Thai Communist Party. This
raises the possibility that during the time of bad feelings between
Hanoi and Peking in 1968-69 the TPF left China and set up headquarters in Laos or North Vietnam.

THE MCP AND "CRUSH MALAYSIA"

In the Malay world another broad strategic commitment as
important to Peking as its commitment to North Vietnam also provided a tactical incentive for a new twist in the armed struggle. As
pointed out in our discussion of the Jakarta-Peking axis, Sukarno's
"crush-Malaysia" campaign was seen as providing a unique opportunity
for the promotion of the united front between China and Indonesia,
on the one hand, and the PKI and Sukarno, on the other. China thus
became one of the most vociferous opponents of Malaysia.

297

Prime Minister Tunku Abdul Rahman, concerned over the possibility of a future communist victory in Singapore, in May 1961 proposed the merger of Singapore and Malaya and the British Borneo colonies of Sarawak and Sabah (formerly North Borneo) and the protected state of Brunei. The three Borneo states were included to restore the demographic balance that would have been upset by a merger only with Singapore. While the objectives of neutralizing Chinese chauvinism and communist ideology have been accepted as the major motivation in the original creation of Malaysia, there were also elements of Malay nationalism and Moslem ideology in the inspiration to build a Malaysian nation.[157]

In the new federation, the Malays and other "natives" were to receive "special privileges" in the economic field and in the civil service; and in addition, the central government was to maintain control over internal security. Lee Kuan-yew, who had all along proposed a merger with Malaya as the only viable economic arrangement for Singapore, seized upon the broader concept of Malaysia on these terms. The left wing of the PAP, however, was opposed to Malaysia, as was the communist organization in Sarawak. It was at this time that the left broke with the PAP and established the Barisan Socialis. This new Peking-oriented party called for full self-government for Singapore, to be followed by a "genuine reunification" in which Singapore would become a state in the Federation of Malaya with its citizens having all the rights and privileges of any other citizen of the federation. This proposal was a straight amalgamation, which would have provided the Chinese a near majority in the population, with no special political powers for the Malays, a situation that remained unacceptable to the Malay leaders.

The MCP could clearly see that the political objective of the Tunku's proposals was explicitly to create a situation that would prevent a future communist takeover in Singapore. On the other hand, the objective of the MCP was a merger on terms that would provide the greatest prospect for the assertion of communist influence throughout the Malayan peninsula. In a referendum on the question of Malaysia held in Singapore on September 1, 1960, 90 percent of the eligible voters participated and 25 percent cast blank ballots, as called for by the procommunist groups.

Despite the MCP's opposition (expressed through its front groups in Singapore) to Malaysia, the PRC in 1961 made no major comment on the matter.

Although Peking did not at first protest against Malaysia and made only perfunctory denunciations of the Association of Southeast Asia, by 1961 it was attacking the Federation of Malaya as having "all along been a state subservient to the U.S."[158] Peking made no public reference to the MCP at this time, but as we will see, it

298

was still deeply involved in the policies and the politics of the organization.

THE MCP AND THE PKI SPHERE

The political situation within the MCP in the early 1960s is confused, but apparently a division appeared within the party that still lurks beneath the surface today. The split was apparently along the same lines that divided the Burmese communists in 1955, 1963, and 1967: the continuation of armed struggle versus acceptance of the government's amnesty terms. According to a later MCP statement, in 1961 the party revised and corrected the "capitulationist" line of 1954 and reestablished a revolutionary line of persisting in armed struggle to the end. In the case of the MCP, an additional, and perhaps the major, issue would be the question of the party's relationship with the Indonesian Communist Party (PKI).

Possibly as early as 1961, Peking discussed with the PKI (and by 1964 perhaps with Sukarno or his representatives) a coordination of strategies in Southeast Asia and areas of responsibility. In the party realm, the Philippines and the Northern Borneo States were apparently put under the general jurisdiction of the PKI. The position of Malaya and Singapore is less certain, but as we concluded in our chapter on Indonesia, it seems reasonable to guess that these areas also were made the fraternal responsibility of the PKI. Apparently this decision created a serious division in the Malayan Communist Party.

In December 1961, the PKI came out publicly against Malaysia, and according to one report sometime between February and April 1962, the MCP agreed to recognize the PKI's regional leadership, provided the PKI endorsed the Peking line and in effect accepted China's ideological hegemony.[159] This may have been the view of an extreme pro-Peking faction in the Malayan party in Singapore, but it is doubtful that the main MCP group in Malaya led by Chin Peng actually agreed to accept PKI guidance or authority. Nevertheless, the Chin Peng group did approve of the "crush-Malaysia" campaign, and thus it was prepared to cooperate to a limited extent with the Indonesians. There was very likely an increasing liaison between the MCP, the PKI, and China on the question of Malaysia. Contact may have been established by the PKI with the MCP forces on the Thai-Malayan border area or through Penang from Sumatra. In addition a new Nasakom-type* effort was made at this time by the

---

*Sukarno's concept of nationalism, religion, and communism.

MCP to win over the Moslem people in the Thai border provinces. New front groups were set up to appeal to the separatist sentiment among the Malays living in this border area of Thailand.

The December revolt in Brunei against the "British plot" of Malaysia provided the occasion for Sukarno's own declaration against the amalgamation concept. When Indonesia launched its "crush-Malaysia" campaign, China was quick to respond with pledges of support for Indonesia's "just stand in opposing the neocolonialists' scheme." Beginning at this time and for the next two years, hundreds of Chinese youths from Malaysia reportedly went to Indonesia for guerrilla training and reinfiltration back into the country. Tunku Abdul Rahman claimed in 1964 that 2,000 youths from Sarawak and Sabah, 300 from Singapore, and about 200 from Malaya had gone to Indonesia for such training in the previous two years.[160] Whatever their numbers, prisoners taken from among the terrorists have confirmed that these youths were associated with the procommunist organizations in Sarawak or with front groups of the Malayan Communist Party in Malaya and Singapore.

In September 1963, after the collapse of the Maphilindo concept and after the renewal of Sukarno's fierce opposition to Malaysia, China denounced "the reactionary ruling clique of Malaya" and pledged itself "to support the peoples of North Kalimantan [the Borneo States], Malaya and Singapore in their struggle to exercise their right to national self-determination."[161] In 1963 China, the PKI and Sukarno, North Vietnam, and the various communist parties in Southeast Asia all began to emphasize the interrelationship between their respective struggles and objectives. Also at this time the PKI began to stress its international and revolutionary role in Southeast Asia, and Peking began to praise the Indonesian party as a model for "certain" other countries.

In June 1964, the MCP released a statement that claimed that the party leadership had successfully launched "a new phase of the struggle . . . against the dangerous imperialist scheme of Malaysia." And it proclaimed that the "crush Malaysia" campaign needed to be intensified and heightened "to coalesce with the general anti-U.S. imperialist struggle now reaching new heights in Southeast Asia."[162]

In November 1964 a spokesman for an MCP front organization proclaimed that "we fully realize the great significance the victories of the people of Vietnam have in relation to our struggle against Malaysia . . . we pledge ourselves to stand firmly together with the people of Vietnam as we've always done in carrying through our common struggle to the end."[163] And, as we have seen, by early 1965 the government of Indonesia had also formally acknowledged that all of the "anti-imperialist revolutionary movements" in Asia, including its own "crush-Malaysia" campaign, formed "an integral whole."

But this strategy created dissension in the communist ranks, particularly in Singapore, where the extremist wing had completely accepted the Peking-PKI line. In the spring of 1964, opposition within the MCP to alignment with the PKI and involvement in the "crush-Malaysia" campaign came to life in the Chinese city. On May 4, 1964, Lee Siew-choh, the militant pro-Peking chairman[164] of the Barisan Socialis, and seven other high functionaries resigned, charging that the Barisan had become "infected with compromise and capitulation."[165] Lee and seven others resigned over the Barisan's rejection of Lee Siew-choh's call for a boycott of national service (draft) registration. The basic issue however was Lee's insistence on a hard line.[166]

Lee Siew-choh's reflection of Jakarta-Peking policies was implicit in his many speeches and articles:

> The political situation in the whole of Southeast Asia is developing more and more favorably with each passing day for the new emerging forces (of which the left wing movement in Malaya is a part) on the one side and more unfavorably for the old decadent forces (of which imperialists and their local reactionary allies form a part) on the other.[167]

While Lee was still at loggerheads with the Singapore Barisan, the MCP moved ahead with its PKI-Indonesian orientation by the creation of a new front group for the party, the Malayan National Liberation League (MNLL), which called for the smashing of Malaysia and for the reunification of Singapore and Malaya.[168]

Some elements within the mainland branch of the MCP also may not have been attracted to a policy of fighting for a communist Malaya under Indonesia's hegemony. This was suggested when the London-published but Peking-controlled Malayan Monitor on June 20, 1964 denounced a group of "Modern revisionist comrades who tried to infect their ideas of rapprochement with Malaysia or of toning down the confrontation." These "comrades" in the Malayan Communist Party, the article claimed, "had virtually accepted Malaysia as a fait accompli and are trying to foist their betrayal policy on their comrades." The article charged that such "parochial and peaceful revolutionaries" had plagued certain sections of the liberation movement, and they must be "obliterated from the ranks of the Malayan National Movement."[169]

It is unclear, however, whether the "parochial and peaceful revolutionaries" were found only in the Singapore branch of the MCP or whether the division in the party also extended to the mainland branch. As the intraparty polemics imply, the dispute involved not only the issue of strategic relationship with the PKI and Indonesia but also the question of basic internal strategy for the MCP.

Since the end of the emergency in 1960, the remnants of the military arm of the party had stuck to their strictly defensive military posture in the Thai-Malayan border jungles. The concurrent political strategy of the party was basically one of "constitutional struggle"—that is, the establishment of various front groups and the infiltration of opposition political parties, principally the Labor Party of Malaya (LPM).[170] The "defeatists" in the MCP, at least in Singapore, wished to continue this policy. But in conjunction with the party's commitment to the "crush-Malaysia" line a more militant policy of mass struggle was adopted by the MCP.

MCP militancy, however, unlike that of the communists in Sarawak, was at this time limited to agitation and demonstrations. Throughout the period of Sukarno's policy of "confrontation," against the establishment of Malaysia, the Malayan National Liberation Army itself engaged in no new acts of terrorism. It remains a matter of conjecture why it did not do so. Probably Chin Peng was not yet ready to initiate military action, although in 1961 the "revisionist" line had been repudiated and a policy of armed struggle reasserted. Perhaps also at this early stage of "confrontation," the largely ethnic Chinese MCP did not wish to compromise the Indonesian effort to enlist the support of Malay nationalism. Most likely, it was simply an expression of the cautious approach developed by Chin Peng over the years in following the Peking line in actual deeds in contrast to mere words. Years of struggle had taught the MCP the danger of widening too much the gap between theory and practice.

The intended path of the revolutionary movement in Malaya—at least as seen in Jakarta and Peking—was in fact further indicated when in the fall of 1964 Indonesia began its infiltration of guerrillas into the Malayan Peninsula. Indonesia and the PKI hoped to exploit Malay nationalism as the MCP had never been able to do. Shortly afterward, the new MNLL's tie-in with Indonesia was demonstrated when the organization, with a largely Malay staff, set up its headquarters in Jakarta in February 1965.[171] Indonesian officials immediately pledged support to the MNLL's struggle to "liberate Malaya" —a struggle that the MNLL claimed to have been leading since 1948.[172]

On March 9, 1965, the pro-Indonesian line seemed established in the Singapore branch of the MCP when Lee Siew-choh and his colleagues once again took up their posts in the Barisan Socialis "in the interest of unity" and the MNLL issued an eight-point program reiterating its "crush-Malaysia" policy.[173]

The Indonesian design was also suggested by Jakarta's efforts to make common cause with extremist opposition groups in Malaya and to foster the idea of a "greater Indonesia." In 1963, a "revolutionary government" of the "Republic of Malaya" (NRM) and its military arm, the National Army of Malaya (TNM), were proclaimed by clandestine radio from Indonesia. Nothing much came of the NRM, and the next year the MNLL was formed as the major united-front organization that presumably would embrace the communists as well as the extremist Malay nationalists. Sukarno also began to focus on the existing opposition groups in Malaya. The chairman of the socialist front and the vice president of the Pan Malayan Islamic Party were both arrested by the Malaysian authorities in early 1965, and both allegedly confessed to receiving money from the Indonesian Government. They also reported plans for setting up a Malayan government in exile with Indonesia's help and for the eventual creation of a "Greater Indonesia."[174] It was to this prospect of Malay dominance that some elements on the MCP and its various front groups apparently had objected. But the line of cooperation with the PKI, as approved in Peking, was apparently accepted at least in theory in the Malayan party.[175] Immediately after Lee Siew-choh's return to head the Barisan, the Chinese Communist Party, for the first time in many years, publicly greeted the MCP on the occasion of the latter's anniversary. The Central Committee of the Chinese party in its message praised the MCP as a "stanch Marxist-Leninist contingent in the international communist movement" and lauded its persistent struggle against Malaysia. The Chinese party also asserted that the "international situation was promising to the revolutionary cause of the MCP," and, apparently in return for the MCP's cooperation with the Peking-PKI strategy, the Malayan Communist Party, for the first time, publicly was pledged support from China in the achievement of its own revolutionary goal:

> The Chinese Communist Party and the Chinese people
> have always shown concern about and have supported the
> just struggle of the Malayan Communist Party and the
> Malayan people. . . . the Malayan people can count on
> the resolute support and energetic help of the Chinese
> people no matter how many difficulties you encounter
> on the road of your advance.[176]

These events also took place within the context of the serious escalation of the Vietnam war in early 1965 and of the feeling in Peking and Jakarta that the final battle to oust the United States and the United Kingdom and to form a new international order in Asia had begun. By this time, all factions in Peking, the PKI, and very likely Sukarno himself were agreed that the "crush-Malaysia" campaign would have to be exploited to bring the revolution to a new stage in Indonesia (that is, the ousting of the anticommunist army leaders) and subsequently to bring a new approach to the achievement of a Marxist-Leninist revolution in the Malay world, a world that would be under the influence of Jakarta but that on a broader scale would orbit about Peking. Had Sukarno and the PKI succeeded in "consolidating the revolution in Indonesia," the next stage of the strategy would probably have been a major effort by Indonesia working under the MNLL front to promote a pan-Malay revolutionary movement in Malaya. The ethnic-Chinese-dominated MCP would have been expected to have renewed its efforts among the Chinese in Malaya and Singapore but to have acknowledged the leadership of the pro-Indonesian Malay elements—elements that ironically were also extreme Malay nationalists and thus tended to be anti-Chinese.

THE CHINESE COMMUNISTS OF SARAWAK

A similar situation faced the Marxist-Leninist forces within the Chinese community in Sarawak on the island of Borneo.

The communist organization in Sarawak, like the MCP, is made up largely of ethnic Chinese (of Sarawak's 1960 population of 800,000, about 230,000 were Chinese),[177] but it is a much younger and more shadowy organization. Embryonic communist cells were not formed in Sarawak until 1951, when they appeared among a group called the Sarawak Overseas Chinese Democratic Youth League, which organized itself to study Marxism-Leninism and the thoughts of Mao Tse-tung. The communist organization itself has put the beginning of its struggle as 1952.[178]

The communists gained a stronghold among the Chinese community of Sarawak for several reasons. First, about one-half of the Chinese population were poor farmers, who generally proved more vulnerable to communist organizational tactics than their city cousins.[179]

Secondly, until the 1960s, Chinese schools in Sarawak were virtually free of government control or supervision, and their education had a strongly chauvinist flavor. Finally the British colonial authorities were remarkably tolerant of communist propaganda and indoctrination not only in the schools but in the press as well. Up until confrontation in 1962, many Chinese newspapers in Sarawak primarily carried news stories from Peking and in their editorials employed communist and Maoist terminology.

The authorities, however, did try to suppress clandestine communist organizations in the colony. In 1952 the Democratic Youth League was banned, and a number of suspected Chinese communists were deported to China. Subsequently, several other communist front groups appeared, such as the Sarawak Advanced Youth Association and the Farmers Association. The principal organization, however,

304

appeared to be the Sarawak Liberation League. Lacking any over-riding name of their own, these various organizations were dubbed the Clandestine Communist Organization (CCO) and later the Sarawak Communist Organization (SCO) by the security authorities.[180]

Beginning in 1959 the SCO put a major effort into infiltration of the newly created, left-wing and ethnic-Chinese-dominated Sarawak United People's Party (SUPP)[181] in much the same way that the MCP attempted to take over the PAP in Singapore. By 1962 the communists were in a much stronger position in the SUPP than they had ever attained in the PAP. A majority of the party's 54 local branches were thought to be under the control of SCO elements, and while the top leadership was in the hands of noncommunist moderates, Ong Kee-hui and Stephen Yong, the central organs were dominated by the activist pro-Peking elements. Although they possessed this strong base in the Chinese community, the communists in Sarawak needed to avoid the path trod by the MCP—that is, to avoid becoming an insurgent and terrorist group, while they remained an ethnic minority party. This reality was apparently recognized by the SCO, and "racial work" (that is, organization among the natives) was being emphasized at this time. International events, however, precipitated the Sarawak communists into premature exposure, and, subsequently, much of the organizational structure they had painstakingly built up over the years was suppressed.

In 1962 the SCO apparently established secret contact with the PKI in Kalimantan. In December, the Brunei rebellion spilled over into some areas of Sarawak, but the communists were apparently not involved and even appeared to have been taken by surprise. But, after the revolt, the security authorities in Sarawak began to arrest members of the SUPP left wing, and, as a consequence, 700 to 800 young procommunist Chinese slipped across the border into Indonesia. The short-lived Brunei revolt initiated the first stage of Indonesia's confrontation policy, as Jakarta supported Sheikh Azahari's move-ment to overthrow the Sultan of Brunei. Thus, the young Sarawakians were welcomed into Indonesian Kalimantan, where they were trained by the Indonesian Army, armed with old weapons, and formed into guerrilla units.[182]

According to one former Sarawakian official in Azahari's government, as a precaution against a reversal of Indonesian policy, only about 300 of these men were put directly under the Indonesian Army, while the remainder set up base camps in the border region.[183] In 1965 a crack Siliwangi Brigade was assigned to West Kalimantan as part of Sukarno's military build up against the British and Malay-sian forces in Sarawak. The brigade commander was General Supardjo, a PKI sympathizer and possibly a clandestine party member, who was to become the principal military officer involved in the aborted coup later in the year. But, in the meantime, his assignment to West Kalimantan improved liaison between the army and the Sarawakian communist forces.

The moderate Chinese leaders of SUPP denounced the Brunei rebellion and Sukarno's confrontation, but three of the party's 16-member working committee fled to Indonesia.[184] Other leaders of the party—including Bong Kee-chok and Wen Ming-chuan, who had earlier been deported to China—also showed up in Jakarta at this time.[185]

These developments suggested some tactical coordination between the communist movements of China, Indonesia, and Sarawak, but generally they reflected individual decisions to seize the revolutionary opportunity presented by the Brunei revolt and by the beginning of "confrontation."* However, while there is no documentation, it appears reasonable to conclude that Peking was prepared to acquiesce in the primary influence of the PKI and Indonesia in the North Borneo (or North Kalimantan) area. All of the communist organizations concerned were obviously in agreement that the Sarawak communists should not be a part of the MCP, since "confrontation" was about opposition to the union of Sarawak (and Sabah) to Malaya (and Singapore). On the other hand, if it was anticipated at that time that Sarawak (or North Kalimantan) was to be independent,† the communists would have fulfilled the Maoist model and formally declared a communist party of Sarawak or of North Borneo. In fact, neither the communists in Sarawak nor those in Peking referred to the existence of a formal communist party organization as such in North Kalimantan until 1969, when a directive referred to the need to establish a party organization. Finally in March 1970, the North Kalimantan Communist Party was formed.[186] This suggests that China in the mid-1960s was either holding open its options in regard to the eventual political status

---

*A former leading member of the militant wing of the SUPP in an interview in 1969 said that he believed the communists in Sarawak had only received indirect guidance from Peking as to strategy and tactics. There was probably an office somewhere in Peking, he said, which concerned itself with Borneo or Sarawakian affairs, and there may have been occasional direct contact with members of the communist underground in Sarawak, but generally the organization followed Peking's line from listening to Peking Radio and from reading the Chinese press.

†Peking supported the "liberation struggle" of the people of North Kalimantan but never expressed support for Sheikh Azahari's "government" of "Kalimantan Utara" (North Borneo). Nor did Peking pick up Azahari after his Indonesian backers lost power in 1965.

and strategic alignment of North Kalimantan or else had accepted PKI-Indonesian preeminence in this area.

After the collapse of the one-day Brunei revolt, Azahari was left with only a paper organization, the "Unitary State of North Borneo," which neither Peking nor Jakarta officially recognized, although both supported "the struggle of the people of North Kalimantan." The only substance to the North Kalimantan Nation Army (TNKU) was the guerrilla units formed by the Sarawakian communists in Kalimantan, a group that paid only lip service to Azahari's organization.

China apparently left the handling of Azahari and the Kalimantan situation completely in the hands of the Indonesians. During the 10th anniversary celebrations of the Bandung conference, Azahari approached Chou En-lai with a request for weapons assistance for his TNKU. According to one source, Chou agreed to lend support but said that it would have to be channeled through the Sukarno government.[187]

The Sarawak communists in late 1964 set up their own united front organization for the area—the North Kalimantan National Liberation League (NKNLL). The NKNLL came into existence shortly before the MNLL mission arrived in Jakarta (and at about the same time as the formation of the Thai Independence Movement). The military arm of the NKNLL, the guerrilla units in Kalimantan, made sporadic small-scale incursions into Sarawak, and in mid-1965 in coordination with the organization within the state they began a terrorist campaign. But the Sarawak communists had hardly begun their armed struggle when events in Indonesia in 1965 suddenly wiped out their "reliable rear base."

With the settlement between Indonesia and Malaysia in June 1966, the Sarawakian insurgent forces in West Kalimantan found themselves in an ironic position. Not only were they wanted as rebels by the authorities in Sarawak, but by October 1966, they were also being hunted down by the Indonesian Army, which had previously been their mentors. These Chinese-Sarawakian insurgents broke into two main groups separated geographically and also by splits in the leadership. These two forces were called the People's Guerrilla Troops of Sarawak (PGRS) and the North Kalimantan People's Liberation Army (PARAKU).[188]

The PGRS took refuge in the mountainous northwest portion of West Kalimantan, where their situation was not unpromising. The wild terrain of this area was inhabited by Dayaks living in widely separated longhouses. In addition there were 60,000 or more residents in the area; many of these were either traders or small farmers. This topographical, political, and demographic situation was somewhat similar to that existing in the MCP redoubt on the Thai-Malaysia border, and it was possible the PGRS could have built a strong rear base in West Kalimantan, provided it did not provoke the Indonesian military authorities. This appeared to be the approach of the PGRS and the PARAKU in the year and a half following the collapse of the PKI-Peking working alliance with Sukarno.

In the summer of 1967, however, the PGRS went on the offensive against the new Indonesian Government. On July 16, 1967 a group of Sarawakian and Indonesian communists attacked an Indonesian airbase at Singkawang (midway between Ledo and Sanggua) and made off with a substantial number of weapons. Peking subsequently called this raid the "first military attack on the enemy"[189] and "the first shot in the armed revolution in West Kalimantan."[190] This raid was followed up with occasional assassinations of teachers and other local Indonesian officials. The Indonesian Government in late 1966 had begun a sporadic campaign to suppress the former trainees from Sarawak, but the terror offensive by the Sarawakian communists stirred Jakarta into more vigorous action. After the July attack on the airbase, military forces in the area were reinforced, the suppression campaign was intensified, and for the first time tactical cooperation and coordination were established with the Malaysian security forces.

The PGRS decision was obviously shaped in large part by the Indonesian campaign against the PGRS, but its reaction was more than defensive and proved to be its undoing. Perhaps a major reason for the decision was that one section of the PGRS did contain some Indonesian-PKI members; one of its leaders was Sajid Ahmad, the PKI first secretary for West Kalimantan, and Sajid and his compatriots gave equal or greater stress to the revolutionary movement in Indonesia. Chinese-Sarawakian leaders of the PGRS, such as Bong Kee-chok, Lai Pak-kah, Liem A-liem, and Lai Chun, were concerned primarily with events in Sarawak, but they, too, were probably influenced by Radio Peking's exhortations to revolutionary violence—exhortations issued in both the context of the North Kalimantan and the Indonesian revolutionary movements.

The major error of the PGRS was committed on September 20, 1967 when armed units killed nine Dayak chiefs in the Sanggau Ledo area near the Sarawak border. This triggered a "blood war" of Dayaks against not only the PGRS but against all Chinese in the area. The Indonesian Army reportedly attempted to exploit the animosity of the former headhunting Dayaks against the PGRS, but very soon the situation was out of hand. From 50,000 to 60,000 Chinese refugees (virtually the entire Chinese population) fled to the coastal cities in the course of this little-noted tragedy. Hundreds and perhaps thousands of Chinese residents were killed.[191]

With the effective elimination of the potentially sympathetic Chinese population, the PGRS situation became increasingly more desperate, and the suppression campaigns of the Indonesian Army began to take a high toll. As with the communist parties of Indonesia and Burma, the premature rush down the path of armed struggle by the PGRS resulted in a heavy toll of its top leaders, and by the beginning of January 1969 the original PGRS band of several hundred, according to Indonesian claims, had been reduced to about 70.[192]

Meanwhile, by 1969 the PARAKU forces in the northeastern sector of West Kalimantan opposite the third and fourth divisions of Sarawak had been reduced to a hard core of possibly 200. But the PARAKU, unlike the PGRS, had followed a more defensive strategy, and by 1969 appeared to have established a fairly reliable "rear base" in this most remote area of Indonesian Borneo.

But in 1969, the communists reportedly adopted a strategy that called for accelerated preparations for armed struggle inside Sarawak. In January 1970 Peking Radio quoted Liberation News as calling for the creation of a new "Red People's Army" as well as a communist party organization.[193] The remnant PGRS forces re-formed within the state's first division, and groups of PARAKU terrorists began to return to Sarawak's third division from Indonesian territory, leaving only residual units behind. This decision to carry the war back to the home country coincided with the return of substantial Malayan Communist "Liberation Army" units to West Malaysia from their hideouts in the Thai border area. As in West Malaysia, terrorist attacks and ambushes increased markedly in East Malaysia in 1970 and 1971.[194]

The year 1970 was said to have been a period of "unprecedented development in the revolutionary struggle" in which the communist side for the first time "began to take the initiative" in certain localities,"[195] and in May 1971 it was proclaimed that "revolutionary base areas" had been established within Sarawak.[196]

In addition to the setbacks suffered by the military units of the SCO in Indonesia in 1967-69, confrontation and its aftermath had meant that the communist political organization in Sarawak had been steadily suppressed. This situation was probably a major factor in the communist decision to concentrate on developing armed struggle and base areas within the state.

After the July 1970 election, SUPP, which had been the outspoken foe of Malaysia in the 1960s, made the surprise decision to join in a coalition with the conservative Moslem Party, Bumiputra, and to cooperate with the Alliance Party (with which Bumiputra was associated) in the Malaysian Federal Parliament.

After the disaster of 1967, Peking still occasionally referred to the activities of the revolutionary forces in Kalimantan but in a more restrained manner. Although almost all guerrilla activity in West Kalimantan was carried out by Sarawakian Chinese, Peking distinguished between two different struggles—one being carried out in the context of the Indonesian revolution and the second in the context of the North Kalimantan (or Sarawak) revolution. In June 1968, Radio Peking in an Indonesian broadcast described the revolutionary armed struggle in West Kalimantan as one of the two major areas of revolution "under the leadership of the PKI" (East Java being the second area). The "West Kalimantan people's guerrilla unit" was said to be "developing its revolutionary base areas along the mountain regions."

> In West Kalimantan, with its high mountains and dense
> jungles, a people's armed forces was founded, while in
> many rural areas, people's guerrillas and armed workers
> teams have been formed. Following the successful attack
> on the Singkawang airfield in July last year, in which hun-
> dreds of cases of enemy rifles and ammunition were
> seized, within half a year toward the end of last year the
> people's armed forces dealt more heavy blows against
> the enemy in dozens of attacks against the Suharto-
> Nasution fascist soldiers.[197]

Most of these attacks were the work of the PGRS or the PARAKU, but Peking was anxious at the time for evidence of armed struggle in Indonesia, and it chose to point to them as part of the Indonesian struggle and thus as bringing "immense encouragement to all the Indonesian people."[198]

By the end of 1968 Peking had modified its revolutionary optimism of mid-1967 in regard to North Kalimantan. NCNA's summary of the North Kalimantan situation at the end of 1968 reported that the people's armed forces were "carrying on mobile guerrilla war in the hilly regions bordering upon Indonesia and in the jungles of Sarawak."[199]

By 1970 Chinese comment concentrated almost entirely on revolutionary activities within Sarawak. Peking publicized and apparently approved of the strategy, wherein the remnants of the PGRS and the PARAKU returned to Sarawak and concentrated on developing armed revolutionary bases within the state and on the rebuilding of a political organization.

MALAYSIA AFTER CONFRONTATION

In January 1966, four members of the central committee of the Malayan National Liberation League were expelled from Jakarta and

310

the MNLL soon joined the ranks of other front organizations in Peking. The Malayan League and its chief representative in Peking, P. V. Sarma, attempted to carry on as if Indonesian "confrontation" were still a relevant strategy. Sarma bravely repeated the pledge to crush Malaysia and to raise the level of revolutionary violence in Malaya.[200] And in November, the MCP in a message to the Albanian Workers Party Congress denounced Rahman and Lee Kuan-yew as "faithful dogs of English imperialism." Occasional NCNA broadcasts also carried the same run-of-the-mill insults. It was clear, however, that the defeat of the PKI-Sukarno strategy had resulted in uncertainty as to the future path of the revolution in Malaya.

The strategy of providing Malay-Indonesian elements an important role in the Malayan revolution, or more correctly the strategy of accepting this theoretical principle, was revised by the force of events. As noted, the pro PKI policy had not totally appealed to the ethnic-Chinese-dominated MCP. This change was marked by the demise of the Peking-backed and Malay-dominated Malayan National Liberation League and the formation in November 1968 of a new Malayan National Liberation Front as the new mass revolutionary organization led by the MCP. (Interestingly, Peking ignored the new MNLF and, until June 1970, continued to refer to the MNLL. P. V. Sarma, however, dropped out of sight in 1968.)

During the next several years the party continued to stress long-term preparations for a renewal of armed struggle, but it was to remain very patient about when this struggle would begin. In the meantime, the policy of militant "mass struggle" was stepped up, particularly in the form of illegal demonstrations organized by the LPM and the Malayan People's Party (PRM). In Singapore the Barisan Socialis intensified its extraparliamentary struggle and took to the streets in several violent demonstrations. In October 1967, the LPM National Executive Committee issued a policy statement, allegedly drafted under MCP direction, which pointed out that "mass struggle" should take precedence over the parliamentary struggle.[201] Shortly thereafter the LPM organized violent demonstrations against the devaluation of the Malaysian currency (following the British devaluation), demonstrations that resulted in a bloody racial riot in Penang. This action led to the arrest of several LPM members and the proscription of many LPM and PRM branches and divisions.

Through 1967, Peking, in the midst of its Cultural Revolution and with radicals in control of the Foreign Ministry, proclaimed that the international situation had never been better for armed struggle and that a high tide of revolutionary violence was sweeping Southeast Asia. China's policies were increasingly affected by ideology and by the internal struggle for power in Peking. During the course of the year, pro-Peking communists in the Philippines, Burma, Sarawak, and Indonesia responded to China's strident exhortations with either new acts or new proclamations of armed struggle. The MCP, however, under Chin Peng's cautious leadership seemed to be not fully cooperative. In 1967 it was still proclaiming that the party was in a transitional stage:

> Our basic policy at the present stage of the revolutionary struggle within our country is neither to fight decisive battles nor to withdraw, but to advance forward step by step and to accumulate our strength at the same time. Tactically we should wage face-to-face struggles against the enemy; strategically, we should advance forward by meandering along.
>
> The people of the various classes being engaged in the revolutionary movement within our country are at neither the stage of high tide nor low ebb; they are at a stage between the high tide and the low ebb, but in transition towards the high tide. The duration of this transitional period will be determined by the development of the various kinds of contradictions within our country, by the speed at which the gap between the strength of the enemy and that of ours is narrowed and by the degree of repercussion cast by the international political situation, particularly the political situation in Southeast Asia.[202]

The military arm of the MCP, the Malayan National Liberation Army (MNLA), was in fact slow in taking action even with a symbolic attack. Throughout 1967 and into the first half of 1968, the MCP guerrillas in the border area continued to avoid provoking the Thai authorities—the party's local propaganda frequently reiterated that it had no argument with the Bangkok government. (On the rare occasion when a Thai was killed in a patrol clash with the guerrillas, the MCP often wrote an apology to the Thai authorities.) There had been one serious ambush in August 1966 of a joint Thai-Malaysian force, but in general the MNLA had avoided initiating attacks on Thai forces. Moreover, the MCP had been surprisingly slow in publicly espousing the new Cultural Revolution in China and in proclaiming itself to be guided by Mao's thoughts. The party's front organizations also did not yet talk of armed struggle.

Why was the MCP tardy in taking up the slogans of the Cultural Revolution in reiterating its position on the Sino-Soviet split and in proclaiming its renewal of armed violence? Very likely there was dissension within the party on these questions. Ching Peng was probably skeptical about Peking's new radicalism, but others in the party pushed for closer alignment with the Chinese line. There is no direct evidence (such as there was in the intraparty polemics of 1964) of such a dispute but only vague suggestions. Whereas the Burmese party was quick to ape the Cultural Revolution and to answer Mao's call for a general onslaught on the reactionaries, the MCP was much more restrained.

Near the end of 1967, however, the MCP did begin to clarify its stand. In December, well after similar pronouncements by the Thai, Indonesian, and Burmese communists, the "organ of the mission of the MNLL in China" reported that the MNLA was studying and carrying out Mao Tse-tung's thoughts in order to throw out the "puppet cliques."[203] Later the same month NCNA reviewed revolutionary armed struggles in Southeast Asia, as reported by the People's Tribune published in Singapore.[204] No mention was made in this article of the revolutionary situation in either Singapore or Malaysia—perhaps a hint that a new phase or at least a declaration of armed struggle in Malaya was overdue.

There was another suggestion—although only that—of hesitance within the MCP on the advisability of following the violent line then being put out by Peking. In early January—two months after the event—NCNA carried a statement issued by the MCP Central Committee on the occasion of the 50th anniversary of the Russian October Revolution. This was the first official MCP Central Committee message on the Sino-Soviet split since the end of "confrontation," and it took a strong pro-Peking line, praising Mao as "the Lenin of our time" and China as the "center of world revolution."[205] Whatever the reason for its tardiness, the MCP had once again fallen into step with Peking in its verbal policies. In February it was announced from Peking that the MNLA was indeed persisting in armed struggle, had increased its strength, and had expanded the guerrilla zone.[206] The same article gave the first hint of a new posture by the MNLA, when it asserted that

> Although the path of revolution is tortuous and the tasks
> arduous, under the leadership of the MCP, and with the
> brilliant guidance of Mao Tse-tung's thought, the revo-
> lutionary Malayan people will win greater achievements
> in 1968.

In March, NCNA in a Thai-language broadcast on the "expanding armed struggle in Southeast Asia" included (as it had not in the December review) the struggles of the MNLA.[207] A few days later Peking Radio broadcast an article by P. V. Sarma entitled "The Malayan People's Armed Struggle in Perspective," which appeared to lay down a future strategy of renewed armed struggle.[208] Moreover, in

May Peking quoted an April 28 article from <u>Barisan</u>, which stated that a "vigorous struggle by the revolutionary masses was sweeping across Malaya."209

Finally in June 1968, the MCP Central Committee in a long statement on the 20th anniversary of the national liberation war in Malaya announced that "the international situation was excellent," and it predicted "the outbreak of a new revolutionary storm in Malaya and Singapore." The present task, the statement concluded, was to "launch a sustained and vigorous offensive."210 Experience has proved, the statement said,

> that armed struggle must be the main form of struggle and the army the main form of organization, while other forms of mass organization and mass struggle must be directly or indirectly coordinated with the armed struggle. It follows therefore that the center of gravity of revolutionary work must be in the rural areas, and thus it is imperative to consolidate and expand the rural base areas.211

Indication of another important change in the public policy of the MCP also appeared in early 1968, this time in regard to the Thai Government. In contrast to the previous tactic of attempting to avoid provoking the Thai authorities, the MCP in its propaganda began for the first time to link its struggle with that of the Thai Communist Party. In January 1968 an anniversary message of the Central Committee of the MCP to the TCP was broadcast over the Voice of the People of Thailand. (The message was, however, allegedly dated over one month before, on December 1, 1967.) The MCP praised the revolutionary struggles of the TCP because "it powerfully supports the national liberation war of our people." The parties and peoples of the two nations, the MCP message said,

> have stood side by side in a common struggle. We have supported each other in the past and we will do so in the future. The Malayan Communist Party will cooperate with the great Chinese Communist Party with the party of Thailand and with all brotherly Marxist-Leninist parties to fight imperialism, modern revisionism and all reactionaries.212

It was at this time that Peking again began to emphasize the need for oppressed peoples in Southeast Asia "to coordinate closely with and support each other, some striking at its head [U.S. imperialism] and others at its feet."213 Shortly after the MCP message, the TCP also began for the first time to talk of the struggle in neighboring Malaya.[214] The political, although at that time not yet physical, union of the MCP and the TCP revolutionary movements was suggested by the TCP's reporting of ambushes in the border area, apparently carried out by the MNLA, as having been accomplished by "our forces."[215] Peking comment also began to refer to armed struggle along the border as both the MCP and a TCP operation.[216] During the next year, TCP forces steadily increased their armed activity in the southern provinces.

This joining of hands with the Peking-backed TCP was a significant new political stance by the MCP, and within a few months its tactical possibilities were indicated. On June 4, 1968, MNLA guerrillas attacked a 10-man Thai patrol near the border town of Betong and killed three Thai policemen. And on June 17, a few days after the conclusion of the five-nation defense talks in Kuala Lumpur, the MNLA in its bloodiest attack in years ambushed a Malaysian security force convoy near the border town of Kroh and killed 15 Malaysian policemen.

No general guerrilla or terrorist offensive followed these symbolic attacks, but other evidence appeared that suggested that the MCP was speeding up its preparations for a new stage of violence in Malaya. Beginning in May 1968, the Malaysian police began to uncover Maoist ideological training camps, mostly in Johore state, bordering on Singapore. The largest raid on June 16 resulted in the arrest of 123 suspects.[217] In addition, there were reports of increasing numbers of young recruits being given military training in the MCP camps in South Thailand.

On November 10 the Malaysian authorities arrested 116 alleged subversive elements, many of them LPM members, and released a "white paper" charging that the MNLA terrorists had switched from an evasive posture to an aggressive one and that the MCP had decreed a return to armed struggle.[218] Occasional encounters between the MNLA and Thai and Malaysian patrols continued, and Thailand and Malaysia again stepped up their joint efforts at suppression.

By mid-1969, the polarization of the races in Malaya due to the communal conflict that followed the May general elections opened up new possibilities for the MCP and Peking. The election results reflected a further polarization of communal politics. A large percentage of the Malays voted for the extremist Malay party, PMIP, while many ethnic Chinese Malaysians deserted the conservative Chinese component of the Alliance Party and supported the Chinese-led opposition.

Although the Alliance maintained a clear majority in Parliament, many Malays feared that the outcome signaled the eventual end of Malay political dominance. Provocative "victory" demonstrations by some of the more chauvinistic young Chinese in Kuala Lumpur set the stage for a riot of Malays in the capital against the Chinese on May 13. According to official accounts, 143 Chinese were killed, as compared to 25 Malays.[219]

NCNA on May 20 charged that the "reactionary Rahman clique" had created the incidents of large-scale bloodshed among the "Malayan citizens of Chinese descent" in order to save its "tottering rule." NCNA also charged that in recent years the Kuala Lumpur Government had "collaborated still more closely with U.S. imperialism and Soviet revisionism and intensified its anti-people, anti-communist and anti-China counter-revolutionary policy. . . ." Nevertheless Peking avoided any implication that China had any responsibility for protecting the Chinese community in Malaysia.

After the May riots, the MCP issued a lengthy statement, which charged that the "big-scale sanguinary massacre" was the logical result of the Malaysian Government's policy of "Malay chauvinism" and that 90 percent of the victims of the riots had been Chinese. The victims were described as "of Chinese nationality" rather than as "Malayan people of Chinese origin."[220]

The MCP charge of "Malay chauvinism" against the Kuala Lumpur government and its denunciation of "special Malay rights" seemed to risk the alienation of what little Malay support the party possessed.

As the government in Kuala Lumpur wrestled with the problem of finding some way to guarantee Malay political dominance, the MCP hoped that once again it would be the only vehicle for resistance by the Chinese to a bloody pogrom and thus would again possess a class-transcending issue. As the MCP had exploited anti-Japanese nationalism 30 years before, it now expected to exploit the breakdown of multiracial democracy to rally the ethnic Chinese while still appealing on the basis of class struggle for the support of the poor Malay peasant. But a new pogrom did not in fact develop, and stability returned to the relatively prosperous country.

Although parliamentary democracy resumed in Malaysia in 1970, constitutional changes were made that allowed the government to suppress criticism of the "special" political rights of the Malays. The regime now had a stronger hand in dealing with Chinese chauvinism. This development in turn would make the government feel more confident in its dealings with China.

In April 1970, the MCP proclaimed a new nine-point program, which reflected a basically chauvinist approach to building its support in the country.[221] It was an approach that dropped the previous official line of catering to the interests of Malay nationalism, a line allegedly foisted on the party at the time of the "revisionist" Peking leadership of Liu Shao-chi and Chou En-lai. The Party's previous program of eight points, which had been announced in December 1955, specifically enjoined "respect for the position of the Sultans," a feudal institution that the Malays value as a guarantee of Malay political dominance.[222] In contrast, the 1970 program called for abolition of the "feudalist system" and the establishment of a "People's Republic."

Point five of the 1955 program had proclaimed that "the Chinese, Indian and other nationalities should unite around the Malay nationality . . ." and that "the Government should pay attention to developing the economy and culture of the Malay nationality." There was, however, no such focus on the central position of Malay culture or on the special needs and privileges of the Malays in the 1970 program, which dealt with the whole communal problem with the promise to "implement equal rights for all races in all fields" and to "develop a new culture of all nationalities." This was the sort of program that would appeal to the ethnic Chinese citizens and not to the Malays, who feared that, without special privileges for themselves, the country would be dominated politically and culturally, as well as economically, by the Chinese. Significantly, the 1955 program had been issued as part of the preparation for peace talks with the government and under pressure from China, whereas the 1970 program came as the Malayan party's second major effort at armed struggle was getting under way but as China itself was beginning slowly to turn away from revolutionary diplomacy.

Although official reports were inclined to overplay the communist threat for political purposes, it was apparent that after the May 13 incident, MCP organizational and propaganda activity increased on the Malaysian side of the border. More important, terrorist activity inside Malaysia began; the MNLA was moving back across the frontier. In July, another six members of a Malaysian security force were killed in ambush; in October, road mines were employed by the guerrillas, and in December, a railroad bridge was destroyed and a border police station attacked. Also, in late 1969, a powerful clandestine radio, the Voice of the Malayan Revolution, began broadcasting in Malay and Mandarin from a station about 1,500 miles north of Kuala Lumpur somewhere in southern China. This station was obviously provided by the Chinese authorities and operated with their consent.

At the same time, there were indications that the MCP was again making greater efforts to stir up separatism in South Thailand among the Moslem population.[223] By 1969 the MNLA reportedly had grown to 1,000 armed men, divided into three regiments, the smallest of which was comprised mostly of Malays and local Thai Moslems led by an MCP Malay leader, Rashid Mydin.[224] By 1971 official figures talked of 1,000 to 2,000 terrorists in the border area.

Thai communist guerrillas also gradually appeared further south, and by late 1969 the TPLA for the first time was active along the border in the general operating area of the MNLA. In November of that year, the Thai communists made their first major attack on Thai Government forces in the border area, killing 18 policemen.

By 1970 the revolutionary struggle in Southeast Asia had passed an important milestone—the physical union of the communist forces in Thailand and Malaya, similar to the united front of communist forces in Indochina. The MCP, by agreeing to a coordination of political and military tactics with its fraternal party in Thailand, had thus accepted the internationalization of its own struggle. There would be no more apologies by the MCP to the Thai authorities. In the spring of 1970, there were reports that 200 TCP guerrillas under the command of a Chinese Thai allegedly trained in Peking, Prasit Thiensiri, were in regular contact with the MCP forces. The Malayan communists were reportedly providing training to young TCP recruits, who had previously been sent for training to North Vietnam.[225]

In 1971 Peking officially proclaimed that the Thai and the Malaysian revolutionaries in the border areas had forged a militant friendship and had fought "in closer coordination in the last few years." Since the second half of 1970, the Thai guerrillas, according to Peking, had extended their fighting zones into southern Thailand and had effectively supported the Malayan National Liberation Army. Similarly, the MNLA was said to have "encouraged and supported" the Thai insurgency.[226] The Thai communists also hailed the solidarity and mutual support now existing between the two liberation armies.[227]

In turn, the Malaysian and Thai governments stepped up their cooperation. A joint antiguerrilla command was established in late 1969, and in March 1970 it was agreed that troops of both sides could cross into each other's territory.

Throughout 1970 the MCP also had gradually gained in strength and expanded its operations inside Malaysia. In June 1971 security forces uncovered a communist camp 70 miles south of the Thai border in the state of Perak.[228] The communists themselves claimed to have moved into "vast areas" of the states of Kedah and Kelantan as well as Perak.[229]

But despite its renewed activity across the border, the Malayan party continued to be cautious in its pursuit of the revolutionary goal, for the MCP leaders knew that there was still little hope that in the foreseeable future China could provide its Malayan comrades significant direct support. Paradoxically, as the MCP appeared to be making some advances, Peking and Kuala Lumpur began moving toward accommodation.

In Singapore, developments after the 1965 separation from Malaysia suggested that the fear of a communist takeover of an independent Singapore (which fear was the original impetus to the Malaysia concept) had been exaggerated. Nevertheless, Singapore's Malaysian episode provided the context in which the communist forces were weakened inside the former crown colony. Ironically, Singapore's separation from Malaysia and its independence in 1965 also had the same effect. The communists in Singapore after 1963 had progressively weakened their own influence because of their adamant position against Malaysia and their support and indeed cooperation with Indonesia's confrontation policy. But after 1965 their insistence on rejecting the independence of Singapore as a sham had the same effect.

In the 1963 elections the Barisan Socialis received about 33 percent of the popular vote (about the same percentage that had cast blank ballots against Malaysia in the 1961 referendum). The following year, a split developed in the ranks of communist elements in Singapore and Malaysia over the issues described above—"confrontation," the "Greater Indonesia" concept, and PKI influence. At this time the MCP operated through its legal front, the Barisan Socialis (Socialist Front), but in addition it reportedly directed a network of underground cadres associated with a clandestine People's Revolutionary Party (PRP) of Singapore, from a base on the nearby Indonesian Rhio Islands.[230] These cadres may have had a hand in fomenting communal riots in Singapore in the summer of 1964 and in the series of terrorist bombings in the city, of which there had been approximately 40 by mid-1965. Immediately after the separation of Singapore from Malaysia in August 1965, a plot by the PRP to assassinate the Singapore ministers and officials was exposed.[231]

The Barisan Socialis, after having consistently denounced Singapore's membership in Malaysia, put itself in the unique position of attacking Singapore's breakaway as an Anglo-American plot, and of denouncing Singapore's independence as a fraud. Consistent with MCP policy, the Barisan Socialis called again for a merger of Singapore and Malaya—that is, without the Borneo territories.

A difference was immediately apparent between the attitude of the communists in Singapore and China, on the one hand, and that of the Sukarno-Indonesian Government, on the other. Jakarta eagerly proclaimed Singapore's departure from the federation as a "grand victory" for its policy of "confrontation," and Foreign Minister Subandrio immediately announced that Indonesia would recognize Singapore's independence and open diplomatic relations with it.[232] Probably Indonesia and the PKI were inclined to welcome the independence of

Singapore because in the long run Indonesian influence could be better established over Malaya (and over the MCP) without the Chinese city of Singapore. China's reaction to events in Singapore was less enthusiastic, and it ascribed the withdrawal as due simply to "inner contradictions" and to Indonesia's correct policies.

The subject of Singapore was discussed by Chen Yi and Sukarno during the former's important mid-August visit to Indonesia,[233] and a joint position on the issue was worked out. The Indonesians apparently agreed at this time to move back to the Chinese and the MCP position, for the joint policy that soon emerged rejected the reality of Singapore's independence. On August 30, the Malayan National Liberation League (the new united front for the MCP under Malay-Indonesian-PKI influence) in Jakarta issued a statement on Singapore, which proclaimed that Lee Kuan-yew was still a puppet of the imperialists and that Singapore was still a "new-type colony." The people of Malaya and Singapore were called upon to continue their struggle and to "reunite" Singapore with the peninsula.[234] This statement came only a few days after the exposure of the plot to assassinate the Singapore leaders. On September 3, Subandrio reversed his earlier position and proclaimed that Indonesia would not recognize Singapore as long as British bases existed, Lee Kuan-yew having already made clear that the bases would remain indefinitely.

The collapse of the Peking-Jakarta axis, the destruction of the PKI, and the ending of Indonesia's confrontation with Malaysia left the communists in Singapore as well as in Sarawak and on the Malayan peninsula in an embarrassing, confused, and awkward position. Nevertheless, the Barisan Socialis, the MCP, and China stuck to their policy of denying the legitimacy of Singapore's independence and insisting that the city was still an integral part of Malaya. The Barisan Socialis followed this policy through to its logical end; it boycotted parliamentary proceedings and by-elections, and by October 1966 all of its members had resigned from the Singapore parliament. The Barisan did not take part in the February 1968 election. The MCP at this time also attempted to take the struggle to the streets and create chaos and disorder in Singapore.

These policies, however, were opposed by some members of the Barisan Socialis as self-defeating, and thus another division in the ranks of the communists occurred. Even the founder and secretary general of Barisan Socialis, Lim Chin-siong, gave up the struggle in July 1969. Lim announced that he had completely lost confidence in the international communist movement and that he "wholeheartedly supported Singapore's Independence."[235] Lim confessed that his party had "completely misjudged the mood of the People."

The Singapore government also worked successfully to undermine communist influences in the schools and trade unions of Singapore.

Thus by 1969, while the extent of communist strength and sympathetic support within Singapore was difficult to measure, the MCP could clearly see that its influence in the Chinese city-state was at a low ebb, a fact that was due in no small part to the party's having obediently followed the line from Peking.[236]

The Marxist forces in the city-state by this time perhaps also realized that a communist takeover of Singapore could actually compromise their long-range efforts in Malaya and Indonesia. The establishment of a communist outpost in the Chinese city of Singapore would inflame Malay nationalism and possibly drive Malaysia and Indonesia together into an anticommunist, anti-Chinese alliance. In accordance with Mao's dictum, the capture of the city—Singapore—should wait until the fall of the countryside—Malaya.

After the end of confrontation, Peking maintained a relatively low posture toward Singapore. In general, Peking limited itself to carrying MNLL and MCP diatribes against the Singapore Government. Toward the end of 1968 Peking hurled another salvo of its own verbal thunderbolts at the "puppet Lee Kuan-yew clique," charging it with spearheading the formation of an "aggressive military bloc in Asia" and turning Singapore into "a base of U.S. imperialism for military and economic aggression."[237]

RESURGENCE OF THE BANDUNG LINE
IN THE PHILIPPINES

China's policy toward the Philippines in the first half of the 1960s closely followed the line set by Indonesia. During this period, Sukarno launched a concerted diplomatic campaign toward the Philippines reminiscent of China's Bandung offensive toward Thailand and Malaya from 1955 to 1958. Indonesia, of course, had a considerable advantage in that it already had diplomatic relations with the Philippines. Indonesia's campaign was similarly conducted at the three levels of state, party, and people. The Indonesia leaders attempted to exploit rising nationalism in the Philippines and the fortuitous event of a Philippine claim on Sabah (North Borneo) in order to win over the Philippine Government and people to a neutralist foreign policy and ultimately to identification with Indonesia.

The administration of President Macapagal instituted a "new look" foreign policy that attempted to assert an independent and significant Philippine voice in Southeast Asian affairs. The establishment of closer ties with Indonesia, the assertion of the claim to North Borneo, and opposition to Malaysia all coincided with a wave of anti-U.S. sentiment in some parts of the Manila press and intellectual circles. This sentiment was fed by a number of procommunist front groups that had been slowly building up in Manila and that were to a limited but possibly important extent financed by the Indonesian Embassy.[238]

In 1964 some procommunist elements in the Philippines apparently entertained the hope that Macapagal, who had begun to talk of completing the "unfinished Philippine revolution," might just possibly be encouraged to play the role of a Philippine Sukarno.[239] The Philippine communists at this point, like the PKI, probably hoped to exploit confrontation with Malaysia as a device to seize leadership of the nationalist movement, Accordingly, Peking carefully avoided offending the Manila government.

Peking's first significant comment on the Philippines for many years came in December 1964, in a People's Daily "Commentator" article entitled "U.S. Get Out of the Philippines." This article praised the recent anti-U.S. demonstration, which had demanded the removal of U.S. bases, but it carefully avoided criticizing the Philippine Government.[240] In January, "Commentator" was excited by further anti-U.S. demonstrations in the Philippines to express the opinion that the islands had become a "growing volcano." This struggle in the Philippines, although it was still aimed at a "united-front-from-above" with the governing authorities against the United States, was also linked with the other struggles against U.S. "imperialism" and colonialism.

At the same time, important developments were occurring within the Marxist-Leninist movement in the Philippines.

As a formal organization, the traditional leadership of the PKP was in poor condition. Most of its Politburo had been in jail since 1950, where they were joined by the major party figures (Luis Taruc in 1951 and Jésus Lava, captured in 1964). Nevertheless, these party elders maintained visiting rights and communication with the outside and in effect attempted to assert control over the movement from their prison cells. (Taruc was pardoned September 11, 1968 by President Ferdinand Marcos, and a court decision in May 1969 cleared the way for release of Lava and 13 other Politburo members). This traditional element of the PKP was controlled by members of the Lava and Taruc families. During the early and mid-1960s the PKP underground was led by Pedro Taruc and the Huk by its military commander, Simulong (Faustino del Mundo), both of whom were operating in Central Luzon.

But in 1960 a new and younger group of Marxist-Leninist intellectuals in Manila began to organize and challenge the traditional PKP elements for leadership of the movement. These young Philippine intellectuals organized and operated through the development of procommunist and anti-American popular front groups among labor, youth, and the peasantry. The leaders of these front groups divided into old pro-Moscow moderates, Maoists, and a group of leftist nationalists who were not communists.

These groups were not strictly divided, and they overlapped in many organizations. The first and third groups, however, largely dominated the Labor Party (Lapiang Manggagawa, or LM), the Free Farmer's Association (MASAKA), and the Bertrand Russell Peace Foundation (Philippine Committee) and included such figures as Cipriano Cid, Felixberto Olalia, Francisco Nemenzo, Jr., and Ignacio Lacsina.

The pro-Peking group, which began to emerge in 1960, was headed by young José Maria Sison (born 1939), chairman of the Youth Movement (Kabataan Makabayan, or KM), which was founded on November 30, 1964, and editor of the Maoist-leaning Progressive Review.[241]

Despite differences among the leftist movements in the Philippines, there was in the early 1960s a general orientation toward Sukarno-Indonesia and a tendency to look to the PKI for inspiration.[242]

As indicated earlier, the Philippine party's organizational tie with the Chinese communists was always nebulous, and unlike the MCP and the TCP, the PKP was never in a position of being "guided" by the Chinese party.

During confrontation, highly nationalistic and anti-American columnists in the press as well as communist-connected intellectuals pushed for all-out alignment with Indonesia. Sison in particular was reportedly described by Philippine security services as in "closest touch" with the Indonesians.[243] In 1962, Sison was in Indonesia on a grant from the Jakarta government, and when he returned he became (in 1963) the executive director of the Philippine-Indonesia Friendship and Cultural Association. In June 1963 he became editor of the new and at that time pro-Indonesian Progressive Review, possibly under subsidy of the Indonesian Embassy.

After the disaster for the communists in Indonesia at the end of 1965, the procommunist elements in the Philippines found themselves again at a loose ends. Although they nominally joined together in 1967 in a united front, the issue of strategy would again divide them along Peking–Moscow lines. Sison, having lost his Indonesian connections, led the faction that turned to Peking for guidance and support.

POSTCONFRONTATION POLICY DEVELOPMENTS

Even before the events of September 30, 1965 in Jakarta, the Philippine Government had begun to have second thoughts about its ties to Sukarno-Indonesia, particularly after Indonesia's escalation of "confrontation" in 1964 into the Malay peninsula itself. The fall of Sukarno and the ending of the "crush-Malaysia" campaign were no great disappointment to the Philippine Government.

But the destruction of the PKP caught Peking without much of an operational policy toward the Philippines. For the next year, China seemed to continue one aspect of Indonesia's diplomatic line by heavy stress on "people's diplomacy" and a propaganda emphasis on the alleged benefits of trade relations. In December 1965, Peking Radio, for example, began regular Tagalog broadcasts (10.5 hours per week), and in 1966 with the relaxation of a Philippine government ban on travel to communist countries, there was a sudden rush of Filipino journalists, academicians, and politicians visiting China, usually financed by organizations in Peking. These visitors generally returned with high praise for the communist regime. In March 1966, as the Philippine Government was debating the dispatch 2,000 combat engineer troops to Vietnam, a delegation headed by Senator Maria Kalaw Katigbak, a member of the Liberal Party, was warmly welcomed in Peking, which described her group as an "exploratory mission." On several occasions, Senator Katigbak was told that "in the promotion of friendly contacts between the two people and trade relations between the two countries there were no difficulties from the Chinese side."[244] The "exploratory mission" was received by Chen Yi, who said that the presence of U.S. bases in the Philippines, while deplorable, should not prevent the opening of friendly Chinese-Philippine relations.[245] Chen reportedly said that the major U.S. bases threatening China were not in the Philippines, but in Japan, Okinawa, South Korea, and Taiwan.[246] In May, Chen also stressed the need for friendly Philippine-Chinese relations to a press delegation and a "trade study group," both from the Philippines.[247] A group of Philippine students also slipped into China in December without official approval and were likewise received by the Chinese foreign minister.[248]

But the year 1966 also saw the continuation of the growth of Huk activity in central Luzon and occasional government claims that such activity was being supported by the Chinese. President Marcos, for example, on NBC's "Meet the Press" program, September 10, 1966, stated that agents "coming from Peking" were aiding the Huks. Reports also appeared in Manila papers charging that infiltrators from China were running military training camps for the Huks and that counterfeit pesos were coming from the mainland.[249] The substance behind these reports is impossible to fathom, and, indeed, Marcos occasionally reversed himself and stated that the Huks received no aid from Peking.

It was always difficult in the Philippines to ascertain what was Huk activity and what was simply banditry; or when it was apparent that the Huks were involved, to what extent the activity was connected with or represented the policy of the outlawed PKP. The Huks or HMB (from the Tagalog words meaning People's Liberation Army), numbering probably in the hundreds remained concentrated in central, western, and southern Luzon under the command of Simulong and Pedro Taruc.

Possibly in the early and mid-1960s there was some increased financing provided to the Huks by the pro-Peking element in the Philippine-Chinese community. The resurgent Huk activity, however, had begun in 1965, and this did not seem to fit in with Peking's modified Bandung offensive toward the Philippines at that time.

The Peking press had made little reference to armed struggle in the Philippines since 1955, but near the end of 1966 and after the ouster of Liu Shao-chi, Peking began to lump the Philippines with Laos, South Vietnam, Thailand, Indonesia, and Malaysia as Asian areas where armed struggle had gained new successes. According to NCNA in December 1966, "unabated armed struggle coupled with anti-imperialist demonstrations" had marked the growing revolutionary situation in the islands. No specific treatment, however, was given the struggle of the Philippine People's Liberation Army until the spring of 1967.

Hints of a change in Peking's policy were accompanied by important activity on the part of the Marxist elements in the Philippines. José Sison made several trips to China in 1966, and during the year the two major procommunist front groups in Manila, the Labor Party and the Youth Movement, mobilized demonstrations against the Vietnam war, culminating in the violent protest of October 24, 1966 at the time of the Manila conference of U.S. Asian allies. On February 8, 1967, the Movement for Advancement of Nationalism (MAN), described as the "broad National Democratic Alliance" embracing all the "progressive and patriotic forces in the Philippines,"[250] was formed. Leading figures from all the various leftist and anti-American factions including pro- and noncommunist elements were represented in MAN.

The chairman of the MAN was the respected noncommunist nationalist and socialist Senator Lorenzo M. Tanado;* the general secretary, however, was José Sison, who described the MAN as "an

---

*Tanado had a reputation for integrity and independence. As solicitor general after the war, he was the chief prosecutor in the trial of collaborators. Following in the footsteps of his late associate Senator Claro M. Recto, Tanado was a fiery proponent of neutralism.

attempt to create a united front of the working class, peasantry, petty bourgeoisie and patriotic businessmen."[251]

The objectives and principles of the MAN were nationalistic and reformist. But as Sison pointed out in Maoist terms, the objective of the united front as he saw it was

> to accomplish the national democratic phase of the Philippine Revolution. If national democracy is a minimum and immediate goal, socialism is a maximum and long-range goal. Let us take the first step before the taking the second. A socialist perspective now can serve to prevent nationalism from degenerating into chauvinism or fascism.[252]

The proper united front having been created, the Maoist model now required that the communist party establish its own independent policy and work to establish hegemony over the front and that armed struggle or the preparation for armed struggle should commence. Efforts to move in this direction followed in short order.

On May Day 1967, the Labor Party transformed itself into the Socialist Party of the Philippines (SPP). Ignacio Lacsina was elected party chairman and Sison became first deputy chairman.[253] Two years later Sison's group formed a new communist party, but in 1967 they may have hoped that the Socialist Party of the Philippines would become the revolutionary core. The SPP associated itself with the national-democratic front, which in the Philippines was now the MAN.

While at this time many Filipino leftists were dismayed with the violence of Mao's Cultural Revolution, Sison made explicit his Maoist predilections, praising the Chinese chairman as "the great leader of the world Socialist revolution . . . whose thoughts inspire the present era of the world socialist revolution."[254] More important, together with a MAN regional official and former priest, Milario A. Lim, he traveled to China in May 1967 at the invitation of the Chinese People's Institute of Foreign Affairs.[255] Two others later identified with the Maoist group in the Philippines, Arthur Garcia and Nilo Tayag, also reportedly traveled to China at this time.

While Sison was in China, a new stage of the Philippine revolution was declared by the Maoist faction speaking in the name of the Philippine Communist Party. Peking praised this development and at the same time dropped the earlier sporadic "diplomacy-from-above" aimed at the Philippine Government and pledged political support to a communist-led insurrection in the islands. On May 21, NCNA reported from Peking that the Politburo of the PKP had issued a statement that pledged the PKP to a policy of armed struggle with a "national united front under the leadership of the working class." This statement also seemed to put the PKP squarely on the side of the Chinese in the struggle with Moscow.

> The Communist Party of the Philippines is committed to an uncompromising struggle against modern revisionism with the Soviet revisionist ruling clique at its center. There is no middle road between modern revisionism and the proletarian revolutionary line. The outlawed situation of the Party dictates clearly that there is no path to a national and social liberation except true armed struggle.[256]

On May 23, Peking Radio in a Tagalog broadcast carried the text of this statement, and on May 29 NCNA proudly announced the first victories that had allegedly resulted from the new policy when it declared that the "Philippine People's Liberation Army led by the Philippine Communist Party has recently stepped up its guerrilla warfare on Luzon Island and secured one victory after another."

This new declaration of subversion against the Philippines was clearly connected with Sison's visit to China, which occurred during the ferment of the Cultural Revolution and the dominance of the ideologues in the Foreign Ministry. Sison probably presented the PKP's statement for Chinese approval, although it may have been jointly drafted. In any event, it seemed clear that the new policy was heartily endorsed by the radical faction in Peking as another reversal of Chou En-lai's Bandung diplomacy. Five years later, Chou En-lai indicated that Lin Piao had been responsible for China's open support of Sison's group.[257]

However, it soon developed that Sison only represented one faction within the PKP and within the People's Liberation Army. Sison had hinted at this split at the time of the forming of the SPP when he warned of "malicious intriguers" bent on keeping the SPP out of the MAN. In fact, many leaders in the Labor Party had refused to go along with the formation of the SPP.

The traditional and pro-Moscow groups within the communist movement continued to advocate concentration upon the urban scene and on front groups and legal activity. The Politburo of the PKP, the anti-Sison pro-Moscow faction, soon issued its own statement to refute the May 1 "statement of the PKP" as carried by Peking and the pro-Maoist New Zealand People's World (May 10, 1967).

The pro-Moscow Politburo statement as published in the "Information Bulletin" of the World Marxist Review described the May 1 document as the "spurious" work of a "small but reckless anti-Party group." It denounced this group for "seeking international recognition by waving the banner of the thoughts of Mao Tse-tung" and for urging an immediate "call to arms" without consideration of the objective conditions and subjective forces in the Philippines.[258]

Upon Sison's return, a serious split occurred in the Philippine movement. Dr. Francisco Nemenzo, Jr., Felixberto Olalia, and other moderates clashed with Sison and broke their connections with the Progressive Review. A new, more restrained leftist journal, Heritage, soon appeared on the scene as well as a new youth organization, Union of Free Filipino Youth (MPKP), to compete with Sison's KM.259 Sison also failed in his attempt to dominate the MAN and turn it into a copy of the TPF and the MNLL. By 1970 the MAN, like the Thai Patriotic Front and the Malayan National Liberation League, was dying if not dead, and the SPP, under Lacsina, was following a relatively cautious line, attempting to hold onto its legal status. These organizations were no longer of any use to Sison. A new united front group, the Movement for a Democratic Philippines, was formed in early 1970 without establishment representation, as existed in the MAN.

Unlike the communist parties in Thailand, Malaya, Indonesia, and Burma, the pro-Peking faction of the PKP did not immediately follow up its earlier pronouncement in favor of armed struggle and Mao Tse-tung's thought with similar declarations. However, Sison and the pro-Maoists in the movement were apparently busy with organizational efforts. A so-called Congress of Re-establishment of the PKP was opened by the Maoists on December 26, 1968 (the 75th birthday of Mao Tse-tung). This congress denounced the "revisionism and opportunism" of the "city-based Lava clique" and the bourgeois line of the Pedro Taruc-Simulong leadership in Central Luzon. The Lava group was said to be following a policy of mostly legal and parliamentary action, and the Liberation Army, under Taruc and his "close relative," Simulong, was charged with following a counter-revolutionary policy of rejecting armed struggle. Simulong was also charged with corruption in his position as the HMB's national finance officer. This "black bourgeois line," according to the Maoists, was related to the right opportunism of "Lavaism," which had existed within the PKP since the mid-1930s.

After 1964, "those upholding Mao Tse-tung's thought," led by José Sison, now calling himself Comrade Armado Guerrero, rose up to "criticize and repudiate modern revisionism, Lavaism and Tarucism" and thus prepared the way for the "reestablishment and rebuilding of the Communist Party of the Philippines under the supreme guidance of Mao Tse-tung's thought."260

Under the leadership of Guerrero, the "Congress of Re-establishment" ratified a new party program and constitution, both of which were said to have been "inspired by Mao Tse-tung's thought." The new program, like those of the other Maoist parties in Asia, called for a protracted city-encircling armed struggle, employing the peasantry as the main force under the leadership of the "working class."

Following Mao's example, the program's immediate aim was said to be the establishment of a "new democracy," which would include a private economic sector respecting the individual initiative and enterprise of the "petty and the national" bourgeoise. The long-term goal, however, was frankly stated to be the achievement of socialism. In discussing the national united front, the new party's program suggested that the Movement for the Advancement of Nationalism was still dominated by the "national bourgeois," and because of this it was becoming a "vapid ineffectual group." The true foundation of a national united front, the program stated, was its leadership by the communist party.

The most striking characteristic of the new PKP (ML)* program and constitution was the party's open and enthusiastic acceptance of Mao's ideological guidance and of China's political leadership in the international arena.

> The most significant development in the entire history of the Filipino people so far is the re-establishment and rebuilding of the Communist Party of the Philippines as a Party of Mao Tse-tung's thought.
>   . . . the countryside of the world, Asia, Africa and Latin America, has a reliable, well-consolidated central base in China.
>   . . . It [the PKP (ML)] regards the People's Republic of China as an iron bastion of the world proletarian revolution and as a reliable friend of all oppressed peoples, including the Filipino people.[261]

In keeping with Maoist tenets, the new PKP (ML) proclaimed that, in addition to party-building and united-front work, its main task was development of armed struggle. In this connection, the most important advance for the Philippine Maoists was their recruitment of an important segment of the HUKs or (HMB). In early 1969, an ideologically oriented group broke with the Huk leader, Commander Simulong. In March 1969, the politically oriented revolutionaries among the guerrillas headed by Commander Dante (Bernabe Buscayno), who had attended the formation of Sison's new Party in December, broke away from the Huks and formed the New People's Army (NPA) in Tarlac Province. Dante was elected to the Central Committee of the PKP (ML), which proclaimed that the NPA was to "propagate and apply Mao Tse-tung's thought as the highest development of Marxism-Leninism in the present era."

---

*ML, Marxist-Leninist.

329

In March 1970 one Filipino official, quoting military statistics, reported that Dante's NPA was run by a central committee of 22 members and consisted of 361 regular armed troops, 417 "general utility" men, 1,038 self-defence corps members, and a mass base of 41,000.[262]

The traditional Lava-Taruc faction of the PKP continued to adhere to the Moscow line, and five unnamed Filipino delegates attended the June 1969 Moscow World Communist Conference.

Throughout 1969 and the first half of 1970, China made no reference either to Sison's pro-Maoist PKP (ML) or to the Maoist New People's Army. After its sudden spurt of enthusiasm in May 1967, Peking only occasionally referred to active guerrilla warfare being conducted by the Philippine People's Liberation Army "under the leadership of the Philippine Communist Party."[263] Throughout the next two years, Peking's reporting of events in the Philippines seemed to imply that armed revolutionary action was not actually in existence in the islands, for it usually referred only to an "anti-U.S. struggle."[264] In regular Peking reviews of armed struggles in Asia in 1968 and 1969, the Philippines again were not reported as being part of the "revolutionary storm."[265]

Peking failed even to refer to "armed struggle" in commenting on the Manila riots in early 1970, describing them as a "revolutionary mass movement." It was also significant that Peking's comment did not identify President Marcos as the target of the rioting students. In fact, Peking continued to avoid any direct personal attack on Marcos.

Finally in August 1970 (a year and a half after the formation of the pro-Maoist PKP faction and its military arm), China featured the activities of the New People's Army, noting approvingly that in addition to its guerrilla activities, the NPA was busy propagating Mao's thought to the Filipino peasant. This comment was also the first reference by Peking to the "recreated" PKP (ML).[266] Nevertheless, the Chinese statements still did not personally abuse Marcos.

Again, one can only speculate as to the reasons for China's delay in acknowledging the efforts of the New People's Army and for its suggested lack of enthusiasm for Sison and his efforts to create a Maoist wing in the Philippine communist movement. Conceivably, the Chinese accepted advice not to identify themselves too closely with any Philippine movement lest they undercut its nationalist appeal. But until some other evidence appears, we are left with the possibility that this odd behavior toward a revolutionary group prepared to pay political obeisance to Mao's thought was involved in some way with internal politics in Peking, as well as with China's interest in the Manila government's sporadic and tentative movement toward neutralism in 1969.

Lin Piao and his allies apparently seized upon support of Sison as part of their drive to assert control over foreign affairs under the banner of radicalism. The moderates inside the Chinese leadership may have succeeded in slowing down the embrace of Sison by warning that the new PKP (ML) might split itself asunder in internecine struggles (as the BCP did in 1967). Various rumors indicated that trouble had already developed between Dante and Sison over the Chinese and Vietnamese tactics Sison had tried to impose on the NPA. For example, the building of Viet-Cong-like tunnel complexes was said to have reduced the mobility of the guerrillas and to have incriminated peasants who lived nearby.[267] In addition, Arthur Garcia, who had reportedly been trained in China as an ideological adviser, was said to have been killed or assassinated near the end of 1969 because Dante suspected he was attempting to gain control of the movement.

But more significant was China's return to a peaceful coexistence diplomacy and the unprecedented steps taken by the Marcos government in 1969 toward a more neutralist foreign policy. These steps will be described in the next section of this chapter, but in short, Marcos by his campaign stance and by such moves as the withdrawal of the Philippine Army contingent from Vietnam suggested to Peking a possible opening for a united front-from-above policy.

Therefore it may be that the more traditional and pragmatic policy-makers in Peking, in urging restraint in China's attitude toward the Philippines, argued for the wisdom of feeling out the intentions of the Philippine Government. Foreign Minister Chen Yi, in fact, was reported to have sent a conciliatory message to Marcos in late 1969 through the novelist Han Su-yin. The radicals pushed forward a strong line in support of the New People's Army just on the eve of the 2d Plenum of the Chinese Party's Central Committee. Very likely they did so in the hope of preventing criticism of their line toward insurgent parties.

Whether or not this was the sort of calculations that lay behind Peking's prolonged silence on the New People's Army in the Philippines and its sudden renewal of attention in August 1970, a new Bandung approach was on the way.

REASSESSMENTS BEGIN

In the mid-1950s the governments of Malaya, the Philippines, and Thailand believed that security would best be served by relying on military alliances with one or more of the Western powers. At the same time, each of these governments believed that a policy of isolation from the PRC was both possible and desirable—for internal as well as external reasons.

The leaders of China at this stage were willing, for a complex of reasons, to establish a "united-front-from-above" with the noncommunist and "bourgeois" governments of these three states. But shortly after Peking's diplomatic overtures had been rebuffed, a 10-year period of radical internal development in China began, accompanied by intensification both of the Sino-Soviet conflict and the wars in Indochina. The combination of isolationist policies toward China, the radicalization of the Chinese leadership and that leadership's concern with its strategic interests in Vietnam and Indonesia and its political objective of splitting the communist camp in Asia led to growing hostility between Peking and the pro-Western states of Southeast Asia. China had renewed its interest in the communist parties in these states because they were useful tactical weapons to counter allied moves in Southeast Asia and also because the Chinese were then attempting to build their own communist movement in Asia on the claim that Peking was more opposed to the United States and more diligently served the interests of fraternal parties, whether ruling or insurgent, than Moscow.

By the early and mid-1960s China was providing open encouragement and in one case material support for communist insurgencies in these countries. Furthermore, in 1967, foreign affairs in China was taken over by a group that was intent upon overturning the Bandung policies of the past, both for ideological reasons and in order to discredit those who had shaped such policies—that is, Liu Shao-chi and Chou En-lai. Even Burma, which followed a neutralist course, was caught up in the internal upheaval in Peking. Inevitably those countries that had persisted in isolating themselves from China and in joining Western anti-China alliances suffered a sharpening of Chinese interest in their respective internal conflicts.

But ironically, shortly after the Cultural Revolution began, the governments in Bangkok, Kuala Lumpur, and Manila began to show interest in the possibilities of accommodation with China. This was in striking contrast to their isolationist policies 10 years earlier, when China itself had been making friendly overtures.

The softening of public positions on China in the allied capitals reflected important strategic reassessments. While because of the radicalism of the Cultural Revolution, isolation from China seemed perhaps even more desirable to these governments than before, its feasibility was now being questioned. The development of a Chinese nuclear capability that covered most of Southeast Asia gave a new dimension to China's potential in the area and also a strong motivation to consolidate a relationship of coexistence. But probably more important was the question of the credibility of the Western alliances as effective deterrents.

The beginning of the British pullout of its military forces "east of Suez" and doubts whether after the Vietnam experience the United States would ever again commit its troops to the Asian mainland altered the security calculations of the Asian governments. It was apparent that in the future the Western powers would probably not assist directly in putting down internal communist insurrections and that even the ability and willingness of the West to deter direct intervention by China was also less certain than 10 years before.

Thus, as the 1960s drew to an end, the allied governments in Asia began slowly to move to a policy of seeking security through accommodation with all the major powers including the Soviet Union and China. They began to look for stability through a multipolar balance of interests in the area rather than in taking sides in a bipolar world. Peaceful coexistence with the communist powers on the basis of mutual respect was cautiously reexamined in the allied capitals.

The search for a broader balance of power in the area at first centered on improved relations with the Soviet bloc.

Beginning in 1967, Bangkok, Kuala Lumpur, Singapore, and Manila began to establish or improve ties with Moscow and the Eastern European countries. In November 1967, Malaysia established diplomatic relations with Moscow, and Singapore followed in June 1968. The remarkable advance in Soviet-Malaysian relations was manifested in March 1969 when the Soviet minister of Foreign Trade, N. S. Patolichev, paid an official visit to Kuala Lumpur and offered Malaysia long-term credits.

In the Philippines a bill was introduced in the Senate in 1968 that called for open trade with communist countries, and several trade deals were concluded with Eastern Europe. That year the first commercial Russian ship arrived in Manila to pick up cargo. Also in 1968 a 17-man Soviet cultural and scientific delegation visited Manila, and in 1969 four stars of the Bolshoi Ballet arrived, as did a group of Soviet and East European newsmen.

Thailand, which had established diplomatic relations with the USSR after the end of World War II, also began to improve its ties with the Soviets. In early 1970 Bangkok signed its first trade agreement with Moscow.

PEKING'S MOUNTING ALARM

At first, China and the Maoist parties in these countries charged that these moves toward better relations with the Soviet bloc were aimed at stifling the communist movements and colluding against

China.[268] For example, José Sison protested that the Philippine policy of gradually opening up trade and diplomatic relations with the bloc was "in line with the U.S. imperialist policy of maintaining a global alliance with the Soviet Union in opposing China, the people, revolution, and communism."[269]

Most worrisome for China were public expressions by some of the pro-Western leaders of interest in the Soviet proposal for a "collective security" arrangement for Asia. In the course of a trip to the United States in early 1970, Thai Foreign Minister Thanat Khoman said that Brezhnev's proposal for Asian collective security—first advanced in June 1969 at the Moscow meeting of communist parties—"seems to envisage the departure from the scene of the Western powers and the eventual occurrence of a power vacuum which may be filled by a large nation presently inimical to Russian interests.[270] If this were to be the case, Thanat Khoman suggested, it would be in the interest of Asian nations to have the Soviets playing a role in the area.

The Malaysian deputy premier, Tun Razak, shortly after Brezhnev floated his suggestion on Asian security, also rejected suggestions that the Russian naval presence in the Indian Ocean posed a threat to countries in the region. The same view was explicit in Singapore's later announcement that its port and repair facilities would be available on a commercial basis if requested by Soviet ships. Russian warships, Lee Kuan-yew said, could usefully serve to counterbalance the expansion of other big navies in the Indian Ocean and the South China Sea.[271] In July, the first Soviet naval vessels anchored in Singapore.

China also became increasingly concerned about the Japanese role in the area. Numerous articles appeared in Peking media warning of the evil intentions of the Japanese in expanding their trade and investments in Thailand, Malaysia, Singapore, and Indonesia.

Peking feared that Japanese economic influence was bound to lead to political interests and ultimately to a Japanese role in the security of the area. The Chinese press began to charge that Japan was dreaming again of a "greater East Asia Co-Prosperity Sphere" and that the Japanese had their eyes on the Straits of Malacca.

CHINA RETURNS TO PEACEFUL COEXISTENCE

By 1969, Chinese absorption with the Soviet menace, the diminishing U.S. threat in Indochina and U.S. military retrenchment throughout Asia, increased Chinese concern with expanding Japanese influence in Asia, signs of a breakdown in the isolationist policies

of the governments of Southeast Asia, and the rise of the moderate
faction in Peking, all resulted in the beginning of a shift in Chinese
policy back toward a broad united-front peaceful-coexistence line.
The more accommodating posture toward China by the government
of Malaysia, and to a lesser extent those of Thailand and the Philippines, promised to open up a diplomatic alternative for the assertion
of Chinese interests and the countering of Soviet and Japanese influence. The PRC could no longer afford to bank its interests in
these countries on the future success of Maoist insurgents.

Moreover, because Peking's policy of polarization had failed
in regard to the communist parties of Indochina, North Korea, Japan,
and Indonesia and because no pro-Maoist insurgents anywhere seemed
on the verge of seizing power, Peking had little to lose by adopting
policies that conflicted with the ideological premises upon which it
previously had hoped to split the socialist camp. The ideological
damage incurred by China because of its decisions in 1970-71 to treat
with such "reactionary cliques" as those in Kuala Lumpur, Manila,
and Rangoon did not reduce Chinese political influence in any effective
way. On the contrary, these moves strengthened China's hand in
countering its main rivals in the area—the USSR, the United States,
and Japan.

In the 1970s, China's interest in Southeast Asia would no longer
focus on its contest with the USSR for leadership of the international
movement and on countering U.S. military presence and threats, but
rather on discouraging the expansion of Soviet and Japanese military
and political power in the area. These objectives required, among
other things, that Peking make credible its intention to coexist peacefully with the noncommunist governments of Asia and that it play
down its support and involvement with insurgent parties in these
countries.

EFFECT OF PEKING POLITICS

The rapid erosion of radical influence in Peking after 1969 was
an important element in the shift in Chinese priorities in Southeast
Asia. In addition, the triumph of Chou En-lai, the father of the "Bandung spirit," over Lin Piao in 1971 likewise facilitated the return to
the diplomatic line.

As noted in the chapter on Burma, China's relations with Pro-
Peking revolutionary groups was one of the issues separating Lin
Piao and Chou. Beginning with his 1965 treatise, Lin Piao had established himself as an authority on "people's wars" in Southeast Asia,
and he was outspoken during the Cultural Revolution in proclaiming

China's support and identity with the communist revolutionaries of the area.

Chou, on the other hand, had been closely associated with Peking's peaceful coexistence policies of the 1950s, which several Southeast Asian Maoist parties later condemned as having also involved pressure on them to give up armed struggle.

Although after 1968, Lin, in keeping with Peking's evolving diplomatic line, increasingly stressed a broader anti-U.S. united front, he still persisted in his 1969 report to the Ninth Party Congress in according attention to revolutionary movements in those countries, such as Burma, Malaysia, and India, with which to varying degrees Peking was preparing to move toward normalization of relations.

Certain glaring inconsistencies in 1970-71 between Peking's public treatment of revolutionary insurgents and its developing diplomacy may have been a reflection of differences on this question between the two Chinese leaders.

The influence of Lin and the civilian radicals, for example, possibly accounted for the appearance of an NCNA article in May 1971 that broke the new pattern in Chinese public treatment of the insurgents in Burma and Malaysia by originating its own favorable comment on their revolutionary struggles and again stressing the "coordination" of all the insurgent movements in the area.[272]

The Chinese are fond of describing their political intrigues by literary allegories. For example, Liu Shao-chi's group first came under attack for the play Hai Jui's Dismissal, which was said to be a veiled criticism of Mao's policies. The existence of a conflict between Chou and Lin over the proper interpretation of "international proletarianism" and over policy toward the Third World was likewise suggested in a revised version of a Peking "revolutionary opera" entitled On the Docks, which appeared some months after Lin's fall.

The villain of the plot, Ch'ien Shou-wei, urges a stevedoring team to upset the original plan to load rice seed for an African country and instead load a ship with fibreglass for a "north European port." Ch'ien was said to have planned "to flee to another country if his scheme failed," an apparent allusion to Lin Piao's aborted effort to flee to the Soviet Union. The villain is foiled by the dock's party committee chairwoman, Fang Hai-chen.

This opera, which according to Shanghai Radio embodied "Mao's revolutionary diplomatic line," suggested that the villain (Lin Piao) not only objected to economic aid to noncommunist countries but that he held a narrow view of international proletarianism compared to the broader more responsible outlook of the character Fang (Chou En-lai?).

RULES OF ACCOMMODATION

In keeping with his pragmatic view, Chou gradually returned China to a selective and flexible approach in dealing with both the allied governments and Maoist parties of Southeast Asia. In regard to those countries that indicated a willingness to accommodate the vital interests of the People's Republic and to divorce themselves from involvement in the Indochina war—the most clearcut example being Malaysia—Chou sanctioned a "classic right" strategy giving priority to state relations. The PRC's vital interests for which Chou sought accommodation included recognition of the PRC's internal legitimacy and its world role.

Chou's strategy called for China to drop its open identification with and encouragement of illegal communist parties in those countries that met these minimum terms and to return its support for fraternal friends back to the clandestine level.

The new style also required a cessation of attention to exile organizations in Peking from those Southeast Asian countries that showed promise. The Malayan National Liberation League office in Peking and its head, P. V. Sarma, for example, disappeared from view. Even the Thai Patriotic Front and its spokesmen in Peking dropped out of the public eye. Eventually, relations with those exile groups that continued to operate in the open (like the Indonesian and Burmese delegations) were put more on a strictly party basis. For example, beginning in 1971, a separate reception on the eve of National Day (October 1) was given by the CCP's Central Committee, which the resident communist exiles attended, thereby missing the official government reception. Likewise, NCNA stopped publishing National Day greetings from the communist parties.

The "Chou En-lai doctrine" also called for a return to the post-Cultural Revolution posture toward overseas Chinese. Peking would not claim dual nationality for overseas Chinese, nor would it interfere in attempts by the Southeast Asian governments to force the pace of cultural integration in their countries; on the contrary, the Chinese leaders would again publicly urge the overseas communities to accept integration. In other words, while still looking upon the overseas Chinese as an economic asset, Peking would not undertake to protect their parochial interests so long as the host governments prevented civil violence against them.

The new policy of peaceful coexistence developed gradually as the external situation evolved and political conditions inside China changed. But by early 1971 the PRC was again following a flexible and selective policy toward the states of Southeast Asia.

337

MALAYSIA—PUSH FOR NEUTRALIZATION

In August 1968, shortly after the CCP's June letter of encouragement to the Malayan communists, the Malaysian Government announced
that it was prepared to become a friend of Communist China if Peking
expressed a similar willingness and gave assurance that she would
pose no threat to the nation.[273] Malaysian Prime Minister Rahman
said that he would consider setting up diplomatic relations with Peking
if China demonstrated that it had no evil intentions toward Malaysian
sovereignty.[274]

Recognition of China's role in Southeast Asia was carried further by the deputy prime minister, Tun Abdul Razak, who in March
1969 said that if Malaysia's independence and integrity could "be
guaranteed by the big powers—America, the Soviet Union and China—
then we can look forward to a stable and peaceful future."[275]

When in September 1970 Razak became prime minister, he
attempted to strike a more nonaligned posture in foreign policy and
to push ahead with a new concept of the neutralization of Southeast
Asia. He and other Malaysian leaders repeated their desire for friendly
relations with China, and they gave substance to this desire by announcing that Malaysia would abstain rather than vote against the
Albanian Resolution in the UN General Assembly.

At the commonwealth meeting in Singapore in January 1971,
Razak boosted his plans for neutralization and made some insightful
comments on the question of China:

> It is a fact that China for the most part has been excluded
> from the mainstream of international affairs for more
> than two decades. I do not think it is profitable, at this
> point of time, to go into the whys and wherefores of this.
> What is of more immediate relevance is that as a result.
> a natural result some might say, China does not accept
> the international order as it exists today and seeks to
> upset it because, in her view, she has been deliberately
> excluded. The countries of Southeast Asia are her im-
> mediate neighbors and are the first to live with the con-
> sequences of her policies.[276]

Responding to Tun Razak's repeated calls for better relations,
Peking in February 1971 offered (U.S.) $208,000 worth of aid for
Malaysian flood victims. And in March the Communist Chinese-
sponsored Silver Star Cultural Group from Hong Kong visited Malaysia and played before packed houses, sanitizing its program of political content.

In April the 14-year-old Anglo-Malaysian defense agreement ended and was replaced by a much looser pact between Malaysia, Singapore, the United Kingdom, Australia, and New Zealand. In the event of an external attack against Malaysia or Singapore, the five countries agreed to "immediately consult together for the purpose of deciding what measures should be taken jointly or separately." In keeping with its policy of not raising fears about its intentions toward Southeast Asia, Peking's comment on this pact denounced it as a British attempt to defend its "remnant colonial interests" but did not attack the motives of the other members nor did it charge that the accord was aimed at China.[277]

Also in April, Kuala Lumpur announced it would establish a consulate in Hong Kong to help boost trade between Hong Kong, Malaysia, and the People's Republic. The next month the first unofficial Malaysian trade mission since 1958 visited China from May 8 to May 16. The mission, although formally a private one, included several officials from the Malaysian Government.

In announcing the arrival of the mission, and in all subsequent references to it, NCNA termed it a Malaysian rather than a Malayan group. Thus, in effect, China accepted the end of "confrontation."

Chou En-lai met with the delegation and said that trade relations were a significant step in bringing better relations between the two people. Chou also made a point of saying that overseas Chinese in Malaysia should live there as Malaysians.[278] Earlier, Peking had notably abstained from criticizing the new constitutional amendment in Malaysia that had prohibited any public challenge of the special position of the Malays or of the language issue.

As a result of the talks, it was agreed to establish direct trade between the two countries instead of through middle men in Hong Kong and Singapore, as had been done in the past. The PRC agreed to consider buying between 150,000 to 200,000 tons of rubber annually, and to explore new purchases of Malaysian timber, palm oil, and copra. In turn, Malaysia would continue to import Chinese consumer goods as well as such new items as light machinery and agricultural equipment.

In addition, it was agreed that all exports would be handled by vessels owned or chartered by the national shipping lines of the two countries.

Shortly after the announcement of President Nixon's visit to Peking, the first official PRC visit to Malaysia took place when a Chinese trade mission visited Malaysia to complete the trade pact. The Chinese delegation paid a call on Prime Minister Razak and extended Chou En-lai's "best wishes."[279] The clock seemed turned back to 1957, when Chou and Mao had greeted the independence of Malaya.

In October, a 47-member Malaysian mission attended the fall
Canton fair. And that same month the Government of Malaysia in the
UN General Assembly voted against the "important question" resolution, which would have required two-thirds to oust the Taipei government, and it voted for the Albanian resolution, as did Singapore.
Kuala Lumpur, however, had the pleasure of having been well ahead
of the pack in declaring its new China policy.

SEPARATING PARTY AND STATE RELATIONS
IN MALAYSIA

Throughout this period, Peking gradually modified its previously
open identification with the MCP.
In the first half of 1970 China's relations with fraternal revolutionary parties were still largely controlled by the radical faction.
In April, on the 40th anniversary of the MCP, the party stressed its
ties to Peking and proclaimed that China was like a "giant standing
boldly in the East . . . the unconquerable bastion of the world revolution . . . making greater contributions to the cause of world revolution."280 The Chinese party in turn praised the MCP for persisting
in the correct road of seizing political power by armed force. Furthermore, the Chinese again reiterated that it was their internationalist duty to "resolutely support the revolutionary struggle of the
Malayan people."281
In the first six months of 1970, NCNA carried 97 separate
articles on Malaysia. Most of these were reports of broadcasts
by the newly established Voice of the Malayan Revolution(VMR) and
of articles by the North Kalimantan Liberation News. But NCNA
also originated its own articles castigating the "Rahman-Razak
clique" for its alleged exploitation of workers, arms expansion, and
"collusion" with the Thai, Japanese, and U.S. governments.
In the second half of the year, which was marked both by the
defeat of the Chinese radicals at the Second Plenum of the CCP Central Committee and by Razak's ascendancy to the premiership in
Kuala Lumpur, the number of NCNA articles on Malaysia dropped by
half. Moreover, Peking itself abandoned the use of the term "Rahman-
Razak clique" and began to cut out most such references from its
own reports of VMR broadcasts. On January 2, 1971, NCNA carried
a VMR editorial reviewing the victories of the MNLA in 1970, but
in Peking's own year-end reviews of the world revolutionary situation, "Malaya" was not specifically mentioned.
China's new diplomatic campaign, which led to its establishment of official contact with the government in Kuala Lumpur, its
tacit recognition of Malaysia, and the dropping of the attack on

Singapore's independence created difficulties with the MCP. A difference was soon apparent between the VMR and the MCP, apparently reflecting a schism among the Malayan communists. The VMR, but not the MCP, was reported as hailing the CCP Second Plenum in September 1970, and on China's National Day the VMR, but not the MCP, was cited by NCNA as having sent a message of congratulations. In 1971 the Chinese party was not recorded as having greeted the anniversary of either the MCP or of its Liberation Army.

After the first official contact between Peking and Kuala Lumpur, the MCP Central Committee sent a message to the CCP on the occasion of the latter's 50th anniversary (July 1). As before, the MCP again praised China as the "impregnable base for world revolution" and as resolutely supporting revolutionary struggle throughout the world. The Malayan communists, however, seemed somewhat less than certain when they stated, "It is our firm belief that, in our common struggle against imperialism, revisionism, and all reactionaries, the militant friendship and revolutionary unity between our two parties and two peoples will be further consolidated and developed."[282] VMR in its own greeting on the occasion extended "our heartfelt thanks to Chairman Mao, the Chinese Communist Party, and the Chinese people for their enormous aid and support to the people of our country in carrying out our revolutionary struggle."

With recent developments in Sino-Malaysian relations in mind, the VMR also proclaimed that, "our enemies will never succeed in their attempt to undermine the revolutionary unity between the Malayan and Chinese Communist Parties and between the peoples of our two countries."[283] The "enemies" referred to may also have included elements within the MCP who had protested China's diplomacy with the "reactionaries" of the Malaysian Government.

EXPLAINING THE UNITED FRONT TO THE MCP

Previous chapters have described China's attempt to explain in theoretical terms its return to a united-front-from-above policy toward "reactionary," as well as "imperialist," regimes. The new Peking diplomacy undermined the ideological basis upon which the Chinese in the 1960s won the loyalty and support of such parties as the MCP in its dispute with Moscow—that is rejection of Khrushchev-type peaceful coexistence with the United States and of the Soviet theory of peaceful transition for Marxist parties. China, however, in 1971 was much less concerned over the consequences of ideological compromise than it was in the 1960s, when it seemed bent on polarizing the international movement. A "great upheaval" had taken place in international politics, and it was in reaction to this transformation that the Chinese shaped what they were to term "Chairman Mao's revolutionary diplomatic line."

Peking's appeal to Maoist parties such as the MCP to fall in with this new line was similar to the appeal made by the CCP during the war against Japan for a united front against China's principal enemy. In 1971 the Maoists were asked to understand the complex world situation in which the primary threat was now the Soviet Union and potentially Japan.

The Chinese made clear to the MCP and other pro-Peking groups in the area that the complex international situation required an active diplomacy by the People's Republic. The Chinese presumably promised the MCP continuing fraternal friendship and possibly limited clandestine financial support if required. Peking could not encourage the MCP to follow a line of peaceful transition—although this would have been in keeping with Chinese foreign policy objectives—because the leaders in Kuala Lumpur made clear that détente with China in no way altered the government's determination to suppress the communists. But, however, the Chinese attempted to explain their position, the MCP's revolutionary momentum would surely suffer.

China's tacit acceptance of Malaysia's legitimacy and Singapore's independence, its friendly intercourse with the Malaysian leaders, and its negotiations with Nixon would inevitably erode the antiimperialist issue of the MCP. The party would no longer have a transcending nationalistic cause with which it could attack the Alliance Government. In the future the MCP would have to base its appeal strictly on internal social and economic issues and parochial appeals to the ethnic Chinese community.

The MCP seemed grudgingly to adjust to Peking's new diplomatic line. In an August 1971 broadcast, the VMR endorsed the interpretations by Sihanouk and Kim Il Sung of the forthcoming Nixon visit to China as a U.S. defeat.

The VMR also came to grips with improvement in the PRC-Malaysian relations, declaring that "Razak and his ilk" by their moves toward China were attempting "to extricate themselves from crisis."

The VMR did not discuss Chinese motivation, but at least limited approval was suggested in the radio's greeting to the CCP, which praised Mao's "revolutionary diplomatic line"—a synonym for the new united-front-from-above policy—and the "big victories" this line had won. These statements all originated with the China-based VMR, which was presumably more influenced by Peking's wishes than the MCP Central Committee.

Nevertheless, Peking and the MCP leadership seemed to come to a meeting of the minds. Chin Peng apparently agreed not to complain about China's diplomatic line and in return Peking apparently agreed not to interfere with the MCP's revolutionary policy or with its internal leadership. Shortly before the establishment of diplomatic relations between the PRC and Malaysia in 1974, Peking for the first time since the 1950's publicly acknowledged Chin Peng's leadership. This came in an NCNA article of February 3, 1974 which carried excerpts of a VMR broadcast on the 25th anniversary of the Malayan National Liberation Army. The article contained Peking's first public reference to Chin Peng since the 1950s. Meanwhile the new offensive which Peking had urged upon the MCP in the late 1960s sputtered along with no great success. The party failed to establish an operational base inside Malaysia and Chin Peng in late 1973 ordered more stress on other forms of struggle, although armed struggle would continue to play the major role.

EAST MALAYSIA

Although the PRC tacitly acknowledged the legitimacy of Malaysia in the spring of 1971, it continued for some time to provide favorable propaganda coverage of the "liberation struggle" in "North Kalimantan" or East Malaysia. Peking and other interested communist parties also continued to avoid defining the preferred political status of "North Kalimantan."

The MCP program of April 1970 promised to support the people's struggle in North Kalimantan "to determine the fate of the country and nation," suggesting that independence or even continued association with Malaysia was possible. A preference for independence, however, was suggested by the reported formation of the North Kalimantan Communist Party in 1970.[284] A broadcast from Peking citing an article by a "North Kalimantan" journalist concluded that an "independent, peaceful, democratic, and prosperous North Kalimantan is sure to appear!"

China, however, was careful not to involve itself in the politics of Sarawak. It did not comment, for example, when the SUPP, which the communists had once hoped to control, joined with the Alliance Party Bumiputra in forming the new government in Kuching in July 1970 and also participated in the Alliance cabinet in Kuala Lumpur. In March 1974 the armed struggle in Sarawak appeared to be dealt a death blow. Bong Kee-chok, one of the insurgent leaders, brought 481 of his almost 700 strong guerrilla force out from the jungle under the promise of a virtual amnesty and the right to participate as individuals in political activity. Bong, who had gone to China in 1962 and then returned to lead the insurgency, said that basic peace had been restored and that his agreement with the government would help Sarawak oppose imperialism and colonialism, and safeguard national independence and sovereignty. On April 8, NCNA carried a statement by Wen Ming-chuan, chairman of the Central Committee of the North Kalimantan Communist Party. This was Peking's first mention of Wen and its first public recognition of the NKCP. Wen denounced the surrender of Bong's group and rather lamely proclaimed," our party still leads a fairly strong armed force. We will continue to use armed struggle as the main form of struggle." Wen indicated that the target of the revolution was the "Malaysian reactionary regime" not the concept of Malaysia. Although the surfacing of a seperate party for North Kalimantan implied that independence was the goal, Wen did not discuss the political status of the state. In any event, for a long time to come, the Communists would have little to say about the future of Sarawak.

SINGAPORE NO LONGER A SHAM

The Singapore government was less enthusiastic than Kuala Lumpur about accommodation with China, as it feared the effect of such a move on the building of a "Singapore identity." The PAP wished for more time to create a cohesive national consciousness among the largely ethnic Chinese population.

But for Peking, rationalizing China's party and state interests in regard to Singapore was less complicated than in the case of Malaysia; there was no real liberation struggle in existence in Singapore to which the Chinese party had committed itself, and Singapore had no ties with Taipei. The MCP still considered Singapore part of Malaya,[285] but the question of reunification became increasingly a nonissue. The official organ of the procommunist Barisan Party in May 1970 noted that "the problems confronting the Malayan people . . . are in the end still a question of political power. They concern neither national unification nor parliamentary democracy."[286]

Peking virtually stopped its attention to Singapore affairs, and by 1971 it had dropped the phrase "Rahman-Razak-Lee Kuan-yew clique."

In May, Premier Lee Kuan-yew ordered the detention of three executives of a Chinese-language newspaper in Singapore on the charge that they had switched to a policy of glamorizing communism and stirring up communal and chauvinistic sentiments over language and culture. The paper had not only allegedly been stirring up the grievances of the Chinese-educated in Singapore (about 40 percent of the population) but had also been printing too much news about

China.[287] A few days later Lee publicly charged that the English-language Eastern Sun, although it was anticommunist, was subsidized by Peking as a long-term asset. China neither reported nor mentioned any of these events in Singapore.

In October, the first Singapore Chinese Chamber of Commerce trade mission to China since 1956 visited the Canton fair and toured other parts of the country. The mission was accompanied by a number of Singapore reporters. While in Peking, the group sought China's assistance in breaking the monopoly over freight rates out of Singapore held by members of the Far Eastern Freight Conference. The People's Republic agreed to send 10 vessels to Singapore every month to pick up cargoes destined for European ports (the first China-chartered ships arrived in February 1972).

Singapore, like Malaysia, voted for the Albanian resolution to seat China, and it also responded to China's invitation to participate in the Afro-Asia Tennis Friendship Invitational Tournament in Peking in November. Unlike their Malaysian colleagues, however, Singapore officials continued occasionally to express doubts about the rush to accommodation with China. Culture Minister Jek Yuen Thong, for example, in speaking about relations with China warned that the communist threat in Malaysia had a "very direct bearing" on Singapore, which had always had a "communist threat" in its midst.[288]

Nevertheless, in July 1972, when a Chinese ping pong team toured Singapore, the PRC implicitly acknowledged the legitimacy of Singapore's independence. In reporting the teams' call on Lee Kuan-yew, NCNA made the first straightforward reference to his title as "Prime Minister of the Republic of Singapore."

In the September 3 elections, the PAP won all 65 seats in the new elections to Parliament. Nevertheless Lee Kuan-yew was disturbed that the opposition had polled 30 percent of the vote, and he clearly intended to keep a tight rein on internal security. Shortly after the elections, one of the new opposition leaders was arrested. NCNA on September 17 reported the election and the swearing in of the new cabinet of the "Republic of Singapore." The People's Republic of China was now prepared to accept Singapore and to deal with its elected government.

MALAYSIA-SINGAPORE ECONOMICS

A revisionist slip had been showing in China's relations with Malaysia and Singapore for some time. Despite frequent charges that the United States and Japan were exploiting the two countries, Peking continued to expand its own trade relations with both Malaysia and Singapore, importing raw materials and exporting finished products.

China ceased rubber purchases in Malaysia in 1963, but after its own break with Indonesia in 1967 it reentered the Malaysia market. By 1968 China was the fourth largest purchaser of Malaysia rubber and in fact of all Malaysian exports. Malaysia meanwhile had become the sixth largest market for China in the noncommunist world.

In 1970 Malaysian exports to China amounted to (U.S.) $27.4 million worth of rubber, while imports from China of light manufactures and consumer goods totaled $77.7 million. Singapore was an even more important market for China; in 1970 the People's Republic exported $127.2 million worth of goods to Singapore, while it imported only $22.9 million of Singapore goods, again largely rubber.[289]

In contrast to China's very favorable balance of trade with these two countries, the Soviet Union consistently ran a deficit with both.

BANDUNG SPIRIT REVIVES IN THE PHILIPPINES

In the Philippines, as in Malaysia, new talk of a modus vivendi with Communist China appeared during the time of the Cultural Revolution. As early as November 1968, President Marcos said that in the event of an American withdrawal from Asia, some arrangement with China would be necessary. The new foreign secretary of the Philippines, Carlos Romulo (who had talked with Chou En-lai at Bandung), also offered "friendship and mutual respect" to Communist China,[290] and he said he did not think that relations with China would pose any danger to the Philippines. Later, Romulo even suggested that China would be welcome to join the Asian and Pacific Council (ASPAC),[291] and in December he repeated Razak's suggestion for a guarantee by the superpowers, including China, of the neutrality of Asia. For such a treaty to be possible, Romulo said, there can be no foreign bases in any of the countries of Asia.[292]

Student riots in Manila in early 1970, in which the Maoist-leaning youth organization KM played an important role, temporarily cooled Marcos's interest in a new China policy. Peking's belated recognition of the activities of the Maoist PKP (ML) in mid-1970 further prejudiced the chances for early détente. But in order to meet the demands of nationalism as well as of a changing order in Asia, Marcos continued to probe for an opening to the communist world. A consensus was reportedly emerging among Filipino congressmen favoring a relaxation of policy toward China.[293] During this time, China was careful not to prejudice future possibilities by directly attacking Marcos or his actions.

Only three months after its first recognition of the New People's Army, Peking launched its united front diplomacy toward the Philippines. In November the Chinese Red Cross sent an $83,000 contribution to flood victims in the Philippines, and in March 1971, Peking returned within 24 hours a hijacked Philippine Airline jet. After the beginning of Sino-U.S. ping pong diplomacy and the relaxation of the U.S. trade embargo on China, Marcos permitted an unofficial 30-man Philippine trade mission to visit China. Premier Chou En-lai received the delegation and said that Peking was waiting with "open arms" to establish diplomatic relations with the Philippines but was ready as a first step to enter into trade relations and friendly exchanges, as these would "inevitably lead" to government ties. Chou also said that he was pleased to hear that the Philippines had changed its Independence Day so that it no longer coincided with that of the United States.[294] Out of this visit there developed a private barter deal of Chinese rice for Philippine coconut oil, which was allowed by the Philippine Government despite the official ban on such trade. People's diplomacy with Manila was back in full swing.

As the U.S. Government had already announced that it was reviewing its policy on the Chinese representation issue in the UN, Marcos told a press conference in May 1971 that the Philippine Government was also restudying its position on this question. Marcos at this time said he did not believe the PRC was trying to export revolution for the domination of Asia.[295]

About this time a minor territorial dispute between China and the Philippines over several small islands in the South China Sea also surfaced, but Peking did not personally attack Marcos over his claim to these islands. Rather, China's intention seemed to be to make a pro forma declaration of its own long-standing claim.[296]

Following the announcement of Nixon's invitation to Peking, Marcos told newsmen that he approved of the visit, as it would reduce tension in the area. Marcos also said that this event made necessary a reassessment of Philippine relations with China and that his Foreign Policy Council had decided tentatively to vote for admission of China into the UN but to oppose the expulsion of the Republic of China. Manila was in fact the only pro-Western Southeast Asian state to vote "no" on the Albanian Resolution.

In mid-August a grenade attack on a Liberal Party political rally in Manila caused Marcos to suspend the right of habeas corpus and to declare that an armed rebellion was under way led by those of a "Marxist-Leninist-Maoist ideology" and supported by a "foreign power." He did not name the foreign power, but apparently he meant China.[297] Marcos continued sporadically to renew this charge while still pursuing better relations with Peking.

After Peking's victory in the United Nations and a rush of diplomatic recognition of the People's Republic, the Philippines speeded
up its own rapprochement efforts. An official press release on February 12 reported that the president's Foreign Policy Council had
decided to open trade with all communist countries, including China.
Foreign Secretary Romulo also reportedly told the House Foreign
Affairs Committee that Manila would enter into diplomatic relations
with both Peking and Moscow before the end of Marcos's presidency.

In the first half of 1972 a stream of Philippine visitors paraded
into Peking, including senators, doctors, agriculturists, and journalists. Later in the year the PRC sent its first ship to Manila carrying 2,104 tons of relief goods for Filipino flood victims.

Semiofficial contact began early in the year with a nine-day
visit to Peking by Marcos's brother-in-law, Benjamin Romualdez,
governor of Leyte, who held a two-hour meeting with Chou En-lai.
After Romauldez's return, Marcos said that his brother-in-law had
gone to Peking as his authorized representative to explore various
questions, including the following: Would the PRC agree to cultural,
trade, and other links, short of diplomatic relations? If not, would
it agree to establish diplomatic relations without disturbing existing
relations between Manila and Taipei? And would the PRC "refrain
from stirring up overseas Chinese or other groups in the Philippines"?

Chou En-lai answered that links could be established short of
diplomatic ties if desired, but that the latter could not be considered
with any country that maintained diplomatic relations with Taipei.
In reply to the third question, Chou reiterated China's commitment
to the Bandung principles of nonintervention in the domestic affairs
of other states. Chou said that China did not believe that revolution
could be exported and that its support of "national liberation" was
only in an imperialist context.298

Nevertheless, Marcos continued to make charges of Chinese
involvement in the Philippine insurgency. In April, for example,
he charged that Filipino communist leaders had been trained in
China.299 But, as we have seen, there is no evidence that China ever
provided significant material assistance to the communists in the
Philippines. Throughout 1971 Peking media had continued to carry
about one news article each month on the activities of Sison's group.
This publicity was apparently the extent of Chinese involvement in
the Philippine insurgency, other than the inspirational element provided by Mao's thought.

The Maoist group in the islands was relatively unaffected by
China's friendly governmental contacts with Manila. Members of
the heavily ethnic-Chinese Malayan Communist Party could only
be bewildered by Peking's kind words for the leaders in Kuala Lumpur; the course of Chinese chauvinism in Malaysia no longer had

the sanction of hostility between China and the Malaysian Government. But Maoist morale in the Philippines was probably little affected by signs of a rapprochement between Manila and Peking.

Sino-U.S. détente presented a bigger political problem to the New People's Army, as it tended to undermine the validity of the "U.S. imperialist" issue. Nevertheless, the New People's Army continued to expand by exploiting domestic grievances.

On September 23, 1972, Marcos declared martial law in the Philippines following a series of bombing incidents in Manila. The government closed down newspapers and radios and detained leading critics of the regime including several members of Congress. Marcos claimed that the New People's Army now had 10,000 armed men and 100,000 supporters. The presidential press secretary, Francisco Tatad charged that the rebellion was supported by a foreign power, and he linked the Chinese Communist Party to the attempt by the Philippine communists to overthrow the government.[300]

No doubt Marcos's action was primarily shaped by internal factors, but it also followed a developing pattern in which the anti-communist governments of Southeast Asia sought to strengthen their domestic control in order to deal with the international changes taking place. The leaders of these countries wished to make their adjustments with China without the pressures and harassments of democratic institutions.

THAILAND—CONFRONTATION TO CONTACT

New parliamentary elections were finally held in Thailand in February 1969. The two neutralist and socialist parties, the Economic Front and the People's Party, which campaigned for recognition of and trade with China, won only six of the 219 seats in the House of Representatives. The leader of the Economic Front was none other than Thep Chotinuchit, who in 1958 had been one of the chief figures in the neutralist Socialist Front of that time. Thep Chotinuchit was defeated in his own campaign in a constituency in the communist-infiltrated northeast region.

Nevertheless, the government party, the United Thai People's Party, won only 75 seats in the House, and many other opposition members, in addition to the six leftisits, began to speak out again in favor of reconciliation with Peking.

The foreign minister, Thanat Khoman, proclaimed that Thailand was ready to sit down for discussions with the Chinese communists and that a stable settlement for Southeast Asia would require the agreement of China.[301] Thanat spoke of "carrying the offensive for peace and stability to Peking"[302] and of negotiating a trade pact with China.[303] The president of the Chamber of Commerce went further in saying that there was an "urgent need" for trade with China.[304]

In early 1970, as the Chinese-built road in Laos edged nearer the Mekong River, and as Thai troops were fighting in Laos, Khoman called for another Bandung conference and a "revival of the Bandung formula with necessary modifications." If the smaller nations could cooperate, he said, "they might convince China at such a meeting to come to terms with its neighbors."[305]

In keeping with Chou's approach to other insurgent movements, China at this time began to alter its propaganda support of the "Thai people's struggle." While NCNA continued to originate its own articles—as well as to carry VPT broadcasts—on the guerrilla war in Thailand, references to China's support for the revolution began to drop off in 1970.

Official and semiofficial Chinese pronouncements and editorials in regard to Thailand were limited to subjects involving Thailand's activities in Indochina. Peking continued to publish messages from the TCP Central Committee hailing various events in China, but no further Chinese party statements on Thailand were recorded. On the TCP anniversary on December 1, 1971, Radio Peking's Thai-language broadcast for the first time in six years failed to comment on the occasion. The TCP's own statement on this anniversary failed to mention Mao's contribution to the party's struggle.

In September 1970, Thanat suggested that his remarks on China constituted a "public offer" by the Thai Government to "sit down and meet with Peking representatives."[306] Communist China, Thanat was quoted as saying, "will become pivotal to peace, security and freedom in Asia as it turns from internal preoccupations to outside interests and as the United States tries to sneak out of the Asian scene."[307] When in 1970 China allowed former Premier Pridi Phanomyong to leave for exile in Paris, the Thai Government reportedly awarded him a pension and a passport. Rumors spread that he would act as a go-between for the two governments.

While making conciliatory noises about relations with Peking, Thanat, in the spring of 1970, also reopened talks with Hanoi on the repatriation of the 40,000 Vietnamese living in northeastern Thailand. Although no agreement was reached in the joint communiqué of May 25, 1970, the talks were said to have taken place in the "spirit of mutual understanding," and both sides agreed to maintain contact.[308]

Both Hanoi and Peking at this time were probably impressed with Bangkok's decision to withdraw from South Vietnam and not to send troops to Cambodia to help Lon Nol fight the communists and Sihanoukists.

In 1971, Thanat also began to complain more bitterly of the drop in U.S. economic aid to Thailand, the American "intrusion" in the world rice market, and U.S. press and congressional criticism of Thailand.[309] Some observers believed that Bangkok was attempting to pressure the Americans for more assistance and a greater defense commitment as the price of its future cooperation.

In May, after Sino-U.S. ping pong diplomacy had begun, Thanat sounded optimistic about Sino-Thai relations, claiming that through third parties China and Thailand had made indirect exchanges leading to better mutual understanding.[310] Thanat also used the term "People's Republic of China" for the first time, and he said that the policy of relaxing tension with China had been approved by the prime minister and the cabinet.[311]

Premier Thanom Kittikachorn was, however, not entirely pleased. After a June visit to Kuala Lumpur, he expressed serious doubt about the success of neutralization. And in July he reportedly informed his cabinet that he opposed commercial or other contact with the PRC until Peking stopped its sponsorship of insurgency in his country.[312] The number-two man in the regime and then reputed successor to Thanom, General Prapat Charusathien said he agreed because he believed such contact would open up opportunities for subversion of the Chinese minority in Thailand.

Unlike those in Malaysia and the Philippines, some officials in Thailand expressed dismay at the announcement of Nixon's trip to China. The director of Bangkok's Communist Suppression Operations Command said that Nixon's attitude was an "acknowledgment of defeat."[313] Thanat himself said he did not think Southeast Asian countries would "jump on the bandwagon."

In August, an article by an influential Thai journalist, Theh Chongkhadikij, who was known to be close to Thanat, said that the Thai Government could not fully follow U.S. policy on China because Thailand was a small country, close to China, and with a PRC-supported insurgency and a large ethnic Chinese population. Nevertheless, the article concluded, if the PRC leaders showed they were friendly by "stopping their support of the war of national liberation against us, we could be friendly to them." To demonstrate that Thailand was willing to relax tensions, the article suggested that the government revoke the prohibition on trade with China and allow authorized persons to travel to China.[314]

While Malaysia had announced that it would vote for the Albanian resolution to seat Peking in the UN and oust Taipei, Thailand decided to cosponsor the U.S. dual representation resolution. This decision was denounced by the Voice of the People of Thailand as tailing after the United States and "antagonizing the Chinese people,"[315] but Peking did not directly comment on the Thai position.

After the U.S.-supported resolution failed, Thailand, for the
first time, abstained, rather than voting against the Albanian resolution. In addition, the Thais withdrew their candidacy for one of the
vacated seats on the UN Economic and Social Council after Peking
expressed a desire to become a member. Personal contact between
diplomats of the two governments also began at the UN when the Thai
and Chinese Ambassadors each attended receptions given by the other.

Despite difficulties over Thailand's support of U.S. policies
in Indochina and in the UN, Peking indirectly attempted to encourage
further gestures of accommodation from Thailand. A Harvard professor and author, Dr. Ross Terrill, who had recently spent some
time in China with an Australian delegation, told Thanat in a published interview on July 30 that "the Chinese are interested in your
proposal for a dialogue with them and in particular your personal
proposal." However, Terrill said, nothing had come of this proposal
perhaps because "there have sometimes come different voices from
Thailand." Thanat agreed that there were differing views on the
question of relations with China.[316]

China's victory in the UN brought forth an increased swell of
pressure in Thailand for a new China policy. Newspapers and opposition politicians again clamored for a change. Three members
of Parliament cabled congratulations to Mao, and both Chinese- and
Thai-language papers in Bangkok increased their coverage of events
in the PRC.

Pridi was quoted in the Bangkok press as saying in Paris that
the People's Republic of China was now recognized "de facto and de
jure" as a big power and that Thailand should recognize the PRC
immediately.[317] Even the Voice of the People of Thailand endorsed
the call for establishment of relations between its enemy, the Thai
Government, and its patron and benefactor, China.[318]

Under Thanat's prodding and public pressure, the Thai Government in early November gave the impression of taking some tentative
steps toward improving relations with Peking. Thailand's National
Security Council, presided over by Premier Thanom, in early November agreed in principle to consider removing the ban on trade with
China, to relax anticommunist laws, which restricted relations with
China, and to allow sports and cultural relations. The council also
reportedly approved of Thanat's efforts to sound out Peking through
third parties. As explained by the Ministry of Economic Affairs,
trade with China, if allowed, would be on a government-to-government
basis through a public corporation such as that which handled Malaysia's trade with China. The council reportedly ruled out diplomatic
relations with China in the near future and decided against allowing
travel to China by political figures.[319]

The premier made clear that the government was not rushing into anything and that no changes would be made until the "details" had been considered over a "reasonable period of time." Furthermore, Thanom said that the council had strongly endorsed a close relationship with Taiwan.

On the other hand, Thanat was busy painting a rosy picture. He again suggested that his efforts were bearing fruit and that China had responded to his proposal for a dialogue through a third country.

On November 13 Thanat again said that the PRC had signaled its readiness to enter a dialogue, and he claimed that the cabinet had authorized ambassadorial talks with the PRC.[320]

On November 17, however, Thanom and a junta of generals, in a repeat of Sarit's 1958 coup against his own government, dissolved the cabinet, abolished Parliament, suspended the constitution, and declared martial law. Responsibility for foreign affairs was taken away from Thanat.

Thanom and the generals abandoned the new democratic experiment for several reasons. A squabble was developing within the cabinet (centering around Thanat), and in addition the politicians in Parliament were demanding economic development projects for their home provinces, for which they were prepared to slash the military budget. Members of the government's United Thai People's Party were threatening to vote against the budget if their "pork-barrel" demands were not met. While many of the parliamentarians may have been moved by corrupt motives, the generals in 1971, as in 1958, were essentially annoyed with the criticism and the obstructionism of the parliamentary system; authoritarian impatience again carried the day.

But relations with China also once again played an important role. Thanom explained that he feared a swing to communism by Thailand's Chinese population as a result of Peking's entry into the United Nations. In his list of reasons for the coup, the marshal cited first the need to forestall a small but growing movement among some politicians to begin exploring new relations with China and to retain the reins of foreign policy firmly in his own hands.[321]

The situation was very different, however, from that of 1958, when Sarit rejected neutralization and accommodation with China. At that time China was itself offering the hand of friendship to Thailand, there was no Chinese-supported communist insurgency in Thailand, the United States was discouraging the Thai Government from adjusting its relations with China, and the credibility of the U.S. commitment to stop communism in Indochina was on a rapidly rising scale. Fourteen years later, the United States itself was courting China, pulling out of Indochina, and cutting back elsewhere in Asia. Moreover, Thailand was paying the price for having backed the United

States and having turned its back on China—a major and costly insurgency in Thailand. Thanom did not have the same options as Sarit.

Consequently, the generals did not intend to end the exploration
of a dialogue with China, but rather they wished to keep tight control
over the development of this major policy change. Elimination of
public pressure on the issue would allow the generals to continue at
a more measured and cautious pace. Indeed, 10 months later, the
Thai Government accepted a ping pong invitation to Peking and sent
along a government official to sound out the Chinese on their attitude
toward Thailand.[322]

Interestingly, Peking, as in 1958, did not directly comment on
the military takeover in Bangkok.

Malaysia, Singapore, and the Philippines were not directly involved in the Indochina conflicts and thus their state-to-state accom-
modations with China were easier. Bangkok, on the other hand, was
the most important U.S. ally in Southeast Asia, and the Thai Government's attitude toward China had been the least flexible of any of
the pro-Western governments (except perhaps for post-Sukarno Indonesia).

Nevertheless, Peking was still ready to include Bangkok in its
policy of détente despite continuation of the Indochina wars.

The Thai, like the Malaysian, leaders insisted that détente with
China depended upon Peking's cessation of support for the insurgency
in Thailand. However, the Thai leaders never indicated what adjustments they in turn were willing to make in their alliance with the
United States or in their relations with Taiwan. At the beginning of
1972, Bangkok still believed that Thailand's security very much depended on the defeat of the communists in Indochina and that U.S.
bases in Thailand were essential to this objective. As long as this
situation existed, the Chinese, while ready to improve state relations,
were likely to continue to pressure the Thai Government through its
support for the communist insurgency. In the Chinese interpretation,
this support could still be justified as antiimperialist because of
Thailand's continued role in the Indochina conflict.

Nevertheless peaceful coexistence on some level could develop.
Peking gave unusual publicity to the Thai ping pong team, which took
part in the tournament held in the Chinese capital in September 1972.
The "adviser" to the Thai team was Prasit Kancharawat, deputy head
of the Directorate of Finance, Economy, and Industry of the ruling
National Executive Council. Prasit was received by Chou En-lai on
September 5.

According to Prasit, Chou took a conciliatory line and said that
if there were obstacles on the Thai side to immediate diplomatic
relations, China could wait. But in the meantime, Chou suggested,
China and Thailand should begin to promote relations in other fields

such as sports and trade. As with his Philippine visitors earlier
in the year, when the question of insurgency was raised, Chou said
that the Chinese did not interfere in the internal affairs of other countries but did support the fight for freedom of various peoples against
foreign imperialism.[323]

Chou reportedly took for granted U.S. military presence in
Thailand and apparently did not discuss the issue of Thai involvement in Laos.[324] The Chinese foreign minister also told Prasit
that overseas Chinese should be loyal to their countries of residence
and should obey their laws. And the Chinese deputy minister of Economic Relations with Foreign Countries informed Prasit that China
was ready to trade with Thailand on a government-to-government
basis or on a government-to-people basis.

Chou's personal touch was reflected in his expression of greetings, conveyed by Prasit, to the Thai King, and the two top military
leaders, Thanom Kittikachorn and Prapat Charusathiara. The Thai
leaders decided to open commercial relations, and a delegation was
dispatched to the Canton Trade Fair in October.

NEUTRALIZATION

Tun Razak's efforts to promote a neutralization policy for
Southeast Asia were speeded along by the sudden U.S. movement to-
ward détente with China in 1971 and by the People's Republic's ad-
mission into the United Nations. The Thai and Indonesian generals,
fearful of China's intentions, were apprehensive of such a plan; Lee
Kuan-yew as noted wanted more time for nation-building; and the
Marcos Administration, beset by its own Maoists, was in no hurry.
Yet events moved all these countries along the road blazed by the
Malaysians.

An ASEAN foreign ministers meeting took place in Kuala Lumpur from November 25 to 27 (Thanat represented Thailand although
he was no longer foreign minister), and a declaration of neutralization
was issued. The vague declaration was considerably short of what
the Malaysians had desired. Yet for the first time, the pro-Western
states of the area declared themselves in favor of creating a "zone of
peace, freedom and neutrality" in Southeast Asia. Neutralization
was declared a desirable objective, although the meaning of the term
was not defined—nothing was said about military bases or defense
pacts. It was also agreed to establish a committee to study what
further steps should be taken to bring about the realization of this
objective.

Peking maintained a prudent silence on the neutralization declaration. The Malaysian Trade Delegation that visited Peking in May, however, reported that Chou En-lai had reacted favorably to the idea.[325] Chou, of course, had unsuccessfully pushed a similar concept in the mid-1950s, and he very likely viewed the pronouncement by the ASEAN ministers as the beginning of an evolutionary process that could lead to the neutralization of the ASEAN states on the pattern of Burma, Nepal, and Ceylon.

Before 1964, China had also supported the concept of a "zone of peace" and a "nuclear-free zone" in Asia, as it believed these principles would promote China's security and political interests. In the earlier period, Chou saw neutralization as a way to reduce Southeast Asia as a "sphere of influence" for the United States and the United Kingdom.

By 1971, the Chinese were again attracted to the idea of neutralization for Southeast Asia but for different reasons. The Soviet Union and Japan were now major contenders for influence in the region, and neutralization would tend to deter these two powers from taking up the slack that promised to result from U.S. retrenchment. At the same time, China's new, more powerful but less militant image, the ebbing of the old Western alliances, and U.S. détente with China made neutrality and coming to terms with Peking a more attractive choice for most of the allied states.

Probably the Chinese did not expect the ASEAN declaration to have much substantive effect on Southeast Asia until there was a settlement of the Indochina conflict. In the meantime, China concentrated on selectively improving its bilateral relations with the ASEAN governments, more confident than ever that the old policies of isolation were being cast into the dustbins of history.

THE STRAITS OF MALACCA

A concrete example of China's rising fear of the strategic consequences of Soviet and Japanese intrusions into Southeast Asia arose over the question of the Straits of Malacca. In November 1971, Malaysia and Indonesia agreed that since both countries had extended their territorial waters from 3 to 12 miles, the Malacca Straits were no longer to be considered international shipping lanes, and they reserved the right to intercept or forbid any ship from using the straits. Use of the straits would continue to be granted in accordance with the principle of innocent passage. Singapore participated in the talks but only "took note" of this position, although it agreed that the safety of navigation was the responsibility of the coastal states concerned.

The Soviet Union in discussions with the Japanese insisted that the straits were an international waterway and must be kept open for free passage by foreign ships. This principle was important to the Soviet Navy, as its ships stationed in the Indian Ocean traversed the straits on their way to and from their main base at Vladivostok.

As Japanese tankers carried 90 percent of Japan's oil requirements from Persian Gulf ports through the Malacca Straits, Japan naturally agreed with the Soviet stance. Later the United States also approved acceptance of the principle that extension of territorial waters to 12 miles should not be allowed to change the long-standing international character of the important straits.

With no oceangoing fleet of its own, China had mutual security interests with Malaysia and Indonesia in restricting the use of the Malacca Straits by the superpowers. In March 1972, Peking denounced Moscow's expansionist naval activities and the use of the Malacca Straits by large numbers of Soviet warships, which threatened the security of countries in the area.[326] Chinese media also favorably reported the remarks of Malaysian officials on the issue.

This question not only reflected Peking's alacrity in exploiting an opportunity to reduce Soviet maneuverability and to make diplomatic points but also suggested the shifting of security concerns by the allied governments of Southeast Asia. As their perception of a Chinese threat diminished, Soviet and Japanese presence loomed larger.

NOTES

1. David A. Wilson, "Communism in Thailand," in Ralph Trager, ed., Marxism in Southeast Asia (Stanford, Cal.: Stanford University Press, 1959), p. 86.
2. J. H. Brimmell, Communism in Southeast Asia (London: Oxford University Press, 1959), p. 114.
3. Voice of the People of Thailand (VPT) clandestine broadcast, December 2, 1967. Wilson in Trager, op. cit., pages 19-93, quotes a TCP pamphlet in the early postwar years which stated that a group of communists had been in existence since about 1925 and organized as a party since 1935. Apparently the TCP was in an embryo state for so long that the communists themselves could not remember when it actually had been conceived. However, we may now take the 1942 date as the last word on this subject.
4. Brimmel, op. cit., p. 101.
5. Ibid., p. 104.

6. Renze L. Hoeksema, "Communism in the Philippines; An Historical and Analytical Study of the CCP and Its Relations to the Communist Movement Abroad" (unpublished doctoral thesis, Harvard University, 1956), p. 87.

7. Justus M. van der Kroef, "Philippine Communists and the Chinese," China Quarterly, no. 30, April-June 1967, p. 117.

8. Luis Taruc, He Who Rides the Tiger (New York: Praeger Publishers, 1967), p. 33.

9. Hoeksema, op. cit., p. 109. For another history of the PKP see series by Ildefonso T. Runes, "The Red Chapter" in the Manila Chronicle, February 13-19, 1967. Also "The Communist Movement in the Philippines," an unattributed pamphlet (by SEATO) published in Bangkok, 1970.

10. See David Jules Steinberg, Philippine Collaboration in World War II (Ann Arbor: University of Michigan Press, 1967). For information on Malay nationalism's greater concern with Chinese rather than British domination, see W. R. Roff, The Origins of Malay Nationalism (New Haven: Yale University Press, 1967).

11. Gene Z. Hanrahan, The Communists in Malaya (New York, 1954), cities Japanese estimates of 2,300 Japanese casualties in Malaya during the entire war including the drive on Singapore. Hanrahan notes that estimates of "collaboraters" killed by the MPAJA are considerably higher. Brimmel, op. cit., notes estimates that of the 25,000 persons killed by the Huks, only some 5,000 were Japanese.

12. See excerpt from Ang Bayan in Philippine Herald, March 1, 1970.

13. L. Taruc, op. cit., p. 33.

14. Ibid., p. 34. Another PKP leader, José Lava, reports the same story in his book Milestones in the History of the Communist Party in the Philippines (Manila, 1950), p. 96.

15. Hoeksema, op. cit., p. 268.

16. Armado Guerrero, Philippine Society and Revolution (Hong Kong: Ta Kung Pao, 1971).

17. Luis Taruc, Born of the People (New York, 1953), pp. 75-76. This book was published before Taruc surrendered in 1954. Near the end of the war, this "Hwa Chi" squadron reportedly withdrew to one of the southern islands and according to both Taruc and Lava had no further contact with the Huks.

18. Brimmel described the MCP at this point as being in fact an extension of the Chinese Communist Party. Whether or not this was ever true, it is no longer accurate.

19. The indirect nature of the relationship was revealed in Taruc's report that the Huks used Edgar Snow's Red Star over China as a textbook. Taruc, He Who Rides, op. cit., p. 33.

20. The MCP leader at this time, Loi Tek, according to Malayan Government reports, twice visited China in 1946. The Basic Paper on the MCP, vol. 1, part 2, p. 31, Federation of Malaya Legislative Council, Kuala Lumpur, 1959.

21. Taruc, He Who Rides, op. cit., p. 34.

22. Another ranking member of the PKP, José Lava (captured 1964) disallowed any connection between the PKP and the CCP. See van der Kroef, op. cit. Basic Paper of the MCP, op. cit., refers to a conference of communist representatives from Thailand, Burma, the Philippines, Vietnam, and China held in China in 1946. Such a conference would seem to have been a natural occurrence at that time and may well have taken place, although as McLane, op. cit., p. 313, comments, no other sources have referred to this meeting.

23. This meeting was referred to by VPT broadcast in Thai of August 19, 1968. Although the place of the meeting was not given, Prasert was said to have been in attendance.

24. Brimmel, op. cit., p. 215.

25. See Hanrahan, op. cit., pp. 51-52, for translated portions of Loi Tek's speech.

26. Brimmel, op. cit., p. 204.

27. Wilson in Trager, op. cit., p. 92-93.

28. Brimmel, op. cit., p. 210.

29. It is not clear, however, whether this delegation had any connection with the PKP. See McLane, op. cit., p. 418.

30. Guerrero, op. cit., p. 70.

31. Lava, op. cit., p. 96.

32. VPT, December 2, 1967.

33. VPT broadcast in Thai of statement by "spokesman of the TCP," August 19, 1968. It is implied that the revisionist line was then rejected, but subsequent developments and the realities of the existing situation suggest that a policy of armed struggle was not being contemplated at that time.

34. Van der Kroef, op. cit., p. 123.

35. Taruc, He Who Rides, op. cit.

36. George Weightman, "The Chinese Community in the Philippines" (unpublished MA thesis, University of the Philippines, 1952), p. 132, cited by van der Kroef, op. cit., p. 119.

37. Edgar O'Ballance, Malaya, the Communist Insurgent War 1948-60 (London: Faber, 1966).

38. McLane, op. cit., p. 399.

39. Ibid., p. 400, cites an unauthenticated British intelligence report of the arrival of 20 Chinese communist agents in Singapore in November 1948; their mission was allegedly part of a Chinese communist project "To build up and develop all of the Communist parties of the south seas."

40. Ibid., p. 400.

41. According to the 1960 census, there were 181,625 alien Chinese in the Philippines; other estimates, however, run from 300,000-500,000.

42. See Chou En-lai's report on foreign affairs, supplement to People's China, no. 19, September 1, 1954. Chou also strongly supported the Soviet Government's proposal for a similar "system of collective security in Europe," a parallel that suggests that the two proposals were indeed cut from the same cloth. This period forms an interesting contrast to China's reactions to the Soviet proposal in 1969 for a "system of collective security in Asia."

43. NCNA, December 29, 1950; SCMP, no. 30, December 1950.

44. See NCNA report, November 21, 1952 and December 24, 1952; SCMP, no. 458, November 1952, and 480, December 1952.

45. President Eisenhower, in an address on April 10, 1953, called for "united action" in Southeast Asia, and in March 29, 1954, in an important speech, Secretary of State Dulles reiterated the need for collective defense in the area even if it meant "serious risk."

46. NCNA, February 23, 1954; SCMP, no. 755, February 1954.

47. NCNA, March 13, 1954; SCMP, no. 766, March 1954.

48. NCNA, May 17, 1954; SCMP, no. 810, May 16, SCMP, no. 811, May 19, 1954.

49. People's Daily, July 17, 1954.

50. Ta Kung Pao, July 16, 1954.

51. People's Daily, July 29, 1954.

52. Pridi, it should be noted, was always thought of as being more amenable to China than most Thai leaders. This was true of his attitude before the communist takeover in China as well as after. It was under Pridi's premiership in 1946 that Thailand established diplomatic relations with Nationalist China. See George Modelski, "Thailand and China," in Policies Toward China, A. M. Halpern, ed. (New York: McGraw-Hill, 1966).

53. See for example, NCNA, June 11, June 25, July 14, 1954; SCMP, nos. 827, 837, 848.

54. Article by NCNA commentator Wu Min, August 16, 1954; SCMP, no. 870 August 1954.

55. People's Daily commentator Wu Chuan, August 7, 9, 16, 1964; SCMP, nos. 864, 870, August 1964. There was much less attention to the membership of Pakistan, which had established relations with China, than to the membership of the Philippines and Thailand.

56. Cited in George Kahin, The Asian African Conference (Ithaca, N.Y.: Cornell University Press, 1956), pp. 13-14.

57. Ibid., pp. 14-15. While there conceivably could be some political potential or subversive assets for China in the Thai

autonomous region, Chou's explanation of the innocence of the situation was probably substantially correct. Since armed struggle began in Thailand in 1965, there have been no substantiated reports of Thais from Yünnan being employed by the communist forces.

58. Ibid., pp. 15 and 26. For the text of Chou's speech in which he refers to these points, see pp. 56-62 of Kahin's work.

59. Ibid., pp. 15 and 26.

60. Ibid., p. 27.

61. Supplement to People's China, June 16, 1955.

62. For a good review of the political parties and newspapers, see David Wilson's "Thailand and Marxism," in Trager, op. cit.

63. George Modelski, SEATO: Six Studies (Melbourne: F. W. ChesAire pty. Ltd., 1962), pp. 125-126.

64. See article in People's Daily by Yi Mei-hou on Sino-Thai relations, June 21, 1955; SCMP, no. 1076, June 1955.

65. Klaew Norapat, Yiam Pakking (Visiting Peking) (Bangkok, 1957), cited by David A. Wilson, "China, Thailand and the Spirit of Bandung" China Quarterly (July-September 1967), pp. 110-120.

66. Ibid., pp. 235-244.

67. NCNA, May 3, 1956, SCMP, no. 1283, May 1956; and NCNA, June 14, 1956, SCMP, no. 1312, June 1956.

68. Wilson, in China Quarterly, op. cit., p. 124.

69. NCNA, May 3, 1956.

70. People's Daily, July 25, 1956, SCMP, no. 1348, August 1956, article by Ching Feng. The article went on to detail the economic woes brought to Thailand by "U.S. monopolistic and exploitative controls."

71. See Wilson, in China Quarterly, op. cit., p. 115.

72. See David A. Wilson, China Quarterly op. cit., pp. 97-101; and Modelski, SEATO, op. cit., pp. 124-127.

73. VPT broadcast in Thai of statement by "spokesman for the TCP," August 19, 1968.

74. Ibid. A similar struggle is also said to have occurred in 1953.

75. Ibid.

76. NCNA, January 12, 1957, SCMP, no. 1451, January 1957.

77. Donald E. Nuechterlein, Thailand and the Struggle for Southeast Asia (Ithaca, N.Y.: Cornell University Press, 1965), p. 131.

78. This information comes from personalities in Bangkok, some of whom were actors in the affairs of this period.

79. Ibid.

80. Apparently Peking did not comment upon this election.

81. NCNA, July 20, 1957, SCMP, no. 1576, July 1957.

82. Frank C. Darling, Thailand and the United States (Washington, D.C.: Public Affairs Press, 1965), pp. 182-183.

83. Told to the author by a reliable individual in Bangkok who was informed of this cable at the time by one of the editors concerned.

84. McLane, op. cit., p. 462.

85. See for example, NCNA, January 7, 1955, SCMP, no. 972, January 1955; and NCNA March 23, 1955, SCMP, no. 1014, March 1955.

86. See for example, NCNA, November 22, 1955, SCMP, no. 1176, November 1955; and NCNA, November 30, 1955, SCMP, no. 1181, December 1955.

87. NCNA, April 1955, SCMP, no. 1035, April 1955.

88. Harry Miller, A Short History of Malaysia (New York: Praeger Publishers, 1965), p. 196.

89. Brimmel, op. cit., p. 334.

90. Ibid., p. 335.

91. People's Daily article by Chin Chang, December 28, 1955, SCMP, no. 1199, December 1955. The article denounced as a vile scheme efforts to portray Chin Peng as a representative of the Chinese communists.

92. People's Daily article by Chin Chang, January 8, 1956.

93. "Hold High the Great Red Banner of Marxism-Leninism-Mao Tse-tung Thought and March Forward Courageously," Voice of the Malayan Revolution in Mandarin, 0515 GMT, April 26, 1970, Statement of the MCP Central Committee on the Party's 40th Anniversary.

94. Ibid.

95. On April 24, 1956, NCNA reported an MCP statement on "the present situation," which again called for a reasonable solution that would grant "democratic rights and political freedom to the people of Malaya including the Communists." Under these terms, the MCP said it would welcome the reopening of talks.

96. NCNA January 25, 1957, SCMP, no. 7461, January 1957.

97. NCNA, August 29, 1957, SCMP, no. 1604, September 1957; NCNA, August 30, 1957; SCMP, no. 1604, September 1957.

98. People's Daily and Ta Kung Pao, August 31, 1957, SCMP, no. 1604, September 1957.

99. Nan Chun, "On the Independence of Malaya," Current Affairs, no. 16, August 21, 1957; Extracts from the Chinese Mainland Magazines, no. 106, November 4, 1957.

100. Brimmel, op. cit., p. 336.

101. Nan Chun, op. cit., Some communist-front groups in the city after 1959 did begin to call for immediate independence for Singapore. This line, however, was never supported by the Malayan Communist Party or the PRC. It is uncertain what lay behind this position, if indeed it was a deliberate MCP policy.

102. In 1961, Lee Kuan-yew gave a long series of talks over Radio Singapore in which he revealed the history of the communist struggle for power within the PAP.

103. Miller, op. cit., p. 211.

104. NCNA, August 29, 1956, SCMP, no. 1363, September 1956.

105. NCNA, April 11, 1957, SCMP, no. 1512, April 1957.

106. Miller, op. cit., p. 215.

107. NCNA "Commentator," August 22, 1958, SCMP, no. 1841, August 1958.

108. People's Daily, "Commentator," June 4, 1959, SCMP, no. 2030, June 1959.

109. NCNA, October 29, 1955, SCMP, no. 1160, November 1955.

110. One other important visit during this time was that of Manila's vice mayor, Jesus Marcus Roces, who with a group of newsmen visited Peking in July-August 1958. Roces praised China and called for recognition. NCNA, August 8, 1958, SCMP, no. 1382, August 1958; NCNA, August 3, 1958, SCMP, no. 1872, August 1958.

111. A. Doak Barnett, Communist China and Asia (New York: Harper and Brother, 1960), p. 242.

112. NCNA, March 6, 1959, SCMP, 1972, March 1959.

113. People's Daily, "Commentator," February 5, 1959, SCMP, no. 1952, February 1959.

114. NCNA, April 22, 1959, SCMP, no. 2000, April 1959.

115. People's Daily, editorial May 30, 1959, SCMP, no. 2026, June 1959.

116. People's Daily, May 30, 1959, SCMP, no. 2026, June 1959.

117. NCNA, September 30, 1959.

118. Radio Peking broadcast article on the TCP, December 5, 1967, in Thai.

119. NCNA (English), April 10, 1962.

120. This information was confirmed by 20 captured personnel who attended the school. See Stanley Karnow, "Insurgency in Thailand: Looking Glass War," Far Eastern Economic Review, nos. 17-23, 1967; and J. L. S. Gilling, "Northeast Thailand: Tomorrow's Vietnam," Foreign Affairs, January 1968. Some of the Thai recruits also spent several months in training with the Pathet Lao in Laos at least as early as 1963. See testimony of former terrorists in Straits Times, September 14, 1968.

121. The Thai Communist Party coordinator of activities in the Northeast, Thong Jamsri, was captured in Sakon Nakhon Province in 1967. Thong received training first in 1952 at the Marxist-Leninist Institute in Peking and later at the institute set up in Chungking (See Asian Analyst, December 1967). At least four of the 33 TCP leaders arrested in a sweep in August 1967 were trained in China (Bangkok Post, September 1, 1967).

122. Article in Ta Kung Pao, July 31, 1964, SCMP, no. 3273, August 1964, by "noted Thai public figures" Saing Marangkul and Suchint Akrakhai.

123. NCNA, October 1, 1964.

124. See Bangkok Post, January 21 and January 23, 1965. According to some reports purchases in the first part of the year had totaled 20 million bahts.

125. The following year C. L. Sulzberger reported that 45 percent of all bombing attacks against North Vietnam originated in Thailand. New York Times, April 15, 1966.

126. NCNA, April 16, 1965.

127. Ibid., March 11, 1965.

128. See for example, People's Daily, April 28, 1965.

129. Ibid., October 7, 1965.

130. VPT broadcast, August 7, 1967.

131. Ibid., December 31, 1968.

132. NCNA, January 14, 1966.

133. See for example, People's Daily, April 27, 1966.

134. Ibid., August 18, 1966.

135. Tirana Radio, November 6, 1966; see also Asian Notes, no. 82, November 28, 1966. On April 9, 1966, NCNA carried a statement from the TCP on events in Indonesia.

136. VPT broadcast, January 7, 1967.

137. Ibid., August 7, 1967.

138. Straits Times, January 18, 1969.

139. July 8, 1968 TCP communiqué dated June 20, 1968.

140. On November 11, 1969, seven Thai policemen were killed by Thai communists in Sengkhla Province only nine miles from the border. Straits Times, November 13, 1969. The TCP took credit for this attack in a VPT broadcast of November 13, 1969.

141. VPT, December 6, 1968.

142. Ibid., February 4, 1969.

143. Ibid. An NCNA (English) January 11, 1968 report on the "short-term policy" referred to "the right of autonomy" for the ethnic minorities.

144. VPT, December 31, 1968, TPLAF Supreme Command communiqué of January 1, 1969.

145. Ibid. This transition was forecast three years previous: "Only when the people's armed struggle is expanded to people's war can we destroy the enemy's armed forces and win final victory" (TPF, New Year message 1966, NCNA English, January 14, 1966).

146. VPT, December 31, 1968, op. cit.

147. Ibid.

148. NCNA, August 5, 1971.

149. For example, PRC Foreign Ministry Statement of January 19, 1967, NCNA, January 19, 1967.

150. NCNA April 3, 1967.

151. Ibid., April 18, 1967.

152. VPT, June 3 and 13, 1968. The provocative acts were said to be (1) the dispatch of U.S. spy planes from Thailand; (2) stationing of B-52's in Thailand; (3) propaganda attacks; and (4) Thai cooperation with Chiang Kai-shek.

153. People's Daily, January 9, 1969.

154. NCNA, January 3, 1969.

155. Peking Radio in Thai, May 21, 1967.

156. Ibid., June 3, 1967.

157. An interesting insight is provided in a letter by Prime Minister Rahman to the Sultan of Brunei, Sir Omar Ali Saifuddin, dated July 10, 1961: "When I visited Sibu and Kuching recently I was told by the Sarawak Malays that the only way to protect the Sarawak Malays was for them to unite with their brothers the Malays in the Federation of Malaya under the Malay rulers." Text of this letter was in an official Brunei Government exhibit in Brunei Town, September 1968. Brunei eventually chose not to join Malaysia.

158. People's Daily, editorial, March 12, 1961

159. Arnold C. Brackman, Southeast Asia's Second Front (New York: Praeger Publishers, 1966), p. 252. This report is not sourced.

160. Later estimates by the Malaysian Government put the figure from Sarawak at 700-800.

161. People's Daily, "Observer" September 29, 1963, SCMP, no. 3073, October 1963.

162. Malayan Monitor, June 30, 1964. This article was published as a pamphlet by Foreign Languages Press, Peking, 1965.

163. Tahir bin Muhamad, Representative of the Malayan National Liberation League on November 25, 1964, at the International Conference for Solidarity with the Vietnamese People Against U.S. Imperialism and for the Defence of Peace, Malayan Monitor 18, 1 (January 31, 1965).

164. Lim Chin-siong while in prison remained secretary general.

165. Malayan Monitor, May 31, 1964, p. 7, quoted in Brackman, op. cit., p. 252.

166. A summary of Lee Siew-choh's denunciation of the defeatism of his party opponents is contained in a newssheet produced by Lee and 7 others called "Comment on the First Article in the Barisan Newsletter No. 3," February 6, 1964.

167. Lee Siew-choh, mimeographed statement March 9, 1965.

168. In May 1965, two members of the MNLL attended the 4th Afro-Asian Solidarity Conference as official delegates of the MCP.

169. Malayan Monitor, June 30, 1964.

170. The national chairman of the LPM in a recantation issued after his release from arrest related how he had joined the Anti-British League, an underground MCP organization, in 1955 and

subsequently had been instructed by the MCP to "penetrate" the LPM. Straits Times, November 10, 1968.

171. See Straits Times, January 9, 1967.

172. Indonesian Herald, July 23, 1965.

173. Malayan Monitor, March 31, 1965. Koo Young, deputy leader of the Barisan, was arrested in June 1967 and defected from the party. On January 27, 1968, Koo on Singapore TV confirmed that Lee had been reinstated on the instructions of the MCP. See Sunday Times (Singapore) January 28, 1968.

174. Bangkok Post, February 14, 1965; and New York Times, March 1, 1965. See "White Paper" in Straits Times, March 1, 1965.

175. By 1965 several leaders of the MCP (and the Barisan Socialis) had taken refuge in Indonesia. These included En Chooi-yip, Fung Chuang-pi, Chan Sun-wing, and Wang Soon-fong (Straits Times August 28, 1965).

176. NCNA, April 29, 1965, SCMP, no. 3450, May 1965.

177. The immigration of Chinese farmers was encouraged by the "white rajas" of the Brooks family who ruled Sarawak for about 100 years. Steven Runciman, The White Rajahs (London: Cambridge University Press, 1960).

178. The communist organization itself has put the beginning of its struggle as 1952. Liberation News, 110, quoted by NCNA (English), January 14, 1970.

179. See Communism and the Farmers (Kuching: Government of Sarawak, 1961).

180. For government reports on the history of the communist organization in Sarawak, see The Danger Within (Kuching: Sarawak Information Service, 1963); and The Communist Threat to Sarawak (Kuala Lumpur, 1966).

181. The SUPP (formed in June 1959) claimed about one-half non-Chinese among its 40,000-50,000 members. In the 1963 elections it won 24.5 percent of the votes cast; generally it received the overwhelming support of the Chinese community.

182. Communist Threat to Sarawak, op. cit., p. 2.

183. I am indebted for this piece of information to Professor Richard Solomon of the University of Michigan, who interviewed the source in 1969.

184. Brackman, op. cit., p. 66.

185. Malayan Times, November 7, 1963. When represented "North Kalimantan" at the 1966 Afro-Asian Writers Conference but has not been heard from since that time.

186. "The Threat of Armed Communism in Sarawak" (Kuala Lumpur: Malaysian Government, 1972).

187. From Professor Richard Solomon, who interviewed a former Sarawakian communist who attended the celebrations with Azahari.

188. According to Peking the PARAKU was formed on October 26, 1965, shortly after the failure of the PKI, and the PGRS was "built before" this date. NCNA (English), October 26, 1969, citing a handbill.

189. NCNA, January 11, 1968.

190. Ibid., December 29, 1968.

191. For reports of the Dayak uprising, see Straits Times, November 21, 28 and December 18, 1967; Sarawak Tribune, January 9, 1968.

192. Estimate of TNI General A. J. Witono, Sunday Tribune, Sarawak, January 12, 1969.

193. NCNA, January 14, 1970.

194. "Threat of Armed Communism, " op. cit.

195. NCNA, February 23, 1971, citing News Bulletin.

196. Ibid., May 19, 1971.

197. Peking Radio in Indonesian, 0500 GMT, June 28, 1968.

198. NCNA, December 29, 1968.

199. Ibid., December 28, 1968.

200. Ibid., January 12, 1966.

201. Ibid.

202. Quoted in The Path of Violence to Absolute Power (Kuala Lumpur: Government "White Paper," 1968).

203. Malayan Bulletin, quoted by NCNA, December 11, 1967.

204. People's Tribune, quoted by NCNA, December 28, 1967.

205. NCNA, January 8, 1968.

206. Malayan Bulletin, cited by NCNA, February 23, 1968.

207. NCNA (Thai), March 26, 1968.

208. NCNA, March 31, 1968.

209. Ibid., May 7, 1968. According to the report of a guerrilla defector, the MCP in early 1968 had decided to renew and revive its work among the masses (Anthony Polsky, "Chin Peng Bides his Time," Far Eastern Economic Review, October 16, 1969).

210. NCNA, June 18, 1968.

211. Ibid.

212. VPT, January 5, 1968.

213. People's Daily, "Commentator," March 23, 1968.

214. VPT, March 20, 1968

215. Ibid., September 10, 1968.

216. NCNA, September 17, 1968.

217. Straits Times, June 17, 19, December 2, 1968.

218. Ibid., November 10, 1968; Path of Violence, op. cit.

219. The May 13 Tragedy, report of National Operations Council (Kuala Lumpur, October 1969). Foreign press reports asserted that the death toll was considerably higher.

220. NCNA, August 9, 1969.

221. MCP 40th anniversary statement, NCNA, April 28, 1970.

222. Brimmell, op. cit., pp. 333-334.

223. Polsky, "Chin Peng," op. cit.,

224. Straits Times, November 24, 1969, quoting the general officer commanding in chief, West Malaysian Major General Mohamed Sany bin Abdul Ghafar.

225. Ibid., April 30, 1970, quoting General Saiyud Kherdphol, director of Operations of the Communist Suppression Operations Command.

226. NCNA, May 20, 1971.

227. VPT broadcast, February 1, 1971, NCNA, February 2, 1971.

228. "The Resurgence of Armed Communism in West Malaysia" (Kuala Lumpur: Government of Malaysia, October 2, 1971).

229. NCNA, January 1, 1972.

230. Yearbook on International Communist Affairs (1966) op. cit., p. 378

231. The leader of this plot, who was arrested at the time, Sim Siew-lim, was identified as secretary-general of the Singapore Town Committee of the MCP. Sim had returned from Indonesia, where he allegedly had received his instructions from the MNLL (Straits Times, August 27, 28, 1965).

232. Jakarta Herald, August 10, 1965.

233. Ibid., August 11, 1965.

234. Ibid., August 30, 1965.

235. Straits Times, July 24, 1969. Lim was released from prison and went to United Kingdom for studies.

236. For an interesting discussion of the political situation in Singapore through 1964, see Justus M. van der Kroef, "Singapore's Communist Front," Problems of Communism, September-October 1964, pp. 53-62.

237. See for example NCNA (English), December 16, 1968.

238. There were numerous reports of such financing by the Indonesian Embassy as well as indirectly by Communist China, but there is little documentation on the subject. See for example, Justus M. van der Kroef, "Philippine Communism and the Chinese," China Quarterly, no. 30 April-June; and Manila Times, April 1, 1966.

239. In this connection see an article by the pro-Peking communist leader José Maria Sison, "Political Turmoil in the Philippines," which appeared in Eastern World (London), February 1964, and which saw signs of a new and promising foreign policy in the Philippines.

240. People's Daily, December 30, 1964, SCMP, no. 3370, January 1965.

241. For a collection of Sison's early Marxist-Leninist-Maoist views, see José Ma. Sison, Struggle For National Democracy (Quezon City: Progressive Publications, 1967).

242. When Jésus Lava was captured in May 1964, correspondence between himself and the secretary general of the PKI, Aidit, came to light, as did a copy of a translation of Lessons from the History of the PKI (Brackman, op. cit., p. 255).

243. Weekly Graphic (Manila), February 24, 1965. Manila Times, May 11, 1964.

244. NCNA, March 14, 1966. See also Manila Times, April 1, 1966.

245. Manila Times, April 1, 2, 1966, articles by Isagani Yambot on the Katigbak visit.

246. Ibid.

247. NCNA, May 9, 1966, SCMP, no. 3616, May 1966. In early 1967 there were reports that China had offered to sell rice to the Philippines. See Bernardino Ronquillo, "Shyly Willing," Far Eastern Economic Review, March 2, 1967, p. 357.

248. Asian Notes, no. 87, February 13, 1967, NCNA, December 6, 12, 1966.

249. Van der Kroef, "Philippine Communism and the Chinese," op. cit., p. 67.

250. Progressive Review, Manila, no. 10, 1967. For documents and speeches of the Founding Congress, see Movement for the Advancement of Nationalism Basic Documents and Speeches, Founding Congress, printed by Phoenix Press, Quezon City, 1967.

251. Progressive Review, no. 10, 1967, p. i.

252. Sison,op . cit., p. 119.

253. Manila Times, May 2, 1967. In 1933 a Socialist Party had also been formed as a front for the outlawed PKP.

254. Sison, Struggle for National Democracy, op. cit., p. 110.

255. NCNA, May 6, 1967.

256. Ibid., May 27, 1967, giving a summarized version of the PKP statement.

257. Hong Kong Standard, May 7, 1973, quoting an interview with Marcos by Crocker Snow of the Boston Globe. Chou reportedly told this to Marcos's representative, Benjamin Romauldez.

258. World Marxist Review, no. 11, December 20, 1967.

259. The KM took part in the student demonstration of late 1968 against the United States and the United Kingdom for their position on Manila's claim to Sabah. The KM, however, did not support the claim itself, charging that it was a diversion from domestic problems. (See Peter Forzman's two interesting articles on the Philippine left in the Far Eastern Economic Review, October 13 and October 24, 1968.) What may be taken as Peking's view on the issue was expressed in an article in Malayan Monitor (September 1968), which declared that Sabah belonged to neither Malaysia nor the Philippines but to the people of Sabah, who are the "only claimants with unimpeachable credentials."

260. Ang Bayan, official organ of the new PKP (MC). Documents captured in June 1969. Published in the Philippines Herald, March 1, 1970.

261. Ibid.

262. Paper by Maximino B. de Gusman in Report of the Seminar on Village Defence and Development (Bangkok, March 15-21, 1970).

263. See for example, NCNA, September 2, 1967. In October 1968 Peking referred to the "unrelenting struggle of the Philippine people's armed forces" but did not refer to any role for the PKP.

264. See for example NCNA reporting of President Nixon's visits to Manila on July 26 and 27, 1969.

265. For example, an NCNA commentary of March 26, 1968 entitled "The Flame of the Armed-Struggle in Southeast Asia Is Blazing Higher and Higher" described revolutionary situations in Malaya, Thailand, Burma, Vietnam, Laos, India, and Indonesia, but it failed to mention the Philippines. Year-end summaries by NCNA in 1968 and 1969 also failed to include an article on the Philippines, and Lin Piao in his report to the Ninth Congress of the CCP in April 1969 failed to mention the Philippines in his review of revolutionary struggle. Hanoi in November 1969, however, noted the "continually expanded guerrilla movement" in the Philippines (VNA, English, November 20, 1969). But again no mention of the PKP (ML) or the New People's Army.

266. On October 27, 1970, NCNA carried a statement by Armado Guerrero acclaiming Mao's May 20, 1970, statement "People of the World Unite and Defeat the U.S. Agressors and All Their Running Dogs !" However, no statement was carried from the PKP (Marxist-Leninist) on China's National Day, October 1.

267. Francis Starner, "Whose Ballot, Whose Blood?," Far Eastern Economic Review, October 17, 1970.

268. NCNA, November 25, 1967, carried an early attack on Soviet-Malaysian ties. Abdul Razak, deputy prime minister and defense minister of Malaysia, visited the Soviet Union from May 23 to 25, 1968. Peking subsequently charged that the Soviet Union was preparing to supply arms to Malaysia to "suppress the people's struggle" (NCNA, May 28, 1968). The MNLL organ, Malayan Bulletin, in June denounced Soviet ties to Malaysia and Singapore in the same terms (NCNA, June 27, 1968).

269. Armado Guerrero, Philippine Society and Revolution (Hong Kong: Ta Kung Pao, 1971).

270. Far Eastern Economic Review, March 26, 1970 p. 26.

271. South China Morning Post, April 8, 1971.

272. NCNA, May 19, 1971.

273. Straits Times, August 20, 1968.

274. Sarawak Tribune, March 8, 1969.

275. Straits Times, March 11. 1969.

276. Foreign Affairs Malaysia 4, 1, March 1971.

277. NCNA, April 19, 1971.

278. Straits Times, May 24, 1971.

279. South China Morning Post, August 25, 1971.

280. VMR, statement of the MCP, April 28, 1970.

281. NCNA, message of the CCP Central Committee, April 29, 1970.

282. VMR, June 30, 1971 (NCNA, July 1, 1971).

283. VMR, June 30, 1971.

284. "The Threat of Armed Conflict in Sarawak," (Malaysian Kuala Lumpur: Government White Paper, 1972).

285. VMR, April 28, 1970, MCP 40th anniversary statement.

286. VMR, May 17, 1970.

287. Dick Wilson, "A Long View—or Bogey," Far Eastern Economic Review, August 7, 1971.

288. Straits Times, August 5, 1971.

289. Current Scene, August 7, 1971.

290. Daily Express, Kota Kinabalu, January 3, 1969.

291. Straits Times, June 17, 1969.

292. Interview with Agence France-Presse, Manila, December 9, 1969.

293. Hong Kong Standard, October 10, 1970.

294. Ibid., May 11, 1971.

295. Manila Times, May 5, 1971.

296. NCNA, July 17, 1971.

297. In April 1972 Marcos again charged that Filipino communist leaders had been trained in China. Hong Kong Standard, April 10, 1972.

298. Philippine Government report on Romauldez's trip released to the press February 24, 1972. Manila Times, February 25, 1972.

299. Hong Kong Standard, April 10, 1972.

300. Sunday Post-Herald, September 24, 1972.

301. Straits Times, February 27, 1969. Also, interview in the Far Eastern Economic Review, February 20, 1969.

302. Thanat speech at Parliament. Bangkok Post, March 25, 1969. In July Thanat said it was not yet time to recognize China or support its admission to the UN.

303. Bangkok World, April 17, 1969.

304. Hsing Hsien Wan Pao (Bangkok), March 31, 1969.

305. Straits Times, February 26, 1970.

306. News conference, September 10, 1970, Bangkok Post, September 10, 1970. Thanat said he presumed Peking had not responded to the offer because it wanted secret talks.

371

307. Bangkok Post, September 14, 1970.

308. The meetings resumed in October 1970 but were interrupted in November.

309. See Thanat's open letter to Defense Secretary Melvin Laird, February 8, 1971. Royal Thai Consulate General Press Release, Hong Kong.

310. Bangkok Post, May 14, 1971.

311. Ibid., May 15, 1971.

312. Ibid., July 5, 1971.

313. Nation, Bangkok, July 26, 1971.

314. Bangkok Post, August 22, 1972.

315. VPT, October 29, 1971, NCNA, November 2, 1971.

316. Bangkok Post, August 1, 1971.

317. Ibid., November 7, 1971.

318. VPT, September 7, 1971.

319. Bangkok World, November 3, 1971.

320. Bangkok Post, November 13, 1971.

321. New York Times, November 21, 1971.

322. Nation, August 4, 1972.

323. Bangkok Post, September 15, 1972.

324. Nation, September 15, 1972.

325. Kuala Lumpur Radio, May 18, 1971.

326. NCNA, March 11, 1972.

6

Chinese international behavior is the product of a complex interaction of China's internal politics and capabilities and its assessment of the intentions and capabilities of other powers. China has the physical assets of a near superpower, and its politics and international behavior are influenced by a history of greatness and revolution, by its memory of humiliation, and by a totalitarian structure and universalist ideology. Moreover, the thrust of the most massive nationalism in history and the drive to modernization on an unprecedented scale provide a unique dynamism to the political processes of the People's Republic of China.

There are few things inevitable about Chinese policies in Southeast Asia or elsewhere. In the case of Burma and Indonesia, we have observed the importance of the unexpected and the unwanted event upon the course of China's policies; and perhaps in all of our studies there is testimony to what Hannah Arendt has called the hallmark of history— the disparity between cause and effect. Moreover, the political and psychological proclivities of different decision-makers render possible many alternative courses of action and reaction.

But one thing does seem unavoidable: China will increasingly assert its power and influence in Asia. This development would seem to be the inevitable consequence of history and of geopolitical reality, and its realization should be a major part of the role required of any Chinese leader. This inexorable truth is also brought home by the simple fact that, despite occasional and sometimes self-inflicted setbacks, China's military, industrial, and nuclear power continues every day to add another stone to what will be the towering edifice of Asia and one of the great powers on earth.

In light of Chinese culture and cuisine, the assertion of Chinese influence need not be an unpleasant experience. Indeed, it was once the fitful hope of U.S. policy in the 1930s and early 1940s that China would be established as the preeminent power in Asia in balance with Russia and Japan.

The defeat of Japan and its subsequent close ties to the United States, together with the victory of the communists in China and their alliance with the Soviet Union, changed the U.S. perception of China's role in Asia. Even after the breakup of the Sino-Soviet alliance, the United States continued to see China as the main threat to its own position in Asia.

But the Soviets, with much greater economic and military muscle than the Chinese, began a steady process of expanding their role in Asian affairs; by 1972 they were the dominant outside power in South Asia, the main ally of the North Vietnamese, and the principal benefactor of the partial political vacuum created by the Nixon doctrine. In addition, the Soviets were hastening to improve their ties to Japan and to involve Japan in economic ventures in Siberia, which also had political and strategic implications. At the same time, Japan had become the third largest industrial power in the world, its looming economy threatening to outspace the United States in many areas.

While the Soviets and the Japanese were coming on strong, the United States was harassed by its own economic and social troubles and was drained financially and emotionally by the Indochina wars. The United States could no longer hope to fight off Chinese as well as Soviet influence in Southeast Asia.

Consequently, after more than 20 years of U.S. efforts to contain and weaken China, the Nixon visit to Peking in 1972 suggested that the United States again saw China as a useful balancing force in Asia. Although Peking is likely to remain essentially a U.S. rival and Japan essentially the main American ally in Asia—a reversal of the pre-World War II relationships—the People's Republic of China is no longer seen as an inherent adversary, and both sides will, in the future, appreciate their coincidence of interest in preventing any other power from establishing hegemony in Southeast Asia.

What is important to the Southeast Asians is the manner in which China's future influence will be asserted. The approach employed may be fierce and intrusive, or it may be marked by self-confidence and mutuality. Obviously the nature of the ultimate relationships that evolve will be largely shaped by the way in which Chinese influence grows.

The manner in which China chooses to make its voice heard in Southeast Asia has taken and will continue to take different forms. The choice, we have observed, is determined by the policies toward China of the governments concerned, by internal developments in China, and by China's perception of other great-power intentions and capabilities in the area. We have observed that the differences within the leadership in interpreting external threats and opportunities in Southeast Asia were primarily along the lines of great-power versus more limited national interests, of boldness versus caution, and of long-term goals versus short-term gains. Moreover, the differences became acute when there were sharp contradictions of national interests caused by perceived threats from the outside, and when power struggles within the regime accentuated policy disputes.

In Vietnam in 1965, actions by the USSR and the United States posed various dilemmas of policy for the Chinese leadership, dilemmas that eventually contributed to a violent split within the Chinese party on the interpretation of national priorities. Six years later, an even more horrendous splintering occurred over the question of relations with the two giant rivals of China.

In Sukarno's Indonesia, personal factors were not the major determinant of Peking's actions because no conflict existed between national and ideological or sovereign and great-power goals. Thus there were no contradictions between party and state relations upon which internal disputes in Peking could play. Developments in Indonesia in the first half of the 1960s probably represented for all the Chinese leadership the optimum evolution of international politics in Asia.

But a sharp conflict between party and state relations had always existed in Sino-Burmese affairs and the institutional and psychological effects of the radical internal campaign in 1967 presented the opportunity for a reversal of priorities—subordinating security interests to the revolutionary ideal. Clearly in the case of Burma, the political and psychological climates created by the internal situation in China were paramount.

In regard to policy toward Malaysia, Singapore, Thailand, and the Philippines, a consensus probably existed among the Peking elite in the 1960s. There were no conflicts in interpreting the proper political role of China in regard to these states; there was no contradiction between party and state relations or between sovereign and great-power interests, because there were no state relations and sovereign interests were not at stake. Although the radicals in Peking also had ideological goals, broader strategic issues were the major influence in China's relations with these countries in the 1950s and 1960s.

There has been no suggestion in our studies that China has territorial ambitions or that it entertains any notion of using military power aggressively or without provocation in Southeast Asia. Moreover, beginning in 1971, China adopted a self-effacing policy that renounced any pretension to superpower status. Instead of striving to polarize the Third World, China began to seek only to champion that world against the superpowers and their alleged hegemonic ambitions. Likewise, Peking abandoned, at least temporarily, the attempt to set itself up as the alternate center of world communism. But during most of the 1960s, China by its own proud boast, saw itself as the center of an expansionist ideological movement. Mao, Lin Piao, and their radical colleagues dreamed of global conquest—of the worldwide victory of Mao's "thought." Such a victory was not seen in terms of armies marching across borders, but neither was it to be simply a process of spiritual osmosis. Advancement toward the goal was explicitly pictured in terms of power and organization; and while the main force of this advance was said to be the people of each nation, assistance and support from the "rear base" (China) was explicitly recognized as important and sometimes critical.

Although China no longer seeks to promote a communist community in Asia centered on Peking and on the thoughts of Mao Tsetung, to deny that this national-ideological objective may again motivate China's behavior is to make the same mistake as those who, in the 1930s and 1940s, refused to believe that the leaders of the Chinese Communist Party were serious and sincere communists. This goal remains the utopian international objective of the Chinese communist movement, just as internally the goal of transition into true communism is the theoretical ideal.

Both of these ideological goals—internal and external—conflict with present-day reality and the attainment of practical ends. It is the task of the totalitarian leader, however, to resist the corruption of reality and as much as possible to keep alive his movement's utopian goals. If he fails, the movement ossifies and dies. This was the insight of Mao Tse-tung.

The Chinese have used the fraternal parties of Southeast Asia as instruments of China's foreign policy. Changes in Peking's relations with these parties have been shaped largely by China's cold war with the US and its allies and by its ideological conflict and rivalry with the Soviet Union. Often the question of fraternal commitments versus diplomatic interests has been caught up in the internal power struggle in Peking. Sometimes serious miscalculations have been made about the prospects of revolution. In the end, China adjusts its fraternal relations to serve its national interests in terms of security, prestige, and influence. Yet a core of concern and commitment will always remain; for a global mission in the name of a transnational ideology serves the power interests of a regime and the drive for personal power and immortality by its leaders.

378

321-322, 323-324; and Sarawak,
305-306, 307; September 30
movement, 114-120; and Singapore, 570-571; and Union of
Soviet Socialist Republics, 90-
91, 94, 97-98, 104, 120, 138n.;
and the United Nations, 94, 100,
101; and the United States, 83,
98, 108-110, 120, 129, 132, 133
Indonesian Communist Party, 84,
96-97, 107, 109, 111-113, 117-
118, 119, 132, 136, 141n.; and
China, 82-83, 84, 88-92, 97, 110,
112, 116-117, 121-122, 123-125,
126, 128-131, 133-134, 137n.,
143n., 299-300, 306-307, 335;
guerilla activity by, 127-128,
132-133, 308-309; and Malaya,
92, 99, 121, 299, 302; and Malayan Communist Party, 299-300,
301-303, 310-311; and Malaysia,
90-91, 92, 94, 95, 96, 102-103,
299-303; and the Philippines,
299, 323; and September 30
movement, 114-121, 122-123,
143n.; and Singapore, 319; splits
in, 128-129; and Sukarno, 85-88,
90, 92, 93-94, 96, 108-109, 110,
111, 114-115, 115-116, 117, 118,
125-126; and Union of Soviet
Socialist Republics, 84, 86, 90-
91, 93, 94, 117, 122-123, 126,
128-130, 143n.

Japan, 72, 374; and China, 180,
334-336, 356-357
Indonesia, 132, 134; and the
United States, 374
Japanese Communist Party, 53,
54-57, 84, 335
Johnson, Lyndon B., 24, 28, 30,
32, 32n., 47-48, 65-66, 79n.,
80n.

Khmer Rouge, 16, 145, 147-148,

158; and China, 150, 156; and
Vietnam, 150, 156, 157
Khrushchev, Nikita, ix, 16, 18, 20,
22, 27, 29, 74n.
Korea, North, 30, 53, 55, 65, 84, 97
Korean conflict, 6, 8, 9, 10-11, 38,
66

Lamson, 113-173
Lao Dong, 19, 22, 30, 51, 183
Laos, 10, 16, 22, 35, 60; and China,
162-164, 165, 170-171; Geneva
conference on, 21-22; and Union
of Soviet Socialist Republics,
22, 165; and the United States,
26, 34, 165, 169-170, 171-172;
and Vietnamese revolutionary
movement, 162-164, 169-170,
171-173
Lee Kuan-yew, 282, 283, 310, 320,
344, 345, 355, 362n.
Liao Cheng-chih, 208-209, 214,
222, 249n.
Lin Piao, ix, x, 375; and Burma,
213, 227, 224-225, 230, 235, 237,
239-240, 241; and Chinese
foreign policy, 64; and Chinese
internal political disputes, 40,
44-46, 59, 62-63, 71, 124, 158-
159, 164-165, 175, 176-177, 178-
179, 186, 209, 216, 224-225, 234,
236, 238-239, 241, 335-336; and
Indonesia, 108, 131; and
Philippines, 327, 331; and
Thailand, 289, 291; and Vietnamese revolutionary movement,
49-50; 80n., 169, 178
Liu Shao-chi, 55, 193, 202; and
Burma, 194-195, 196, 197-198;
199-201, 202, 203-205, 206, 208,
219, 230, 232-233; and Chinese
internal political disputes, 36,
38-40, 53, 54-55, 125, 179, 186,
236, 243, 332; and Indonesia,
108, 124; and Malaya, 278-279,

316; and the Union of Soviet
Socialist Republics, 49-50, 62,
77n., and the United States, 63-
64
Lo Jui-ching, 38, 44, 46, 49, 59,
77n.,
Lon Nol, 147, 150, 151, 152-154,
155, 156-157, 185

Malaya, 254, 261, 311; and China,
65, 98, 99, 121-122, 261-262,
270, 276, 278, 279-280, 284, 285-
286, 287-288, 297, 300, 315, 321,
331-332; and Indonesia, 91-92,
98, 99, 121-122, 297, 300, 302-
303; and Indonesian Communist
Party, 91-92, 99, 121, 302; and
Singapore, 282-283, 284, 298;
and the Union of Soviet Socialist
Republics, 276, 278-279
Malayan Communist Party, 218,
253-255, 256-257, 260, 277-278,
280, 286, 302, 304, 316-317, 320,
343, 362n.; and China, 68, 84,
251-252, 257-258, 260-261
262, 267, 276-277, 278-281, 287,
298, 300, 301, 302-303, 312-314,
315, 316, 317, 319, 321, 337, 340-
342, 358n., 365n., 366n., 367n.,
368n.; and Indonesian Communist
Party, 299-300, 301-302, 311-
312, 320; and Malaysia, 300-
302, 303, 316; and Singapore,
282, 298, 319-321, 344; splits
within, 299-302, 340; and Thai
Communist Party, 294-295, 314-
315, 318-319; and Vietnam, 301,
Malaysia, 94-95, 110-111, 297-298;
309, 311, 316, 356; and China,
ix, 91, 95-96, 98, 100, 251, 299-
300, 315-316, 334, 338-340, 341-
342, 346, 351, 370n.; and Indonesia, 42, 90-91, 92, 94, 95-97,
80, 100, 102, 107, 110-111, 299-
303, 321; and Indonesian Com-

munist Party, 89-91, 91, 94, 95,
96, 298-303; and Malayan Communist Party, 300-302, 303, 316;
and Singapore, 297-298, 318-319;
and Union of Soviet Socialist
Republics, 91, 333-334, 357,
371n.
Mao Tse-Tsung, x, xi, 3, 8, 35, 64,
67, 100-101, 375; and Chinese
internal political disputes, 38-
40, 41-46, 52, 53-55, 57, 58, 62,
70-71, 124, 134, 158, 159-161,
169, 178, 209, 214, 217, 222, 230,
289; and Indonesia, 89-90, 91-92,
96, 100, 111-112, 117-118, 121,
124-125, 265; and Malaya, 280;
and Philippines, 329; and Southeast Asia Treaty Organization,
268-269; and Thailand, 289, 293;
and Union of Soviet Socialist
Republics, 56, 57, 179-180; and
the United States, 180-181
Marcos, Ferdinand, 324, 349; and
China, 330-331, 346-347, 355,
364n.
Minh, Ho Chi, 1-4, 7, 8, 11-12, 17,
19, 70

National Liberation Front (of Vietnam), 30, 60, 97-98, 148, 156
Ne Win, ix, 196-198, 199, 200, 201,
203, 204-205, 208, 212-213, 218,
219-220, 224, 228-230, 231, 232-
233, 236-237, 243n., 250n.
Nixon, Richard M., 15; and Cambodia, 156; and China, xii, 66, 71,
160, 166, 170, 174, 178, 180, 184;
and Laos, 170; and Vietnam, 17,
66, 67, 68, 80n., 153, 154, 162,
174, 177
Nu, U., ix, 191, 192, 193, 195, 196,
228-230, 231

Pathet Lao, 16, 22, 25, 26
Peng Chen, 38, 43, 53-56, 59, 110,

104; and United States, 109, 110

Teng Hsiao-ping, 38, 40, 45, 53, 55
Thai Communist Party, 218, 252-
253, 256, 257, 259, 267, 268, 271,
272-273, 288-289, 291-292, 294-
295, 297, 318, 358n., 359n., 363n,
364n.; and China, 251, 252-253,
257, 258, 270-271, 290, 293-294,
296-297, 350, 364n.; and Malayan
Communist Party, 294-295, 314-
316, 317-318
Thai Patriotic Front, 290, 291-
294, 295, 296, 297, 338
Thailand, ix, 61, 83, 84, 293-294,
315; and Cambodia, 275-276; and
China, 251, 252, 262, 262-266,
268-271, 273-276, 285-286, 287-
290, 291-293, 295-296, 332, 349-
355, 360n., 361n., 371n., 375;
and Southeast Asia Treaty Organization, 264; and Union of
Soviet Socialist Republics, 333-
334; and United States, 263-264,
274, 275, 276-277, 288-289, 290,
291-292, 293, 295-296, 350-351,
353-354, 361n.; and Vietnam,
291-292, 296, 297, 356, 364n.
Thakin Ba Thien Tin, 192, 196,
219-220, 222-224, 233, 234, 236,
243n.
Thakin Than Tun, 192, 196, 200-
201, 202, 207-208, 222-223, 243n.,
248n.
Thanat Khoman, 349-353, 356
Thanom Kittikachorn, 351, 352-
353, 355
Tonkin Gulf resolution, 26, 29, 31-
32, 41

Union of Soviet Socialist Republics,
xi, 1; and Burma, 195, 201, 204,
206, 220, 224, 237; and Cambodia,
150, 154, 155; and China, viii, x,
10, 20, 21-22, 23, 24, 30, 33, 35,

36-44, 45-46, 47, 48-49, 52-53,
55-59, 61-62, 63, 64-65, 67-68,
69, 70-71, 76n., 77n., 94, 95-96,
100, 104, 118, 125, 128-130, 131-
132, 134, 155, 159-160, 165-166,
167, 168-169, 171, 174, 175-179,
180-182, 186, 206, 216, 217, 220,
224, 231-232, 235, 237, 260, 286-
287, 291, 331-332, 333-334, 335-
336, 341, 355, 356-357, 360n.,
370n.; foreign policy of, 10-11,
29-30, 35-36, 63, 67-68, 102-
103, 260, 261; and India, 237; and
Indonesia, 90-91, 94, 97-98, 104,
118-119, 120, 129-130, 138n.,
356; and Indonesian Communist
Party, 84, 86-87, 90, 91, 93, 94,
122-123, 125-126, 128-130; and
Indo-Pakistan war, 103, 181;
and Japan, 356; and Laos, 22; and
and Malaya, 276, 278-279; and
Malaysia, 90, 333-334, 347, 356;
and the Philippines, 328, 330,
333, 348; and Singapore, 333-
334, 346; and Southeast Asia,
10, 84, 174, 333, 335-336, 355;
and Thailand, 333-334; and
United States, 18, 20-21, 31-35,
41, 42, 46, 52, 71, 83, 155, 175,
176-178, 179, 180, 181, 184; and
Viet Cong, 33; and the Viet Minh,
7, 18; and Vietnam, 3-4, 7, 10,
12, 18, 19-22, 27-28, 30, 33,
35n., 41, 44, 52, 59, 65, 80n.,
155, 170, 174, 175, 184; and
Vietnamese revolutionary movement, 1, 2, 4, 6, 7, 8, 11, 15-16,
17, 18, 27, 29-30, 35, 36-37, 38-
39, 40, 41-42, 52, 67-68, 103-
104, 171, 183-186, 375
United Nations, 71; and Cambodia,
154; and China, 100-102, 135,
345, 347, 351-352, 355; and Indonesia, 94, 100, 101
United States; and Burma, 193-194,

ABOUT THE AUTHOR

JAY TAYLOR is a Foreign Service Officer who has specialized in Chinese affairs for the past 14 years. He has served in Taiwan, Malaysia, and Hong Kong, and traveled throughout Asia (including India and the People's Republic of China). He has also followed Chinese affairs in the Department of State in Washington.

Mr. Taylor has published articles in several journals including Asian Survey, Current Scene, and the American Foreign Service Journal. He holds degrees from Vanderbilt University and the University of Michigan at Ann Arbor.

CHINA AND THE GREAT POWERS: Relations
with the United States, the Soviet Union, and
Japan
edited by Francis O. Wilcox

CHINESE AND SOVIET AID TO AFRICA: An
Economic and Political Analysis
edited by Warren Weinstein

CHINA'S AFRICAN POLICY: A Study of
Tanzania
George T. Yu

SINO-AMERICAN DÉTENTE AND ITS POLICY
IMPLICATIONS*
edited by Gene T. Hsiao

SOUTHEAST ASIA UNDER THE NEW BALANCE
OF POWER*
edited by Sudershan Chawla, Melvin Gurtov,
and Alain-Gerard Marsot

THE NEUTRALIZATION OF SOUTHEAST
ASIA
Dick Wilson

*Also available in paperback as a PSS Student Edition